THE SAMARITAN MISSION
IN ACTS

V. J. SAMKUTTY

t & t clark

Published by T&T Clark
A Continuum imprint
The Tower Building, 11 York Road, London SE1 7NX
80 Maiden Lane, Suite 704, New York, NY 10038

www.tandtclark.com

British Library Cataloguing-in-Publication Data
A catalogue record for this book is available from the British Library

Typeset by Free Range Book Design & Production Ltd
Printed on acid-free paper in Great Britain by Biddles Ltd, Kings Lynn, Norfolk

ISBN 0567044645 (hardback)

LIBRARY OF NEW TESTAMENT STUDIES
328

Formerly the Journal for the Study of the New Testament Supplement series

Editor
Mark Goodacre

CONTENTS

ACKNOWLEDGEMENTS

This work was originally submitted as a thesis for my PhD at the University of Sheffield, where I was able to pursue my interest in the portrait of the Samaritans in Luke-Acts. It has been a privilege to conduct research at the university and to interact with faculty members and fellow students in the Department of Biblical Studies. There are many people to whom I am grateful for their assistance and support.

First of all, I wish to thank my supervisor, Canon Professor Loveday C.A. Alexander, who provided expert guidance at every stage of my research. Her continuous support and encouragement was of inestimable value in bringing the work to its fruition. For this I am most grateful. I also wish to thank Professor Martin D. Goodman, Professor of Jewish Studies at the University of Oxford and Dr. Diana V. Edelman, Reader in Biblical Studies at the University of Sheffield, for their useful comments on, and contributions to, Chapter 3. I am also grateful to Rev. Dr David Wenham of Wycliffe Hall, Oxford, for his assistance and insights in the early stages of the research.

I would like to acknowledge my sincere thanks to Dr R. Barry Matlock and the Graduate Selection Committee of the Department of Biblical Studies for granting me a Department Scholarship, and to the committee of Universities UK for an award from the Overseas Research Scholarships (ORS) scheme to support the research. I also remember with gratitude my friends and families who supported me financially during my three-year stay in Sheffield.

Special thanks are due to the departmental staff, Mrs Alison C. Bygrave and Mrs Gill Fogg, for their help and willingness to assist in practical matters. I also wish to thank the staff at the University Main Library for their assistance in helping me to obtain the necessary resources for my research.

I am most appreciative to my colleagues at All Nations Christian College, where I currently teach New Testament Studies and Greek. The college has given me much encouragement in bringing this work to its final completion and publication.

Particular thanks must go to my parents, John and Achamma Daniel, who never gave up hope of having a child, and to whom I was born after ten years of tireless prayer and waiting. Their commitment reflects the words of Hannah: 'I prayed for this child, and the Lord has granted me what I asked of him. So now I give him to the Lord. For his whole life he will be given over to the Lord' (1 Sam.1:27-28).

Finally, this book is dedicated to my wife, Kochumol, who has constantly supported and encouraged me during my studies and ministries and has taken primary responsibility for looking after our two children, Jeremiah and Christopher, during this project.

V.J. Samkutty
All Nations Christian College
England

May 2006

ABBREVIATIONS

AASOR	*Annual of the American Schools of Oriental Research*
AB	Anchor Bible
ABD	Anchor Bible Dictionary
AbrN	*Abr-Nahrain*
AJ	Josephus' *Jewish Antiquities (Works*, ed. H. St. J. Thackeray, R. Marcus, A. Wikgren and L.H. Feldman, 9 vols. LCL, Cambridge, MA: Harvard University Press, 1926–1965).
AnBib	Analecta Biblica
ANRW	*Aufstieg und Niedergang der römischen Welt*
ASMS	American Society of Missiology Series
b.	*The Babylonian Talmud*, I. Epstein (ed.), *Hebrew-English Edition of the Babylonian Talmud*, London: The Soncino Press, 1984–1994.
BBB	Bonner biblische Beiträge
BDAG	W. Bauer, F.W. Danker, W.F. Arndt, and F.W. Gingrich. *A Greek-English Lexicon of the New Testament and Other Early Christian Literature*, ed. and rev. F.W. Danker, 3rd edition, Chicago: University of Chicago Press, 2000.
BDF	F. Blass, A. Debrunner and Robert W. Funk, *A Greek Grammar of the New Testament and Other Early Christian Literature*, a Translation and Revision of the ninth-tenth German edition, Chicago: The University of Chicago Press, 1961.
BECNT	Baker Exegetical Commentary on the New Testament
BEThL	Bibliotheca Ephemeridum Theologicarum Lovaniensium
Bib	*Biblica*
BA	*Biblical Archaeologist*
BAIAS	*Bulletin of the Anglo-Israel Archaeological Society*
BAR	*Biblical Archaeology Review*
BI	*Biblical Interpretation*
BJ	Josephus' *Jewish War*
BJRL	*Bulletin of the John Rylands University Library of Manchester*
BNTC	Black's New Testament Commentary
BR	*Bible Review*
BTB	*Biblical Theology Bulletin*
BWANT	Beiträge zur Wissenschaft vom Alten und Neuen Testament

BZ	*Biblische Zeitschrift*
BZNW	Beihefte zur Zeitschrift für die neutestamentliche Wissenschaft
CBQ	*The Catholic Biblical Quarterly*
CBR	*Currents in Biblical Research*
CIS	Copenhagen International Seminar
CRB	Cahiers de la Revue biblique
CRINT	Compendia rerum Iudaicarum ad novum testamentum
EEM	East European Monograph
EKKNT	Evangelisch-Katholischer Kommentar zum Neuen Testament
EvQ	*Evangelical Quarterly*
ExpTim	*Expository Times*
GNS	Good News Studies
GTA	Göttinger theologische Arbeiten
HOS	Handbook of Oriental Studies
HTKNT	Herders theologischer Kommentar zum Neuen Testament
HTR	*Harvard Theological Review*
HUCA	*Hebrew Union College Annual*
Hom	*Pseudo-Clementine Homilies*
ICC	International Critical Commentary
IEJ	*Israel Exploration Journal*
Int	*Interpretation*
JBL	*Journal of Biblical Literature*
JJS	*Journal of Jewish Studies*
JPTS	*Journal of Pentecostal Theology*, Supplement
JQR	*Jewish Quarterly Review*
JRS	*Journal of Roman Studies*
JSJ	*Journal for the Study of Judaism*
JSJSup	*Journal for the Study of Judaism*, Supplement
JSNT	*Journal for the Study of the New Testament*
JSNTSup	*Journal for the Study of the New Testament, Supplement series*
JSOT	*Journal for the Study of the Old Testament*
JSP	*Journal for the Study of Pseudepigrapha*
JSS	*Journal of Semitic Studies*
JSPSup	*Journal for the Study of Pseudepigrapha*, Supplement
JTS	*Journal of Theological Studies*
KEKNT	Kritisch-Exegetischer Kommentar über das Neue Testament
LCL	Loeb Classical Library
LSJ	H.G. Liddell, R. Scott and H.S. Jones, *A Greek-English Lexicon*, With a revised supplement, Oxford: Clarendon Press, 1996.
m.	*The Mishnah, Translated from the Hebrew with Introduction and Brief Explanatory Notes* by Herbert Danby, Oxford: Oxford University Press, 1933.

NCB	New Century Bible
Neot	*Neotestamentica*
NIBC	New International Bible Commentary
NovT	*Novum Testamentum*
NovTSup	*Novum Testamentum*, Supplement series
NSBT	New Studies in Biblical Theology
NTS	*New Testament Studies*
NTG	New Testament Guides
OCA	Orientalia Christiana Analecta
PEQ	*Palestine Exploration Quarterly*
PGM	*Papyri graecae magicae*
PNTC	Pelican New Testament Commentary
PTMS	Pittsburgh Theological Monograph Series
RB	*Revue Biblique*
Rec.	*Pseudo-Clementine Recognitions*
Ref.	Hippolytus' *Refutatio*
RevE	*Review and Expositor*
RevQ	*Revue de Qumran*
RSV	Revised Standard Version
RSR	*Religious Studies Review*
SANT	Studien zum Alten und Neuen Testament
SBEC	Studies in the Bible and Early Christianity
SBF	Studium Biblicum Franciscanum
SBLDS	Society of Biblical Literature Dissertation Series
SBLMS	Society of Biblical Literature Monograph Series
SBLSP	Society of Biblical Literature Seminar Papers
SBS	Stuttgarter Bibelstudien
SBT	*Studies in Biblical Theology*
Spec. Leg.	*De Specialibus Legibus*
SCJ	Studies in Christianity and Judaism
SE	*Studia Evangelica*
SES	Société d'Etudes Samaritaines
SJC	Studies in Jewish Civilization
SJLA	Studies in Judaism in Late Antiquity
SNTSMS	Society of New Testament Studies Monograph Series
ST	*Studia Theologica*
SPA	*Studia Philonica Annual*
SWR	Studies in Women and Religion
TDNT	*Theological Dictionary of the New Testament*, ed. G. Kittel and G. Friedrich, 10 vols. Trans. & ed. G.W. Bromiley, Grand Rapids: Wm.B. Eerdmans Publishing Co., 1964–1976.
ThHKNT	Theologischer Handkommentar zum Neuen Testament
ThR	*Theologische Revue*

Tos.	*The Tosefta,* Jacob Neusner (trans.), *The Tosefta,* New York: Ktav, 1979–1997.
TSAJ	Texts and Studies in Ancient Judaism
TU	Texte und Untersuchungen
TynBul	*Tyndale Bulletin*
TZ	*Theologische Zeitschrift*
VT	*Vetus Testamentum*
WBC	Word Biblical Commentaries
WTJ	*Westminster Theological Journal*
WUNT	Wissenschaftliche Untersuchungen zum Neuen Testament
WuD	*Wort und Dienst*
y.	*The Jerusalem Talmud*
ZNW	*Zeitschrift für die neutestamentliche Wissenschaft*
ZRGG	*Zeitschrift für Religion und Geistesgeschichte*
ZTK	*Zeitschrift für Theologie und Kirche*

Part I

Introduction and Survey

Chapter 1

INTRODUCTION

1.1 Purpose and Rationale

That Luke has a special interest in the Samaritans as a separate category of people, apart from his broader interest in the Gentiles, is undeniable. Only Luke-Acts contains various literary types of material about the Samaritans: a narrative on Jesus' sending of messengers into Samaria (Lk. 9:51-56), a parable of the compassionate Samaritan (Lk. 10:25-37), a miracle of the grateful Samaritan (Lk. 17:11-19) and an extensive account of the evangelization of Samaria (Acts 8:4-25). Also, in Acts, Samaria is mentioned at important points at 1:8; 8:1; 9:31 and 15:3. Luke's interest in and portrait of the Samaritan mission in Acts 8:4-25 seems to have a more significant place than it appears in demonstrating the advancement of the gospel, as it has been set in between the account of the mission to the Judeans and that to the Gentiles.

The purpose of the present study is to examine the significance of the portrait of the Samaritan mission in Acts 8:4-25. This study will be of a comprehensive and extensive nature exploring the historical, literary and theological aspects of the account in Acts 8:4-25, aiming to enhance the analysis of the text in order to evaluate the significance for Luke of the portrait of the Samaritan mission.

It is somewhat intriguing, given Luke's significant interest in the Samaritans, that there is to date not much extensive work exploring the significance of the Lukan portrait of the Samaritan mission in Acts 8:4-25.[1] However, a recent study of Martina Böhm on *Samarien und die Samaritai bei Lukas*,[2] is an exception where the author extensively argues that Luke considers the

---

1. The Gentile mission has been the focus of many studies. For example, S.G. Wilson, *The Gentiles and the Gentile Mission in Luke-Acts* (SNTSMS 23; Cambridge: Cambridge University Press, 1973); J.B. Tyson, 'The Gentile Mission and the Authority of Scripture in Acts', *NTS* 33 (1987), pp. 619–31; F. Hahn, *Mission in the New Testament* (London: SCM Press, 1965); J. Jeremias, *Jesus' Promise to the Nations* (London: SCM Press, 1956).

2. Subtitled *Eine Studie zum religionshistorischen und traditionsgeschichtlichen Hintergrund der lukanischen Samarientexte und zu deren topographischer Verhaftung* (WUNT: Reihe 2; 111; Tübingen: Mohr Siebeck, 1999).

Samaritans to be part of Israel. Other studies on Acts 8 have focused on the roles of isolated individuals like Philip or Simon Magus[3] or on the relationship between water-baptism and baptism in the Holy Spirit[4] or on the identity or role of the Samaritans.[5] As the history of research will demonstrate, no attempt has been made to evaluate specifically what Luke is doing in the entire narrative of Acts 8:4-25 in view of the setting, the events and the characters he brings in to describe this particular account of the *mission* to the *Samaritans*. The task of engaging in the study of Luke's mission portrait of the Samaritans should also consider his treatment of the Samaritans in the Gospel and the socio-political and religious context of the Samaritans in the New Testament period.

The Jewish attitude towards the Samaritans, as we shall see, was very ambiguous and ambivalent. Some Jews considered them as a hostile people and treated them negatively as social outcasts and religious apostates. But others treated them favourably. The Gospel of Matthew has a mission prohibition by Jesus to the Samaritans: 'Go nowhere among the Gentiles, and enter no town of the Samaritans' (10:5b). Luke does not seem to share these views as he shows a positive affinity towards them. He has Jesus himself take the initiative to go through Samaria and also bring no charge against the Samaritans when they fail to receive him and his messengers (Lk. 9:52, 55). The parable of the compassionate Samaritan overturns the popular prejudice of the Jews against the Samaritans and exhorts them to be neighbours to anyone in need just like the merciful Samaritan (Lk. 10:36, 37). Likewise, Jesus commends the one Samaritan who was healed of leprosy and who came back to Jesus to offer him worship in gratitude (Lk. 17:18-19). Any readers of these stories of Luke would find themselves feeling an affinity towards the Samaritans and challenged to behave like the merciful Samaritan traveller and

3.   C.R. Matthews, *Philip: Apostle and Evangelist: Configurations of a Tradition* (NovTSup.105; Leiden: Brill, 2002); *idem*, 'Philip and Simon, Luke and Peter: A Lukan Sequel and Its Intertextual Success', *SBLSP 1992*, pp. 133–46; F.S. Spencer, *The Portrait of Philip in Acts: A Study of Roles and Relations* (JSNTSup.67; Sheffield: Sheffield Academic Press, 1992); Bernd Kollmann, 'Philippus der Evangelist und die Anfänge der Heidenmission' *Bib* 81 (4, 2000), pp. 551–65. For a sample of the major studies on Simon Magus, see Stephen Harr, *Simon Magus: The First Gnostic?* (BZNW 119; Berlin: Walter de Gruyter, 2003); R. Bergmeier, 'Die Gestalt des Simon Magus in Act 8 und in der simonianischen Gnosis-Aporien einer Gesamtdeutung' in *Das Gesetz im Römerbrief und andere Studien zum Neuen Testament* (WUNT 121; Tübingen: Mohr Siebeck, 2000), pp. 238–46.

4.   J.C. O'Neill, 'The Connection between Baptism and the Gift of the Spirit in Acts', *JSNT* 63 (1996), pp. 87–103; D.A. Koch, 'Geistbesitz, Geistverleihung und Wundermacht: Erwägungen zur Tradition und zur lukanischen Redaktion in Act 8:5-25', *ZNW* 77 (1986), pp. 64–82.

5.   Böhm, *Samarien*; David Ravens, 'The Role of the Samaritans and the Unity of Israel', in *idem*, *Luke and the Restoration of Israel* (JSNTSup.119; Sheffield: Sheffield Academic Press, 1995), pp. 72–106; J. Jervell, 'The Lost Sheep of the House of Israel: The Understanding of the Samaritans in Luke-Acts', in *Luke and the People of God: A New Look at Luke-Acts* (Minneapolis: Augsburg, 1972), pp. 113–32.

the grateful Samaritan leper. Hence these stories in the Gospel seem to function as a positive preparatory agenda for Luke to portray the legitimacy of the Samaritans and their sharing in the blessings of the Kingdom as narrated in Acts 8:4-25.

However, Luke's composition of the mission to Samaria raises a number of significant issues. First of all, Philip's mission to the city of Samaria in Acts 8:5 may contradict the saying of mission prohibition in Mt. 10:5b, as does Jesus' sending of messengers into a Samaritan village in Lk. 9:51-56. Whether or not some Jewish Christians still shared this prohibition in Luke's day, the significant interest of Luke in portraying the successful mission to the Samaritans needs to be accounted for. Next, the apostles remained in Jerusalem when the mission was in progress only to come later to Samaria after the Samaritans accepted the word of God by the ministry of Philip. It is their own part of ministry, which enables the baptized Samaritans to receive the Holy Spirit, and the only part which confronts the intentions of Simon Magus. This brings up the issue of why Philip, who was successful in converting the Samaritans including Simon Magus, could not convey the Holy Spirit to them and why the Jerusalem apostles had to share in the mission to Samaria. There is nothing in the text to suggest that the Samaritans were not genuinely converted so that they could not receive the Holy Spirit. A cursory reading of Luke's portrait of Philip reveals the successful nature of Philip's ministry and there is nothing in the text to claim that Luke stigmatized his ministry[6] nor does he seem to suggest the apostles as the only custodians of the Holy Spirit (cf. Acts 9:17). Likewise, Luke does not suggest that the apostles came to redo or undo what Philip has already done. Therefore, the reason why Luke composes the account of the Samaritan mission in this particular way demands other explanations in the light of fresh investigations.

The Simon Magus episode also raises further issues in the account of the Samaritan mission. Why does Simon Magus occupy most space in the narrative of this new mission development in Samaria? What is the significance for the theology and narrative of Luke of the Simon Magus episode in the context of the Samaritan mission? Likewise, the delay of the Holy Spirit upon the Samaritans and the separation of the laying on of hands from baptism and its attachment to the reception of the Spirit raise theological issues at least for those who think otherwise. These issues in the present account of the Samaritan mission should not be seen primarily as Luke's attempt to formulate a systematic theology meant to contribute to the doctrines of various churches of our day; rather, their significance should be explored in the context of the mission to the Samaritans.

---

6.   Spencer, *Portrait, passim*, explores the successful role of Philip as the pioneering missionary, the dynamic prophet and the co-operative servant, who stands in the line of the Old Testament prophets, Jesus and the apostles.

The focus of our study, however, is to evaluate why Luke presents the Samaritan mission in the way it is narrated in Acts 8:4-25. I argue the thesis that Luke tries to show the Samaritan mission as equally valid with the Jewish mission and that he intends to defend the divine origin and legitimacy of Samaritan Christianity. Hence, Acts 8:4-25 may function both as an apologetic against those who question the validity of the mission to Samaria and the origin of Samaritan Christianity and as a catalyst for the ongoing mission of the early Church to the non-Judaeo-centric community of Luke's day. This apologetic purpose of Luke in the portrait of the Samaritan mission may throw further light on considering the overall purpose of Luke-Acts as apologetic.[7]

Since Luke has references to the Samaritans in his Gospel as well as narrating the proper mission to them in Acts, a few statements about the unity of Luke's Gospel and Acts need to be made here. There is disagreement among scholars as to the question of whether the Gospel and Acts are to be treated as separate, independent volumes or whether they form a single unit.[8] It is maintained in our study that for Luke, his second volume is the continuation of what he says in his first and that whether or not Luke's Gospel and

---

7.   The purpose of Luke-Acts as apologetic against various groups has been noted by various scholars. See for example, L.C.A. Alexander, 'The Acts of the Apostles as an Apologetic Text', in M. Edwards, *et al.* (eds), *Apologetics in the Roman Empire: Pagans, Jews and Christians* (Oxford: Oxford University Press, 1999), pp. 15–43; P.J. Tomson, 'Gamaliel's Counsel and the Apologetic Strategy of Luke-Acts', in J. Verheyden (ed.), *The Unity of Luke-Acts* (BEThL CXLII; Leuven: Leuven University Press, 1999), pp. 585–604; P.F. Esler, *Community and Gospel in Luke-Acts: The Social and Political Motivations of Lucan Theology* (Cambridge: Cambridge University Press, 1987); R.L. Brawley, *Luke-Acts and the Jews: Conflict, Apology, and Conciliation* (Atlanta: Scholars Press, 1987); A. Neagoe, *The Trial of the Gospel: An Apologetic Reading of Luke's Trial Narratives* (Cambridge: Cambridge University Press, 2002).

8.   H.J. Cadbury, *The Making of Luke-Acts* (London: Macmillan, 1927), considers Luke and Acts as a single continuous work and says, 'Acts is neither an appendix nor an afterthought' (p. 9). For detailed works on the unity of Luke-Acts, see J. Verheyden (ed.), *Luke-Acts*. Among others who view Luke and Acts as a unity are R. Tannehill, *The Narrative Unity of Luke-Acts: A Literary Interpretation*, 2 Vols. (Philadelphia: Fortress Press, 1986, 1990); R.F. O'Toole, *The Unity of Luke's Theology: An Analysis of Luke-Acts* (GNS 9; Wilmington: Michael Glazier, 1984); I.H. Marshall, *Luke: Historian and Theologian* (Grand Rapids: Zondervan, 1970); G.E. Sterling, *Historiography and Self-Definition: Josephos, Luke-Acts and Apologetic Historiography* (Leiden: E.J. Brill, 1992), pp. 331–2. Sterling goes on to suggest that the author had in mind Acts when he wrote the Gospel and that he followed the procedure of making outlines of his works before he wrote the episodes, as it was customary among the authors of antiquity to do so (pp. 333–8). However, contrary to the above views, see M.C. Parsons and R.I. Pervo, *Rethinking the Unity of Luke and Acts* (Minneapolis: Fortress Press, 1993), pp. 20–1; Pervo, 'Must Luke and Acts Belong to the Same Genre?', *SBLSP 1989*, ed. D.J. Lull (Atlanta: Scholars Press, 1989), pp. 309–16, claims that 'the argument for generic unity begins in obscurity and ends in absurdity, the obscurity of seeking no more than a convenient label and the absurdity of challenging the completeness of any gospel' (p. 316); also C.J. Hemer, *The Book of Acts in the Setting of Hellenistic History* (WUNT 49; Tübingen: J.C.B. Mohr, 1989), pp. 30–43.

Acts differ in their purpose and genre, one cannot easily separate them in terms of their narrative and theological unity. In other words, the unity of Luke-Acts could be assumed in terms of their prefaces and theological unity.

Regarding the prefaces, scholars advocate that the prefaces of the Gospel and Acts do not stand independently; rather they form a single preface where the latter refers to the former work.[9] In this regard, it is worth noting that the secondary preface in Acts is linked to the primary preface of the Gospel, a custom in antiquity of dividing long works by introducing a preface that provides a summary of the preceding volume and the intro-duction of the next.[10] Loveday C.A. Alexander cites various ancient works that use the recapitulation statements at the beginning of successive volumes. According to Alexander, such recapitulation at the beginning of a book cannot be described in any way as customary in Greek historiography.[11] Though the preface in Acts refers to the former work, it is questionable whether the preface in the former presupposes the latter.[12]

Regarding the theological unity of Luke-Acts, scholars have noted that Luke-Acts have one particular central theme. For example, Marshall and Robert O'Toole have insisted that the theme of salvation becomes the central motif in the theology of Luke-Acts.[13] However, this position on the theological unity of Luke-Acts is challenged by Parsons and Pervo who claim that in matters of resurrection, the saving significance of the death of Jesus, eschatology, and the dimensions of salvation, the two volumes differ. According to them, the missionary speeches in Acts do not stress Jesus' death as a salvific event; eschatology and salvation are not imminent and immediate, but futuristic.[14] Thus, they maintain that the 'existence of the two volumes is the evidence that the problem of the theological unity of Luke and Acts is first and foremost the problem of continuity, of the relation of the life and activity of the Church to the "Christ-event"'.[15] It may be that certain differences in perspectives, for example, the saving significance of Jesus'

---

9.   H.J. Cadbury, 'Commentary on the Preface of Luke', in F.J. Foakes-Jackson and K. Lake (eds), *The Beginnings of Christianity: Part I. The Acts of the Apostles*, vol. 2 (Grand Rapids: Baker Book House, 1922), pp. 489–510, 491–2; Sterling, *Historiography*, pp. 331–2; W.C. van Unnik, 'The Rules of Hellenistic Historiography', shares the view that 'Acts is indeed the second part of a work in two volumes and that the prologue to the Gospel introduces the entire work and not just volume one' (p. 40).

10.   Cf. e.g. Sterling, *Historiography*, p. 248.

11.   L.C.A. Alexander, 'The Preface to Acts and the Historians', in B. Witherington (ed.), *History, Literature and Society in the Books of Acts* (Cambridge: Cambridge University Press, 1996) pp. 73–103, 79–82, 89–92.

12.   For a discussion of this issue, see L.C.A. Alexander, *The Preface to Luke's Gospel*, SNTSMS 79 (Cambridge: Cambridge University Press, 1993), pp. 128–30; *eadem*, 'Preface to Acts'; Sterling, *Historiography*, pp. 333–6.

13.   Marshall, *Historian*, pp. 92, 94–102; O'Toole, *Unity, passim*.

14.   Parsons and Pervo, *Rethinking*, pp. 87–9.

15.   Parsons and Pervo, *Rethinking*, p. 86.

death, do not change the theological unity of Luke-Acts; rather it reflects the primitive tradition, which also appears elsewhere in Pauline letters. On the one hand, Acts is not foreign to the saving significance of the death of Jesus (20:28; 5:30; 10:40; 13:29 cf. Lk. 22:19-20), but on the other, just like the Pauline letters (1 Cor. 15:3-4; Rom. 1:3-4; 4:24-25; 10:9-13; Phil. 2:6-11), Acts reflects the primitive tradition where the offer of salvation is ascribed to the exalted Lord (Acts 2:33-36; 10:43).[16] It is to be noted that for Luke, christology, soteriology and eschatology are very much rooted in history. His intention is not to produce a theological treatise or a systematic theology, but to write the programmatic development of Christian mission rooted in history and centred on the Christ-event. The changes in perspective of the theological elements may also be due to the programmatic fulfilment of history in accordance with the plan of God in Christ and his ongoing work in the church. What scholars often overlook in the theology of the author of Luke-Acts is his theology of mission. It is crucial for both volumes as this is the only means by which the gospel can be preached and thus bring people to salvation. Even from the beginning of his Gospel to the end of Acts, Luke has succeeded in portraying the birth, growth and the development of Christian mission. Mission to Gentiles is in focus throughout Luke-Acts. Particularly, the stage is set for the Samaritan mission in the Gospel, and their mission is well portrayed in Acts. It must be noted that Luke has not changed his theology of mission in Acts from that depicted in his Gospel and that both the Gospel and Acts reflect unity in mission.

In this study I will use the term 'Luke' to refer to the author of Luke-Acts. He could be identified with the 'we' – narrator and a companion of Paul who on their journey stayed with Philip in Caesarea (Acts 21:8-10).[17] It should be noted that the use of the first person in the 'we'-sections can be understood in various ways: (a) It is a historical device of the author to show that he is an eyewitness of the events recounted in the narratives.[18] (b) It reflects the itinerary diary of the author.[19] (c) It is a literary device of the author to use

---

16.   See the discussion in I.H. Marshall, 'The Resurrection in the Acts of the Apostles', in W.W. Gasque and R.P. Martin (eds), *Apostolic History and the Gospel*, Biblical and Historical Essays presented to F.F. Bruce on his 60th Birthday (Exeter: The Paternoster Press, 1970), pp. 92–107.

17.   For a discussion on this view, see Hemer, *Acts*, pp. 309–64.

18.   J. Dupont, *The Sources of Acts: The Present Position* (London: Darton, Longman & Todd, 1964), pp. 75–93, 94–112, gives us a survey of various studies carried out on the 'we'-sources of Acts, and then suggests that the author uses the first person plural deliberately because he 'wishes it to be understood that he has personally taken part in the events he is recounting' (p. 167).

19.   J.A. Fitzmyer, *Luke the Theologian: Aspects of his Teaching* (New York: Paulist Press, 1989), pp. 16–22, thinks that the 'we'- passages come from a record that the author himself kept during his travels with Paul, and later he made use of it in his narrative in Acts. For the view that Luke, the author of Acts himself had possessed an itinerary diary, see M. Dibelius,

the first person as in the context of sea voyages of the first-century Greco-Roman literature.[20] It may be that the author took part in some of the events described in Acts, and that he is also the author of the 'we'-passages (16:10-17; 20:5-15; 21:1-18; 27:1–28:16).[21]

1.2. *Preview of the Research*

Part I (Chapter 2) is a survey of research which has been done on Acts 8:4-25.

Part II is a historical exploration of the socio-religious and ethnic background of the Samaritans up to and including the New Testament period (Chapter 3). This is not meant to provide a history of the origin of the Samaritans; rather it is to highlight the overall situation of the Samaritans during the first century CE which in turn, would enable us to evaluate the significance of Luke's account of Jesus' encounter with the Samaritans (Chapter 4). Here, I will also argue the possible identification of Luke's mention of the 'city of Samaria' (Acts 8:5) with Sebaste, the capital city of the Old Testament Samaria. The significance is that Luke tries to portray the mission to the Samaritans carried out in a place where they lost their socio-political and religious identity as part of the people of God and that he intends to show their new identity in Christ as they believed in the gospel. Chapter 4 will examine the Samaritan references in the Gospel of Luke, which form part of the *Sondergut* of Luke, and will bring out the role they play in the mission to them described in Acts. It will also explore the theological significance for Luke of his positive portrayal of the Samaritans. The main argument in this chapter is that the Samaritan references in the Gospel of Luke signify an anticipation of a Samaritan mission, an anticipation which

Studies in the Acts of the Apostles (London: SCM Press, 1956), pp. 5–8. B. Witherington, *The Acts of the Apostles: A Socio-Rhetorical Commentary* (Michigan: Wm.B. Eerdmans Publishing Co, 1998), pp. 167–71, suggests that the 'we' passages are Luke's expansion of his own notes taken while travelling with Paul.

20.   V.K. Robbins, 'By Land and By Sea: The We-Passages and Ancient Sea Voyages' in C.H. Talbert (ed.), *Perspectives on Luke-Acts* (Edinburgh: T. & T. Clark, 1978), pp. 215–42. For a different view that the author of Acts has utilized a continuous independent source probably discovered in the course of his investigation, see Stanley E. Porter, 'The "We" Passages', in David W.J. Gill and Conrad Gempf (eds), *The Book of Acts in Its First Century Setting. vol. 2: The Book of Acts in Its Graeco-Roman Setting* (Grand Rapids: Wm.B. Eerdmans Publishing Co., 1994), pp. 545–74. Also see J. Wehnert, *Die Wir-Passagen der Apostelgeschichte: Ein lukanisches Stilmittel aus jüdischer Tradition* (GTA 40; Göttingen: Vandenhoeck & Ruprecht, 1989); for a summary of various views, see S.M. Praeder, 'The Problem of First Person Narration in Acts', *NovT* 29 (1987), pp. 193–218.

21.   If the author was not a companion of Paul, it is highly unlikely that he would retain the first person plural form 'we' instead of the third person in the narrative of these events. For this view, see Marshall, *Acts*, pp. 36–9; A.D. Nock, *Essays on Religion and the Ancient World I and II* (Harvard: Harvard University Press, 1972), pp. 821–32; J. Jervell, 'The Future of the Past: Luke's Vision of Salvation History and Its Bearing on His Writing of History', in Witherington (ed.), *History*, pp. 104–26.

is rooted in the initiative of Jesus himself and which forms part of Luke's legit-imating device for authenticating Samaritan Christianity in Acts 8:4-25. In other words, Part II is designed to lay the foundation for placing the Samaritans in perspective to understand Luke's purpose for the way he portrays the Samaritan mission in Acts.

Part III focuses on the study of the portrait of the Samaritan mission in Acts 8:4-25 by employing structural (synchronic) and exegetical analyses of the text. Chapter 5 provides a structural analysis of the text to explore the literary technique Luke employs and the theological purpose he intends to achieve. It is argued that Luke employs a technique of 'reversal' to portray the successful mission to the Samaritans and to authenticate Samaritan Christianity. An exegesis of the text is undertaken in Chapter 6 to evaluate the theological motivation of Luke in his portrayal of the Samaritan mission. This study will further expose the legitimating purpose of Luke in Acts 8:4-25. Chapter 7 reiterates the rhetorical and theological function of the Lukan portrait of the Samaritan mission, especially in light of the historical and narrative analyses of the text. It will reaffirm the significance of Acts 8:4-25 in that Luke defends the divine origin and legitimacy of Samaritan Christianity and contends that his purpose may be apologetic. Chapter 8 is a summary and conclusion of the findings of the research.

1.3. Methodologies Employed

This study will employ various methodological approaches appropriate to the particular area of interest under investigation in each chapter. It will take up tradition-historical, redaction-critical and literary critical methods, which may be deemed relevant at various points of the research. The traditional methods of source- and textual-critical analysis are retained in the present study of Acts 8:4-25. Since the Samaritan references are uniquely Lukan materials, one needs to ask whether Luke had enough sources and traditions for what he narrates in Acts 8:4-25. If he had, how can we detect their presence in the present text and to what extent are they reliable? Did they come to Luke in the way they are given in the text or did he himself combine various traditions?

However, historical-critical analysis of Acts has its own problems and limitations.[22] This is partly because of the lack of parallel materials to check the available data and partly because of the literary creativity of Luke. The

---

22. See discussions in R.A. Culpepper, 'Story and History in the Gospels', *RevE* 81 (1984), pp. 467–77; L.E. Keck, 'Will the Historical-Critical Method Survive? Some Observations', in R.A. Spencer (ed.), *Orientation by Disorientation: Studies in Literary Criticism and Biblical Literary Criticism, Presented in Honor of William A Beardslee* (PTMS 35; Pittsburgh: Pickwick Press, 1980), pp. 115–27.

difficulty has long been stated by Cadbury: 'It need not be supposed that Luke knew all that history himself, but he diligently and carefully embodied what thus came to him into a new comprehensive publication, editing it in accordance with the conventions of his time, adapting it to his purpose and in part stamping it with his own personality'.[23] Luke's personality or individuality is reflected in his writing style and it affects the accuracy of his work.[24] Likewise, M. Dibelius who applied the methods of form-criticism and style-criticism to the book of Acts claimed that Luke was able to greatly extend his literary freedom in Acts because, unlike in his Gospel, he had no predecessors to follow their example for narrating the events he describes.[25] E. Haenchen, following the work of Dibelius, argued that Luke did not have enough sources at his disposal for the composition of Acts as no tradition existed about the words and deeds of the apostles. [26] For him, the words and deeds of Jesus were the object of tradition during the apostolic period and so there was no possibility for the formation of an apostle-tradition.[27] H. Conzelmann strongly suggested that Luke had used sources for the composition of Acts, but their reconstruction is impossible as Luke reworked his materials as he did with his sources in the Gospel.[28] J. Dupont in his extensive study on *The Sources of Acts*, offered a survey of various theories proposed by scholars regarding possible sources of Acts. He concludes, 'it has not been possible to define any of the sources used by the author of Acts in a way which will meet with widespread agreement among the critics'.[29]

Despite the limitations of the historical-critical method, the attempt to probe behind the text to the underlying traditions in Acts has not fully been given up. G. Lüdemann's work on the task of separating tradition from

23.   Cadbury, *Luke-Acts*, p. 110.

24.   Cadbury, *Luke-Acts*, says that it is not the author's identity, his name or even his own part in the events that affects the reliability of the work, but his own personal habits of mind. Thus, Cadbury claims: 'Authorship by a companion of Paul is in itself no guarantee of trustworthiness' (p. 363).

25.   Dibelius, *Studies*, argued that the first part of Acts (chs 1-12) is not based on any source, but Luke joined together separate stories of very unequal value in the style of legend, by inserting speeches, composing connecting-links, and interpolating other details to present a story of the development of an early community. 'At least there is no philological criterion which would permit us to establish a unified source in this part of the book' (p. 105). But, according to Dibelius, Luke has a 'thread' for chapters 13-21, for he had an itinerary of Paul's journey, which he filled out with stories of varying historical value. Here we do not have old traditions, but 'the communications of a well informed man upon what he was able to ascertain' (p. 105).

26.   Haenchen, *The Acts of the Apostles: A Commentary* (Oxford: Basil Blackwell, 1971), pp. 81–2.

27.   Contrary to this position, see Jervell, 'The Problem of Traditions in Acts', *ST* 16 (1962), pp. 25–41, reprinted in *Luke and the People of God*, pp. 19–40.

28.   Conzelmann, *The Acts of the Apostles* (Philadelphia: Fortress Press, 1987), pp. xxxvi–vii; also Bruce, 'Historical Record', pp. 2588–9; H.C. Kee, *Understanding the New Testament* (New Jersey: Prentice-Hall, Inc., 1983), p. 174.

29.   Dupont, *Sources*, p. 166.

redaction in Acts is an ideal example for this.[30] He admits that Luke has used some traditions to write Acts, but questions the historical value of these traditions. He raises two reasons, as were also identified by other scholars mentioned above, for the considerable difficulties in discovering these traditions. (1) The literary character of Acts: (a) Because Luke has fused the material he uses into his own language, the 'vocabulary statistics' method of literary criticism is not helpful, (b) the 'tensions' do not always reflect the pre-existing material, but it can arise from the redaction of the author. (2) None of the material on which Acts was based has been preserved (apart from the OT quotations and the reference back to the Gospel of Luke).

As an alternative approach to the historical-critical method and due to an awareness of the need for a more literary study of the scripture, literary criticism has found a place in biblical studies.[31] By this method the reader finds the meaning in the text by engaging with the text itself rather than looking for meaning through the text. This approach sees the ancient text not as a 'window' into the historical situation of the then time and place but as a 'mirror' reflecting the present existence of the reader. Within the literary discipline, the narrative-critical study of biblical texts has dawned, which views the text as a story and seeks to find meaning in the text from the perspective of its 'implied reader'.[32] Using narrative criticism, studies on the overall structure and literary patterns of Luke's narrative come into focus.[33] Since Acts is taken as a narrative that conveys a complex message and promotes values and beliefs, the narrative-critical approach has become a literary discipline also in Acts studies. Tannehill's *The Narrative Unity of Luke-Acts* is an obvious example of this approach to the Lukan studies. He says that narrative criticism is employed in Acts 'in order to understand this narrative's message, a message that cannot be confined to theological state-

---

30.   G. Lüdemann, *Early Christianity according to the Traditions in Acts*, trans. J. Bowden (London: SCM Press, 1989), p. 9.

31.   For a useful discussion on various methodologies in the study of biblical texts, see W.A Beardslee, *Literary Criticism of the New Testament* (Philadelphia: Fortress Press, 1969); S.D. Moore, *Literary Criticism and the Gospels: The Theoretical Challenge* (New Haven: Yale University Press, 1989); J.B. Green (ed.), *Hearing the New Testament: Strategies for Interpretation* (Grand Rapids: Wm.B. Eerdmans Publishing Company, 1995); J. Barton (ed.), *The Cambridge Companion to Biblical Interpretation* (Cambridge: Cambridge University Press, 1998).

32.   See Mark Allan Powell, *What is Narrative Criticism?* (Minneapolis: Fortress Press, 1990).

33.   The literary style of Luke was already noted by Cadbury, *Luke-Acts*; other studies on the literary character of Luke include, C.H. Talbert, *Literary Patterns, Theological Themes and Genre of Luke-Acts* (SBLMS 20; Missoula: Scholars Press, 1974); *idem, Reading Luke: A Literary and Theological Commentary on the Third Gospel* (New York: Crossroad, 1982); L.T. Johnson, *The Literary Function of Possessions in Luke-Acts* (SBLDS 39; Missoula, Montana, 1977); D.P. Moessner, *Lord of the Banquet: The Literary and Theological Significance of the Lukan Travel Narrative* (Minneapolis: Fortress Press, 1989).

ments but encompasses a rich set of attitudes and images that are embedded in the story and offered for our admiration and imitation'.[34] It is evident that recently there has been an increasing interest in approaching the character of Luke-Acts as narrative.[35]

Like narrative criticism, structuralism also has been found to be a useful tool in the study of biblical texts.[36] Though it has been applied to various texts, no effort has been made to study the Acts texts structurally.[37] The word 'structure' is used to mean a 'pattern' or 'arrangement' of a text as in rhetorical criticism. It is also used in the structuralist sense to mean the 'hidden or underlying configuration that can offer some explanation for the more or less visible or obvious pattern in the text'.[38] The complexity of the nature and application of structuralism is reflected when David C. Greenwood says, 'No scholar has so far succeeded in providing a definition of structuralism which is universally acceptable'.[39] This is because of the disagreement as to whether or not structuralism is a philosophy, science or a discipline.[40] However, structuralism involves both decomposition and recomposition of a narrative and fabricates all the *possible* meanings from its structure.[41]

Structural analysis, as a method, is a development of 'structural linguistics',[42] and historically it is the application of principles derived from

---

34.   Tannehill, *Luke-Acts* II, p. 4.

35.   Other recent studies include S.M. Sheeley, *Narrative Asides in Luke-Acts* (JSNTSup.72; Sheffield: Sheffield Academic Press, 1992); W.S. Kurz, *Reading Luke-Acts: Dynamics of Biblical Narrative* (Louisville: Westminster Press, 1993); W.H. Shepherd, *The Narrative Function of the Holy Spirit as a Character in Luke-Acts* (SBLDS 147; Atlanta: Scholars Press, 1994).

36.   D. Patte, *Structural Exegesis for New Testament Critics* (Minneapolis: Fortress Press, 1989).

37.   Patte, *The Gospel According to Matthew: A Structural Commentary on Matthew's Faith* (Philadelphia: Fortress Press, 1987); however, the study of Roland Barthes, 'Structural Analysis of a Narrative from Acts X-XI', in A.M. Johnson, Jr. (ed.), *Structuralism and Biblical Hermeneutics: A Collection of Essays* (Pennsylvania: The Pickwick Press, 1979), pp. 109–43, is an exception in Acts.

38.   Dan Via, *Kerygma and Comedy in the New Testament: A Structuralist Approach to Hermeneutic* (Philadelphia: Fortress Press, 1975), p. 7.

39.   Greenwood, *Structuralism and the Biblical Text* (New York: Mouton Publishers, 1985), p. 2.

40.   Barthes, 'Acts X-XI', says that structural analysis of a narrative 'is not yet a science nor is it even properly speaking a discipline' (p.109), and can not be treated as a 'biology or even as a sociology' (p.111). Likewise, Richard Jacobson, 'The Structuralists and the Bible', *Int* 28 (2, April 1974), pp. 146–64, contends: 'In large measure, structuralism, which is not quite a science but an array of methods, is very much in the process of "speaking itself"' (p.146).

41.   Barthes, *Critical Essays*, trans. R. Howard (Evanston: Northwestern University Press, 1972), pp. 217–18, says: 'The object of structuralism is not man endowed with meaning but man fabricating meaning'.

42.   Barthes, 'Acts X-XI', p. 110.

Saussurian linguistics.[43] It is concerned with the linguistic paradigm of the text without aiming at what the author meant.[44] Whether or not the author intended this structure is not relevant but it affirms that the 'meaning' is in the semantic dimension of the 'language'. It assumes that when language imposes itself upon the author, significations are also imposed upon him. The 'meaning' of a text includes the author's intentions and various unconscious constraints, which impose themselves upon him. According to D. Patte, this meaning is produced by the interaction of three types of constraints or structures or (structural levels) within a text.[45] (1) The structures of enunciation, which are the constraints of the author's intentionality and his *Sitz im Leben*, (2) the cultural structures, which are constraints common only to a specific group of people and (3) the deep structures, the unconscious constraints which impose themselves on any author. Therefore, a text becomes meaningful only when it evokes for the readers all these structures which preside over the creation of the text.

When historical investigation is possible in the level of enunciation and cultural level, structural analysis aims to study all the structures, especially the deep structures, and thus to deconstruct the 'meaning effect' of a text. Structural analysis implies a plurality of 'structural meanings'[46] and different structural levels expose different structural meanings. Each structural study

43.   Ferdinand de Saussure, *Course in General Linguistics* (New York: McGraw Hill, 1966), pp. 13–14, proposed the distinction between *langue* (language) and *parole* (speech), where *langue* is 'the sum of word-images stored in the minds of all individuals', and *parole* is a specific message. The structure of a language is a relational network where the words are organized into a system. The words are signs in which each sign has two components: *signifier* (sound-image) and *signified* (content). The process by which signifier and signified are united into a sign is signification. L. Hjelmslev, *Prolegomena to a Theory of Language* (Madison: University of Wisconsin, 1961), who is another linguist, uses the terminology, *expression* (for Saussure's signifier) and *content* (for Saussure's signified) and *relation* (for Saussure's signification); Greenwood, *Structuralism*, p. 2.

44.   There are various analogies, which structuralists use for illustrating the structural activity. For example, the imagery by Levi-Strauss of (1) musical performance (the musical score with horizontal and vertical dimensions); (2) geological stratum (a landscape comprising hills, valleys, trees, etc.) and (3) traffic lights (from the colour spectrum, three colours, which are Green, Red and Yellow, are apprehended by the human brain as a signal system). For details see, Levi-Strauss, *The Raw and the Cooked: Introduction to a Science of Mythology* I, trans. J. & D. Weightmann (New York: Harper & Row, 1969); R.A. Spivey, 'Structuralism and Biblical Studies: The Uninvited Guest', *Int* 28 (2, April 1974), pp. 133–45. Patte uses the imagery of a hand-woven blanket, where the creativity of the author, the loom and the set of coloured threads determine the final form, *What is Structural Exegesis?* (Philadelphia: Fortress Press, 1976), pp. 21–5.

45.   Patte, *Structural Exegesis?*, pp. 22–5.

46.   Barthes, 'Acts X-XI', p. 118, says that the Structural analysis differs from the Philological analysis because it does not seek to establish 'the' meaning or 'one' meaning of the text, rather it attempts to establish 'the possible basis of meanings, or rather the plurality of meaning or the meaning as plural'. He further mentions that for Structural analysis, 'all the roots of the text are up in the air' (p. 119).

points out a plurality of meanings; that is, a given structure is a set of semantic potentialities of the text. Analysis of the deep structure involves formalization of the text. Formalization is to fit the text into a grid composed of horizontal (Syntagm) and vertical (paradigm) axes. When each element of the text is associated with elements, which precede and follow it in the text, it is a linear, chain-like, syntagmatic reading of the text. Paradigmatic reading of the text is the gathering together of the elements, which manifest in a given structure. A structural approach is synchronic in contrast to the diachronic, linear horizontal historical study of the text.

Our study will also adopt structural analysis, which will include both syntagmatic and paradigmatic reading of Acts 8:4-25, and will integrate various approaches, mainly those of Roland Barthes and A.J. Greimas. Barthes' analysis of the text is relatively unscientific and arises from the 'paradigm of difference'.[47] It seeks to understand the structure of a narrative in terms of its difference from a fixed model. It portrays the generative structure of the historical subject. Barthes' method incorporates both diachronic and synchronic elements and therefore there is no antithesis between history and structure.[48] Greimas' methodology is both scientific and 'deductive' and aims to uncover the semantic structures of the narrative.[49] According to him, each narrative structure includes six distinct elements: sequence, syntagm, statement, actantial model, function, and actant.[50] The major feature of his method is the 'actantial analysis', where the actants are divided into three opposing pairs: (1) Subject versus Object, (2) Sender (*Destinateur*) versus Receiver (*Destinataire*), and (3) Helper (*Adjuvant*) versus Opponent (*Opposant*). We will analyse the relevant texts using this model in Chapter 5 of this book.

47.   R. Barthes, *Image, Music and Texts* (New York: Hill and Wang, 1977), pp. 79–124.

48.   Since structural analysis focuses only on the literary work, the major objection against structuralism is that it is a- or anti-historical, and that it is a 'Formalist Fallacy'. This is because of the claim that Structural analysis is synonymous with Russian Formalism, a method which does not consider other factors such as socio-cultural and historical information beyond the literature itself. According to this objection, structural analysis, like Russian Formalism, neglects the 'content' and the ethnographical context of the literary works and is incompatible with history. However, many structuralists claim that these factors themselves make Structuralism distinct from Formalism, and the former it is claimed, is compatible with historical research. On this issue, see C. Levi-Strauss, 'Structure and Form: Reflections on a Work by Vladmir Propp', *Structural Anthropology* II, trans. M. Layton (New York: Basic Books, 1976), pp. 115–45; A.M. Johnson, 'Structuralism, Biblical Hermeneutics, and the Role of Structural Analysis in Historical Research', in Johnson (ed.), *Structuralism*, pp. 1–28.

49.   Greimas, 'The Interpretation of Myth: Theory and Practice', in P. Maranda and E.K. Maranda, *Structural Analysis of Oral Tradition* (Philadelphia: University of Pennsylvania, 1971), pp. 81–121.

50.   See Greimas, *Structural Semantics: An Attempt at Method*, trans. D. McDowell, *et al.* (Lincoln: University of Nebraska Press, 1983). Theoretical explanation of these terms will be illustrated in the structural analyses of the passages under consideration in Ch. 5.

Any attempt to understand the significance of the Lukan portrait of the Samaritan mission in Acts 8:4-25 cannot completely overlook the socio-historical world of Luke's time for the sake of exploring his story world or vice versa, especially since the Samaritans play a part in Luke-Acts. That the knowledge of the socio-historical world of Luke is essential in the narrative-critical study of Acts is evident in the comments of Tannehill:

> ... an understanding of first century society and of historical events within it may be important for understanding Acts as a narrative. ... I believe that study of first-century Mediterranean literature and society may illuminate unspoken assumptions behind the narrative and may also suggest specific reasons for emphases in the text.[51]

That historical investigation is still valued is further evident from what M.A. Powell says: 'Literary criticism of the book of Acts will never replace traditional-historical and theological modes of interpretation. It is unlikely that people of faith will ever be satisfied to read these stories of faith simply as stories, without wanting to inquire into the history that lies behind them'.[52]

There are Lukan studies that combine both the historical context and the narrative context of the text. For example, M.C. Parsons' *The Departure of Jesus in Luke-Acts* is a combined approach of diachronic and synchronic analyses of the ascension narratives in Lk. 24 and Acts 1. He comments: 'Preoccupation with historical questions, coupled with disregard for the literary context of the passage, may easily lead to a distortion of the significance of the pericope for understanding the larger story of Jesus and his followers in Luke-Acts'.[53] A recent attempt to demonstrate the interpenetration of story and history is Samuel Byrskog's work on *Story as History – History as Story,*[54] where the author employs the oral history approach and argues for the connection between history and story in the early Christian literature. According to him:

> ... it becomes obvious that the absolutizing of the narrative world of a story focuses too much on the interpreted history and neglects the widespread notion and practice of the interaction between history as a past event and history within the story. All too often our analytical methods tend to silence the oral history and the living voice of the ancient people, burying them under the sophisticated patterns of various literary strategies![55]

---

51. Tannehill, *Luke-Acts* II, pp. 4–5.
52. M.A. Powell, *What are they Saying about Acts?* (Mahwah: Paulist Press, 1991), p. 107.
53. Parsons, *The Departure of Jesus in Luke-Acts: The Ascension Narratives in Context* (JSNTSup.21; Sheffield: Sheffield Academic Press, 1987), p. 15.
54. Byrskog, *Story as History – History as Story: The Gospel Tradition in the Context of Ancient Oral History* (WUNT 123; Tübingen: Mohr Siebeck, 2000).
55. Byrskog, *Story*, p. 266.

The interplay between the interpretative and narrativizing procedures concerns much more than literary and argumentative techniques, reaching its climax as history is narrativized into a coherent story that exhibits the author's own conceptual framework. ... The historians' grand patterns of interpretation functioned as a bridge between the two worlds, bringing history and story together.[56]

The preceding comments and works of scholars make it clear that the historical and literary approaches to a text are not incompatible with each other. Since one approach would enhance the other, this study also will employ both historical or diachronic approach and the narrative or structural synchronic analysis to determine the function and purpose of the Lukan text on the Samaritan mission in its historical and narrative contexts.

---

56. Byrskog, *Story*, pp. 303–4.

Chapter 2

A SURVEY OF RECENT DISCUSSIONS ON ACTS 8:4-25

2.1. Introduction

The aim of this chapter is to present various views and issues arising out of previous scholarly discussion of the Samaritan mission episode in Acts 8:4-25. As we shall see, Acts 8:4-25, which comprises the Samaritan mission of Philip, including the conversion of Simon the magician (vv. 4-13), the intervention of the Jerusalem apostles, Peter and John and the delay of the Holy Spirit (vv. 14-17), and Peter's confrontation with Simon (vv. 18-25) raises, for many scholars and for various reasons, considerable difficulty in interpreting the text. The first section of the present survey is categorized into source-critical, narrative and theological approaches as they have emerged from previous scholarship in its examination of individual units or of the whole narrative in Acts 8:4-25. Since the questions on the coming of the apostles and the delay of the Holy Spirit, and the confrontation with Simon Magus have been the focus of much discussion, they will be treated separately in the subsequent sections. However, no effort will be made to explore the Lukan theology of baptism and the Holy Spirit, as they are beyond the scope of our research. The present survey will help us to benefit from earlier research as well as to identify the gaps in laying out a possible and reasonable option in ascertaining the function of Acts 8:4-25.

2.2. The Samaritan Mission of Philip: Views and Issues

2.2.1. Source-Critical Approaches
In 1906, Hans Waitz in his source-critical study of Acts 8 insisted on the existence of a Petrine *Grundschrift* underlying the text of Acts 8:5-25.[1] According to him, Peter, not Philip, was the main figure in both the story of the Samaritan mission and the conversion of the Ethiopian eunuch. Since Luke said in Acts 8:1 that the apostles remained in Jerusalem during the persecution, he could only substitute Philip for Peter.[2] Therefore, Luke ascribes to

---

1. Waitz, 'Die Quelle der Philippusgeschichten in der Apostelgeschichte 8,5-40', *ZNW* 7 (1906)', pp. 340–55.
2. Waitz, 'Quelle', p. 352.

Philip what was originally carried out by Peter in Acts 8. This view of Waitz was overturned by Julius Wellhausen in 1914 when he claimed that the reference to Peter is only a Lukan construction, for the story originally depicted Simon's offer of money not to Peter, but to Philip to buy the ability to heal the sick.[3] This opinion is based on the link, which Luke makes between Acts 8:18b and v. 13b on Simon's amazement. These two extreme and diverse claims of Waitz and Wellhausen – Petrine tradition versus Philip's tradition – show the complexity of the problem involved in interpreting the text.

Similar to the view of Waitz, Dietrich-Alex Koch has argued for a Peter-Simon tradition behind Acts 8:18-24.[4] Koch begins his reconstruction of the entire narrative by separating Simon from the tradition of the missionary activity of Philip in Samaria and his contact with Philip himself. He claims that the information about Simon in the Philip narrative of vv. 9-11, 13 is originally part of the Peter-Simon tradition but Luke in his redactional activity brought Philip and Simon together in order to expand rather scanty materials on Philip.[5] He thinks that Peter, given his prominent place in early Palestinian Christianity, is the natural choice to be the best opponent of Simon. And, he conjectures that there lies an oral tradition of a sharp conflict between Peter and Simon.[6] This pre-Lukan tradition was aimed at the complete defeat of Simon and his followers. Koch thinks that the original issue of the conflict was the possession of the Spirit, not the ability to induce the Spirit.[7] The evidence he presents for his case is the phrase δωρεὰ τοῦ θεοῦ in v. 20 which is taken to mean in Koch's view the Spirit itself, rather than the ἐξουσία in v. 19.[8] Koch points to the ambiguous and indecisive conclusion to the Peter-Simon encounter in v. 24 as Luke leaves the Simon story open-ended and does not say explicitly whether Simon repented and was restored to the Christian fellowship. In Koch's view this ambiguous conclusion to the conflict between Peter and Simon in vv. 21-24 is a Lukan redaction since it is incompatible with an oral tradition of a sharp conflict found in the pre-Lukan tradition.[9] He assumes that it was not possible for Luke to portray

---

3. Wellhausen, *Kritische Analyse der Apostelgeschichte* (Berlin: Weidmann, 1914), p. 15.
4. Koch, 'Geistbesitz', pp. 64–82.
5. Koch, 'Geistbesitz', p. 78.
6. Koch, 'Geistbesitz', pp. 71–4.
7. Koch, 'Geistbesitz', p. 76.
8. Lüdemann, *Traditions*, p. 99, says that 'such a differentiation is over-sharp, and is no use for dividing redaction from tradition, especially as the theme of the Spirit dominates the section vv. 14-17 which Koch also sees as redactional, and the special theme of the laying on of hands and the bestowal of the Spirit fits smoothly with vv. 14-17'. The text in vv. 19-20 implies that the power to bestow the Holy Spirit, like the Spirit itself, is the free gift of God. See Shepherd, *Narrative Function*, p. 182.
9. Koch, 'Geistbesitz', p. 71.

Simon as an authentic convert to Christianity (8:13) and at the same time to make a conclusion as to his being someone outside the Christian community (v. 24). If Luke had portrayed either Simon's absolute submission to Peter or his rejection by Peter, the presence of the continued existence of Simonians would have proved the opposite and so also would prove Peter's curse ineffective. However, Koch does not claim that the original tradition contained Simon's submission to Peter. Therefore, in Koch's view, Luke takes a middle ground where he maintains the superiority of the apostles and an ambiguous end of Simon's fate.[10]

In 1939, O. Bauernfeind who tried to separate tradition from Lukan composition in Acts 8:4-25 claimed that in 8:4-25 Luke had conflated two originally independent sources, one about the Samaritan mission of Philip, and another about Peter and Simon Magus, and combined them with a redactional bridge of vv. 14-17.[11] Based on this view, Dibelius, Haenchen and Conzelmann argued that Luke had composed a traditional story originally about the Philip-Simon encounter with fabricated material concerning the apostles.[12] It was Wellhausen who originally presented this view and later on it was carried over by Dibelius and others. Dibelius comments: 'Originally, Simon probably asked Philip himself if he could buy the gift of performing miracles and was refused by him; but our text misses the point of this refusal as it takes place in an atmosphere half of cursing and half of regret and with no result'.[13] According to Haenchen, 'there was no initial connection between the stories of Simon and Philip'.[14] This is because he thinks that Philip ministered among the Samaritan Jews and Simon worked among the Gentile population of Samaria. He also claims that in order to show Philip's success of ministry in converting even Simon Magus, Luke downgraded Simon from the rank of an incarnate god to that of a magician. Again, Simon offered money not to the apostles, but to Philip; not to buy the gift of conferring the Spirit, but that of the miraculous powers of Philip. Haenchen claims that the whole episode in vv. 14-25 is a Lukan creation: 'Luke has done no less than to take the combination of baptism, laying-on of hands and reception of the Spirit, which in the belief and custom of his time formed one indissoluble whole, and divide it among Philip and the apostles in such a way that the former got the beginning and the latter the end'.[15]

---

10.   Koch, 'Geistbesitz', pp. 78–80.
11.   Bauernfeind, *Die Apostelgeschichte* (ThHKNT 5; Leipzig: Deichert, 1939), pp. 124–5.
12.   Dibelius, *Studies*, p. 17; Conzelmann, *Acts*, pp. 62–3; Haenchen, *Acts*, pp. 307–8.
13.   Dibelius, *Studies*, p. 17.
14.   Haenchen, *Acts*, p. 307.
15.   Haenchen, *Acts*, p. 308.

In his analysis of tradition and redaction in Acts 8:4-25, Lüdemann claims the Lukan influence and the redactional motivation as clearly featured on the text. He suggests that the activity of Philip in vv. 5-8 is in all probability a historical fact, for it is based on 'the tradition of a spirit-filled activity of the preacher Philip in Samaria'.[16] The tradition about Simon underlying vv. 9-13 is 'part of a written or oral tradition from the Hellenist circles which reported the clash between the supporters of Simonian and Christian religion'.[17] He further suggests that this Hellenist tradition 'would have contained not only an account of the successful mission to the Gentiles in Samaria but also an account of the victory over the god of the Simonians'.[18] Thus Lüdemann claims that the Hellenists clashed with the Gnostic Simonian religion in Samaria and that here Luke is working on a reliable tradition. Though Lüdemann sees the section as thoroughly Lukan in language, he identifies the designation Δύναμις Μεγάλη for Simon as part of the tradition. That both the Lukan account and the early Christian sources report that Simon had a significant number of followers in Samaria affirms a tradition about Simon. Thus he is able to say, 'the tradition which Luke works on in Acts 8 is reliable in this detail'.[19] For him, the bestowal of the Holy Spirit and the Peter-Simon encounter in vv. 14-24 is a Lukan composition, for it is 'redactional in both language and content'.[20]

Jervell has argued in a similar line that Luke's interest in the Samaritans goes beyond and above the tradition and that there is more than a source and a tradition in Acts 8 taken over by Luke without revision.[21] His main claims are the following. (1) The language and style in Acts 8 are typically Lukan. (2) It is only Luke who associated the Jerusalem apostles with the Samaritan mission. (3) The theological comments are typically Lukan, as in Acts 1:8, 9:31 and 15:3 where the Samaritans are specifically mentioned. (4) The Lukan insertion of the special materials into the Gospel (Lk. 10, 17) indicates a particular interest in the Samaritans.

F.F. Bruce while referring to the absence of Philip's role in vv. 14-24 suggests that Luke here draws on a Jerusalem source, departing from the Hellenist source which he used for the previous narrative.[22] Likewise, Fitzmyer thinks that the information that Luke uses in this episode of Peter and Simon about the role of the Spirit in the Christian life 'has undoubtedly come to him from a prior tradition, most likely of Palestinian origin'.[23] This

---

16. Lüdemann, *Traditions*, p. 98.
17. Lüdemann, *Traditions*, p. 98.
18. Lüdemann, *Traditions*, p. 99.
19. Lüdemann, *Traditions*, p. 101.
20. Lüdemann, *Traditions*, p. 96.
21. Jervell, 'Lost Sheep', pp. 113–32, 115.
22. Bruce, *The Acts of the Apostles* (Michigan: Wm.B. Eerdmans Publishing Co., 1990), p. 220.
23. Fitzmyer, *The Acts of the Apostles: A New Translation with Introduction and Commentary* (AB; Garden City, New York: Doubleday and Co., 1998), p. 401.

view of Bruce and Fitzmyer contradicts that of Haenchen, Lüdemann and others who claim that vv. 14-25 is entirely Lukan redaction.[24]

C.K. Barrett raises some historical and literary issues on the relationship of the narrative of Acts 8:4-25 to the traditional material:

> What sources did Luke use? How did he combine them? What was their historical value, and how far was any historical value they may originally have possessed preserved and how far destroyed in the editorial process? These are not questions that can be answered with confidence, and those who discuss them should remember that they are usually guessing, even when their guesses are guided by observation and probability.[25]

Barrett raises the issue of the uniformity of Lukan style and vocabulary with regard to Acts 8:4-25. He says, 'Luke has not only imposed his own style on the material but has organized it into a straightforward narrative', and the passage does not shed much light on the sources and traditions used by Luke.[26] He thinks vv. 5-13 and vv. 14-25 must originally have been distinct, as Philip is the central figure in the former and he is absent in the latter and the apostles are in the centre of the stage.[27] He goes further to say, 'Luke in Acts 8 goes out of his way to integrate into each other the activity of the Seven and that of the twelve in a composite narrative'.[28] It means that any implied relation between Philip and the apostles is a Lukan product rather than tradition.[29] This is based on the geographical consideration of Philip's movements in the rest of the chapter and on the action ascribed to him in the narrative. Luke knew little more than that Philip was one of the Seven and that while this group founded the church at Antioch, Philip was to be connected with Caesarea. Barrett also claims that the pre-Lukan tradition did not connect Philip and Simon together. This is because he thinks that v. 13 is the only verse that brings Philip and Simon together and that it is probably an editorial supplement designed to connect them.[30] It was Simon who was firmly located in Samaria and it was traditions about Simon, not about either Philip or Peter that fixed the events in Acts 8:4-25. It means that 'Simon is not a piece of cement holding Philip and Peter together ... he is rather a piece of traditional material existing in his own right'.[31] The arguments of Barrett

---

24.   Lüdemann, *Traditions*, p. 96; Matthews, 'Philip', p. 145.

25.   Barrett, 'Light on the Holy Spirit from Simon Magus (Acts 8,4-25)', in J. Kremer (ed.), *Les Actes des Apôtres: Traditions, Rédaction, Théologie* (BEThL 48; Louvain: Louvain University Press, 1979), pp. 281–95, 283.

26.   Barrett, *The Acts of the Apostles: A Critical and Exegetical Commentary* I (Edinburgh: T. & T. Clark, 1994), p. 395.

27.   Barrett, *Acts* I, p. 395.

28.   Barrett, 'Light', p. 282.

29.   Barrett, *Acts* I, p. 396; *idem*, 'Light', p. 285.

30.   Barrett, 'Light', pp. 283–4.

31.   Barrett, *Acts*, I, p. 396.

resemble that of Haenchen as both agree on the dissociation of Philip and Simon in the original tradition; for the former the reason is historical (that Philip and Simon worked in different locations) and for the latter it is literary (that only v. 13 combines them together).

C.R. Matthews makes an attempt to illustrate the presence of intertextual appropriation of canonical Acts in the redactional development of the story of the Peter-Simon encounter in the Apocryphal Acts of Peter (hereafter APt).[32] He contends that what we encounter in the early Christian stories involving Peter and Simon is 'a tantalizing piece of Lukan inventiveness'.[33] It means that the Peter-Simon encounter in the present text of Acts 8:18-24 is not based on any tradition, rather, it is a Lukan redaction and therefore Luke is responsible for the later expansions of the Peter-Simon contest in APt. This stands contrary to Koch's view that the conflict between Peter and Simon is based on Luke's tradition. Commenting on the nature of intertextual operation in the story of Peter-Simon contest in APt, Matthews says: 'It was Luke's juxtaposition of these two figures, in the absence of any substantiating traditions, that provided the impetus for the various successive (and successful) elaborations of this entertaining and edifying episode'.[34] He makes further remarks:

> If Luke first learned of Simon 'the magician' in connection with a tradition based on Philip's activity in Samaria, and, if he in the absence of any traditional information brought Simon into contact with Peter, then subsequent stories concerning Peter and Simon have their sufficient cause in Luke's transfer of a traditional element from Philip's 'biography' to Peter's.[35]

On the one hand, Matthews' claim may help us to raise the issue of the unhistorical nature of the Peter-Simon encounter in APt, for he supposes it to be based on the variations on the Lukan account. On the other hand, it raises the objection whether it is reasonable to cast a relatively earlier account of Luke as dubious and unhistorical, because an embellished version of the same story emerged after a century in APt. Matthews undoubtedly considers the activity of Philip in Samaria as depending on pre-Lukan tradition, though 'the possibility of reconstructing any underlying written source for these verses has been foreclosed by the thoroughly Lukan nature of the existing narrative'.[36] Later, Matthews broadens the Lukan text from 8:18-25 to 8:14-25 as to the extent of Lukan creation and assumes that Luke took advantage of Simon's presence in Samaria to bring him into contact with Peter in his redaction. Though Matthews does not provide any new evidence for

---

32. Matthews, 'Philip', pp. 133–46.
33. Matthews, 'Philip', p. 133; *idem, Philip*, pp. 63–4.
34. Matthews, 'Philip', p. 133.
35. Matthews, 'Philip', pp. 138–9; *idem, Philip*, pp. 50–54.
36. Matthews, 'Philip', p. 141.

his claim except to support a pre-Lukan tradition of Philip because of his 'unprecedented evangelizing activity' in Samaria, his view is similar to that of other scholars mentioned above.

F. Scott Spencer's monograph, *The Portrait of Philip in Acts*, remains one of the major works produced within the last few decades on the role of Philip himself. Regarding the issue of sources behind Acts 8:4-25, Spencer says:

> But in probing behind the present form of the text to uncover the sources which Luke utilized, many have detected a number of seams which supposedly betray a patching together of discrete traditions. Resulting from such analyses are nagging doubts about Luke's compositional skills and prevailing opinions that any supposed unity in 8.4-25 is more illusory than real.[37]

However, Spencer thinks that any attempt at getting behind the present text of 8:4-25 will bring us to a similar version of the text: 'If we insist on peering through Luke's story in search of what lies behind it, we may only be able, given the story's careful design, to envisage an original model which more resembles than deviates from the final version'.[38] That Spencer neither wants to bury any 'nagging doubts' nor wants to envisage an 'original model' is evident when he avoids the tradition-historical discussions on the narrative.

P.L. Dickerson seeks to reconstruct the sources utilised by Luke in Acts 8:5-25.[39] He begins with the question raised by scholars on the original connection between Philip and Simon in Luke's narrative. The reasons for claiming no connection between them can be either historical or literary. Dickerson avoids the historical question of whether Philip actually encountered Simon and this is because, he says: 'We may not know enough about the historical circumstances surrounding Simon's career and teaching to get past these historical problems'.[40] Therefore, he attempts to see whether Luke has created a literary link between Philip and Simon. He says that Luke has at least two sources: the first is Philip converting Samaria including Simon and the second the conflict between Peter and Simon. In other words, Philip was originally connected with Simon in the (first) source and Luke is not merging any sources to have a literary link between them. His reconstruction is based on the following arguments: (1) Luke is employing a stylistic device in 8:9-14, what Dickerson calls, 'New Character Narrative', which consists of the introduction, description and the story of a new character. Here, the new character Simon has to be introduced first (8:9a), and then to be described (8:8b-11) before Luke could actually begin the story involving Simon (8:12). Thus, Luke begins his narrative with an account

---

37. Spencer, *Portrait*, pp. 28–9.
38. Spencer, *Portrait*, p. 31.
39. Dickerson, 'The Sources of the Account of the Mission to Samaria in Acts 8:5-25', *NovT* 39 (3, 1997), pp. 210–34.
40. Dickerson, 'Sources', p. 212.

about an old character Philip and then introduces the new character Simon at the appropriate point. Therefore, that Philip and Simon do not appear together until 8:13 does not suggest Luke's merging of two sources, rather the connection between Philip and Simon in the source.[41] Dickerson's explanation here thus refutes the view of Barrett who claims the seemingly odd combination of Philip and Simon in 8:13 as Lukan redaction. (2) Based on Beyschlag's comparison of the portrait of Simon and Philip in 8:5-13, Dickerson argues that the similarity between the description of Simon and Philip is 'embedded in the narrative, but one must go looking for it'.[42] He continues: 'This makes sense if the comparison reflects the source but is obscured when Luke edits the source for his own purposes'.[43] Also, the information found in the description of the new character, Simon (9-11), reflects a source. 'As a rule, Luke is not particularly creative as regards the content of the description'.[44] Therefore, it is likely that Luke has a source, which says that the people of Samaria first followed Simon, then they (including Simon) followed Philip. Thus Dickerson, following the view of Barrett, suggests that Acts 8:14-25 reflects two different sources. So his conclusion is this: it may be that Luke has joined three sources for the entire narrative in 8:5-25: the Philip-Simon (vv. 5-13), the spirit-reception (vv. 14-16) and the Peter-Simon (vv. 17-24).

Witherington, while discussing the narrative in 8:4-25, claims that there are neither written sources other than Luke's own notes nor long histories of transmission and editing of material.[45] This is based on the view that Luke was sometime a companion of Paul including during the time when Paul visited Philip in Caesarea (Acts 21:8-10) and that he had direct access to Philip and/or his daughters over the few days of their stay and took his own notes. Therefore, for Witherington, the stories in Acts 8 are not a Lukan construction: 'In fact, this material at various points appears not to have received the benefit of much, if any, editing, and certainly not of a final literary polishing'.[46] He says further that the story of Philip and Simon (8:4-13) is very much attached to that of Peter and Simon (8:14-25) by the presence of Samaritans and Simon in each part, and the latter presupposes and depends on the former.[47] In other words, the story of Peter's activity in Samaria and his confrontation with Simon is not an independent narrative standing by its own. This position stands contrary to Haenchen, Lüdemann and others who think that there was no original connection between the story of Philip's activity in Samaria and that of the Peter-Simon encounter.

---

41. Dickerson, 'Sources', pp. 214–15.
42. Dickerson, 'Sources', pp. 215–19, 217.
43. Dickerson, 'Sources', p. 217.
44. Dickerson, 'Sources', p. 217.
45. Witherington, *Acts*, pp. 280–81.
46. Witherington, *Acts*, p. 281.
47. Witherington, *Acts*, p. 281.

The opinions of scholars arising out of the source-critical discussion of Acts 8:4-25 can now be summarized:

1. A Petrine *Grundschrift* existed underlying the story of Acts 8:4-25, but Luke substituted Philip for Peter in the original version of the story. Therefore, the presence of Philip in the narrative is a Lukan construction.
2. The story originally contained a tradition of Philip's activity in Samaria including Simon's offer of money to Philip for the ability to perform miracles. But it was Luke who constructed the involvement of the apostles in the story of the Samaritan mission.
3. Only the encounter between Philip and Simon derives from a tradition, though it was originally separate, the other Peter-Simon conflict is a Lukan construction.[48] It also means Philip and Simon worked in different cities.
4. The event in 8:4-13 is based on a single source without any merging of traditions, but 8:14-17 is entirely a Lukan construction.
5. The association between Philip and Simon in the narrative reflects one single source without merging of separate sources, and likewise the Peter-Simon encounter also reflects another single source.
6. The tradition about Simon Magus underlying vv. 9-13, is part of a tradition derived from Hellenist circles, which narrated the clash between the Simonians and the Christians. Because the theme of money is a favourite theme of Luke, the fact that Simon offers money to buy the ability to bestow the Holy Spirit by the laying on of hands in vv. 18f. does not reflect a tradition, but a redaction with v. 20.[49]
6. The tradition originally narrated a clash between Peter and Simon without the inclusion of Philip, and Luke in his redaction brought Philip and Simon together in order to expand the scanty material on Philip's missionary activity.[50]
8. The question of the exact location of Philip's missionary activity is raised as it is referred to as 'a/the city of Samaria' in Acts 8:5. Also the issue of how significant the 'city of Samaria' is for Luke for the portrayal of the Samaritan mission, though he does not specify what city it is, needs to be discussed.

Source-critical approaches reveal unanimity in the opinion that Luke is at least partially reliant on sources or traditions in this section. But there are strong disagreements as to who really the ideal figure was for such a mission activity in Samaria and who actually encountered Simon. On the one extreme,

---

48. Haenchen, *Acts*, pp. 305–6.
49. Lüdemann, *Traditions*, pp. 98–100.
50. Koch, 'Geistbesitz', p. 78.

Wellhausen, Dibelius, Haenchen, Conzelmann and Lüdemann who claim the presence of a Philip-Simon tradition in Acts 8:4-25 believe that the coming of Peter to Samaria and his encounter with Simon are not based on any tradition but are a Lukan creation. Conzelmann, despite his historical scepticism of Acts, admits that Hellenist traditions lie behind the account of the Samaritan mission in Acts 8, though he claims that they originally had no account of the apostles.[51] On the other extreme, those who insist on a Peter-Simon tradition argue that the presence of Philip in the narrative is a Lukan creation. There are others who, while claiming traditions for both Philip and Peter, disagree on the questions of the original connection of Simon to Philip and Peter, and the Lukan merging of different sources in the narrative.

Since source-critical analysis is beyond the scope of our present study, a critical appraisal of the various views outlined above is only briefly to be mentioned here. Mission to Samaria is thought to be a major breakthrough and an important stage in the evangelizing activity of the early church and Philip is said to be the first one to conduct such a mission. The fact that Philip's ministry was the first of its kind suggests that Luke may have received some information about the ministry of Philip either from fellow Hellenist Christians in Antioch or from Philip himself. Given this consideration, it is possible, as Matthews rightly suggests, that there could have existed a pre-Lukan tradition of Philip's mission in Samaria, because he was the first one to start an 'unprecedented evangelizing activity' in Samaria.[52] Luke's knowledge about Philip is evident from the fact that he is included in the Seven (6:5) and that he is mentioned again in 21:8-9 as dwelling in Caesarea and that he had four daughters who prophesied. If the traditional identification of the we-narrator with the author is accepted, then we may see an implied claim to have met Philip in Caesarea as he was among the companions of Paul (Acts 21:8-10). According to Lüdemann, the stay with Philip in 21:8-9, 'may have been part of the source'.[53] He also thinks that the account of Philip's four prophetic virgin daughters is 'in all probability part of the tradition' because it fits the traditions of the Spirit-filled activity of the Hellenists.[54] That there existed a Philip tradition is further evident when Eusebius reports that Polycrates of Ephesus and Papias received information about Philip and his virgin prophetic daughters who lived at Hierapolis.[55] The description of Philip in the conversion story of the Ethiopian eunuch in 8:26-40 also shows that Luke had a cycle of stories of a Philip tradition at

51. Conzelmann, *Acts*, p. 62.
52. Matthews, 'Philip', p. 141.
53. Lüdemann, *Traditions*. It is interesting to note his comments here, 'Luke does not invent stories, but reports them on the basis of tradition' (p. 233).
54. Lüdemann, *Traditions*, p. 233.
55. See Eusebius, *Church History* III, 31.3; 39.9. For a summary of various views on the second century references to Philip and his daughters, see Matthews, *Philip*, pp. 15–34.

his disposal. Thus, it is possible that Luke made use of a Philip tradition for his account in Acts 8:4-13. Therefore, the claim of Koch that Luke introduced Simon into the activity of Philip in order to elaborate the scanty material which he had on Philip is untenable and unjustifiable in the light of Luke's apparent knowledge about Philip and the next Philip-Ethiopian eunuch episode that he narrates in 8:26-40.[56] For Luke, as we will see later in our study in Chapter 6, Philip makes an ideal figure for the mission in Samaria.

For Luke the activity of both Philip and Simon probably took place in the same 'city of Samaria'. Even if Philip's ministry was limited only to the Samaritans, as Haenchen claims,[57] there is no reason to think that Simon also limited his activity only to the Gentiles. As a magician, Simon would have amazed people irrespective of their ethnic and religious convictions. If Simon the magician was most probably a Samaritan, as will be argued in Chapter 6, in all probability he would have come across Philip and his ministry among the Samaritans. This becomes clear when Luke says that after Simon's conversion, 'he followed Philip everywhere, astonished by the great signs and miracles he saw' (Acts 8:13). Had there not been an association in the original tradition between the activity of Philip and Simon's conversion, it would have enabled Luke to bring Peter straight away into confrontation with Simon instead of separating a Philip-Simon tradition (vv. 5-13) from a Peter-Simon tradition (vv. 18-25). In other words, if there existed an earlier tradition that attributed the conversion of Simon the magician to Peter's ministry, then Luke would hardly have substituted a lesser figure for Peter.[58] Thus it is probable that the source originally contained a Philip tradition and it is unlikely that Luke smuggled Philip into a Peter-Simon tradition for Acts 8:4-13.

Was there an original connection between the events in 8:4-13 and 8:14-25? The implied relation between the Seven (or Philip) and the Twelve (or Peter and John) is often considered as a Lukan product rather than tradition.[59] It is true that the apostles are absent in the former and Philip in the latter and they both do not appear to meet together in the narrative. This is due to the *spatial* difference in the former as the apostles remained in Jerusalem when Philip ministered in Samaria, whereas the *temporal* difference of the latter account brought them to the scene of Samaria. It is only after the Jerusalem apostles heard that Samaria accepted the word of God, they decided to send Peter and John. However, a connection between the two events seems not only literarily likely but also historically possible. The

---

56. Koch, 'Geistbesitz', p. 78; *Contra* Koch, see Lüdemann, *Traditions*, p. 99.
57. Haenchen, *Acts*, p. 307.
58. Haenchen, 'Simon Magus in der Apostelgeschichte', in K.W. Tröger (ed.), *Gnosis und Neues Testament* (Gütersloh: Mohn, 1973), pp. 267–79, 277.
59. Barrett, *Acts* I, p. 396.

event in vv. 14-25 has its base in vv. 4-13 because the Samaritan Christians formed from Philip's ministry in the earlier part are the objects of the Jerusalem apostles' ministry in the later section. Also, Simon who was a follower of Philip in the earlier section becomes the object of Peter's encounter in the latter. It means that both the Samaritan Christians and Simon are the common denominators in both the events. As Witherington says, the former section 'serves as a necessary preparation for what happens when Peter and John show up ... The latter part presupposes and depends on the former. This means that the part about Peter and Simon probably never stood alone as an independent narrative.'[60] Barrett thinks differently when he says that Simon 'is not a cement holding Philip and Peter together', rather 'a piece of traditional material existing in his own right'.[61] However this view does not seem to exclude the possible link between Simon and Peter in the tradition. Thus it is reasonable to think that the original setting of the Peter-Simon narrative is what is narrated in vv. 14-25 itself and that it is not merely the presence of Simon who brings this narrative into the story of Philip.

On the basis of the above discussion another point needs to be emphasized. The strong presence of various non-canonical traditions of Simon would nevertheless suggest that the magical elements of his activities can be supposed to be a historical kernel of truth in accord with what is known of him from Acts 8.[62] It means that he did not lack the power to perform magical deeds. Therefore, the claim of scholars that in the original story Simon tried to buy the power to do miracles rather than the power to confer the Spirit is unlikely. And therefore, the notion of critics that Luke remodelled the story of Simon in order to bring the apostles into the ministry of Philip should be rejected. The critics have not given sufficient attention to the text in discussing the traditional or redactional elements in Acts 8:4-25. Their reconstruction is merely based on assumptions and hypotheses without having taken into consideration the overall unity, the dominant theme(s) and the objective of the narrative. Now we will turn to the narrative approaches.

2.2.2. *Narrative Approaches*
An important work in its approach to reading Acts as a narrative is that of Tannehill's *Narrative Unity of Luke-Acts*. In the account of the Samaritan mission, Tannehill highlights the important role Philip plays as a successful evangelist in fulfilling the commission of Jesus in Acts 1:8. He asserts that Philip's ministry of preaching and performing miracles is described in the same way as that of Jesus and the apostles.[63] That the apostles do not

---

60. Witherington, *Acts*, p. 281, n. 10.
61. Barrett, *Acts* I, p. 396.
62. See the brief discussion on Simon tradition in Chapter 6.
63. Tannehill, *Luke-Acts* II, p. 104.

initiate the mission to Samaria does not make them unimportant, instead they 'become the stabilizing, verifying, and unifying element' in the new mission.[64] They shift their role from the *initiator* to that of the *verifier* as the mission moves to new areas and people beyond Jerusalem and Judea. That the apostles must send representatives to Samaria suggests the fact that the mission took place without their authorization or control. Simon functions in the narrative to emphasize the greatness of Philip's signs over against the power of magic as well as to evoke the danger in mission which leaders must avoid in their attempt to be seen as divine or great and trying to use the Spirit as a commodity for selfish purposes. Tannehill considers the narrative on the coming of the Holy Spirit to the Samaritans from the perspectives of both Philip's mission and the Jerusalem apostles. From the perspective of Philip's mission, says Tannehill, 'faith and baptism are incomplete without the gift of the Spirit, which means that Philip's mission is incomplete until the coming of Peter and John'.[65] Here Tannehill rules out the view that the Spirit can be received only through the laying on of the apostles' hands. From the perspective of the apostles, the coming of the Spirit was a visible sign that God has included the Samaritans also in salvation brought by Jesus and thus they could verify Philip's ministry and confirm the Samaritan mission.

The approach of Tannehill may solve some of the issues in the text which source-criticism fails to account for. It takes into consideration the presence of both Philip and the apostles in Samaria and their respective ministerial roles in the mission to the Samaritans. The success of Philip's ministry is considered neither defective nor subordinate to that of the apostles, rather it is depicted as fulfilling the commission of Jesus in Acts 1:8. The role of the apostle as verifier of the mission is a possible hypothesis but it does not explain why their function is reduced to such a model when it came to the Samaritan mission given that Jesus' commission (1:8) to go to Samaria still implies an initiator role. The question why the apostles did not initially go to Samaria in the first place is as important as why they did go there afterwards. If it was the persecution that brought Philip to Samaria, it is true that the mission took place without the apostles' plan but Philip did not plan it either. The view that 'Philip's mission is incomplete until the coming of Peter and John' also fails to explain why his mission to the Ethiopian eunuch was successful and complete in the absence of any of the apostles. Therefore, we must ask why, of all the 'scattered missions', does Luke choose only the Samaritan one for detailed writing up and portray it in this way?

Another example of narrative approach is that of Spencer who tries to draw out the significance of Philip's ministry to the Samaritans by placing 8:4-25 within the overall context of Lukan narrative. After analysing all the Samaritan references in the Gospel of Luke and comparing them with the

---

64.   Tannehill, *Luke-Acts* II, pp. 102, 104.
65.   Tannehill, *Luke-Acts* II, p. 104.

ministry of Philip in Acts 8:5-13, he states that the 'ministries of the Lukan Jesus and Philip are remarkably similar in substance and setting'.[66] In his encounter with Simon Magus, Philip stands out in his greatness and superiority as a 'prophet like Moses', and resembles the ministries of Jesus and Paul.[67] Luke does not portray Philip's role as subordinate to the superior, Spirit-imparting missionary, Peter, rather as a partner in mission.[68] Philip's limited potential to confer the Spirit on the Samaritan Christian community 'does not reflect a deficiency or abnormality in his mission', but 'an overarching compatibility and continuity between pairs of prominent ministers'.[69] It is interesting to note Spencer's attempt to draw a *forerunner-culminator* model for the ministry of Philip and Peter in Acts 8-11. As John the Baptist, the forerunner, baptizes in water and prepares the way for Jesus the culminator who will baptize with the Spirit, Philip functions as a forerunner to Peter's Spirit-imparting mission.[70] Spencer's discussion of several key elements in the Samaritan ministry of Philip leads him to say that Luke portrays Philip as an authentic and distinguished missionary ranking to the vocations of Jesus, Peter and Paul.

Spencer's thesis is attractive and similar to that of Tannehill. However, there are considerable difficulties with his arguments. (1) He stretches Peter's role too far at the expense of keeping John the fellow apostle always behind the scene. (2) Philip could not be seen as a forerunner, for Philip's ministry in Samaria matches that of Peter. Like Peter, Philip also casts out evil spirits (5:16 cf. 8:7), heals the paralysed or lame (3:1-10 cf. 8:7), does great signs and miracles (2:43 cf. 8:13), proclaims the good news of the kingdom of God (2:14-41 cf. 8:12), and baptises the converts (2:41 cf. 8:12). (3) The Spirit-imparting mission of Peter as a culminator model is improbable, because there is no evidence for such a model either in the event of Pentecost (2:1-4) or in the episode of Cornelius (10:44-45). Moreover, Luke does not always follow a consistent order of reception of the Spirit after baptism. And further, in the Ephesian Pentecost (19:1-7), Paul's ministry could not be considered as a culminator model, for he himself serves as a forerunner as well, and also John's mission is defective (cf. 19:1-7).

2.2.3. Theological Approaches
One example of a theological approach to Acts 8:4-25 is that of Joseph A. Fitzmyer. According to Fitzmyer, Luke uses the narrative of 8:4-25 in order to teach a message about the role of the Spirit in Christian life.[71] Luke

---

66. Spencer, *Portrait*, p. 87.
67. Spencer, *Portrait*, p. 127.
68. Spencer, *Portrait*, p. 219.
69. Spencer, *Portrait*, pp. 240–1.
70. Spencer, *Portrait*, pp. 220–1.
71. Fitzmyer, *Acts*, pp. 400–1.

teaches us that the gift of the Spirit comes only through the apostles or at times through those sent forth by them. The texts that Fitzmyer quotes for this claim are Acts 8:14-17; 10:44-48; 18:25-27; 19:2-6; 20:29-30. He further says that this story 'also tells of the incorporation of splinter groups into the main stream church; Samaritans who are baptized *become fully Christian* by such an apostolic relationship'.[72] Simon is introduced into the narrative 'to offset any identification of the effect of the Spirit with magic practices'.[73] The gift of the Spirit has nothing to do with magic or money and no outsider can acquire the power to confer the Spirit, but is 'bestowed only by apostolic invocation'.[74] Here the claim of Fitzmyer that the apostles are the only authority to bestow the Spirit stands contradictory to that of Tannehill who thinks otherwise. In brief, the main intention of Luke in the story of the Samaritan mission, according to Fitzmyer, is to depict the Spirit-guided Christian community in Acts and to portray the apostles or their emissaries as the sole authority to bestow the Spirit. It is true that the Holy Spirit is a prominent theme for Luke and he has something to say about the Spirit in Acts 8:4-25. However, one must see how other themes in the narrative may relate to this allegedly important teaching. The significance of Luke's story of the Samaritan mission needs to be considered in view of his special portrait of the Samaritans in his Gospel and also his plot in Acts 1:8. Fitzmyer's claim will be discussed along with other similar views in the following section of the study on the visit of the apostles and the delay of the Spirit.

To summarize the foregoing approaches, the issues on the Samaritan mission of Philip fall into three types of arguments:

(1) *Historical*: the question of the original association between Philip and Simon on the one hand, and Philip – and Peter – tradition on the other. Did Luke have enough sources and traditions for his portrait of the Samaritan mission and how reliable were they? Did Philip and Simon work in the same place and did they really come into contact with each other as the present text says? It further raises the issue of the likely location for the activity of Philip: what does it mean when Luke refers to the place as 'a/the city of Samaria' (Acts 8:5)?

(2) *Literary*: the question of Luke merging various accounts. Is Luke creating a literary link between two or more accounts in the present text (a Philip – or Peter – tradition with a Simon tradition) which were originally separate?

72.   Fitzmyer, *Acts*, pp. 400–1, italics mine.
73.   Fitzmyer, *Acts,* p. 404.
74.   Fitzmyer, *Acts*, p. 401; *idem, The Gospel According to Luke* I (Garden City, NY: Doubleday, 1985), says that 'it becomes plain in Acts that the Spirit is given only when the Twelve are present or a member or delegate of the Twelve is on the scene' (p. 231). However, Fitzmyer refers to the case of Paul (9:17-18) as the only exception to this rule.

(3) *Theological*: What is the significance for the theology and the narrative of the author of Acts of the Samaritan mission? Does Luke intend to subordinate Philip to Peter or deliberately choose the apostles as the exclusive authority to bestow the Spirit? Why does he link Philip and the apostles on the one hand, and the Samaritan Christians and the Jerusalem Church on the other?

2.3. The Visit and the Ministry of the Jerusalem Apostles

In Acts 8:14-17, the separation of water-baptism and the bestowal of the Holy Spirit which elsewhere seems to coincide in Acts (cf. 2:38) raises the question of why there was a delay for the coming of the Spirit upon the Samaritan Christians. This dissociation and delay of the Holy Spirit further brings the issue of the failure of Philip to induce the Spirit upon his Samaritan converts. Also the association of the imposition of hands with Spirit-reception and its separation from water-baptism raises a problem for those who maintain that all these elements (or at least baptism and Spirit-reception) are closely connected.

Attempting to solve the above-mentioned problem in Acts 8:14-17, scholars are variously divided on the issues in the Lukan narration of the event.[75] It has been argued that the event mentioned in 8:14-17 is either a unique exception to the norm in Acts that baptism, laying on of hands and Spirit-reception are held together or it is an ad hoc construction. According to G.W.H. Lampe, Hull and Marshall who argue for the former, the Spirit was withheld until the coming of the Jerusalem apostles in order that the Samaritans might be seen to be fully incorporated into the fellowship of the Jerusalem Church who had received the Spirit at Pentecost.[76] Conzelmann looks at the event as an ad hoc construction 'which presupposes precisely the intimate connection between baptism and the Spirit'.[77] For him, the point here is the understanding of the church rather than baptism: 'the Samaritan church is legitimate if it has been sanctioned by Jerusalem'.[78] The concept of a set norm reflects the view of Haenchen mentioned earlier that baptism, laying on of hands and Spirit-reception are 'one indissoluble whole' in Acts, but Luke in his redaction divided them between Philip and Peter.

75. For a useful summary of various views on this event in Acts 8:14-17, see Max Turner, *Power from on High: The Spirit in Israel's Restoration and Witness in Luke-Acts* (JPTS 9; Sheffield: Sheffield Academic Press, 1996), pp. 360–75.

76. Lampe, *The Seal of the Spirit* (London: Longmans, Green & Co., 1951), p. 70; J.H.E. Hull, *The Holy Spirit in the Acts of the Apostles* (London: Lutterworth Press, 1967), pp. 104–9, 118; I.H. Marshall, *The Acts of the Apostles: An Introduction and Commentary* (Leicester: IVP, 1980), p. 157.

77. Conzelmann, *Acts*, p. 65.

78. Conzelmann, *Acts*, p. 65.

The view of Lampe and others raises the issue of the normative and consistent relationship between faith, baptism, laying on of hands and the reception of the Holy Spirit in Acts. According to Acts 2:38, repentance and baptism seem to be the prerequisite for the reception of the Spirit.[79] However, one could also see faith and not baptism as the condition for Spirit-reception.[80] In the case of the Samaritans neither faith nor baptism appears to be connected with Spirit-reception but prayer and laying on of hands.[81] The Cornelius incident (10:44) does not support either baptism or laying on of hands or both as the conditions for Spirit-reception. In any case, faith is the basic factor and the Spirit-reception can either precede or follow baptism, and sometimes with laying on of hands and sometimes without. And, Acts does not give us a normative and consistent association of these elements.[82] If Spirit-reception was the only and final endorsement for the incorporation of new converts into the Church, and even that in the presence of the apostles, then the story of the conversion of the Ethiopian eunuch (8:26-40) is an embarrassment. Whether or not the Samaritan incident is considered as a unique exception, why the incorporation of the Samaritan Christians into the community of believers must depend on the endorsement of the Jerusalem apostles needs to be explored. Why did Luke think that the baptized Samaritans needed further assurance of their incorporation into the fellowship of the Jerusalem Christians? Here, the view of Conzelmann that the Jerusalem Church must sanction the legitimacy of the Samaritan Church is a likely suggestion and to this we will return in Part III of the study.

It has also been suggested that Luke, by bringing the Jerusalem apostles to the Samaritan ministry of Philip, has purposely downgraded the success of Philip's achievements. Käsemann contends that Luke has stigmatized the ministry of Philip as 'defective'.[83] Haenchen, who holds more or less the same view, comments that Philip's success is 'minimized', for 'the most important factor was beyond his control'.[84] He maintains that 'the mission to the Samaritans was not completed by any subordinate outsider, but was carried out in due form by the legal heads of the Church in person'.[85] Bruce also maintains a superior position of the apostles when he considers the visit of

---

79.   So Hull, *Holy Spirit*, pp. 119–20.

80.   Dunn, *Baptism in the Holy Spirit* (London: SCM Press, 1970), pp. 55–68.

81.   F. Bovon, *Luke the Theologian: Thirty-three Years of Research (1950-1983)* (PTMS 12; Allison Park, PA: Pickwick Press, 1987), p. 234.

82.   So Powell, *Acts*, p. 55; Shepherd, *Narrative Function*, says, 'Luke does not present a consistent picture of the relationship among baptism, laying-on-of hands, and the reception of the Spirit' (p. 183).

83.   E. Käsemann, *Essays on New Testament Themes* (Philadelphia: Fortress Press, 1964), p. 146.

84.   Haenchen, *Acts*, p. 304.

85.   Haenchen, *Acts*, p. 306.

the Jerusalem apostles to Samaria as 'their responsibility to supervise the expansion of the faith'.[86] He says that the bestowal of the Spirit, not by the 'freelance evangelist like Philip', but by the laying on of hands by Peter and John, was to give the Samaritans an eloquent assurance that they were fully incorporated into the elect community. This view of Bruce also resembles that of Lampe as both see the bestowal of Spirit as an incorporation of the Samaritans into the Jerusalem Church.

Haenchen and Käsemann consider the arrival of the apostles and the delay of the Spirit from the perspective of the ministry of Philip, rather than that of the apostles or the Samaritans and thus fail to see the event in the context of the overall portrait of the Samaritan mission. In the light of the successful missionary achievements of Philip in vv. 4-13 and vv. 26-40, it is unlikely that Luke intended to portray his ministry as defective. As mentioned earlier, Luke portrays Philip as a prophet and missionary whose work resembles that of Jesus, Stephen, Paul and the apostles and is a clear sign of the work of the Holy Spirit.[87] Nowhere in Acts is it mentioned that the ability to confer the Spirit is the measuring standard to evaluate one's success. Because Philip and Peter perform distinctive roles, it is unreasonable to assume that one ministry is superior to the other.[88]

W. Dietrich has argued that there was an early Jerusalem tradition under-lying vv. 14-17, which reserved the bestowal of the Spirit exclusively for the apostles, and Luke inserted it into his narrative without any alteration.[89] According to this view, Luke is using an early tradition, which credited the apostles as the authorized agents to impart the Spirit. So Philip is respecting the privilege of the apostles. Dietrich's view could be seen in the light of J.D.M. Derrett who explains why only the apostles are important for this role. Derrett thinks that the apostles owned the exclusive power to induce the Holy Spirit because 'they were *de facto* witnesses of Jesus' ministry, sufferings, death, and resurrection'.[90] This view is similar to that of J. Munck who assumes that there was a rule in the early days of the Church that only the twelve apostles were sufficient to confer such a fundamental gift[91] and of Fitzmyer that the Spirit is always connected to the apostles or their emissaries.[92]

---

86. Bruce, *Acts*, p. 220.
87. L.T. Johnson, *The Acts of the Apostles* (Sacra Pagina Series vol. 5; Minnesota: The Liturgical Press, 1992), p. 151; Tannehill, *Luke-Acts* II, pp. 103–4; Spencer, *Portrait*, pp. 271–6.
88. W. Dietrich, *Das Petrusbild der lukanischen Schriften* (BWANT 14; Stuttgart: Kohlhammer, 1972), pp. 249–50; Spencer, *Portrait*, pp. 240–1.
89. Dietrich, *Petrusbild*, pp. 248–9.
90. Derrett, 'Simon Magus (Acts 8:9-24)', ZNW 73 (1982), pp. 52–68, 57.
91. J. Munck, *The Acts of the Apostles* (AB; New York: Doubleday & Co., 1967), p. 75.
92. Fitzmyer, *Acts*, p. 400.

However, one must note that Luke does not portray the apostles as the exclusive authority to confer the Spirit, for it can happen without the laying on of hands by any of the apostles as in Acts 2:38. That Ananias, who is not even a member of the Twelve or Seven, confers the Spirit on Saul (9:17) makes it clear that Spirit is not always connected to the Twelve or their emissaries. In Acts 19, Paul confers the Spirit on the Ephesian disciples though he was not one of the Twelve. If Paul is connected to Jerusalem, his connection, as Shepherd says, is only through Barnabas and he cannot be considered as an emissary of the Twelve.[93] Even if Paul could be considered as an indirect representative of the Twelve as Fitzmyer claims, it raises the difficulty of 'why Philip, who had a more direct connection than Paul, did not suffice as a representative of the Twelve'.[94] Again, Luke has Peter himself say that the Spirit (or the ability to confer the Spirit) is a gift of God (8:20) and cannot be manipulated by money or reserved for any representatives. Here French L. Arrington is right when he says, 'none of the works of the Spirit are limited to the hands of a particular group in the Church'.[95]

It has been argued by Oulton and others that vv. 15-17 does not refer to the gift of the Holy Spirit *simpliciter*, but to his outward manifestation.[96] That means, the Samaritans already received the Spirit, but lacked any external and visible phenomenon. This claim is supported by the following observations. (1) It is apparent from v. 18 that Simon 'saw' the Holy Spirit being given through the imposition of the apostles' hand. (2) The phrase 'as yet he was fallen upon none of them' (v. 16a) is taken to mean 'as yet he was not fallen upon a single one of them'. Luke did not intend to say that the Samaritan converts were without the Spirit, but without any visible or audible manifestation of the Spirit's presence. (3) That the Samaritan Christian community, even before the arrival of Peter and John, 'enjoyed the inner life that is the gift of the Spirit' suggests that this life (vv. 5-13) was similar to that of the Jerusalem converts as described in 2:41-47. (4) In the light of a consistent picture of the relationship of the Holy Spirit in Acts to baptism and laying on of hands, it is unlikely to say that baptism does not convey the gift of the Spirit *simpliciter*, but the imposition of hands. Otherwise, Luke would be 'guilty of a manifest inconsistency' in his account of the Ethiopian eunuch who goes on rejoicing in his way 'after receiving nothing more than water-baptism'.[97] A similar claim is made by Beasley-Murray who mentions Acts 8 in regard to the relation of Spirit-reception to baptism and argues that Luke

---

93. Shepherd, *Narrative Function*, p. 25.

94. Shepherd, *Narrative Function*, p. 25.

95. F.L. Arrington, *The Acts of the Apostles* (Peabody, MA: Hendrickson, 1988), p. 89.

96. J.E.L. Oulton, 'The Holy Spirit, Baptism, and Laying on of Hands in Acts', *ExpTim* 66 (1954–55), pp. 236–40.

97. Oulton, 'Holy Spirit', p. 239.

considered the Samaritan converts as not without the Spirit but without the spiritual gifts.[98] The anarthrous use of πνεῦμα ἅγιον in 8:15-16 signifies the imparting of spiritual gifts, not the Spirit itself. The πολλὴ χαρά in v. 8 shows that the Samaritans received the Spirit when they were baptized.

However, (1) the suggestion that an outward and extraordinary manifestation of the Spirit is needed to justify the admission of new converts into the Church does not have a base in Acts. (2) If the baptized Samaritans had already received the Holy Spirit before the arrival of the apostles, as Oulton and others argue, they would also have had a similar outward manifestation of the Spirit as on the day of Pentecost. It is clear in Luke that the reception of the Spirit is associated with the manifestation of the Spirit (2:4; 10:44-46; 19:6).[99] As Menzies has pointed out, Luke's choice of language in vv. 15-19 suggests that he viewed the gift of the Spirit received by the Samaritans to be identical to the Pentecostal gift (λάμβάνειν πνεῦμα ἅγιον, Acts 8:15, 17, 19; cf. 1:8; 2:38; ἐπιπίπτειν τὸ πνεῦμα τὸ ἅγιον, 8:16; 11:15).[100] It can be assumed that the Samaritans' reception of the Spirit was accompanied by prophetic utterance and *glossolalia* as on the day of Pentecost (8:16-18; cf. 2:4-13; 10:45-46; 19:6).[101] (3) That Luke clearly mentions in v. 16 that 'the Spirit had not yet fallen (ἐπιπεπτωκός) on any of them' contradicts the claim of Beasley-Murray (cf. 10:44; 11:15) and emphasizes that vv. 16-17 refers to the Samaritans' first and only reception of the Holy Spirit.[102] (4) The experience of πολλὴ χαρά in v. 8 is not the result of the Samaritans' reception of the Spirit, rather it springs from the healings and exorcisms performed by Philip. The 'great joy', as Turner suggests, often implies the response to God's saving acts throughout Luke-Acts (Lk. 13:17; 19:37).[103] (5) The anarthrous use of πνεῦμα ἅγιον could equally mean the 'Holy Spirit' rather than the 'gifts of the Spirit', for they are equivalent titles.[104] Also, in Acts the laying on of hands is not associated with bestowing the spiritual gifts, but the Spirit itself (9:17; 19:6).[105]

J.D.G. Dunn tries to explain the coming of the apostles and the delay of the Spirit by establishing that the Samaritans were not really Christians

---

98. Beasley-Murray, *Baptism in the New Testament* (Exeter: Paternoster Press, 1962), pp. 118–20.

99. Derrett, 'Simon Magus', p. 54.

100. R.P. Menzies, *Empowered for Witness: The Spirit in Luke-Acts* (Sheffield: Sheffield Academic Press, 1994), p. 211.

101. Menzies, *Empowered*, p. 211; Haenchen, *Acts*, p. 304.

102. So Turner, *Power*, p. 369.

103. Turner, *Power*, p. 368

104. Dunn, *Baptism*, p. 56.

105. In Acts 9:12, 17 and 28:8, the laying on of hands is associated with healing; in 6:6; 13:3, it is linked to the commissioning of the specially selected people for service and mission.

before they received the Holy Spirit; their initial response and commitment was defective.[106] The following are his arguments: (1) The Lukan account of Philip as preaching τὸν Χριστόν *Simpliciter* (v. 5) and τῆς βασιλείας τοῦ θεοῦ (v. 12) suggests that the Samaritans understood the message in terms of the pre-Christian, nationalistic expectations of the Messiah and the Kingdom. (2) Luke's use of the term προσεῖχον (vv. 6, 10, 11) to describe the Samaritans' attentiveness to both Simon and Philip indicates that their response to Philip was shallow and of the same quality and depth as their reaction to Simon. It implies, says Dunn, that 'the Samaritans' acceptance of baptism was prompted more by the herd-instinct of a popular mass-movement (ὁμοθυμαδόν, v. 6) than by the self-and world-denying commitment'.[107] (3) The use of πίστευω with the dative object in v. 12 (ἐπίστευσαν τῷ Φιλίππῳ) signifies the Samaritans' 'assent of the mind' to Philip's message rather than a genuine commitment to the Word. (4) The defective experience of Simon and the Samaritans in vv. 12-13 suggests that 'they all went through the form but did not experience the reality' of repentance and faith.

Dunn's argument that one cannot really be a Christian unless his or her faith is genuine and that only those who have a genuine faith can receive the Holy Spirit may be true. But this is not what Luke says of the Samaritans. This is obvious from various observations.[108] The task of the apostles was not to repeat what Philip had already done, but to pray for the Samaritans that they might receive the Holy Spirit. There is no indication that the apostles after their arrival had undone or redone the earlier work of Philip. Also, there is no evidence in the Lukan description of the phrases τὸν Χριστόν (v. 5) and τῆς βασιλείας τοῦ θεοῦ καὶ τοῦ ὀνόματος Ἰησοῦ Χριστοῦ (v. 12) that the Samaritans misunderstood Philip's message. These phrases would indicate Philip's message as kerygmatic (cf. Acts 9:22; 17:3; 26:23; 28:31).[109] In 8:4, Philip is portrayed as the one among those who went about εὐαγγελιζόμενοι τὸν λόγον, the kerygma (cf. 2:41; 6:2; 8:14). Further, that the report about the Samaritans' faith that reached Jerusalem (the apostles in Jerusalem heard that δέδεκται ἡ Σαμάρεια τὸν λόγον τοῦ θεοῦ, v. 14a) was similar to that of Cornelius (11:1) confirms that their faith was neither defective nor superficial (cf. 2:41; 17:11).

By using the term προσεῖχον, Luke makes a distinction between the Samaritans' earlier response to Simon (vv. 10f.) and their present response to Philip (v. 6). The Samaritans paid attention to Philip's message about

---

106. Dunn, *Baptism*, pp. 55–72.
107. Dunn, *Baptism*, pp. 64–5.
108. For a critique of Dunn's arguments, see Menzies, *Empowered*, pp. 208–11; Turner, *Power*, pp. 363–7.
109. Marshall, *Acts*, p. 156; Turner, *Power*, pp. 365–6.

Christ, whereas their response to Simon was more of a 'personality fixation, an enchantment with a cult figure'.[110] Their response to Philip (προσεῖχον) is parallel to that of Lydia who gave heed (προσέχειν) to Paul's message and was baptized (16:14).[111] There is no evidence to suggest that the Samaritans were unregenerate till the arrival of the Jerusalem apostles. Again, the construction of πίστευω with dative object is a Lukan phrase to describe genuine faith in God (16:34; 18:8). As Menzies suggests, for Luke, the belief in the message of an evangelist is belief in God himself (16:14; 4:4).[112] Nevertheless, the Samaritans' baptism by Philip indicates that he was aware of their sincerity and genuineness of faith in God.[113] Dunn's argument that Simon was not a genuine Christian was based on Peter's judgement in v. 21: 'You have no part or share in this ministry.' There is no clear evidence to assume that Simon was not truly converted.[114] Peter's comment should be understood in the context of Simon's attempt to buy the ability to confer the Holy Spirit, which, in any way, does not undermine the genuine faith of the Samaritan converts. One must note that Peter (and John) are key figures, being involved for Luke at Pentecost, in Samaria and with Cornelius (the Cornelius incident being explicitly linked to Pentecost, and all three being linked via 1:8). It is also something very important theologically for Luke to do with 'from Jerusalem'.

According to Barrett, the separation of the imposition of hands from baptism and attaching it to the gift of the Spirit is one of the main problems in Acts 8. He argues that the separation of Spirit from baptism in vv. 14-17 is a Lukan product. The following reasons support this view. (1) Luke separates the imposition of hands from baptism and links it to the gift of the Spirit. (2) He intends to integrate the activity of the Seven (or Philip) and that of the Twelve (or Peter and John) by 'apportioning baptism to the one and confirmation to the other'.[115] (3) That the word λόγῳ in the phrase ἐν τῷ λόγῳ τούτῳ (v. 21) is taken to mean 'preaching' implies that 'it is in the context of preaching (not in that of possibly transferable personal δύναμις) that the laying on of hands proves to be the occasion of the gift of the Spirit'.[116] Further, he suggests that the apostles were sent to Samaria in order to 'inspect, so to approve or disapprove, the Christian mission'.[117] Also, they were sent to make up a deficiency of the Samaritan Christian - manifes-

---

110. Spencer, *Portrait*, p. 51.

111. H. Ervin, *Conversion-Initiation and the Baptism in the Holy Spirit* (Peabody: Hendrickson, 1984), p. 32.

112. Menzies, *Empowered*, p. 209.

113. Marshall, *Acts*, p. 156.

114. *Contra*, Witherington, *Acts*, pp. 288–9.

115. Barrett, 'Light', p. 293.

116. Barrett, 'Light', p. 294.

117. Barrett, *Acts* I, p. 410.

tation of the charismatic phenomena of inspiration. Here Luke is sowing the seeds, which would grow into *Frühkatholizismus* in a later period.

If preaching was the context for the bestowal of the Spirit, as Barrett thinks, it would have happened during the preaching ministry of Philip. Luke does not say that the Jerusalem apostles preached before the imposition of their hands on the Samaritan Christians. Further, Luke never separates the manifestation of the Spirit from the reception of the Spirit. Therefore, it is unlikely to mean that the Samaritans did not have manifestation of the charisma, but the Spirit (though Barrett does not say explicitly). Again, if Luke had intended here to integrate the Seven and the Twelve, he could have done so, as in Acts 11, without exclusively attributing the power to the Apostles.

Luke Timothy Johnson makes the suggestion that the apostles come to Samaria to 'fulfil the other part of their mission, which was to pray (Acts 6:4)' and that Luke is interested here to show the new mission 'certified by the Jerusalem leadership'.[118] In 8:4-25, Luke is trying to maintain a continuity between the Hellenist missionaries and the Jerusalem Church which gives his Gentile readers 'their own sense of sharing in God's blessing'. This continuity, says Johnson, is two-fold.[119] (1) Philip's ministry of proclamation and performing mighty deeds is in continuity with that of Jesus and the apostles. (2) The Samaritan community is linked with that in Jerusalem through the validating actions of the apostles. Johnson's view on the success of Philip's ministry is that of Tannehill and Spencer in that all agree on his ministry resembling that of the apostles: ministry of the word, miraculous signs, healing and exorcisms. However, Johnson's view implies that Philip's ministry in Samaria suffered from lack of prayer and that the mission could be successful only by the prayer of Peter and John. This is only a speculation, given the successful activity of Philip. Also, if Luke had intended to demonstrate a continuity between the new community and the Jerusalem Church, he could have made it without attributing the bestowal of the Spirit to the Jerusalem leaders as in Acts 11:22-24.[120] Therefore, the significance of the presence of the apostles in Samaria and the bestowal of the Spirit through their ministry needs to be explored.

Robert P. Menzies briefly examines Acts 8:4-25 in the light of the Lukan pneumatology and argues that the separation of Spirit-reception from baptism or Christian initiation is not inconsistent with Luke, and the text as it stands does not pose a problem.[121] The association of Spirit-reception with the laying on of hands in Acts 8:17 suggests that Luke viewed the gift of the Spirit received by the Samaritans as a prophetic endowment for service in the

118. Johnson, *Acts*, p. 148.
119. Johnson, *Acts*, p. 151.
120. Menzies, *Empowered*, p. 205.
121. Menzies, *Empowered*, pp. 204–13.

mission of the church (cf. 6:6; 13:3). Since the gift is often granted apart from the rite of imposition of hands (2:38; 10:44) and the rite does not always confer the Spirit (6:6: 13:3), Menzies says, 'reception of the Spirit is not integral to the rite but is rather a supplementary element'.[122] Therefore, the laying on of hands in 8:17, as in 19:6, is part of a 'commissioning ceremony' in order to 'incorporate the Samaritans, not into the church, but into the missionary enterprise of the church'.[123] The gift and the rite are linked here because 'those commissioned have not yet received the prophetic enabling necessary for effective service (cf. 9:17; 19:6), unlike the Seven (6:6) or Paul and Barnabas (13:3)'.[124] This suggestion rules out the theory of Dunn that for Luke 'the one thing that makes a man a Christian is the gift of the Spirit'[125] and of Kremer that the gift of the Spirit is given not merely as the source of prophetic power but as the 'means of salvation'.[126]

Menzies' explanation of the text in 8:14-17 is challenged by Turner when he argues that the Spirit in Acts is not merely given as an empowering for mission, but has an important function in the spiritual life of the individual believer and the life of the church. According to Turner, there is nothing in the text by which Luke specifically links the gift of the Spirit to mission in v. 17; the transfer of legal authority found in 6:6 and 13:3 is missing in 8:17 as the new converts receive only the Spirit, not the commissioning.[127] Also for Turner, the empowering function of the Spirit in 8:16-17 fails to explain the 'norm' of 2:38-39, 'a norm which is itself presupposed in 8:16'.[128] Instead, Turner suggests that Luke believed God withheld the Spirit in order for the apostles to approve and seal the first mission beyond Judaism.[129] The claim of Turner and others that Luke has a normative relationship between faith, baptism, Spirit-reception and laying on of hands finds little evidence in Acts. Menzies' claim that the Spirit-reception in 8:17 is to empower the Samaritans for mission is based on the scanty evidence of the function of the imposition of hands in Acts rather than on the importance of the entire Samaritan narrative for Luke's theological purpose. The Seven were set apart from among the Jerusalem disciples for the particular task of charity

---

122. Menzies, *Empowered*, p. 212.

123. Menzies, *Empowered*, p. 212; so also Lampe, *Seal*, pp. 70–8.

124. Menzies, *Empowered*, p. 212.

125. Dunn, *Baptism*, p. 93.

126. J. Kremer, *Pfingstbericht und Pfingstgeschehen: Eine exegetische Untersuchung zur Apg 2,1-13* (SBS 63-64; Stuttgart: KBW, 1973), p. 197.

127. Turner, *Power*, p. 372.

128. Turner, *Power*, p. 373.

129. So also Johnson, *Acts*, p. 151; Lampe, *Seal*, p. 70; Hull, *Holy Spirit*, p. 118; Bruce, *Acts*, p. 220; Shepherd, *Narrative Function*, says, 'The presence of the Spirit now indicates not only divine approval of the Samaritan mission, which had been prophesied by Jesus (Acts 1:8), but also continuity with the apostolic mission' (p. 181).

(6:2) and Paul and Barnabas from the Church at Antioch for a special mission initiated by the Spirit (13:2), where the rite of imposition of hands is involved in both. Since the rite is present in 8:17, the view that Peter and John performed a 'commissioning ceremony' and set apart the Samaritans as missionaries is a mere speculation. In three of the four cases Menzies mentions for the 'commissioning ceremony' (9:17; 19:6; 13:3), the rite is not performed by any of the Twelve. It fails to explain why the apostles came to Samaria and why they had to continue the mission in other Samaritan villages (8:25), if the Samaritans were commissioned for this missionary task. The major views and issues emerging out of Acts 8:14-17 can be summarized into historical, literary and theological categories:

(1) Historically, the event signifies that (a) the Samaritans in fact had already received the Spirit, but did not have the visible manifestations of the Spirit (b) the response and commitment of the Samaritans was defective[130] and that (c) the Spirit-imparting ministry was reserved for the apostles. Luke has inserted this tradition regarding the Spirit into his material without any alteration.[131]

(2) The literary significance is that Luke desired to link the activities of the Seven and the Twelve, and also the new Samaritan Christian community to Jerusalem.

(3) The event is theological in the sense that (a) Luke wanted to stigmatize Philip's ministry as defective[132] and to minimize his success by showing that 'the most important factor was beyond his control'[133] (b) Luke wanted to subordinate Philip to the Jerusalem apostles.

The above survey on the function of the visit of the apostles and the delay of the Holy Spirit is not exhaustive; rather it presents only the major views. As is evident from the study, the opinions of scholars differ on why Luke thinks that the delayed Holy Spirit in Samaria and the coming of the Jerusalem apostles are significant for the portrayal of the Samaritan mission. Some blame the Samaritans as their shallow faith is said to be the reason for this dilemma, others think it is the defective ministry of Philip, and still others blame Luke for trying to combine the Seven and Twelve or making the apostles superior to the former. The dominant view is that Luke wanted to portray the incorporation of the Samaritan Christians into the fellowship of the Jerusalem Church. Our study will maintain this position and will further explore the reason for such a portrayal by Luke. The problem with many of the views is the compartmentalization of the units in vv. 14-17 which unsur-

130. Dunn, *Baptism*, pp. 55–6.
131. Dietrich, *Petrusbild*, pp. 247–8.
132. Käsemann, *Essays*, p. 146.
133. Haenchen, *Acts*, p. 304.

prisingly obscure important elements in the whole narrative of 8:4-25 for understanding the theological function of the visit of the apostles and the delay of the Spirit. Also, as mentioned earlier, the previous scholarship does not seem to consider the function of the entire narrative in the light of the historical context of the Samaritans in the New Testament period and in the light of Luke's overall interest in the Samaritans as is evident from his Gospel. We will engage in this task in Part III of the study.

2.4. *Confrontation of Peter with Simon*

Many studies have been done on Simon of Acts 8 attempting to explore his identity, role and his claim in the light of various traditions and texts pertinent to Simon.[134] Since Haenchen's work on the existence of pre-Christian Gnosis, which served as more or less a catalyst for other scholars, there has been an upsurge in the studies of Simon. Haenchen argued that Simon Magus in Acts 8 is an example of the pre-Christian Gnostic redeemer figure and that the pre-Lukan tradition has disguised the Gnostic Simon as a magician.[135] His claim is mainly based on the *Apophasis Megale* (The Great Disclosure) quoted in Hippolytus, *Ref*.6.9-18, where the term 'the great power' is attributed to Simon as seen in the earlier account in Acts 8. He also depends on the report in Justin Martyr's *I Apology* 26.3 that 'almost all the Samaritans, but also a few among other nations, confess him as the first god and worship him'. Haenchen says that the term, 'the great power' in Acts 8:10b is 'the Simonian designation for that supreme divinity which is opposed and superior to the daemonic rulers of this world'.[136] To claim that the earliest form of

---

134. R.P. Casey 'Simon Magus', in Lake and Cadbury (eds), *Beginnings* I. 5, pp. 151–63; W.A. Meeks, 'Simon Magus in Recent Research', *RSR* 3 (1977), pp. 137–42; K. Rudolph, 'Simon-Magus oder Gnosticus? Zur Stand der Debatte', *ThR* 42 (1977), pp. 278–59; K. Beyschlag, 'Zur Simon-Magus-Frage', *ZTK* 68 (1971), pp. 395–415; *idem, Simon Magus und die christliche Gnosis* (WUNT 16; Tübingen: Mohr, 1974); Lüdemann, *Untersuchungen zur simonianischen Gnosis* (GTA 1; Göttingen: Vandenhoeck & Ruprecht, 1975); *idem*, 'The Acts of the Apostles and the Beginnings of Simonian Gnosis', *NTS* 33 (1987), pp. 420–26; R. McL. Wilson, 'Simon, Dositheus and the Dead Sea Scrolls', *ZRGG* 9 (1957), pp. 21–30; *idem*, 'Simon and Gnostic Origins', in Kremer (ed.), *Les Actes des Apôtres*, pp. 485–91; Barrett, 'Light', pp. 281–95; J.W. Drane, 'Simon the Samaritan and the Lukan Concept of Salvation History', *EvQ* 47 (3, 1975), pp. 131–7; Derrett, 'Simon Magus', pp. 52–68; M. Smith, 'The Account of Simon Magus in Acts 8', in *Harry Austryn Wolfson Jubilee Volume*, English section, vol. 2 (Jerusalem: American Academy for Jewish Research, 1965), pp. 735–49; K. Berger, Propaganda und Gegenpropaganda im Frühen Christentum: Simon Magus als Gestalt des Samaritanischen Christentums', in Lukas Bormann, *et al.* (eds), *Religious Propaganda and Missionary Competition in the New Testament World*, Essays honouring Dieter Georgi (Leiden: E.J. Brill, 1994), pp. 313–17.

135. Haenchen, 'Gab es eine vorchristliche Gnosis?', *ZTK* 49 (1952), pp. 316–49, reprinted in *Gott und Mensch* (Tübingen: Mohr, 1965), pp. 265–97; *idem*, 'Simon Magus', pp. 267–79.

136. Haenchen, *Acts*, p. 307.

Simonian doctrine was purely of gentile provenance, he insists that Simon made his appearance not among the Samaritans, but among the Gentiles of Samaria. This conclusion of Haenchen seems ambiguous for it does not explain how the gentile provenance of Simonianism is linked to the Samaritans and their veneration of Simon as reported by Justin and agreed by Haenchen himself. He associates this Simonian designation to that of the Samaritans: 'It is clear from the history of his movement that "the great power" was a Samaritan designation for the supreme deity'.[137] The claim of Simon is that he is this deity come on earth for the redemption of men.

Haenchen's view on the Lukan treatment of Simon and his reconstruction of the nature and derivation of Simonianism in relation to Acts 8 has been strongly challenged by Karlmann Beyschlag in 1971.[138] Beyschlag, after analysing the various sources that Haenchen and others referred to as the origin of Simonian Gnosticism, objects to the historical value of these materials. The *Apophasis Megale* does not represent any Simonianism at all and may be a Gnostic writing secondarily attached to Simonians. The concept 'the great power' in *Apophasis* is cast into a broad variety of contexts and is not necessarily Gnostic. The term 'the great power' in Acts 8:10b means 'divine man', but later on by imitation of Christian Gnosticism it is transformed into a 'Gnostic revealer'. Acts 8:4-25 is purely Lukan in style and does not provide any evidence for the existence of an earlier pre-Lukan Gnostic version about Simon. He insists that it is quite unjustifiable to treat the historical Simon of Acts 8 as a Gnostic, for the earliest hint to the existence of a Gnostic Simon is a full century later than that mentioned in Acts. Like Beyschlag, R. McL. Wilson also asserts that we cannot trace back to the historical Simon the doctrines of the later Simonian sect, for there is no evidence that he already held such developed Gnostic doctrines.[139] For Wilson, 'there is a gap still to be bridged between the Simon of Acts and the Simon of the heresiologists'.[140]

Lüdemann has attempted to reconstruct the Simon Magus story of Acts 8 in the light of the Simonian tradition attested in the writings of Justin Martyr and Irenaeus.[141] The conclusion he arrived at would nevertheless seem to revive Haenchen's hypothesis of the existence of a pre-Lukan Gnostic tradition: the Gnostic system of the Simonian religion, attested in the second century CE, is already present in Acts 8. Some of Lüdemann's later works also strongly reflect the same argument.[142] For Lüdemann, what Luke is doing is defaming Simon by merely 'depicting him one-sidedly as a magician',

137. Haenchen, *Acts*, p. 303.
138. Beyschlag, 'Simon-Magus Frage', pp. 395–426.
139. Wilson, 'Gnostic Origins', pp. 485–491.
140. Wilson, 'Gnostic Origins', p. 491.
141. Lüdemann, *Untersuchungen*.
142. Lüdemann, *Traditions*, pp. 93–102; *idem*, 'Beginnings', pp. 420–6.

without mentioning his Gnostic identity.[143] The evidences that Lüdemann cites from Acts 8 for his thesis of the date of a Simonian Gnostic system back to the time of Luke's time or his sources are mainly twofold. (1) The designation of Simon given in 8:10b and (2) Luke's use of the word ἐπίνοια (thought) in Peter's response to Simon's request in 8:22.

First, regarding the designation of Simon as 'the great power' in Acts 8:10b, Lüdemann insists that it refers to Simon as the god of the Simonians. This is based on Justin's report in *I Apology* 26.3 that 'almost all the Samaritans, but also a few among other nations, confess him as the first god and worship him'. The designation is part of an 'authentic Simonian tradition' preserved in Acts 8:10 and also a proclamation that Simon made about himself. As to the issue whether the designation is that of a man who identifies himself with God (formula of identification) or that of a Gnostic redeemer figure who appeared as a human being and who claims to be such (formula of recognition), Lüdemann says: 'Only historical considerations can decide, as the evidence from the tradition is not clear'.[144] But without any 'historical consideration', he concludes it as a formula of recognition.[145] Second, the Gnostic identity of Simon is further emphasized by referring to the word ἐπίνοια used in Peter's response to Simon in Acts 8:22. Since this word is used for Simon's female partner Helena in the Simonian tradition, Lüdemann insists that Luke already knew about her from the tradition and thus makes Peter allude ironically to Simon's *syzygos*. In case the original tradition did not contain this word, Luke would have contributed this figure from his own knowledge of the Simon Magus tradition.

Thus, Lüdemann finds in Acts 8 two essential foundations of the Gnostic system attested in Justin Martyr: Simon's proclamation of himself as a god and the tradition about ἐπίνοια as his *syzygos*. This leads him to conclude that Simonian religion was already Gnostic when Philip came into contact with it.[146] Lüdemann thus challenges the thesis of Wilson that 'all attempts so far made have failed to bridge the gap between the Simon of Acts and the Simon of the heresiologists'.[147] As to the question of the historical Simon, he says, 'the bedrock of the tradition about him in Acts 8 is the worship of Simon as a god and the existence of ἐπίνοια as his syzygos'.[148] For him 'Simon can have been a prophet, teacher or miracle worker to whom a Gnostic interpretation was attached'.[149] Also Simon's miracles are part of the tradition,

143. Lüdemann, *Traditions*, p. 101.
144. Lüdemann, *Traditions*, p. 98.
145. Lüdemann, *Traditions*, p. 101.
146. Lüdemann, 'Beginnings', pp. 420–1.
147. Wilson, 'Gnostic Origins', p. 490.
148. Lüdemann, *Traditions*, pp. 101–2.
149. Lüdemann, *Traditions*, p. 102.

but only in the context of historical consideration can it be decided. This scepticism is due to the absence in the early Christian Simonian tradition of any mention of the possession of the Spirit and miracles. Talbert, whose view is similar to that of Haenchen and Lüdemann, assumes that Luke purposely disguises Simon's Gnostic identity in order to idealize the church by portraying the complete unity and orthodoxy of the apostolic age.[150] It implies that Luke is trying to settle the problem of *Frühkatholizimus* of the primitive Church.

Is there clear evidence in Acts 8 to suggest that Luke is dealing with a Gnostic Simon or Gnostic Simonians? One must note that for Luke, Simon is not a Gnostic, but a magician,[151] or possibly more than a magician. It is evident from Acts that Luke never masks what some scholars think contrary to the harmonization of the Church. He clearly exposes various crises the early Church faced – leadership crisis (Acts 1:21ff.), moral crisis (5:1-10), administrative crisis (6:1ff.), theological crisis (15:1-35) and missionary crisis (13:39) – and deals with magic (13:6), sorcery (16:6; 19:13-26) and false gods (17:23; 19:23ff.). If Luke had known Simon as a Gnostic figure, there is no reason to assume that he would not have portrayed him so. Thus, it is unlikely that Luke distorts the Gnostic identity of Simon in order to idealize the apostolic age and to make it an error-free one. And still further, if an early date (70–80 CE) is suggested for Luke-Acts, it is improbable that Luke is attacking a Gnostic heresy, which developed in the mid-second century CE. A reading of the later developed Gnostic ideas into the pre-Gnostic account of Luke is anachronistic. In reconstructing the true identity of Simon, one must be aware that the first source to mention the story of Simon Magus is Acts 8 where Simon is more than a mere magician, but not certainly a Gnostic. And, to identify him as a Gnostic is merely anachronistic. Lüdemann finds no difficulty in considering historical that which he thinks is connected to Simonians. He tries to read Simonianism into the Acts account and claims everything that does not match with the Simonian tradition as Lukan redaction. In other words, only the Simonian religion makes the Acts accounts reliable. But one needs to be aware that Luke does not have Simonians in Acts 8, but only Simon and that Simon's followers in Luke are not the Simonians of Justin and others.

While describing Simon Magus, Morton Smith makes the point that Acts 8:4-25 is a 'Christian propaganda' against the followers of Simon and the primary object of the entire story is to show that Simon was inferior to Jesus and the apostles.[152] Smith goes further, to claim that Simon was a disciple of John the Baptist and that he was at one time baptized by John or one of John's followers. To confirm this claim he focuses on the gospel story of Jesus'

---

150. C.H. Talbert, *Luke and the Gnostics: An Examination of the Lucan Purpose* (Nashville: Abingdon, 1966), pp. 85–6.

151. Barrett, 'Light', p. 286.

152. Smith, 'Account', pp. 735–49.

baptism by John and the story in Acts 19 where the Johannine baptism was followed by a separate gift of the Spirit. 'The story of Simon's baptism looks very much like a Christian's telling against the Simonians the sort of story which the followers of John the Baptist were telling against the Christians to prove Jesus' inferiority to John'.[153]

Smith's claim that Luke is attempting a polemical attack or what Smith calls 'ammunition' against the Simonians may have a historical kernel of truth. Luke has Simon, not the Simonians, in his story of the Samaritan mission because he should have become a major element in the tradition of Luke. In Acts 8:4-25 Luke is describing the programmatic development of Christian mission in Samaria and is also exposing magic and sorcery within the context of mission development. It may be plausible that John the Baptist had preached in Samaria and won disciples though there is not enough evidence to prove it. If those, including Simon, who were converted and baptized by Philip were already baptized by John and his followers, as Smith claims, then why did they still not receive the Holy Spirit in the ministry of Philip?

Wayne A. Meeks, in his short survey article on Simon Magus, briefly discusses the way scholars like Lüdemann and others handled the *Apophasis Megale* quoted in Hippolytus' *Ref.*6.9-18, a source which Haenchen used to reconstruct Simonianism.[154] He then assesses their effect on Haenchen's thesis of the existence of a pre-Christian Gnosis in Acts 8. All of them show in one way or another that there is nothing in this source that is uniquely Simonian. This leads Meeks to say that the 'use of reports about Simon Magus as evidence for a pre-Christian Gnosticism has been effectively refuted' and that the 'burden of proof will lie on anyone who wishes to revive the Haenchen hypothesis'.[155] He also refers to the complexity and the obscurity of the development of Simonianism and its relation to Simon. For example, on the possible relation of Simon to Samaritanism, he says, we 'cannot settle the issue apart from a broader historical investigation'.[156] Meeks agrees with Lüdemann and Beyschlag when he says that they 'see no reason to connect Simon with the Samaritans in the religious sense at all, and they may well be right'.[157] The obscurity is further emphasized: 'The quest for the historical Simon (and Helena) is even less promising than the quest for the historical Jesus'.[158]

---

153. Smith, 'Account', p. 737.

154. Meeks, 'Simon Magus', pp. 137–42.

155. Meeks, 'Simon Magus', p. 141.

156. Meeks, 'Simon Magus', p. 141: This is because he thinks that the arguments of Quispel and Grant are 'vague'; Albright's appendix on the question in the Anchor Bible Volume on Acts is 'superficial and misinformed'; Hans Kippenberg's investigation of some philological parallels in the Samaritan liturgy does not settle the historical issue.

157. Meeks, 'Simon Magus', p. 141.

158. Meeks, 'Simon Magus', p. 141.

C.K. Barrett, in his discussion on Simon Magus, tries to bring the relation of the Holy Spirit to the church in Acts. He comments: 'The story of Simon Magus may prove to touch more of the main themes of Acts than appears at first sight, and also to suggest points that have suffered from unwarranted neglect'.[159] As mentioned elsewhere, according to Barrett, it is the traditions about Simon that fixes the events of 8:4-25, and any implied relation between the Seven and the Twelve is Luke's own product rather than tradition. It means, 'Simon is not a piece of cement holding Philip and Peter together', but he is 'a piece of traditional material existing in his own right'.[160] Barrett emphasizes that Simon in Acts 8 is not a Gnostic, but a magician. His willingness to pay money for the ability to confer the Spirit by the imposition of hands would suggest that he would intend to charge for the magical art when he passed it on. Since Luke has a special concern to show the result or consequences of the proper and improper use of money in relation to holy things, Simon fits into the familiar and characteristic interest of Luke. Simon cannot acquire by money the power to pass on the Spirit to others.

Finally, Barrett draws some implications of the Simon story in the context of Acts. (1) Luke is making a contrast between two persons, the money-making magus and the poor apostle, to show the superior blessedness of giving rather than receiving. (2) The gifts or manifestations of the Spirit are not saleable and are not something which human beings can dispense if suitably rewarded. (3) The Holy Spirit is the one who directs the life and activity of the church, who is not controlled but controls. (4) For Luke, Simon has followers, not the Simonians of whom he does not give any hints about his awareness, but those who follow Simon's theological error and moral perversion, and the readers should guard against them. Barrett concludes that Luke is unaware of the internal problem of the divergences between the Palestinians, represented by the Twelve, and the Hellenists, represented by the Seven. And, this very unawareness means that he did not use the Simon Magus story as a 'smokescreen' to cover up these issues. Through the story of Simon, Luke shows that the church is an institutional home of the Holy Spirit marked by unity and the gift of the Spirit and that it is transcended and controlled by the Spirit.[161]

J.D.M. Derrett has attempted to explain Simon's wishes, his offer and the reason for its refusal by Peter.[162] According to Derrett, Simon intended to buy the ability to induce the Spirit in others because he wanted to develop his divinatory and therapeutic practices for his own exclusive profit. What he offered Peter was not a bribe, but simply a price (as a *quid pro quo*) to

159. Barrett, 'Light', p. 281.
160. Barrett, 'Light', p. 285.
161. Barrett, 'Light', p. 293.
162. Derrett, 'Simon Magus', pp. 52–68.

purchase a 'priesthood' subordinate to Peter. This view is based on the early first century evidence for the availability of Jewish priesthood on sale.[163] Further, it has been suggested that the outlook of Simon was idolatrous, for he was mistaking the charisma as an *'exousia* similar to those notoriously held by priest of idols'.[164] The refusal and rebuke of Peter signifies not only Simon's idolatry and his inappropriate share or lot, but Peter's technique to repeat the diagnosis of the 'crooked and perverse generation'.

Susan Garrett considers that the Lukan portrayal of Simon is 'altogether biased', 'of dubious value for rediscovering the historical Simon', 'marked by oddities' and 'permeated with mythological motifs'.[165] She expresses the complexity of discovering the true identity of Simon: 'All efforts to gain access to the historical Simon via the Acts account will meet with obstacles, perhaps insurmountable'.[166] However, she claims that the Simon Magus story may provide a different sort of historical information regarding the early Christians' view of magic. This is based on her assumption that 'the finished narrative accurately represents Luke's own point of view, whatever sources he may have used'.[167] Garrett discusses the implication for Luke of the title 'the power of God' acclaimed to Simon from the wider context of Luke-Acts, and arrives at the conclusion that Luke sees Simon as associated with the devil. Based on the association of 'magic', 'Satan' and the 'false prophecy' in Jewish and Christian documents of Luke's time, she insists that Luke also regarded Simon as a false prophet. Though he does not explicitly mention this designation, 'one can conclude', Garrett says, 'that Luke has described Simon in such a way that readers would have regarded the designation "false prophet" as apposite'.[168]

The work of Spencer includes a chapter on Simon Magus, in which he attempts to explore the Philip-Simon encounter for elucidating the Lukan portrait of Philip.[169] But this study on Simon is not extensive, in our point of view, for it suffers from not having given sufficient attention to the other part of the story, the Peter-Simon encounter which is of course outside the scope of his study on Philip. He rightly, I suggest, rules out the possibility of a Gnostic fervour of Simon and casts him as a great magician. He argues, in the light of the exodus story, that Philip is cast as a 'prophet like Moses' and his encounter with Simon is analogous to Moses' victory over Pharaoh's

---

163. Derrett, 'Simon Magus', pp. 61–2; see 2 Macc. 4:7-10.

164. Derrett, 'Simon Magus', p. 63.

165. Susan R. Garrett, *The Demise of the Devil: Magic and the Demonic in Luke's Writings* (Minneapolis: Fortress Press, 1989), pp. 61–87.

166. Garrett, *Demise*, p. 62.

167. Garrett, *Demise*, p. 62.

168. Garrett, *Demise*, p. 68.

169. Spencer, *Portrait*, pp. 88–127.

magicians. Luke regards Simon as an 'apostate' in his craving for money and power, for which Philip is not held responsible. In Philip's ministry, Simon Magus 'stands out among the legion of joyful respondents as the *lone example* of a backslider, even as Judas and Ananias and Sapphira are exceptions among Jesus' disciples and the Jerusalem Church'.[170]

L.T. Johnson makes some remarks on the story of Simon. For him, the attempt to understand the literary and theological purposes of Luke on the basis of other sources on Simon is termed as a 'sporadic business' and as 'irrelevant'.[171] It is as a character in the story that Simon is to be considered. This is evident in his following statements:

> ... there are a number of questions that could be discussed concerning the 'historical Simon': Was he truly a magician or rather the center of a cult? Was he a founder of Gnosticism or only a convenient eponym for heresiologists seeking to find roots for that later noxious growth? We leave aside such questions not only because answering them is difficult and distracting (if indeed even possible) but for the more principled reason that the historical Simon is no more pertinent to the understanding of Luke's story than is the 'historical Gamaliel' or the 'historical Paul' or even the 'historical Jesus'.[172]

Johnson regards Simon as one associated at least eponymously with some form of Gnosticism. Since Luke and later Christian writings mention that Simon was a 'magician', this designation may in part have a historical basis and in part reflect a polemical degrading of the claim attached to Simon. It is clear from all sources on Simon that he 'claimed considerable importance in his own sight (and was therefore not simply an effective magician)'.[173] Johnson's view on the theological purpose of this narrative is similar to that of Garrett: Simon the magician is the representative of the demonic powers in Samaria that are resistant to the Kingdom of God and he provides the occasion to demonstrate God's power over Satan and the demonic realm. Unlike others, Johnson reads Simon as a Christian in the narrative, but one who has an attitude of the demonic realm.

Like Barrett and others do, Witherington also rules out the possibility of Simon being a Gnostic in the Lukan account and suggests that none of the later materials on Simon should be read back into the New Testament account.[174] But contrary to Johnson, he insists that Simon was 'only impressed with the apparent miracle-working power of Philip and Peter', and was not converted at all.[175] He draws on several hints in the text to argue that Simon was never converted. (1) Simon is introduced in the narrative in pejorative terms (vv. 9-11). (2) Unlike the case with the Samaritans (vv. 12f.), we are not told what

170. Spencer, *Portrait*, p. 126.
171. Johnson, *Acts*, p. 152.
172. Johnson, *Acts*, pp. 151–2.
173. Johnson, *Acts*, p. 147.
174. Witherington, *Acts*, pp. 279–90.
175. Witherington, *Acts*, pp. 288–9.

Simon believed when it is said that he believed. (3) The καί in v. 13 (ὁ δὲ Σίμων καί) and his separate treatment suggest a distinction between Simon and the Samaritans. (4) The remarks that his heart is not right before God, that he is in danger of going to destruction and that he must repent are suggestive of this. (5) The description of Simon in v. 23, 'trapped in the chain of wickedness', refers to that of an unregenerate person. (6) At the end of the story he does not seem to repent, but is only frightened of the negative consequences spoken by Peter. This view of Witherington is like that of Dunn who claims that Simon, like the Samaritans, cannot have had true faith and had not been truly converted.[176] This is because Dunn thinks that (a) Simon did not receive the Spirit (b) Simon was still in sin and (c) Peter's rebuke indicates that Simon was still a pagan.

It is certain that there exist vivid portrayals of Simon in 8:4-13 and 8:14-25. Simon who believed and was baptized, is said to have followed Philip in vv. 4-13, but later appears to have changed his character and is doomed for destruction in vv. 14-25. However, there is nothing in the initial portrait of vv. 4-13 to suggest that Simon's faith was defective and he was not truly converted.[177] The description of Simon in vv. 9-11 is about his claim and activities for the period *before* (προϋπῆρχεν, v. 9a) he met Philip and believed and was baptized.[178] Thus it is not pejorative, rather a description of his distinct past before he became a Christian. The force of καί in v. 13 indicates the efficacy of the gospel that Philip preached which has power even over mighty figures like Simon and over magical deeds. Also Luke does not seem to portray a difference in the content of Simon's belief. The combination of προσκαρτερῶν with ἐπίστευσεν καὶ βαπτισθείς in v. 13 appears to indicate the new Christian experience of Simon as rather similar to those of the early Christians (cf. 1:14; 2:42, 46; 6:4). The content of the faith, which Simon had, was exactly what the Samaritans also had. Philip does not preach a different message to Simon, nor is Simon said to have misunderstood the message of Philip. It may well be that Philip's miracles amazed Simon and he seemed to be a spectator of these mighty deeds. Further, reading the final description of Simon in vv. 18-24 back into his conversion experience in v. 13 is totally unwarranted. It was not unfamiliar for Luke and his audience to see members of the early Christian community committing sin, as was the case with Ananias and Sapphira (5:1-6) and to undergo serious threat and punishment from the apostles.[179] The very fact that Simon was said to be present among

---

176. Dunn, *Baptism*, pp. 55–6.

177. Pesch, *Apostelgeschichte* I, says: 'Der Text unterstellt ihm dabei keine Heuchelei' (p. 275).

178. Of the only two occurrences of the word προϋπῆρξεν in Luke Acts, the other reference in Lk. 23:12 also stresses a complete break or distinction between the past and the present situation.

179. Hans-Josef Klauck, *Magic and Paganizm in Early Christianity* (trans. Brian McNeil; Edinburgh: T. & T. Clark, 2000), chapter II, pp. 13–29, 21.

the Samaritan Christians while Peter and John prayed for them is a further hint that he was possibly a member of that new Christian fellowship. Therefore, it is all the more likely that Luke thought Simon's response to Philip to be genuine and that of a *bona fide* convert. Thus the above arguments of Dunn and Witherington that Simon was not converted at all are unjustifiable.

The major views emerging from previous studies on Simon can be summarized: (1) On the one hand, it is claimed that there underlies a pre-Lukan source for Simon that has disguised him as a magician and that Simon was already a Gnostic before he came into contact with Christianity and Luke in Acts 8 has degraded the divine redeemer into a mere magician. On the other, the account of Simon in Acts 8 is 'pure Lukan' and there is no evidence for an earlier pre-Lukan version of a Gnostic Simon. (2) The identity of the historical Simon in Acts 8 has been cast into different categories: Gnostic,[180] magician,[181] *theios aner*,[182] and false prophet,[183] a charlatan who was subsequently elevated to the status of a redeemer. (3) The issue of the Christian identity of Simon: did he or did he not become a Christian through the ministry of Philip? (4) The question of the possible relation of Simon to the Samaritans and Simonianism remains open.

The above survey of scholarly discussion shows an increasing interest in identifying Simon with Simonian Gnosticism on the basis of his own claim and that of his followers as reported in Acts 8:9-10. It is also due to the assumption that the Lukan account of Simon is biased and therefore dubious for discovering the historical Simon. Working backward from the evidence from the latest and most complex sources outside Acts, scholars like Haenchen, Lüdemann and Talbert argue that Simon was indeed a Gnostic and the author of Acts had simply degraded him to a mere magician, and that the Lukan text on Simon is an anti-Gnostic polemic. They claim that Luke deliberately distorts the Gnostic identity of Simon and portrays him as a mere magician. This assertion is also based on the possible link between Simon and the Simonian Gnosticism as depicted in the later Christian tradition. As Garrett rightly points out, the tendency of many scholars has been to focus on the question of what information Luke may have hidden on the possible historical connections between Simon and Gnosticism, rather than on how it may help us to understand the early Christian view of magic.[184] Any attempt to understand the Simon of Acts 8 should consider the significance of this episode for the Lukan portrait of the Samaritan mission as a whole.

---

180. Lüdemann, 'Beginnings', pp. 420–1; Haenchen, *Acts*, p. 307; Talbert, *Gnostics*, pp. 83–4.

181. Barrett, 'Light', p. 286.

182. Beyschlag, *Simon Magus*, pp. 122–6.

183. Garrett, *Demise*, p. 68.

184. Garrett, *Demise*, pp. 61–2.

The important issue, for our study, is why does Luke bring the Simon Magus incident into the narrative of the Samaritan mission? Is it just because it happened and was striking? Or is it because Luke knew some heterodox movement associated with the name of Simon? How does this story function in the context of the Samaritans' acceptance of the gospel, the ministry of Philip, the visit of the Jerusalem apostles, and in the overall interest of Luke in portraying the success of the gospel over magic?

2.5. Conclusion

The present survey of scholarly discussion on Acts 8:4-25 reveals a compartmentalization of individual units dominated by the source-critical and theological approaches without taking into consideration the significance of the whole narrative in its historical, literary and theological contexts. What is Luke trying to do in his portrayal of the Samaritan mission? Why does he tell us this story in the way it is narrated in the present text? In other words, what is the rhetorical and theological function of Acts 8:4-25? It is proposed that the function of the narrative will make sense in the historical context of the Samaritans in the first century CE as well as Luke's special interest in the Samaritans as depicted in his Gospel. Therefore, the subsequent chapters of the present study are devoted to exploring the relevant socio-political and religious background of the Samaritans in the New Testament period and the significance of the Samaritan episodes in the Gospel of Luke.

Part II

BACKGROUND TO LUKE'S PORTRAYAL OF THE
SAMARITANS IN ACTS

Chapter 3

SAMARIA AND THE SAMARITANS IN THE NEW TESTAMENT PERIOD

3.1. Introduction

The purpose of this chapter is to review the socio-religious situation of the Samaritans in the New Testament period in order to set the narrative of Acts 8:4-25 in its historical context. Such a review will enable us to demonstrate the ambiguous and ambivalent identity of the Samaritans as is portrayed in Jewish sources and the questionable legitimacy of their socio-religious dynamics which, as we shall see later, are directly relevant to exploring the rhetorical and theological function of the Samaritan episodes in Luke-Acts, especially in Acts 8:4-25. Given the focus of our study, we will not engage here in the reconstruction of the origin and history of the Samaritans,[1] but limit our review to events and conflicts that are related to their socio-religious life, as they will allow us to understand the antagonisms between Jews and Samaritans. This study will also discuss the possible identification of the 'city

---

1. For discussions on Samaritan origins and history, see A.D. Crown (ed.), *The Samaritans* (Tübingen: J.C.B. Mohr, 1989); *idem*, 'Redating the Schism between Judaeans and the Samaritans', *JQR* 82:1-2 (1991), pp. 17–50; *idem*, 'Another Look at Samaritan Origins', in A.D. Crown and L. Davey (eds), *New Samaritan Studies of the Société d'études Samaritaines* (vols. III & IV), Essays in Honour of G.D. Sixdenier (Studies in Judaica No.5; University of Sydney: Mandelbaum Publishing, 1995), pp. 133–55; N. Schur, *History of the Samaritans* (Frankfurt am Main: Verlag Peter Lang, 1989); J. Bowman, *The Samaritan Problem: Studies in the Relationships of Samaritanism, Judaism and Early Christianity* (PTMS 4; Pittsburgh: Pickwick Press, 1975); *idem*, 'The History of the Samaritans', *AbrN* 18 (1978/79), pp. 101–15; R.J. Coggins, *Samaritans and Jews: The Origins of Samaritanism Reconsidered* (Oxford: Basil Blackwell, 1975); F. Dexinger and R. Pummer (eds), *Die Samaritaner* (Darmstadt: Wiss. Buches, 1992); J.A. Montgomery, *The Samaritans: The Earliest Jewish Sect* (Philadelphia: John C. Winston, 1907); M. Gaster, *The Samaritans: Their History, Doctrines, and Literature* (London: Oxford University Press, 1925); J. Purvis, *The Samaritan Pentateuch and the Origin of the Samaritan Sect* (Cambridge: Harvard University Press, 1968); *idem*, 'The Samaritan Problem: A Case Study in Jewish Sectarianism in the Roman Era', in B. Halpern and J.D. Levenson (eds), *Tradition in Transformation*, F.M. Cross Festschrift (Indiana, 1986), pp. 350–83; *idem*, 'The Samaritans', in W.D. Davies and Louis Finkelstein (eds), *The Cambridge History of Judaism*, vol. II: *The Hellenistic Age* (Cambridge: Cambridge University Press, 1989), pp. 591–613; G. Alon, 'The Origin of the Samaritans in the Halakhic Tradition', in *Jews, Judaism and the Classical World* (Jerusalem, 1977), pp. 354–73; R. Egger, *Josephus Flavius und die Samaritaner: eine terminologische Untersuchung zur Identitaetsklaerung der Samaritaner* (NovT; Freiburg,

of Samaria' where Philip's activity took place (Acts 8:5), which seems to have theological significance for the Lukan portrait of the Samaritan mission.

3.2. *The Distinction between 'Samarians' and 'Samaritans'*

The Hebrew הַשֹּׁמְרֹנִים in 2 Kgs 17:29, which the LXX renders as Σαμαρῖται, simply means 'the inhabitants of Samaria' or 'Samarians', but is often translated in English as 'Samaritans'. Originally, the term was an ethnic designation for the racially mixed and religiously syncretistic northern Palestinian population who had been settled in the territory of Samaria by the Assyrians in the late eighth century BCE. Religiously, these colonists and their descendants were seen by their Judahite neighbours to the south as half-pagan and half-Yahwistic (v. 33). Scholars like Coggins and Egger argue that this isolated reference is to be distinguished from the term 'Samaritans', whose religious centre was Mount Gerizim with Shechem as their holy city, and who become an identifiable group only between the end of the fourth century and the second century BCE.[2] Coggins insists that the city of Samaria was never a centre of Samaritanism because the Samaritans were associated not with Samaria but with Shechem.[3] This dual use of the term in Josephus, says

---

1986); C.S. Chang, *A New Examination of Samaritan Origins and Identity in the Light of Recent Scholarship*, (Sydney, Ph.D Dissertation 1990); Z. Zevit, 'The Gerizim-Samarian Community in and between Texts and Times: An Experimental Study', in C.A. Evans and S. Talmon (eds), *The Quest for Context and Meaning: Studies in Biblical Intertextuality in Honor of James A. Sanders* (BI Series 28; Leiden: Brill, 1997), pp. 547–72; M. Cogan, 'For We, Like You, Worship Your God: 3 Biblical Portrayals of Samaritan Origins', *VT* 38 (1988), pp. 268–92; I. Hjelm, *The Samaritans and Early Judaism: A Literary Analysis* (CIS 7, JSOTSup.303; Sheffield: Sheffield Academic Press, 2000); v. Morabito, *et al.* (eds), *Samaritan Researches vol. V: Proceedings of the Congress of the SES 1996/1997* (Studies in Judaica, No.10; University of Sydney: Mandelbaum Publishing, 2000); John P. Meier, 'The Historical Jesus and the Historical Samaritans: What can be said?', *Bib* 81 (2, 2000), pp. 202–32; R.T. Anderson and T. Giles, *The Keepers: An Introduction to the History and Culture of the Samaritans* (Peabody, MA: Hendrickson Publishers, 2002).

2.   R.J. Coggins, 'Issues in Samaritanism', in J. Neusner and A.J. Avery-Peck (eds), *Judaism in Late Antiquity, Part III: Where We Stand: Issues and Debates in Ancient Judaism*, vol. I (Leiden: Brill, 1999), pp. 63–77; *idem*, 'Jewish Local Patriotism: The Samaritan Problem', in S. Jones and S. Pearce (eds), *Jewish Local Patriotism and Self-Identification in the Graeco-Roman Period* (JSPSup.31; Sheffield: Sheffield Academic Press, 1998), pp. 66–78; R. Egger, *Josephus Flavius*; *eadem*, 'Josephus Flavius and the Samaritans', in A. Tal and M. Florentin (eds), *Proceedings of the First International Congress of the Société D'Etudes Samaritaines*, Tel Aviv, April 11–13, 1988 (Chaim Rosenberg School for Jewish Studies: Tel Aviv University, 1991), pp. 109–14; F. Dexinger, 'Limits of Tolerance in Judaism: The Samaritan Example', in E.P. Sanders, *et al.* (eds), *Jewish and Christian Self-Definition*, vol. II (London: SCM Press, 1981), pp. 88–114, 94; J.E. Fossum, *The Name of God and the Angel of the Lord: Samaritan and Jewish Concepts of Intermediation and the Origin of Gnosticism* (WUNT 36; Tübingen: J.C.B. Mohr, 1985), p. 31.

3.   Coggins, *Samaritans*, pp. 8–9; *idem*, 'Issues', p. 66.

Coggins, 'results in confusion both at the geographical and at the religio-political level'.[4] Since there is no secure evidence to identify the 'Samarians' in 2 Kgs 17 with the later religious community of 'Samaritans', the use of the term 'Samaritans' as early as the eighth century BCE has been considered as a Jewish anti-Samaritan polemic, rather than a historical plausibility.[5] As for the Samaritans, they derive their name not from the geographical designation הַשֹּׁמְרֹנִים but rather from the term שֹׁמְרִים meaning 'keepers' or 'guardians' of the Law.[6] Thus, it raises the issue of the origin of the Samaritans chronologically and geographically, and the problem of describing their formation as a political, ethnic, or religious group.

In order to understand how various sources like Josephus treat the Samaritans, the need for making a distinction between 'Samarians' and 'Samaritans' has become more apparent. Egger makes such a distinction and argues that Josephus, when describing events before the time of Alexander (330 BCE), uses the term Σαμαρεῖς or Σαμαρεῖται to refer to the inhabitants of Samaria without clear religious connotation. Therefore, in her opinion, they should be called 'Samarians' rather than 'Samaritans'.[7] Josephus' use of the term to refer to the Samaritans comes from the time of John Hyrcanus, in the second half of the second century BCE. The issue becomes more complex when Egger makes the claim that when we differentiate the references to the Gerizim community from those to the 'Samarians', it is clear that 'Josephus' position was not anti-Samaritan but rather anti-Samarian'.[8] This claim of Egger underestimates the anti-Samaritan polemic that Josephus or his source generally shares. For example, that Josephus links the term 'Cuthaeans' with his description of the Gerizim temple shows his anti-Samaritan polemic.[9] Also, it

---

4.   Coggins, 'The Samaritans in Josephus', in Feldman and Hata (eds), *Josephus, Judaism, and Christianity* (Leiden: E.J. Brill, 1987), pp. 257–73, 258.

5.   Coggins, 'Issues', p. 65. According to Bowman, *Samaritan Problem*, p. 1, what the non-Samaritan sources offer to us is 'not only fragmentary but also polemic and, in addition, filled with contradictions'. Therefore, a review of the first-century Samaritanism has to acknowledge the ambiguity of the available evidence.

6.   The most important Samaritan sources now available are the Samaritan Pentateuch, Targum, the liturgical text called Defter, Memar Marqah and the four Samaritan Chronicles (written between the eleventh and the fourteenth centuries CE.). All the Samaritan texts (except SP and Targum) are to be dated after the fourth century CE. The earliest known MS of Memar Marqah is no older than the fourteenth century. On the issue of the reliability of these sources, see J.D. Purvis, 'The Fourth Gospel and the Samaritans', *NovT* 17 (3, 1975), pp. 161–98, 166; R. Pummer, *The Samaritans* (Leiden: E.J. Brill, 1987), p. 4; Purvis, 'The Samaritans and Judaism', in R.A. Kraft and G.W.E. Nickelsburg (eds), *Early Judaism and its Modern Interpreters* (Philadelphia: Fortress Press, 1986), pp. 81–98, 82–3); Coggins, 'The Samaritans and the Northern Israelite Tradition', in Tal & Florentin (eds), *Proceedings*, pp. 99–108; On the view of Samaritans as 'keepers' of the Law, *idem*, *Samaritans*, pp. 10–11; see also R.T. Anderson and T. Giles, *Tradition kept: The Literature of the Samaritans* (Peabody, MA: Hendrickson Publishers, 2005).

7.   Egger, *Josephus Flavius*; *eadem*, 'Josephus', pp. 109–14.

8.   Egger, 'Josephus', p. 114.

9.   See the discussion on 'Cuthaeans' below.

is likely that every one who was ethnically or religiously a 'Samaritan' was geographically a 'Samarian'. That religious identity emerges gradually because of the Samaritans' explicit attachment to Gerizim and Shechem does not mean that they did not have an ethnic or political identity before. Also, one cannot completely rule out the possibility that the Gerizim community did not have any 'Samarians'. Though Coggins and Egger emphasize the importance of making a terminological distinction in Josephus and speak of the possible identification of the Samaritans after the period of Alexander the Great, the former thinks that Josephus is anti-Samaritan and the latter that he is anti-Samarian. This is further expressed by Feldman: 'Even in Josephus, we cannot always be sure that the word which is translated "Samaritans" may not refer to "Samarians", that is, the inhabitants, not necessarily Samaritans, of Samaria'.[10] On this issue, van den Horst comments:

> Even though there is a growing awareness among scholars that the Greek terms *Samarites* and *Samareus* and the Latin term *Samaritanus* do not necessarily mean 'Samaritan', it is by no means yet common knowledge…. The words concerned can also denote a 'Samarian', which is the recently coined term for an inhabitant of Samaria who is not a member of that religious community.[11]

The above distinction between 'Samarians' and 'Samaritans' implies that chronologically, one can only speak of the 'Samaritans' in the strict sense outside the period of time covered by the Old Testament writings and therefore, a historical derivation of the Samaritans from 2 Kgs 17:24-41 seems quite weakened. It means that the religious community of Samaritans cannot be the Samarians of the city of Samaria at least before the third or second century BCE. The distinction also implies that there is no likely reference to any group, even in the Persian period during the time of Ezra or Nehemiah, which can properly be identified as Samaritans. Mor assumes that it is difficult to believe that the groups mentioned in Ezra 4:1-4 refer to the Samaritans because (a) they are the adversaries of Judah, Benjamin and the people of the land and (b) there is no likely evidence that the Samaritans either tried to join the Jerusalem Temple or planned to build their own temple. [12] This view is shared also by Dexinger, who says, 'It is not possible to speak of Samaritans in the time of Ezra'.[13] So he prefers the term 'proto-Samaritans' to the Samaritans to describe them until the destruction of their temple on Mount Gerizim and of Shechem by John Hyrcanus in 128 BCE.

---

10.   L.H. Feldman, 'Josephus' Attitude Toward the Samaritans: A Study in Ambivalence', in M. Mor (ed.), *Jewish Sects, Religious Movements, and Political Parties, Proceedings of the third Annual Symposium of the Philip M. and Ethel Klutznick Chair in Jewish Civilization held on October 14–15, 1990*, (Nebraska: Creighton University Press, 1992), pp. 23–45, 24.

11.   P.W. van der Horst, 'Samaritans and Hellenism', *SPA* VI (1994), pp. 28–36, 33.

12.   Mor, 'The Persian, Hellenistic and Hasmonean Period', in Crown (ed.), *Samaritans*, pp. 1–18, 6.

13.   Dexinger, 'Limits', p. 94.

Coggins thinks it is possible that 'the tradition embodied in Ezra 1-6 relates to those in the vicinity of Jerusalem who were regarded as opponents by the group responsible for that collection'.[14] References to Samaritans in the Persian period also raise the question of Josephus as a reliable historical source for historical events from Nehemiah to Alexander.[15] The main reason is that he had very little information for the two centuries of history between the end of the Old Testament text and the book of 1 Maccabees. Therefore, it has been claimed that what Josephus offers about this period is 'nothing more than a legend' and cannot be used as authentic.[16]

The distinction between 'Samaritan' and 'Samarian' seems to be reconsidered when Crown claims that the Samaritans are the true descendants of the sons of Israel and were created from Samarians, the old Israel who escaped exile and remained in the land.[17] After the return from the exile there was tension between the returned exiles and the *am-ha'aretz*, who had escaped the captivity and had stayed *in situ*, regarding the identity and role of the new 'true Israel'. Just as the prophets of the early post-exilic period anticipated (Zech. 7:15; Hag. 2:4), the returned exiles were identified as the new Israel and it resulted in a separation of Judah and Israel, in the form of Yahud and Samaria. In this process, according to Crown, many of the *am-ha'aretz* in old Judah, who had stayed *in situ*, may well have joined the *am-ha'aretz* of old Israel thus forming the Samarians. Henceforth, religious ideology is interwoven with political reality, leading to the development of a Samarian body politic, which becomes the Samaritan sect.[18] In this respect, Crown considers 2 Kgs 17 as a post-exilic redaction of the Deuteronomist incorporating the exile of Judah and as a polemic directed against the *am-ha'aretz* of both Judah and Israel.[19] Though Crown's use of the term 'Samarians' refers to the old Israel untouched by exile, his claim implies that the Samaritans, even before their allegiance to Gerizim and Shechem, are part of the Samarians politically, ethnically and religiously.

---

14. Coggins, 'Northern Israelite Tradition', p. 102.

15. M. Smith, *Palestinian Parties and Politics that Shaped the Old Testament* (New York: Columbia University Press, 1971), p. 114; L.L. Grabbe, 'Josephus and the Reconstruction of the Judean Restoration', *JBL* 106 (2, 1987), pp. 231–46 strongly argues that Josephus does not offer us a 'consistent', 'clear' account of the Persian period, and 'the use of any of his data for this time requires a careful historical and literary analysis, along with a good deal of historical scepticism' (pp. 244–5). For a contrary view, see Cross, 'A Reconstruction of the Judean Restoration', *JBL* 94 (1975), pp. 4–18; *idem*, 'Aspects of Samaritan and Jewish History in Late Persian and Hellenistic Times', *HTR* 59 (1966), pp. 201–11; *idem*, 'Papyri of the Fourth Century BC from Daliyeh', in D.N. Freedman and J.C. Greenfield (eds), *New Directions in Biblical Archaeology* (Garden City, NY: Doubleday, 1969), pp. 45–69.

16. Grabbe, 'Josephus', pp. 232, 244–5; Smith, *Palestinian Parties*, p. 114.

17. Crown, 'Samaritan Origins', pp. 133–55.

18. Crown, 'Samaritan Origins', p. 141.

19. For a summary of the source- and redaction-critical analysis of 2 Kgs 17, see S.L. McKenzie, *The Trouble with Kings: The Composition of the Book of Kings in the*

If the term 'Samarians' signifies the original sense of the Hebrew הַשֹּׁמְרֹנִים which is the inhabitants of the city of Samaria, why have they been called 'Samaritans' by ancient sources? It could be that the term 'Samarians' applies to all inhabitants of Samaria, including the Samaritans, and to the Jewish, the pagan and the Christian population, and that the ancient sources do not make a clear terminological distinction.[20] It may also be, as mentioned earlier, that the sources tended to portray the Samaritans' association with the 'Samarians' or at least some 'Samarians' sharing the religious practice of the 'Samaritans', thus showing their ethnic, geographic and religious continuity with the north as opposed to the southern community of Jerusalem. If anti-Samaritan polemic is underlying the identification, then it may reflect the intensity of Jewish hostility towards the Samaritans and the anachronistic tendency of Jewish sources like Josephus to portray the illegitimacy of their origin and socio-religious life. Thus, the reason may be literary and/or theological. The implication in the distinction is that the Samaritans must be identified basically in religious terms and must be associated with their veneration of Mount Gerizim and Shechem. However, it poses the problem of identification when they live away from their religious centre and the temple on Gerizim ceases to exist. For our purpose it is to be noted that Luke does not seem to make a differentiation between 'Samarians' and 'Samaritans' and that, in light of references in his Gospel (cf. Lk. 9:51-57; 10:28-37; 17:11-19) that reflect ethnic and religious tension and features, it seems he is dealing with the ethnic and religious community of the Samaritans.

3.3. Jewish Designations of the Samaritans

Now we will look at some of the designations used in Josephus, intertestamental and rabbinic literature to refer or allude possibly to the religious sect of the Samaritans.

3.3.1. Cuthaeans
Among several terms that Josephus employs in association with the Samaritans, the designation 'Cuthaeans' is particularly prominent. Regarding Cuthaeans, he says:

> As for the Chuthaioi who were transported to Samaria – this is the name by which they have been called to this day because of having been brought over from the region called

---

Deuteronomistic History (Leiden: Brill, 1991), pp. 140–2; For a stylistic reading of the text, J.T. Walsh, '2 Kings 17: The Deuteronomist and the Samaritans', in J.C. De Moor & H.F. Van Rooy (eds), *Past, Present, Future: The Deuteronomistic History and the Prophets* (Leiden: E.J. Brill, 2000), pp. 315–23.

20. R. Pummer, *Early Christian Authors on Samaritans and Samaritanism. Texts, Translations and Commentary* (TSAJ 92; Tübingen: Paul Siebeck, 2002), p. 2.

Chutha, which is in Persia, as is a river by the same name –, each of their tribes – there were five – brought along its own god, and, as they reverenced them in accordance with the custom of their country, they provoked the Most High God to anger and wrath ... those who are called Chuthaioi (Cuthim) in the Hebrew tongue, and Samareitai (Samaritans) by the Greeks ... (*AJ*, IX, 288, 290).

In the above text, Josephus portrays the Samaritans as non-Jews who were brought from Persia to Samaria by the Assyrians and calls them Cuthim, after a Mesopotamian city called Cuthah from which the settlers were said to have been brought. He links them with the Northern kingdom by interpreting the description of the group in 2 Kgs 17:24-41 and Ezra 4:1-5:7ff. as referring to the Samaritans. However, Josephus' association of the term 'Cuthaeans' with the Samaritans raises questions. Egger, as mentioned earlier, insists that Josephus never says that the Cuthaeans who lived in Samaria from the end of the eighth century BCE either sought or had a relationship with Mount Gerizim. The only passage where he associates the term 'Cuthaeans' with Mount Gerizim or its religious community refers to the much later time of John Hyrcanus in the second half of the second century BCE, during the destruction of their temple.[21] In this respect, Hjelm notes that Josephus' use of this term is often linked to his description of the Samaritan temple, especially with its building or destruction and not with questions of the 'legitimacy of the temple' or with political circumstances.[22] As Adrian Mikolasek claims, the Samaritans cannot be identified with 'Cuthaeans' because (a) the term 'Samaritans' הַשֹּׁמְרֹנִים in 2 Kgs 17:29 designates the Israelites of the North expelled into Assyria, not the Cuthaeans and other Babylonians transplanted into Samaria and (b) the Cuthaeans in 2 Kgs 17:24-41 never separated their idol worship from the worship of Yahweh, whereas the Samaritans, because of their special loyalty to the Law did not adopt any syncretistic or polytheistic pagan practices, at least in the early stage of their emergence. [23] Also, there is no evidence that there existed an early controversy with the Samaritans as described in 2 Kgs 17:24-41. However, when Mikolasek claims that Samaritans were the Israelites expelled into Assyria, he is also assuming, wrongly, that the Hebrew term in 2 Kgs 17:29 links historically with later Samaritans. It may be that the later Samaritans are derived in part from 'Cuthaeans'.

When Josephus describes the activities of John Hyrcanus, he mentions both in the *Jewish War* and in the *Antiquities* that Hyrcanus captured 'Shechem and Gerizim and the Cuthaean nation, which lives near the temple built after the model of the sanctuary at Jerusalem'.[24] We should note that the term

---

21.   Egger, 'Josephus', p. 111.

22.   Hjelm, *Samaritans*, p. 216.

23.   A. Mikolasek, 'The Samaritans: Guardians of the Law against the Prophets', in Crown and Davey (eds), *New Samaritan Studies*, p. 92; Coggins, 'Northern Israelite Tradition', pp. 106–7.

24.   *AJ*, XIII, 255–56; Cf. *BJ*, I, 63.

'Cuthaeans' is primarily linked to a geographical location, but for Josephus it has ethnic and religious connotations. The majority of references to this term in Josephus suggests his intention to portray the illegitimacy of the Samaritans' ethnic origin and religious life, which undoubtedly includes the question of their temple as well.[25] The same term 'Cuthaeans' is employed in Rabbinic literature to link the Samaritans with paganism and idolatry (*b.Hullin* 6a; *b.Yoma* 69a).[26]

Josephus also says that the Samaritan community consisted of a breakaway group of Jerusalem priests (*AJ*, XI, 312, 340). According to him, many priests and Israelites left Jerusalem because of their intermarriage with foreigners and they lived in Shechem as 'apostates from the Jewish nation' (ἀποστατῶν τοῦ ᾿Ιουδαίων ἔθνους, *AJ*, XI, 340). If this account of Josephus on the identity of the Samaritans is considered authentic, then his view that they represent a continuum of the older northern traditions is invalid.[27] It also raises the issue of the legitimacy of the Samaritan priesthood. At the outset it seems to contradict his earlier portrayal of them as 'Cuthaeans'. But he links the new breakaway group of many priests of Jerusalem with Sanballat who, according to Josephus, is also a 'Cuthaean'. Thus, he is able to associate the 'Cuthaeans' of 2 Kgs 17 with the 'apostates from the Jewish nation'. Josephus' portrait of the Samaritans as the 'apostates from the Jewish nation', who lived at Shechem from the time of Alexander, as well as his portrait of them as 'Cuthaeans' who were the descendants of foreign settlers, reflects the ambiguous status of the Samaritans in some Jewish circles and the illegitimacy of their ethnic and religious identity according to these rival Jews.

3.3.2. Sidonians
Another term that Josephus employs to describe Samaritans is 'Sidonians' (*AJ*, XI, 340-341). He says that they labelled themselves 'the Sidonians in Shechem' (*AJ*, XI, 342; XII, 257-264). He reports that when the Samaritans met Alexander the Great near Jerusalem, he refused their request to be exempted from tribute in the seventh year: '... when they asked him to remit their tribute in the seventh year ... he inquired who they were that they made this request. And when they said that they were Hebrews but were called the Sidonians of Shechem, he again asked them whether they were Jews' (*AJ*, XI, 343-345). Likewise, during the time of Antiochus IV Epiphanes (175-164

---

25. *AJ*, IX, 288, 290; X, 184; XI, 19-20, 88, 302; XIII, 256.

26. It is debated as to what extent Rabbinic sources provide useful historical information for reconstructing historical facts. For example, one cannot use a fourth century (or later) citation of a second century rabbi as a second century source. For a useful discussion on this issue see a collection of articles in Neusner and Avery-Peck (eds), *Judaism in Late Antiquity*, part III, vol. I.

27. Coggins, 'Northern Israelite Tradition', p. 103.

BCE), the Samaritans wanted to distinguish themselves from the Jews, for which they appealed to Antiochus, repudiating their link with Judaism.[28] Josephus claims that they tried to hide the fact that 'the temple on Gerizim was that of the Most Great God'. Granting their request, Antiochus paganized the temple on Mount Gerizim and proclaimed it to be that of Zeus Hellenios.[29] According to 2 Macc. 6:2, it was quite unwillingly that the Samaritans renamed their sanctuary and called it Zeus Xenios: 'to call the one in Gerizim the temple of Zeus the Friend of Strangers, as did the people who dwelt in that place' (τὸν ἐν Γαριζιν καθὼς ἐτύγχανον οἱ τὸν τόπον οἰκοῦντες Διὸς Ξενίου). One thing to note here is Josephus' choice of the naming of the temple, which is different from that in 2 Macc. 6:2. We will return later to this point.

Who are 'the Sidonians in Shechem'? Various suggestions have been made. (a) Robert Doran suggests that they might be the Hellenized party in Samaria.[30] (b) Mor assumes that it was the Samaritan *Hellenists* who sent the documents in order to break contact with their ancestors' beliefs and customs and to distinguish themselves from the Jews.[31] (c) Bickerman considers the term to mean Phoenicians who were also called Canaanites (Gen. 10:5).[32] (d) Egger goes further to suggest that the Sidonians/Phoenicians were probably in a 'position of power' at the time of Antiochus IV (c.167 BCE) which is evident from their letter to the Seleucid ruler, repudiating their link with the Jews.[33] They were influential, in contrast to the Gerizim-bound Samaritans and the Jews who both were powerless at that time.[34]

Now one needs to ask: does the term 'Sidonians in Shechem' refer to the Samaritans or to a different group? What does this term signify for Josephus? What is clear from Egger's suggestion is that the Sidonians in Josephus are distinct from the religious community of Samaritans. However, some factors need to be reconsidered in identifying the term. There is no religious group apart from the Samaritans at this period that has a strong allegiance to Mount Gerizim. This ties in with the claim of the group to be part of the holy city of Shechem. Also, if the account in which they call themselves 'Hebrews' and Alexander's further inquiry about them being Jews or not is right, then it may fit with Samaritans than any different group. If this term 'Sidonians in Shechem' refers to a group other than the Samaritans as Egger thinks, then their claim that they are distinct from the Jews in race and customs seems less

---

28. *AJ*, XII, 257-264; cf. 2 Macc. 6:2-3.
29. *AJ*, XII, 263.
30. R. Doran, '2 Maccabees 6:2 and the Samaritan Question', *HTR* 76 (1983), pp. 481–5, 482.
31. Mor, 'Persian', pp. 14–15.
32. E.J. Bickerman, *The Jews in the Greek Age* (Cambridge, MA: Harvard University Press, 1988) p. 11.
33. Egger, 'Josephus', p. 112.
34. Egger, 'Josephus', p. 112.

significant to mention in their petition to Antiochus. That, for Josephus, the Samaritans claim themselves that they are a distinct race from the Jews would further tend to identify the group as referring to the Samaritans (*AJ*, IX, 291; XI, 340-341; XII, 257, 262-263). Whether they are the Hellenized Samaritans or not, the use of the term 'Sidonians in Shechem' in Josephus could refer to the religious community of people centred around Gerizim and Shechem. What can also be deduced from their claim made to Alexander and Antiochus is that they do not want to be seen as part of the Jerusalem-bound Jews and the Temple therein.

3.3.3. *Shechemites*

'Shechemites' is another designation that Josephus uses in his discussion about the Samaritans. It appears in his text from the time of Alexander the Great, about 330 BCE. He refers to the Samaritans as living in Shechem: '... the Samaritans (Σαμαρεῖται) whose chief city at that time was Shechem, which lay beside Mount Garizein and was inhabited by apostates from the Jewish nation, seeing that Alexander had so signally honoured the Jews, decided to profess themselves Jews' (*AJ*, XI, 340).[35] In the final section of *Antiquities* XI (346-347), Josephus says, 'Whenever anyone was accused by the people of Jerusalem of eating unclean food or violating the Sabbath or committing any other such sin, he would flee to the Shechemites, saying that he had been unjustly expelled (accused)'. This fits well with the account in 2 Macc. 6:2 of the naming of the Gerizim temple as the 'Protector of Strangers' (Διὸς Ξενίου), as the character of this god, Zeus Ξενίος, is often associated with extending mercy to foreigners and those seeking protection. It implies that the Samaritans themselves are in the category of the Jewish apostates and are those who will gladly accept the same kind of people. However, it is not certain whether the Samaritans would have seen themselves as 'Shechemites' or identified with such a designation.

In light of other Jewish texts - both biblical and non-biblical texts – the implication of the term 'Shechemites' can be drawn. In Genesis 34, the Shechemites were guilty of the rape of Jacob's daughter Dinah and were rejected in spite of their circumcision. This story is taken up in many Jewish texts and elaborated. For example, in the Epic of Theodotus, violence against Shechem is emphasised just as in the story of Genesis 34 (cf. Frag.7-8).[36] It

---

35.   *AJ*, XI, 342, 344, 346; XII, 10.

36.   The authorship and purpose of Theodotus' poem are disputed as to whether the writer was a Jew or a Samaritan and whether its purpose was anti-Samaritan or not. See discussion in M. Daise, 'Samaritans, Seleucids, and the Epic of Theodotus', *JSP* 17 (1998), pp. 25–51; J.J. Collins, 'The Epic of Theodotus and the Hellenism of the Hasmoneans', *HTR* 73 (1980), pp. 91–104; R. Pummer and M. Roussel, 'A Note on Theodotus and Homer', *JSJ* 13 (1-2, 1982), pp. 177–82; Pummer, 'Genesis 34 in Jewish writings of the Hellenistic and Roman Periods', *HTR* 75 (2, 1982), pp. 177–88.

highlights the 'godlessness' of Shechemites, their moral and social perversion and they are condemned for their inhospitality to those who visited them (7:2-5). In the *Testament of Levi*, Shechem is called a city of 'imbeciles' (7:3), and the destruction of the Shechemites is said to have been God's will (5:3-4; 6:8).[37] In *Jubilees*, Levi is praised for his zeal in showing vengeance on Shechemites (30:18). The book of Judith speaks of the Shechemites as 'strangers' (ἀλλογενεῖς, 9:2). Unlike Theodotus and *Testament of Levi*, both *Jubilees* and Judith do not accuse the Shechemites of further wickedness beyond the rape of Dinah, but they both classify them as Gentiles (*Jub.* 30:12-13; Jud. 5:16). According to Philo, who also makes allusion to Genesis 34, Shechem is a place of folly and insincerity and the people are 'fools' (*De mig.*224; *De mut.*193-195, 200). The circumcision of the Shechemites is ignored or denied in the texts of Philo. In Pseudo-Philo's *Liber Antiquitatum biblicarum*, vengeance on Shechem is again mentioned (8:7), but there is no reference to circumcision. None of these sources except *Testament of Levi* (6:6) mentions that the Shechemites were circumcised before the destruction.[38] Whether the treatment of the Shechemites in these various Jewish texts was primarily an anti-Samaritan polemic or not, it never portrays the identity and ethics of these people as legitimate. According to Judges (8-10), the Shechemites worshipped false gods and, therefore, are linked with idolatry and apostasy. If Josephus had in mind the biblical and other Jewish usage of the term 'Shechem' and 'Shechemites', then it may reflect his intention to show the Samaritans' closer relationship, not with the true community of Jews, but with the Jewish apostates and that their action is folly, inappropriate and illegitimate. Thus the term, 'Shechemites' seems derogatory and may reflect the hostility of Josephus and other sources towards the Samaritans.

In view of the above portrait of Shechem and Shechemites both in the Old Testament, and in Josephus and other Jewish texts, we must see how Luke portrays Shechem and, by implication, its inhabitants. (1) The reference in the Epic of Theodotus (7:2-5) to the condemnation of the Shechemites because of their inhospitable nature resembles the story in Lk. 9:51-56 of the Samaritans' refusal to welcome Jesus' messengers and the condemnation upon the Samaritans by James and John. For Luke, Jesus subverts the condemnation and no charge is made against the Samaritans. (2) In contrast to the foolish, inappropriate and illegitimate action of the Shechemites/Samaritans as portrayed in the Jewish texts, Luke has the Samaritan traveller (Lk. 10:30-37) and the Samaritan leper (17:11-19) acting

---

37. For a discussion of relevant texts in the *Testament of Levi*, see T. Baarda, 'The Shechem Episode in the Testament of Levi: A Comparison with other Traditions', in J.N. Bremmer and F.G. Martinez (eds), *Sacred History and Sacred Texts in Early Judaism. A Symposium in Honour of A.S. van der Woude* (Kampen: Kok Pharos Publishing House, 1992), pp. 11–73.

38. On this issue, see Collins, 'Epic of Theodotus', p. 98; Pummer, 'Genesis 34', pp. 178–85.

appropriately and legitimately, unlike their Jewish counterparts in the story. (3) In Acts 7 we have allusions and explicit reference to Shechem which, according to the Samaritans, is the divinely appointed place of worship. In Acts 7:15-16, Shechem is the place where the patriarchs are said to be buried in a tomb that Abraham had bought from the Hamorites.[39] If Luke is depending on a Samaritan tradition for this account of associating the tomb of the patriarchs with Shechem as many have suggested,[40] then his intention to have such a portrait may have to do with his understanding of the Samaritans and the city of Shechem. It may be that he is highlighting the importance of Shechem by alluding to it as the divinely appointed place of worship or linking it with the patriarchs' resting place. It may also be, as Spencer suggests, that for Luke, Shechem represents a symbolic foreign territory where 'even in death Israel's fathers found a home only among the alien Shechemites'.[41] Given their allegiance to Gerizim and Shechem, it is likely that Luke or his traditions would have associated the Samaritans with the Shechemites and thus, in contrast to the popular polemical and derogatory Jewish opinion, Luke's purpose seems to be apologetic and authenticating toward the Samaritans.

It is important to note the combination of designations, 'Sidonians', 'Shechemites' and 'Jewish apostates' in Josephus (*AJ*, XI, 340-341). What is common about the first two terms, according to biblical tradition, is their paganism and idol worship (1 Kgs 11:5; 16:30-32; 2 Kgs 23:13; Jud. 8-10).

---

39.   But this account varies in detail from other traditions found in the Old Testament on the burials of the patriarchs. According to Gen. 50:13, Jacob's tomb is in the cave of Machpelah in Hebron that Abraham bought from Ephron the Hittite. Gen. 33:19 reports that Jacob bought the piece of land in Shechem from the Hamorites and it is there, according to Josh. 24:32, that Joseph's bones were brought from Egypt and buried.

40.   There has been a growing conviction among scholars of a Samaritan source lying behind the narrative of Stephen's speech in Acts 7. This is because the variations of biblical quotations or allusions in Acts 7 seem to resemble the Samaritan Pentateuch but do not agree with either the Massoretic Text or the LXX, thereby reflecting in the speech Samaritan traditions and stylistic peculiarities. Apart from the textual variants, the speech also reflects a Samaritan view of *Heilgeschichte*. See E.H. Plumptre, 'The Samaritan Elements in the Gospels and Acts', *The Expositor*, first series, VII (1878), pp. 22–40; M. Wilcox, *The Semitisms of Acts* (Oxford: Clarendon Press, 1965), pp. 27–33; A. Spiro, 'Stephen's Samaritan Background', Appendix V, *The Acts of the Apostles* (AB 31; ed. J. Munck, rev. W.F. Albright and C.S. Mann; New York, 1967), pp. 285–6; Bowman, *Samaritan Problem*, pp. 57–8; R. Scroggs, 'The Earliest Hellenistic Christianity', in J. Neusner (ed.), *Religions in Antiquity* (Leiden: Brill, 1968), pp. 176–206; Gaston, *No Stone on Another; Studies in the Significance of the Fall of Jerusalem in the Synoptic Gospels* (NovTSup XXIII; Leiden: Brill, 1970), pp. 154–61; M.H. Scharlemann, *Stephen: A Singular Saint* (AnBib XXXIV; Rome: Pontifical Institute, 1968); C.H.H. Scobie, 'The Origins and Development of Samaritan Christianity', *NTS* 19 (1972–73), pp. 390–414; *idem*, 'The Use of Source Material in the Speeches of Acts III and VII', *NTS* 25 (1978–79), pp. 399–421; Purvis, 'Fourth Gospel', pp. 161–98; A.M. Johnson, 'Philip the Evangelist and the Gospel of John', *AbrN* 16 (1975–76), pp. 49–72.

41.   Spencer, *Portrait*, p. 81.

This agrees with the other term, 'Jewish apostates', which implies antinomianism and perhaps, the illegitimacy of the foreign stock. In this light, the use of the term 'Cuthaeans' also makes sense carrying with it a connotation of ethnic-religious illegitimacy.

Set in this context of the anti-Samaritan portrait, especially that of the term 'Shechemites' as idolaters, apostates, and foreign stock, one can make better sense of Luke's reference to Shechem in Acts 7 and his description of Philip's flight to the Samaritans, who are likely to be identified with the Shechemites. Philip flees to Samaria after being expelled from Jerusalem following the persecution after Stephen's death (Acts 8:1, 5). To the alleged illegitimate people of Samaria, the gospel comes with power and they are brought into the Kingdom as they accept Christ and his messengers, in contrast to the Jerusalemite Jews who opposed both the message and the messengers.

3.3.4. *'Foolish people in Shechem' and 'those on Gerizim'*

In the Apocryphal references, the Samaritans are not designated by any distinctive names, but as 'the foolish people that dwell in Shechem' (Sir. 50:26) or as 'the people that dwell in Gerizim' (2 Macc. 6:2). The text in Sir. 50:26 reads: 'Two nations (ἔθνεσιν) my soul detests, and the third is not even a people (ἔθνος): those who live in Seir (οἱ καθήμενοι ἐν ὄρει Σαμαρείας), and the Philistines, and the foolish people that live in Shechem (ὁ λαὸς ὁ μωρὸς ὁ κατοικῶν ἐν Σικιμοις)'.

Purvis considers this text in Sirach as 'a welcome addition to the rather scant collection of early references to Jewish-Samaritan antipathies'.[42] Whether there is a particular incident behind this description in Sirach of the Samaritans as 'the foolish people' or not, it, nevertheless, reflects the animosity and derogatory intention of the Jewish sources against the Samaritans at the beginning of the second century BCE.[43] That the description of the people of Shechem as 'foolish' reflects the overarching emphasis on the folly of the Shechemites as a common Jewish taunt is evident from other Jewish texts mentioned above. It is interesting to note that the above texts of Sir. 50:26 and 2 Macc. 6:2 use only descriptions, instead of proper designations for the people in question. These people are described in relation to their geographical locations. This way of describing the Gerizim- and Shechem-bound people may further illumine why the Jewish lawyer in the Parable of the Good Samaritan responded to Jesus, saying, 'the one who had mercy on him' (Lk. 10:37), rather than using the term 'Samaritan'.

A further motivation for Josephus' association of various terms with the Samaritans may be deduced. First, he claims that the Samaritan temple on Mount Gerizim was built and the new city of Shechem was established only

---

42. Purvis, *Samaritan Pentateuch*, p. 120.

43. Different reasons have been suggested for Sirach's animosity towards the Samaritans. For a discussion on the context, see Purvis, *Samaritan Pentateuch*, pp. 122–9.

during the time of Alexander the Great. Secondly, because it was an offensive and rival temple to Jerusalem, the Jewish sources began to designate the Samaritan religious community in derogatory terms. It is therefore probable that the Samaritans as a distinctive religious sect would have been identified from the end of the fourth century BCE with the erection of their rival temple on Mount Gerizim. And, it is reasonable to say that the various descriptions in Josephus and other Jewish sources – 'Cuthaeans', 'Shechemites', 'Sidonians', 'those on Gerizim' and the 'foolish people that dwell in Shechem' – seem to have more than a geographical significance. It is an attempt to show symbolically that the Samaritans were not true Israelites but syncretists and of pagan origin and thus the association is derogatory. The interpretation of 2 Kings 17 as referring to Samaritans, which became dominant in Jewish sources, would have intended to insist on the inadequacy and illegitimacy of the Samaritan religion.

3.4. *Issues on the Legitimacy of the Temple on Mount Gerizim*

Since the Samaritans can primarily be characterized by their unique devotion to Mount Gerizim and by their hostility towards the Jerusalem Temple, some issues pertaining to the rivalry that existed between the Samaritans and Jews on the legitimate place of worship need mentioning. As noted earlier, it is ambiguous whether it was the Samaritans who opposed the building of the Jerusalem Temple during the reign of the Persian king.[44] But there are references both in Josephus (*AJ*, XI, 340-42) and Talmudic tradition that tell about a conflict between Alexander the Great (332-323 BCE) and the Samaritans, which has indirect bearing on the temple issue. The Babylonian Talmud tells the story of Alexander giving permission to the Jews to deal with the Samaritans who, according to the Jews, plotted against them and their Temple:

> Thereupon Alexander said, 'They are herewith given into your hands'. The Jews then pierced the heels of the Cuthim and tied them to the tails of their horses and dragged them over thorns and briers until they came to Mount Gerizim. And when they came to Mount Gerizim, they ploughed it under and sowed it with vetch, just as the Cuthim had intended to do to our temple. And the day on which they did this was made a festival.[45]

Additional evidence comes from Curtius Rufus and Eusebius, both of whom claim that the Samaritans seized Andromachus, the new Macedonian governor of Samaria, and burnt him alive while Alexander was in Egypt.[46]

---

44.   *AJ*, XI, 19-20; cf. Ezra 4:11-16.
45.   *b.Yoma* 69a.
46.   Curtius Rufus, *History of Alexander the Great* IV.8-10; see also Eusebius, *Chron.* (ed. by Schoene), II, 114: 'Alexander besieged Tyre and conquered Judaea, and being received with honour, he sacrificed to God and honoured the high priest, and as governor of the district he

This was a probably violent reaction to the administrative change in the governorship of Samaria, for since the beginning of the Persian period, Samaria had only had Samaritan governors from the Sanballat family.[47] Because of this revolt, on his return from Egypt, Alexander razed the city of Samaria, executed the murderers, and settled 6000 Macedonian veterans in the city. This revolt appears to have been the occasion of the flight of some Samaritans into the cave at Wadi Daliyeh.[48] After this event, a Macedonian colony at Samaria was established, either by Alexander himself[49] or by the regent Perdiccas after Alexander's death.[50] Thus, Samaria was made into a Hellenistic city by force.

It is possible but not certain that the Jews helped Alexander in revealing the Samaritan caves to the Macedonians or sent an auxiliary force to help Perdiccas subdue the Samaritans during the revolt.[51] But the accounts of Josephus, Eusebius, and the Talmud, despite their contradictions and anachronism in some details,[52] may reflect Alexander's positive dealings with the Jews after the Samaritan rebellion. According to Josephus, Alexander presented the Jews with the 'district of Samaria' in response to their favour towards him.[53] During this period, Samaria was divided into two units under the same governorship: the nation (ἔθνος) of the Samaritans and the Macedonian colony of Samaria.[54] However, the demarcation between the Macedonian Hellenistic city of Samaria and the new Samaritan centre at Shechem remains unclear.[55] It is possible that after the settlement of the

appointed Andromachus, whom the inhabitants of the city of the Samaritans killed; and on his return from Egypt Alexander punished them, and having taken the city, settled Macedonians therein'.

47. Mor, 'Persian', p. 9.

48. F.M. Cross, 'The Discovery of Samaria Papyri', *BA* 26 (1963), pp. 118–19; *idem*, 'Papyri', pp. 41–62; G.E. Wright, *Shechem: The Biography of a Biblical City* (New York: McGraw-Hill, 1965), pp. 170–81.

49. Curtius Rufus IV, 8, 9; V.A. Tcherikover, *Hellenistic Civilization and the Jews* (Philadelphia: Fortress Press, 1966), pp. 103–4; R. Marcus, 'Alexander the Great and the Jews', *Josephus* VI, Appendix C, pp. 523–4; Schürer, *History II*, p. 160.

50. Eusebeus, *Chron.* (ed. by Schoene) II, 118.

51. Marcus, 'Alexander' p. 528.

52. Marcus refers to the contradictions and anachronism which occurred in these texts in terms of personal names and involvement, 'Alexander', pp. 522–3.

53. *Against Apion*, II, 243, cf. I Macc. 11:34; 10:30, 38. See Mor, 'Persian', pp. 10–11; M. Stern, *Greek and Latin Authors on Jews and Judaism* I (Jerusalem: Israel Academy of Sciences and Humanities, 1974), p. 44.

54. *AJ*, XII, 261, 264, 287; 1 Macc. 3:10; M. Avi-Yonah, 'Historical Geography of Palestine', in Safrai and Stern (eds), *The Jewish People in the First Century* I (CRINT; Philadelphia: Fortress Press, 1974), pp. 78–116, 81. Also, see A.H.M. Jones, *The Cities of the Eastern Roman Provinces* (rev. M. Avi-Yonah, *et al.*, 2nd edition; Oxford: Clarendon Press, 1971), pp. 235–40.

55. M. Hengel, 'The Political and Social History of Palestine from Alexander to Antiochus III (333-187 BCE)', in W.D. Davis & L. Finkelstein (eds), *The Cambridge History of Judaism*, vol. II (Cambridge: Cambridge University Press, 1989), pp. 35–78, 43; Jones, *Cities*, pp. 238–9.

Macedonian colony in Samaria, the status of the remaining Samaritans was lost, for they were not given any autonomous civil and political rights as a nation (ἔθνος).[56]

Despite the veracity of the accounts, the significance of the above story, from a Jewish point of view, can be drawn here. It is interesting to note that the Talmud designates the rivals of the Jews as 'Cuthim', just as Josephus uses this term elsewhere, and associates them with Mount Gerizim. It also points to an earlier attempt of this rival group to plot against the Temple of Jerusalem signifying their antagonism towards it. The revenge of the Jews and their humiliating treatment of Mount Gerizim highlight the intensity of their hostility towards the Gerizim-bound rivals. Whether one could clearly identify this group who opposed the Jews as Samaritans or not, their hostile attitude towards Jerusalem and their devotion to Mount Gerizim make them likely candidates. The accounts in Josephus and Eusebius point to the failure and flight of the Samaritans in their attempt to rebel against Alexander and the subsequent loss of their socio-political and ethnic identity as a nation.

Now I will focus on the question of the legitimacy of the Samaritan temple on Mount Gerizim without going into the issue of the historical reliability of the account on the construction of the temple, which Josephus dates in the time of Alexander, around 332 BCE.[57] Wright and Cross have suggested that the Gerizim temple was established by the disenfranchised Samarians after the Macedonian colonization of the city of Samaria by Alexander.[58] But

56.   A. Kasher, *Jews and Hellenistic Cities in Eretz-Israel: Relations of the Jews in Eretz-Israel with the Hellenistic Cities during the Second Temple Period (332 BCE-70 CE)* (TSAJ 21; Tübingen: Mohr, 1990), p. 20; Hengel, 'Political and Social History', p. 43, suggests that the remainder of Samaria did not receive the status of an independent nation (ἔθνος). See also, Strabo XVI.2.2 (C 749); *AJ*, XI, 344; XII, 260; Sir. 50:25-26.

57.   *AJ*, XI, 302-325. Josephus' account has been criticised as unreliable and inauthentic because of several reasons. One reason is that the account has been considered as a variant of the episode mentioned in Neh. 13:28, which occurred nearly a century before Alexander. For discussions on the unreliability of Josephus' account, see Whaley, 'Josephus' *Antiquities* 11.297-347', p. 10; J.G. Vink, 'The Date and Origin of the Priestly Code in the Old Testament', *The Priestly Code and Seven Other Studies* (Leiden: Brill, 1969), pp. 52–3; Rowley, 'Sanballat and the Samaritan Temple', *BJRL* 38 (1955–56), pp. 170–2; Grabbe, 'Josephus', pp. 231–46, 236–7); H.G.M. Williamson, 'The Historical Value of Josephus' Jewish *Antiquities* XI, 297-301', *JTS* 28 (1977), pp. 49–66; Dexinger, 'Limits', p. 92; Anderson, 'Samaritans', *ABD* V, p. 942. However, some scholars maintain the legitimacy of Josephus' account. For example, see Cross, 'Papyri', pp. 41–62; *idem*, 'Aspects', pp. 201–5. For reference to the archaeological evidence for the existence of the temple on Mount Gerizim, see Y. Magen, 'Mount Gerizim and the Samaritans', in F. Manns and E. Alliata (eds), *Early Christianity in Context: Monuments and Documents* (SBF 38; Jerusalem: Franciscan Printing Press, 1993), pp. 91–148; E. Stern and Y. Magen, 'Archaeological Evidence for the First Stage of the Samaritan Temple on Mount Gerizim', *IEJ* 52 (1, 2002), pp. 49–57.

58.   Cross, 'The Papyri and their Historical Implications' (*AASOR* 41; Cambridge, 1974), p. 20.

Kippenberg opposes this idea and argues that after the Assyrian conquest, Samaria was populated by non-Israelite pagans, so it is unlikely that they would begin the Gerizim cult dedicated to Yahweh.[59] Based on the Sanballat-Manasseh story of Josephus, he argues that the Gerizim cult was established not by the political community of Samaria, but by the disenfranchised priests who joined Manasseh from the Jerusalemite community.

Kippenberg's argument raises problems. (a) There is no reason to assume that there were no Yahweh worshippers anywhere in Samaria because Yahweh was worshipped there, even after the Assyrian conquest and throughout the Persian period. (b) The few names ending with the theophoric ending 'iahu' found in the Wadi Daliyeh Papyri would undoubtedly suggest the presence of a Yahwistic religious community in the city of Samaria. (c) It is not certain that all the refugees or the religious community who fled from Samaria following their revolt against Alexander died in the cave of Wadi Daliyeh; it is likely that some of them escaped and survived the flight.[60] (d) Again, if Rowley is right in claiming that Sanballat and his household were Yahwists,[61] it is probable that there were Yahweh worshippers in the political community of Samaria.

Therefore, it is suggested that the Gerizim cult was formed probably in the late fourth century BCE by members of the political community of Samaria, plausibly in association with the disenfranchised priests from Jerusalem who were involved in such marriages as that of Manasseh. In this respect one must assume that the religious community of Samaritans were part of the political group before the Macedonian colonization of the city of Samaria.[62] Their revolt against Alexander the Great led them to flee from the city of Samaria and to settle in the ancient city of Shechem. G.E. Wright suggests that after the Macedonian colonization of Samaria, the Samaritans needed a new centre and thus established one on the old site of Shechem at the foot of Mount Gerizim.[63] They rebuilt the city of Shechem and built their own temple or tabernacle[64] on Mount Gerizim, probably early in the Hellenistic period, *ca.*332 BCE during the time of Alexander. The time of their residence at Shechem, says Purvis, 'proved to be one of the most creative periods in the

59.   H.G. Kippenberg, *Garizim und Synagoge: Traditionsgeschichtliche Untersuchungen zur samaritanischen Religion der aramaeischen Periode* (Berlin: Walter de Gruyter, 1971), p. 47.

60.   Crown, 'Samaritan Diaspora', p. 199, n.24.

61.   H.H. Rowley, 'The Samaritan Schism in Legend and History', *Israel's Prophetic Heritage* (New York: Harper and Row, 1962), p. 208.

62.   Here it is to be mentioned that there are references in Josephus which consider the Samaritans as a nation (ἔθνος) with political aspirations. See *AJ*, IX, 279, 288; X, 184; XVII, 20; XVIII, 85. Feldman notices that Josephus never uses the word ἔθνος to refer to one of the sects of Judaism – Pharisees, Sadducees, Essenes or Fourth Philosophy, *idem*, 'Josephus' Attitude', p. 25.

63.   Wright, *Shechem*, pp. 170–84; also Bickerman, *From Ezra*, pp. 43–4.

64.   See the discussion on the question of the existence of the Samaritan temple given above.

history of the Samaritan people, indeed, the formative period in the history of that community as a religious sect'.[65] In relation to the temple, what is relevant here is the account of the illegitimate priesthood of Manasseh and other disenfranchised priests.

Another report in Josephus says that during the time of Antiochus IV Epiphanes (175-164 BCE), the Samaritans wanted to distinguish themselves from the Jews, to which end they appealed to Antiochus, repudiating their link with Judaism, and requested him to call their temple Zeus Hellenios (*AJ*, XII, 257-264; cf. 2 Macc. 6:2-3). Also, they claimed themselves that they were 'Sidonians in Shechem'. They tried to hide the fact that 'the temple on Gerizim was that of the Most Great God' (τοῦ μεγίστου θεοῦ, *AJ*, XII, 257). Granting their request, Antiochus paganized the temple on Mount Gerizim and proclaimed it to be that of Zeus Hellenios (*AJ*, XII, 263). The point here is the tendency of Josephus to portray the Samaritans' identity with 'Sidonians', their choice to hide the name of their temple, their willingness to live according to the Greek customs and so to accept paganization and their claim to be of a different race from the Jews. All of these relate to the question of the legitimacy of their ethnic identity and of the temple of Mount Gerizim.

The legitimacy question is further evident in the account of Josephus, according to which the Samaritans, during the time of Ptolemy Philometor, disputed with the Alexandrian Jews asserting that their temple on Gerizim was built in accordance with the laws of Moses, but not that of Jerusalem. The text says:

> Now there arose a quarrel between the Jews in Alexandria and the Samaritans who worshipped at the temple on Mount Gerizim, which had been built in the time of Alexander, and they disputed about their respective temples in the presence of Ptolemy himself, the Jews asserting that it was the temple at Jerusalem which had been built in accordance with the laws of Moses, and the Samaritans that it was the temple on Gerizim (*AJ*, XIII, 74).

The above text suggests that there existed rivalry between the temple on Mount Gerizim and that of Jerusalem and that the Samaritans and Jews tried to establish the legitimacy of their respective temple on scriptural grounds.

3.5. The Destruction of the Gerizim Temple and the Identity of the Samaritans

Now I will turn to a brief sketch of the destruction of the Gerizim temple by John Hyrcanus and the subsequent socio-religious life of the Samaritans up

---

65. Purvis, 'Samaritans', p. 596.

to the New Testament period. When Josephus describes the activities of John Hyrcanus (135/4-104 BCE), he mentions both in the *Jewish War* and in the *Antiquities* that Hyrcanus captured 'Shechem and Gerizim and the Cuthaean nation, which lives near the temple built after the model of the sanctuary at Jerusalem'.[66] When Hyrcanus began to Judaize the expanded territories, he adopted the policy of cruelty towards the Hellenistic cities and sympathy towards the other groups in Palestine. Circumcision was the condition for Judaization. While the Idumeans, who had been idol worshippers, were circumcised and accepted into Judaism, the Samaritans, who were already circumcised, were rejected.[67] In this event, he treated the Samaritans just as he did the Hellenistic cities and burned their temple on Mount Gerizim in 128 BC and destroyed the city of Shechem in 107 BC.[68] Why did Hyrcanus destroy the temple and the city of the Samaritans? As mentioned earlier, some of the intertestamental literature belonging to this period that deals with the story of the rape of Dinah by Shechem brings the charge that the Shechemites were not circumcised.[69] The intention of the sources seems to be to associate the Samaritans with Shechemites and so to deny that they were circumcised. This portrait in the sources could legitimize the hostile behaviour of Hyrcanus towards the Samaritans. Also, since the temple on Gerizim stands as a rival to that in Jerusalem, Hyrcanus' action probably reflects the animosity of the Jews towards the Samaritans. According to Josephus, Hyrcanus hated the city of Samaria because of the injuries which 'they had done to the people of Marisa, who were colonists and allies of the Jews'.[70] Thus, it may be that there is a combination of religious motive and political retaliation in the punitive measures of Hyrcanus against the Samaritans.

Josephus says that just before its destruction, Samaria was 'a very strongly fortified city' (πόλιν ὀχυρωτάτην, *AJ*, XIII, 275). After Hyrcanus captured the city of Samaria, says Josephus, 'he effaced it entirely and left it to be swept away by the mountain-torrents, for he dug beneath it until it fell into the beds of the torrents, and so removed all signs of its ever having been a city' (*AJ*, XIII, 281; cf. *BJ*, I, 54-69). His description of Hyrcanus' destruction of the district and city of Samaria may refer, as Kasher suggests, both to the citizens of the city of Samaria and to the Samaritans residing in its vicinity.[71] It would be reasonable to think that the destruction of Shechem forced the Samaritans to leave their city for the immediate vicinity.[72] In brief, Hasmonean rule was a threat to the identity of the Samaritans as they lost their temple, the city

---

66. *AJ*, XIII, 255-256; cf. *BJ*, I, 63.
67. Mor, 'Persian', p. 16.
68. *AJ*, XIII, 255-256; *BJ*, I, 62-63.
69. *Test. Levi* 6-7; *Jubilees*.30:2-6; *Judith* 9:2-4; Theodotus 7-8.
70. *AJ*, XIII, 275; *BJ*, I, 65.
71. Kasher, *Jews*, p. 125. See *AJ*, XIII, 273-274.
72. See Crown, 'Samaritan Diaspora', p. 200; also Wright, *Shechem*, pp. 182–3.

of Shechem and their status as an independent city. This is often regarded as
the moment of separation between the Samaritans and the Jews and it also
expresses the deepest Jewish bitterness towards the Samaritans.[73] It was the
time for the Samaritans to legitimize their identity as distinct from Judaism.

3.6. Jewish – Samaritan Relationship in the New Testament Period

Now I will turn to the nature of the relationship that existed between the Jews
and the Samaritans during the first century CE. Josephus describes an event
during the governorship of Coponius (6-9 CE) when some Samaritans came
secretly into Jerusalem and scattered human bones in the porticoes and
throughout the Temple on the eve of Passover and defiled it. 'As a result, the
priests, although they had previously observed no such custom, excluded
everyone from the temple, in addition to taking other measures for the
greater protection of the temple' (*AJ*, XVIII, 29-30). This incident shows the
resentment on the part of the Samaritans over their lost temple, whereas the
Jews were able to celebrate the Passover in their Temple at Jerusalem.[74] This
act of sacrilege and desecration seems to imply their intention to proclaim
the Jerusalem Temple, the priesthood and the Jews as ritually unclean and
their Passover feast illegitimate. During the reign of Herod, who had married
a Samaritan woman, they seem to have had access to the inner court of the
Temple, but they must have lost this right after his death.[75] In any case, it
suggests the animosity of the Samaritans towards the Jerusalem Temple.

Josephus reports another incident that happened during the governorship
of Cumanus in Judea (48-52 CE) in which Samaritans killed one or more
Galilean Jews who were passing through their territory on pilgrimage to
Jerusalem.

> It was the custom of the Galilaeans at the time of a festival to pass through the Samaritan
> territory on their way to the Holy City. On one occasion, while they were passing through,
> certain of the inhabitants of a village called Ginae ... joined battle with the Galilaeans and
> slew a great number of them (*AJ*, XX, 118).

In revenge for the Samaritans' action, the Jews sacked and burned some
Samaritan villages. When the Samaritans appealed to Quadratus, the Syrian
governor, he punished the Jewish rebels and also found Cumanus guilty.[76]

---

73.   Schur, *History*, p. 42.
74.   Crown, 'Redating', p. 40.
75.   Jeremias, *Jerusalem*, p. 353. J.W. Lightley, *Jewish Sects and Parties in the Time of Jesus*
(London: The Epworth Press, 1925), p. 233 believes that the Samaritans were at this time not
prohibited from entering the Jewish Temple.
76.   *Annals*, XII, 54, 4.

In this incident, the Jews suffered a lot worse than did the Samaritans. Coggins assumes that the references to the Samaritans as the occasion of this episode are merely incidental, since the emphasis is the fair dealing of Roman justice.[77] Three points may briefly be made. First, the hostility of the Samaritans towards the Jews and their festivals led to provocative actions, sometimes even bloody encounters. Second, Cumanus, after being bribed by the Samaritans, armed them against the Jews, which would seem to reflect his favouritism towards the Samaritans. Third, Quadratus' action would indicate that the Roman authorities lost confidence in the ability of the Jewish ruling class to fulfil its function.[78]

Josephus also refers to a Samaritan revolt against the Romans on Mount Gerizim during the Jewish War (*BJ*, III, 307-315), which resulted in the deaths of 11,600 Samaritans. In this account, the Samaritans are neither criticized in relation to their socio-religious identities nor is an attempt made to distinguish them from the Jews, except for the mention that they took 'pride in their own weakness'.[79]

In the Mishnah, there is evidence for Jewish-Samaritan tensions prior to 70 CE. Tractate *Rosh Hashanah* i.3 and ii.2 explains why a new system was introduced to the Diaspora Jews to indicate the day of the beginning of the month so that they would know the days of their various festivals. Instead of the earlier practice of the lighting of beacons, the new system of sending out messengers to the Jewish Diaspora was introduced. According to the above references, certain malpractices of the Samaritans caused this change and it happened before the destruction of the Temple. Though the nature of the malpractice was not specified in the tractate, many scholars assume that the Samaritans lit beacons at the wrong times.[80] It nevertheless indicates their intention to hinder the religious observance of the Jews. The Samaritan Chronicles contains a story that indicates the hostility of the Samaritans to the Jerusalem Temple. It says that the Samaritans substituted a pair of rats for a pair of pigeons in a cage being carried by a Jew to Jerusalem so that it would pollute the Temple and the sacrifice.[81]

In brief, the Jewish – Samaritan relationship in the New Testament period was one of constant tension, hostility and religious animosity. For the

---

77.   Coggins, 'Samaritans in Josephus', p. 268.

78.   M. Goodman, *The Ruling Class of Judea* (Cambridge: Cambridge University Press, 1987), p. 49.

79.   Coggins, 'Samaritans in Josephus', p. 269.

80.   Montgomery, *Samaritans*, pp. 193–4; Gaster, *Samaritans*, pp. 36–7. For a brief discussion on this issue, see T.C.G. Thornton, 'The Samaritan Calendar: A Source of Friction in New Testament Times', *JTS* new Series 42 (October 1991), pp. 577–80.

81.   Paul Stenhouse (trans.), *The Kitab Al-Tarikh of Abu'l Fath* (Sydney: Mandelbaum Trust, 1985), ch. 34, lines 648–658, pp. 155–6.

Samaritans, the Temple of Jerusalem was an illegitimate Temple, and the hostility towards Jerusalem is further confirmed by their resistance to allowing the messengers of Jesus to pass through their territory as reported in Luke 9:51-56.

3.7. Samaritanism: Judaism or Another Religion?

Now we have to ask whether Samaritanism was a variety of Judaism or another religion in the first century CE. To evaluate the evidence, we must take into account the claim Jewish sources try to make that the Samaritans were open to and influenced by foreign ideas, especially Greek culture, from the time of Alexander the Great. Firstly, as mentioned earlier, if the account of Josephus is reliable, then the appeal of some of the Samaritans to Antiochus IV Epiphanes for distinguishing themselves from the Jews and the acceptance of a temple of zeus Xenios on Mount Gerizim indicate that they were not resistant to foreign ideas. And, the building of Hadrian's temple confirms their willingness to adopt Romanization as well as Hellenization. Secondly, the fragments from Pseudo-Eupolemus, the second century BCE anonymous Samaritan historian, and from Theodotus may well indicate the existence of pagan influence on Samaritanism. C.R. Holladay comments on the former that because this fragment 'reflects an outlook which both knows and values pagan mythological traditions, it may be necessary to modify the common view of Samaritanism as a sect immune to outside influence'.[82] Thirdly, the two Samaritan inscriptions found on the Greek island of Delos suggest the presence of a Greek-speaking community and a clear sign of Hellenization as early as the second century BCE.[83] Also Greek inscriptions found in the Samaritan synagogues in Thessalonica, dated possibly fifth century CE, and from Samaria dating fourth to sixth century, confirm the Greek influence on the Samaritans.[84] Fourthly, possible inferences for pagan influence on the Samaritans can be drawn from the Rabbinic writings. For instance, Rabbi Simeon ben Gamaliel said that the Samaritans were more meticulous than Jews in observing those mitzvot which they regarded as binding; but Rabbi Simeon ben Laqish said: 'That was all very well as long as they lived in their own villages; but nowadays they have not a shred of a mitzvah left'.[85] The

---

82.   C.R. Holladay, *Fragments from Hellenistic Jewish Authors* I (Chico, CA: Scholars Press, 1983), pp. 157–88, 160.

83.   P.W. van der Horst, 'Samaritans and Hellenism', in *Hellenism - Judaism - Christianity: Essays on their Interaction* (Kampen: Kok Pharos Publishing House, 1994), pp. 48–58: says that the inscriptions speak about 'the Israelites on Delos who pay their first offering to the sanctuary of Argarizim'. It also shows that they distinguished themselves from the 'Jews' as early as the second century BCE (p. 56).

84.   Van der Horst, 'Samaritans and Hellenism', pp. 56–7.

85.   *y. Pesahim* 27b; cf. *Tos. Pesahim* 1:15.

words of Rabbi Simeon ben Laqish may reflect the Samaritans' less strict observance of religion when they moved outside Samaria. This is further reflected in the comments of Rabbi Abbahu on their economic life – 'they said: your forefathers used to be satisfied with our products. Why do you refuse what we offer? He said: your forefathers were not spoiled in their behaviour, but you have spoiled yours'.[86] It is plausibly an indication of pagan influence on economic life. A second century aggadah says: 'Once Rabbi Simeon ben Eleazar came to a city in the south (*darom*). He went into a synagogue and there he found a teacher, of whom he asked: where can I find wine for sale? The other answered: Rabbi, this has become a Samaritan town, and they do not make their wine in a state of purity as my forefathers used to do'.[87] The words of Rabbi Abbahu and others seem to imply that the Samaritans were influenced by Greek ideologies and were not resistant to pagan religious ideas. These statements in the Rabbinic literature provide sufficient evidence for the Samaritan migration outside Samaria.

Now, we will return to the question: Are the Samaritans Jews or members of another religion? Both Samaritan and non-Samaritan sources try to associate Samaritans with northern Israel, but entirely on different lines. According to the tradition of the Samaritans, they are the true Israelites who are the 'keepers' (שמרים) of the Law. They claim that they are the descendants of Joseph and the only surviving non-Judaean branch of the Israelite nation who remained true to the ancient faith as set forth in the Torah. This link between them and northern Israel within the Samaritan tradition derives from the Samaritan Chronicle II. There are references in Josephus which appear to suggest that the Samaritans were Jews. For instance, Josephus includes the Samaritans along with Galileans and Pereans among the Ἰουδαῖοι (*AJ*, XIII) though he treats them inconsistently in the rest of the *Antiquities*. He writes that when the Samaritans see the Jews prospering they call themselves their kinsmen (συγγενεῖς, *AJ*, IX, 291). His account of the Samaritans' appeal made during the Antiochean persecutions claims that their practices were the same as those of the Jews.[88] In the same account, if Josephus really meant what he says about the Samaritan temple as the 'Temple of the God Most High', it shows Jewish recognition that the Samaritans worshipped the same God as that of Jewish faith.

Another point to note is the Samaritans' relationship with the Qumran community. Bowman and Dexinger among others have shown that there

---

86. *y. Abodah Zarah* 44d.
87. *Midrash Rabbah. Deut.* II:33.
88. *AJ*, XII, 256-260 – the Samaritans defend their right to observe customs which they shared with the Jews. Also *AJ*, IX, 290 – Josephus claims that to this day the Samaritans maintain Jewish practices.

exists a close relationship between the Samaritans and the Qumran community in ritual and doctrinal matters.[89] Based on the textual characteristic of the fragments from Qumran cave 4, Dexinger suggests that the structure of the Samaritan Pentateuch (SP), which is represented at Qumran textually and graphically, would identify the Samaritans as a Jewish group. It is also thought that the actual Samaritan name of the Feast of the Seventh Month, corresponding to the Jewish Rosh-Hashanah, is closer to the biblical terminology and its liturgy represents the status of the pre-Maccabean Jewish liturgy.[90] Common Israelite tradition may well explain this relationship between the Samaritans and the Qumran community.

However, as we have seen earlier, Josephus more frequently portrays the Samaritans as non-Jews who were brought from Persia to Samaria by the Assyrians and he designates them as Cuthaeans, Sidonians and Shechemites (*AJ*, XI, 290, 346-347). He links them geographically with the Northern kingdom by associating them with new immigrant groups mentioned in 2 Kgs 17:24-41 but clearly distinguishes them ethnically as non-Israelites. He also seems to link them to the adversaries headed by Sanballat, who opposed the rebuilding of the Temple in Jerusalem in Ezra 4:1-5:7. His use of the labels Cuthaeans, Sidonians and Shechemites seems designed to show that they were not true Israelites, but syncretists, and thus, the association is derogatory. He also says that the Samaritan community consisted of a breakaway group of Jerusalem priests who originated in the Persian period. This last reported origin contradicts his earlier claims linking the Samaritans to foreign groups moved into Samaria by the Assyrians. In either case, however, his claims refute the common view that the Samaritans represent a continuum of older northern tradition.

In other instances, Josephus portrays the Samaritans as a distinctive race from that of the Jews. For instance, the Samaritans themselves claim, when they see that the Jews are in trouble, that they have nothing in common with the Jews and declare that they are aliens of another race (ἀλλοεθνεῖς). Josephus says,

> ...they alter their attitude according to circumstance and, when they see the Jews prospering, call them their kinsmen, on the ground that they are descended from Joseph and are related to them through their origin from him, but, when they see the Jews in trouble, they say

89. Bowman, *Samaritan Problem*, pp. 91–118; *idem*, 'Contact Between Samaritan Sects and Qumran', *VT* 7 (1957), pp. 184–9; F. Dexinger, 'Samaritan Origin and the Qumran Texts', in Crown & Davey (eds), *New Samaritan Studies*, pp. 169–84; J.M. Ford, 'Can We Exclude Samaritan Influence From Qumran?', *RevQ* 6 (1, 1967), pp. 109–29; A.D. Crown, 'Qumran, Samaritan *Halakha* and Theology and Pre-Tannaitic Judaism', in M. Lubetski, *et al.* (eds), *Boundaries of the Ancient Near Eastern World*, A Tribute to Cyrus H. Gordon (JSOTSup.273; Sheffield: Sheffield Academic Press, 1998), pp. 420–41.

90. Dexinger, 'Samaritan and Jewish Festivals: Comparative Considerations', in Crown & Davey (eds), *New Samaritan Studies*, pp. 57–78.

that they have nothing whatever in common with them nor do these have any claim of friendship or race, and they declare themselves to be aliens of another race (*AJ*, IX, 291).

Also, Josephus explicitly states that Nikaso, the daughter of the Samaritan Sanballat, whom Manasseh had married, was a foreigner (ἀλλοφύλη, *AJ*, XI, 306). It is again evident when Josephus says that during the Antiochian persecution, the Samaritans appealed to Antiochus Epiphanes not to punish them for the charges of which the Jews were guilty, by distinguishing themselves as a distinct race (γένει) from the Jews. These expressions in Josephus could suggest the Samaritans wanted to dissociate themselves from the Jews at certain periods.

Some references in Rabbinic writings regard the Samaritans as equal to the Jews and admit that they strictly observed the commandments of the Law. For instance, R. Simon b. Gamaliel says, 'Every command the Samaritans keep they are more scrupulous in observing than Israel'.[91] Later it was said that a Samaritan is like a full Jew.[92] Samaritan slaughtering of meat was considered to be kosher.[93] There is reference to Samaritans who were accepted to teach the Pentateuch to Jewish children.[94] It is stated that when a Jewish writ of divorce bearing the signatures of Samaritan witnesses was submitted to Rabban Gamaliel, he pronounced it valid.[95] It would seem to imply the trustworthiness of the Samaritans and also their equality with the Jewish *amei ha-aretz*.[96] Many of the early Tannaim considered the Samaritans to be Jews or equivalent to Jews or in halakhic terms 'Israelites'.[97]

However, the Rabbis also called the Samaritans 'Cuthim', a derogatory term that was intended as a stigma to indicate the popular view that the Samaritans all originated from Cuthah in Assyria.[98] This view that the Samaritans were an alien religion and a foreign people (*nokhrim*) may be a reflection of their portrayals in Josephus, the Apocrypha and the Gospels. There are references in the Mishnah, probably dating from the early part of the first century CE, which include the Samaritans among the Gentiles in ritual and cultic matters. Their veneration of Mount Gerizim as a holy mountain, one of the most distinctive features of Samaritanism, caused them to be suspected of being an idolatrous cult.[99] R. Eliezer (*ca.* 90 CE) banned the eating of unleavened bread belonging to a Samaritan at Passover, 'for the Samaritans are not versed in the precepts of the commandments'.[100] He also

91.   *b. Berakoth* 47b; *b. Gittin* 10a; *b. Hullin* 4a.
92.   *m. Nedarim* 3.10; *b. Masseketh Kuthim* 61b (II.2)
93.   b. *Masseketh Kuthim* 61b (II.1).
94.   *Tos. Abodah Zarah* 3.1.
95.   *m. Gittin* 1.5.
96.   Cf. *Tos. Gittin* 1.4; *b. Gittin* 10b; *Tos. Demai* 5:24.
97.   *Tos. Terumah* 4.12, 14.
98.   *b. Hullin* 6a; *b. Yoma* 69a.
99.   *m. Hullin* 2.7; cf. *b. Masseketh Kuthim* 61b.
100. *b. Kiddushin* 76a; *b. Hullin* 4a; *Tos. Pesahim* 1.15.

forbade the eating of an animal killed by a Samaritan 'since an unexpressed intention in a Gentile (while slaughtering) is directed to idolatry'.[101] It was prohibited to accept from a non-Jew or a Samaritan the half-shekel tax, which all Jews were required to give to the Temple, or any sacrifices except those offerings only allowed to the Gentiles.[102] This implies that the Samaritans were treated as non-Jewish. A similar passage, attributed to the early second century Rabbi Akiba, does not mention the Samaritans by name.[103] R. Judah b. Eli (*ca.* 150 CE) said that a Samaritan may not circumcise a Jew, for he would direct his intention towards Mount Gerizim.[104] Rabbi Akiba said that the Samaritans embraced the Torah out of conviction (*gere emet* - true proselytes), to which Rabbi Ishmael responded: 'No, they took on the religion of Israel out of fear' (*gere 'arayot* - because of 'lions', that is, to save their skins).[105] This would indicate that they were not legitimate proselytes. It is also stated that 'the daughters of the Samaritans are menstruants from their cradle',[106] which seems to imply their ritual uncleanness (cf. Lev. 15:19-30; Jn 4:9).[107] In brief, some portions of the Mishnah and the Talmud emphasize the negative view that Samaritans are definitely not Jews.

The Mishnah and the Talmud have contradictory portraits of the Samaritans. They are treated with a certain reservation; many times as Gentiles and sometimes as Jews.[108] The post-Talmudic tractate *Masseketh Kuthim* states: 'When shall we take them back? When they renounce Mount Gerizim and confess Jerusalem and the resurrection of the dead. From that time on he who robs a Samaritan shall be as he who robs an Israelite'.[109] It implies that the Jewish hostility towards the Samaritans is mainly due to their devotion to the holiness of Mount Gerizim. The different portraits of the Samaritans may also reflect the fact that some rabbis were more tolerant than others.

It is clear that both Josephus and the Rabbinic sources provide a divergent picture of the Samaritans. Josephus does not offer us a clear identity of the Samaritans, rather he is ambivalent in his attitude toward them. At times he refers to them as a distinct national entity and at other times as Jews, resulting in ambiguity and ambivalence. In the *Antiquities*, Josephus' treatment of Samaritans appears to be antagonistic. That his attitude shifts from neutrality to hostility would probably be a reflection of the situation

---

101. *m. Hullin* 2:7.
102. *m. Shekalim* 1:5.
103. *Tos. Shekalim* 1:7.
104. *b.Abodah Zarah* 27a; *b. Masseketh Kuthim* 61b (1:9).
105. See *b. Kiddushin* 75b; Rabbi Akiba says that they are *gere tzedeq* (*y. Gittin* 43c).
106. *m. Niddah* 4:1.
107. See discussion in J.D.M. Derrett, 'The Samaritan Woman's Purity (John 4:4-52)', *EvQ* 60 (4, 1988), pp. 291–8; R.G. Maccini, 'A Reassessment of the Woman at the Well in John 4 in Light of the Samaritan Context', *JSNT* 53 (1994), pp. 35–46.
108. *m. Demai* 3.1 cf. 5.9; *b. Berakoth* 47b cf. *m. Shebiith* 8.10.
109. *b. Masseketh Kuthim* 61b (2:7).

in his own day or, as Feldman speculates, Josephus' sources for the *Antiquities* as hostile to the Samaritans.[110] As seen earlier, Josephus several times mentions that the Samaritans sometimes claimed affinity with Judaism, and sometimes rejected any kind of kinship with the community of Jerusalem. Thus, it is clear that the identity of the Samaritans is ambiguously portrayed in Josephus. The Rabbinic sources similarly reflect both affinity and increasing hostility in the Judean-Samaritan relationship. Halakhically, the Tannaim are inconsistent and ambivalent in their treatment of the Samaritans.[111] As Alon points out, the attitude of the Sages towards the Samaritans is 'probably a faithful reflection of popular feeling, and a mirror image of what the Samaritans felt about the Jews'.[112] In general, both Josephus and Rabbinic tradition have a stronger anti-Samaritan than pro-Samaritan bias. They tend to portray the Samaritans as being of pagan origin, and as a corrupt and unscrupulous community.

The ambiguity in placing the identity of the Samaritans in a socio-religious framework is further evident when scholars suggest various claims. One identifiable exception is that of Montgomery who speaks of the Samaritans as the earliest Jewish sect.[113] Purvis, on the other hand, considers Samaritanism as 'an independent activity', with 'a distinct and autonomous status', and at the same time, 'a variety of Judaism'. He refuses to speak of a 'schism'.[114] He suggests that their version of the Pentateuch that emphasized the holiness of Gerizim or Shechem 'drove the permanent wedge between the Samaritans and the Jews'.[115] He gives two main reasons for accepting Samaritanism as a variety of Judaism: Samaritanism should be understood against the religious context of Judaism, and both of the groups are carriers of Israel's sacred traditions.[116] R. Pummer regards them as a branch of Israelite religion, but he adds, 'the orthodox Jews of today do not recognise Samaritanism as a legitimate interpretation of a common religious heritage'.[117] Benyamin Tsedaka, a modern Samaritan, agrees with Pummer's first point. He insists that Samaritanism is not a separate religion evolved out

---

110. Feldman and Hata (eds), *Josephus*, p. 49.

111. After the Second revolt, Rabban Simeon ben Gamaliel said, 'Samaritans are to be classified as Jews'; later his son Judah I said that they were to be classified as 'Gentiles'; finally his grandson Gamaliel II set a regulation stating that meat slaughtered by Samaritans is not kosher. See *Tos. Ter.* 4:12, 14; *y. Berakoth* 11b; *Tos. Pesahim* 1:15.

112. Alon, *The Jews*, p. 562.

113. Montgomery, *Samaritans, passim*.

114. Purvis, 'Samaritans and Judaism', pp. 81–98.

115. Purvis, 'Samaritans and Judaism', p. 89. On the other hand, Coggins concludes: 'There is no evidence that any one decisive event played a special part in widening the breach between Jews and Samaritans', *Samaritans*, p. 164.

116. Purvis, 'Samaritans and Judaism', p. 91. Coggins also views Samaritanism as part of the larger complex of Judaism of the last pre-Christian centuries, *Samaritans*, p. 163.

117. Pummer, *Samaritans*, p. 3.

of Judaism, but both are parallel 'traditions' developed from the common ground of ancient Israelite religion during the Second Temple period.[118] For him, it is the different geographical and historical backgrounds of the period that paved the way for two different traditions, thereby resulting in different identities and ideologies. 'A biblical researcher', Tsedaka says, 'who determines that Judaism is the mother "religion" framework out of which other Jewish units were developed during the first centuries of the period of the Second Temple, clearly bends the historical truth'.[119]

Crown likewise suggests that there exists an Israelite-Samaritan evolutionary nexus both politically and religiously and, therefore, Samaritanism is a phenomenon of continuum with ancient Israel.[120] If the view that the Samaritans are the direct descendants of the Israelites is right, it is likely that they did not show any of the pagan influences credited to them in the Jewish sources, at least during the early period of their existence. It is also likely that during the development of the Samaritans as a dominant sect, they became an unidentifiable group both religiously and politically. 2 Kings 17, Sirach and Josephus deliberately portray them as a community of pagan origin. This is not to say that the Samaritans throughout history remained true to their ancient faith. The Samaritans, who were initially homogeneous were not yet the Samaritans of the post-Alexandrian conquest whose stock was diluted by an influx of Greek colonists.[121]

In light of the available evidence, it is reasonable to say that Samaritanism as a separate entity is neither Judaism nor a foreign religion. It is not Judaism in the sense that geographically, ethnically and religiously the Samaritans do not belong to the southern tribe of Judah and to the spiritual centre of Jerusalem. From a Jewish point of view, the alleged illegitimate origin of the Samaritans, the illegitimacy of their priesthood, the veneration of their temple on Mount Gerizim and of the holy city of Shechem, their separate version of the Torah and their paganization make them a separate sect not belonging to Judaism at all. Anti-Samaritan sources treat them as an ethnically mixed and religiously syncretistic community. At times and by some people, they were treated as socially marginalized. According to Feldman, the fact that the Samaritans insisted on the legitimacy of their own sanctuary on Mount Gerizim against the Jerusalem Temple and worshipped on Gerizim instead of Jerusalem is in itself not sufficient to prove them to be non-Jews. However, it does not prove that they are Jews either. The Samaritans do not

---

118. Tsedaka, 'Samaritanism – Judaism or Another Religion?', in Mor (ed.), *Jewish Sects*, pp. 47–51 asserts: 'It is not the "Jewish religion" nor the "Samaritan religion" posed before us, but a "Jewish tradition" and a "Samaritan tradition", both daughters of the Israelite religion' (p. 51).

119. Tsedaka, 'Samaritanism', p. 49.

120. Crown, 'Samaritan Origins', pp. 133–55.

121. Crown, 'Samaritan Origins', p. 155.

entirely belong to a foreign religion because they belong to the Northern tribe of Joseph, claiming national and religious identities by their loyalty to the God of Israel and the Torah. Their particular attachment to the Pentateuch, Sabbath-keeping and Passover sacrifice place the Samaritans within the Israelite heritage. Samaritanism has a traceable link with the ancient religion of Israel but developed as a distinct entity with its own worldview. As Coggins states, there is no evidence that any one decisive event played a special part in widening the breach between Jews and Samaritans.[122] The separation between them, like that of Judaism and Christianity, was not an *event* but a protracted *process*.[123] In them, one could see the struggle of a community that tried to establish its original ethnic-socio-religious and political identity and ideology, which were lost in the course of differing historical conditions.

Now we must ask, who were the Samaritans for Luke? Where do the Samaritans belong on the mental map of the first century CE readers of Acts? To put it another way, what is the rhetoric of the term, 'Samaritan' and how would a first-century Jew or Jewish Christian view a mission to the Samaritans? Did Luke or his readers share some of the Jewish derogatory portraits of the Samaritans as idolaters and illegitimate people, in contrast to the self-designation of the Samaritans as 'keepers' of the Law? The Gospel of Matthew does not consider the Samaritans as belonging to the 'house of Israel', but it looks anti-Samaritan when it has Jesus say, 'do not go among the Gentiles or enter any city of the Samaritans' (10:5). Unlike the Gospel of Matthew, the Gospel of John is pro-Samaritan, as Jesus has a mission to them and he wins a large crowd (Ch.4).[124] The foregoing review of the socio-religious situation of the Samaritans in the New Testament period clearly demonstrates that, from a Jewish point of view, the identity of the Samaritans is ambiguous and ambivalent, and the legitimacy of Samaritans is in question. In light of this setting, we will explore in subsequent chapters what Luke is trying to do with his Samaritan episodes in Luke-Acts, especially that in Acts 8:4-25.

122. Coggins, *Samaritans*, p. 164.

123. S.J. Cohen, *From the Maccabees to the Mishnah* (Philadelphia: The Westminster Press, 1987), p. 171.

124. See Purvis, 'Fourth Gospel', pp. 161–98; M. Pamment, 'Is there Convincing Evidence of Samaritan Influence on the Fourth Gospel?', *ZNW* 73 (1982), pp. 221–30; E.D. Freed, 'Samaritan Influence in the Gospel of John', *CBQ* 30 (1968), pp. 580–7; *idem*, 'Did John Write His Gospel Partly to Win Samaritan Converts?', *NovT* 12 (1970), pp. 241–56; Maccini, 'Woman at the Well in John 4', pp. 35–46; Jürgen Zangenberg, '"Open Your Eyes and Look at the Fields": Contacts between Christians and Samaria According to the Gospel of John', in Morabito, *et al.* (eds), *Samaritan Researches*, pp. 3.84–3.94.

3.8. The City of Samaria in Acts 8:5

The phrase 'the city of Samaria' in Acts 8:5 needs special attention. Martin Hengel treats this text in 8:5a as 'a difficult and therefore disputed statement'.[125] On the basis of the external evidence,[126] many scholars prefer the textual variant with the definite article to the anarthrous 'city' and render the reading, 'into the (capital) city of Samaria' rather than '*a city* of Samaria'.[127] Which city did Luke mean when he said, 'Philip went down into *the city* of Samaria'? Scholars have given various answers to this question, which can be categorized as follows.

1. 'The city of Samaria' can refer only to Sebaste.[128]
2. It must mean Shechem.[129] The main argument in favour of this claim is the suggestion that Shechem was Samaria's replacement as the Samaritan capital after Alexander's destruction of Samaria in 331 BCE and it was the religious centre of the Samaritans. Also, Philip's mission of preaching 'Christ' does not fit the audience of the Gentile inhabitants of the city of Sebaste, rather the religious community of the Samaritans whose centre is at Shechem.
3. It would possibly be Gitta, the birthplace of Simon Magus.[130]
4. Martin Hengel excludes the possibility of both Sebaste and Shechem and ascribes the name of the city to a 'Samaritan capital' and argues it refers to Sychar.[131] We will take up his arguments in the following discussion. Böhm follows a similar view as that of Hengel but rules out even the possibility of Sychar.[132]

---

125. Hengel, 'The Geography of Palestine in Acts', in R. Bauckham (ed.), *The Book of Acts in Its First Century Setting. vol. 4: The Book of Acts in Its Palestinian Setting* (Grand Rapids: Wm.B. Eerdmans Publishing Co., 1995), pp. 27–78, 70.

126. The external evidence favours *the city* of Samaria: MSS like p74, ℵ, A, B, 69, 181, 1175, 1898, 2344 retain the article τήν with 'city of Samaria'. See also Bruce M. Metzger, *A Textual Commentary on the Greek New Testament* (London: United Bible Societies, 1971), pp. 355–6. If the reading with the article is maintained, then this would mean either Sebaste, the principal city of Samaria in a political sense or the city of Shechem from a religious viewpoint. If the reading 'a city of Samaria' is rendered, then it can be any city of Samaria. On historical, linguistic and theological bases, as it is argued in this chapter, Sebaste could be the most likely setting for the mission in Samaria.

127. For *a city* of Samaria, see Lake and Cadbury, *Beginnings* I. 4, p. 89; Hamilton, *Samaria-Sebaste*, p. 27; Williams, *Acts*, p. 115; Johnson, *Acts*, p. 145; Purvis, 'Samaria (City)', p. 920; Scobie, 'Origins', pp. 390–414, n.2; For the reading, *the city*, see the footnote above.

128. Munck, *Acts*, p. 73; Sanders, *Jews in Luke-Acts*, p. 147, uncritically suggested that presumably it is the main *Samaritan* city of Sebaste.

129. Wellhausen, *Apostelgeschichte*, p. 14; Haenchen, *Acts*, p. 307; Bruce, *Acts*, p. 216–17; Pesch, *Apostelgeschichte* I, p. 272; Roloff, *Apostelgeschichte*, p. 133; cf. Wright, *Shechem*, pp. 175–6.

130. Lake and Cadbury, *Beginnings* I.4, p. 89; Williams, *Acts*, p. 115.

131. Hengel, 'Geography', p. 74.

132. Böhm, *Samarien*, pp. 281–9.

5. Lüdemann refrains from naming the city by suggesting that 'it is not completely clear' whether the mission of Philip took place among the Gentiles of Samaria or the religious community of the Samaritans, although he thinks it probably involved both.[133]

6. There are scholars who do not name the city but only mention that the description of location is 'problematic'[134] or the exact city is 'difficult to determine',[135] or it refers to '(irgend)eine Stadt Samariens'.[136]

In the following discussion, we will take up the arguments of both Hengel and Böhm as they cover similar claims made by other scholars on the same question of Philip's location of ministry in Acts 8:5. Hengel strongly opposes both the reading of the text and the identification of the city as Samaria-Sebaste. He thinks that Luke does not have exact knowledge of the geography of Samaria and that 'the city of Samaria' would probably mean a 'Samaritan "capital" the name of which Luke either no longer knew or left out as being unimportant'.[137] Hengel's main arguments are the following.

(1) Luke never uses Samaria as the name of a city but always to refer to the territory of the ethnic Samaritans. (2) Sebaste was predominantly a Greek city and it was not the religious and ethnic centre of the Samaritans. (3) The name Sebaste very rapidly suppressed the old city name and Josephus, like Luke, uses Samaria for the time after Herod only for the district and no longer for the city. (4) Gentile Sebaste does not provide a 'syncretistic milieu' for the activity of Simon Magus. (5) Those 'who wanted to address the Samaritans as a religious group had to seek them out at their religious centre on Mount Gerizim'. (6) The most likely reference to a Samaritan capital would be Sychar, because it retained its significance after the destruction of Shechem as the nearest place to Gerizim. Like Hengel, Böhm also rules out the possibility of Sebaste. Her arguments are mainly based on linguistic analysis. (1) Philip's preaching of Christ, the long-expected saviour of the Jews does not fit the Gentile audience of Sebaste, but it presupposes that the audience is monotheistic. (2) In the general framework of the scattered mission, Acts 8:4 corresponds to Acts 11:19, where the mission was directed only to Jews. It shows that Philip's ministry was also directed to Israel (those who are in the periphery); therefore, Sebaste is certainly ruled out. (3) When

---

133. Lüdemann, *Traditions*, p. 100; Bauernfeind, *Apostelgeschichte*, p. 125.

134. Garrett, *Demise*, p. 140, n.7.

135. Spencer, *Portrait*, p. 85; Coggins, 'The Samaritans and Acts', *NTS* 28 (1982), pp. 423–34, 429.

136. Böhm, *Samarien*, p. 289.

137. Hengel, 'Geography', p. 76; *idem, Between Jesus and Paul*, p. 126; on this issue, see also A. Lindemann, 'Samaria und Samaritaner im Neuen Testament', *WuD* 22 (1993), pp. 51–76, 61, n. 45.

Luke says that the Samaritans believed and men and women got baptized, there does not seem to arise any problem regarding circumcision. This suggests that the location cannot be Sebaste.[138]

The main objection against the identification of 'the city of Samaria' as Sebaste is twofold: (a) the ancient city called 'Samaria' no longer existed as such in Luke's day and (b) Sebaste was a Hellenistic city whereas the mission in Acts 8:4-25 is to the ethnic Samaritans. The arguments of Hengel and others imply the presupposition that the Hellenistic city of Sebaste did not have any Samaritans and that Philip evangelized only the orthodox Samaritans, if there were any, at or nearby Shechem. It is to be noted that Luke always uses 'Samaria' elsewhere to mean the whole district but when he said 'the city of Samaria' in Acts 8:5, he had a very specific city in mind which is clearly distinguished from the villages of the Samaritans in 8:25. He does not name the city as Sebaste, perhaps to tie it with the programmatic development outlined in Acts 1:8.[139] The reference in 8:14 to Samaria that 'received the Word of God' is primarily to the same city of v. 5 and then probably to cover the district of Samaria.[140] It should also be noted that following Herod's death in 4 BCE, Josephus does not mention the name of Sebaste when he refers to the Roman forces suppressing the Jewish revolt in Galilee and Judaea; instead he uses the name 'Samaria'.[141] Here, the name Samaria may mean both the entire region and the city of Sebaste.[142] It is evident from further references in *BJ*, II, 96; *AJ*, XVII, 319. However, in *AJ*, XV, 246, Josephus clearly uses 'Samaria' to mean Sebaste alone: 'And so he (Herod) suffered from this illness in *Samaria*, (later) called *Sebaste*'. Even Josephus does not use a firm terminology to distinguish between the city dwellers and the inhabitants of the territory of Samaria.

In the remaining discussion of this chapter, it is argued *contra* Hengel, Böhm and others, that Luke may be referring to the city of Sebaste in Acts 8:5. To set the arguments in perspective, we will look at the Samaria of Herod's time, during whose reign the city got its name Sebaste. Pompey in 63 BCE restored and annexed Samaria to the Roman province of Syria and restored it to its own previous inhabitants and gave them the status of *polis* under the proconsul of Syria.[143] It can be assumed that during this restoration process, at least some Samaritans re-settled in the city of Samaria. It is Gabinius in 57–55 BCE who reconstructed the ruined city and restored its

---

138. Böhm, *Samarien*, pp. 294–305.

139. Jervell, *Apostelgeschichte*, p. 259.

140. Cf. A. Harnack, *The Acts of the Apostles* (trans. J.R. Wilkinson; London: Williams & Norgate, 1909), p. 59: Luke is intending to convey that the Gospel, when it was carried from Judaea to Samaria, made its entrance at once into the capital city of that country.

141. *AJ*, XVIII, 220-222, 288-289; *BJ*, II, 16-17, 66-69.

142. Cf. Jones, *Cities*, pp. 235–40.

143. *BJ*, I, 156; *AJ*, XIV, 74-76, 86-88.

citizens. Josephus also reports that in Gabinius' time (58-57 BCE), Samaria was a town where 'colonists were gladly flocking' (*BJ*, I, 166). As a mark of their gratitude to Gabinius, they were called Gabinians (*BJ*, I, 166). Later, the emperor Augustus gave Samaria to Herod the Great, who rebuilt it in *ca.* 30 BCE. Samaria in Herod's time was significant in many ways. He enlarged the city's territory, provided the city with a new constitution, lands for their city *chora*, walls, temples, a forum and a theatre and renamed it Sebaste in honour of Caesar Augustus.[144] He brought both the city and the district of Samaria under his control. Here it is important to notice that Josephus says that Herod selected the city's citizenry: 'And at this time, being eager to fortify Samaria, he arranged to have settled in it many of those who had fought as his allies in the war and many of the neighbouring population' (*AJ*, XV, 296). Who are these settlers, especially 'the neighbouring population' (οἱ ὁμόροι)? If the suggestion of Levine that the residents of the older city and the surrounding territory were the most logical candidates to populate the new city,[145] then οἱ ὁμόροι are to be identified with the rural population of the immediate vicinity. It may be that the population of the newly founded city of Sebaste had some Samaritans.

Josephus says that one of Herod's wives, Malthace, was a Samaritan[146] and Herod felt himself more at home in Samaria than in Jerusalem. The city of Samaria-Sebaste was a base for his military operations against Antigonus and he established it as a stronghold against the Jews.[147] When the Romans needed oil and wine in besieging Jerusalem, he turned to his friends in Samaria for help. Thus, it would seem right to suggest that Herod was favourable to the Samaritans and there were at least some Samaritans in Sebaste. Also, as J.M. Ford says, Herod's reign placed Samaria in a position of antagonism vis-à-vis the anti-Herodian Jews.[148] During this period, Samaria came more under pagan influence because of the Roman and Herodian activities. If citizenship in a Hellenistic city required commitment to pagan worship,[149] it was possible for at least some Samaritans, i.e., the Hellenized Samaritans, to become permanent residents of the city. According to 3 Macc. 2:25-26, Hellenistic cities were glad to accept Jewish people as citizens, though pagan ritual worship was tantamount to apostasy for the Jews.

---

144. *BJ*, I, 403, cf. *AJ*, XV, 296-298. Sebastos is the Greek rendering of the Latin Augustus.

145. L.I. Levine, *Caesarea under Roman Rule* (Leiden: Brill, 1975), p. 16; Kasher, *Jews*, p. 201; Smith, *Historical Geography*, p. 229.

146. *BJ*, I, 562; *AJ*, XVII, 20.

147. *AJ*, XV, 292-93.

148. J.M. Ford, *My Enemy is My Guest: Jesus and Violence in Luke* (New York: Orbis Books, 1984), p. 82.

149. Kasher, *Jews*, p. 178.

The episode in Josephus of a pitched battle between Pilate's troops and the Samaritans (*AJ*, XVIII, 85-89) could give a further clue that there were at least some Samaritans in Sebaste. In this account a reference is made to 'the council of Samaritans' which, according to the revised Schürer, suggests 'a united political organization of the territory'.[150] This is because the Samaritan region was subordinated to the city of Sebaste.[151] It implies that the city territory of Sebaste probably included at least some Samaritan population. In the incident following the murder of the Galilean pilgrims, the Samaritans were armed along with the Sebastenian troops by Cumanus to march out against the Jews, which also shows either the affinity between the Samaritans and the Sebastenians or the hostility of both towards the Jews, or both.

The following arguments are made in favour of the possible identification of the 'city of Samaria' in Acts 8:5 as Sebaste.

1. Neither the city nor the district of Samaria was the centre of a single religio-ethnic settlement during the New Testament period.

In the New Testament period, the majority of the rural population in Samaria were Samaritans.[152] That they spread over into the coastal area is evident from the incidents mentioned in the New Testament and Josephus.[153] Bowman thinks that there were 'probably even more Samaritans than Jews' in the New Testament time.[154] There is no evidence for this probability, so it remains speculation. But it is generally agreed that first century CE Samaria included a large pagan population.[155] The Gentile population was not only in Sebaste but side by side with the Samaritans proper as well. Likewise, the Samaritans were not merely centred around Gerizim but moved to the Gentile territories, probably accepting the Greek way of life. But it is not certain that the Samaritans exceeded the Gentile population of Sebaste. However, as mentioned earlier, the New Testament does not differentiate the Gentile population of Samaria from the Samaritans.

2. Though the Samaritan centre was on Gerizim near Shechem, not all the Samaritans of the first century CE settled at the ruined Shechem or in the city of Sychar; many moved to the Hellenistic cities.

There is evidence of Samaritan settlement outside of Shechem during the third and second centuries BCE, i.e., before the destruction of Shechem by John Hyrcanus. Josephus' description of a quarrel between Jews and

150. Schürer, *History* II, p. 163.

151. Schürer, *History* II, p. 163, states that the Samaritan region was to Sebaste, 'as Galilee was subject to Sepphoris (and Tiberias), and Judaea to Jerusalem'.

152. Avi-Yonah, 'Historical Geography', p. 108.

153. John 4:5; *BJ*, II, 232.

154. Bowman, *Samaritan Problem*, p. 57.

155. André Parrot, *Samaria: The Capital of the Kingdom of Israel* (London: SCM Press, 1958), p. 103 comments that 'Samaria was evidently destined to be the home of a mixed population'; Haenchen, *Acts* p. 306; Scobie, 'Origins', p. 390, n.2.

Samaritans living in Egypt during the reign of Ptolemy Soter (323-283 BCE) concerning the maintenance of their religious practices suggests the presence of a Samaritan community in Egypt.[156] If Josephus' report that the Samaritans participated in the siege of Gaza during the reign of Alexander is right, then it is probable that a Samaritan community was settled in Gaza in the wake of the battle.[157] Arrian says that Alexander repopulated the city of Gaza with 'neighbouring tribesmen',[158] which would have included, as Crown suggests, some of the Samaritans who had served Alexander at Tyre and who had been recruited for garrison duties in Egypt.[159] Josephus also states that the Samaritans in Alexandria engaged in a debate with the Jews over the claims of the Jerusalem Temple and the sanctuary at Gerizim in the time of Ptolemy Philometor (181-145 BCE).[160] If his account is correct, it implies that there was a Samaritan settlement in Alexandria. Two Greek inscriptions dating to 250-50 BCE found on the Greek island of Delos in 1979 make references to Mount Gerizim, apparently indicating the presence of Samaritans at Delos in the second century BCE.[161] The first inscription, dating between 150 BCE and 50 BCE, reads:

Οἱ ἐν Δήλῳ Ἰσραηλεῖται οἱ ἀπαρχόμενοι εἰς ἱερὸν Ἀργαριζεὶν στεφανοῦσιν χρυσῷ στεφάνῳ Σαραπίωνα Ἰάσονος Κνώσιον εὐεργεσίας ἕνεκεν τῆς εἰς ἑαυτούς (The Israelites on Delos who make offerings to hallowed *Argarizein* crown with a gold crown Sarapion, son of Jason, of Knossos, for his benefaction towards them).[162]

The second one, dating around 250–175 BCE, reads: [Οἱ ἐν Δήλῳ] Ἰσραηλεῖται οἱ ἀπαρχόμενοι εἰς ἱερὸν ἅγιον Ἀργαριζεὶν ... ([the] Israelites [on Delos] who make offerings to hallowed, consecrated *Argarizein* ...[163]

P. Bruneau interprets *Argarizein* as the equivalent to Hebrew *Har Garizim* (Mount Gerizim), the holy mountain of the Samaritans. Here it is interesting to note the use of the term 'Israelites' to describe those who devoted to the

---

156. *AJ*, XII, 10. In *AJ*, XI, 345, Josephus mentions Alexander settling Samaritan troops in Egypt. Both Samaritan and non-Samaritan sources support a Samaritan Diaspora during this period and it is reasonable to think of an 'organized group' forming a Samaritan community in Egypt. For the discussion, see P. Stenhouse, *The Kitab al-Tarikh of Abu'l Fath* (Sydney, 1985), pp. 112–13; Crown, 'Samaritan Diaspora', pp. 197–8, suggests the presence of an organized group of Samaritans in Egypt at the time of Alexander's death.

157. Crown, 'Samaritan Diaspora', p. 198.

158. *Arrian*, II, 27:7.

159. Crown, 'Samaritan Diaspora', p. 199.

160. *AJ*, XIII, 74-79. Josephus reports that the Jews won the debate and the Samaritan advocates were put to death.

161. Pummer, 'Samaritan Material Remains and Archaeology', in Crown (ed.), *Samaritans*, pp. 150–1; A.T. Kraabel, 'New Evidence of Samaritan Diaspora was found on Delos', *BA* 47:1 (1984), pp. 44–7; Crown, 'Samaritan Diaspora', p. 202.

162. Kraabel, 'Samaritan Diaspora', p. 44.

163. Kraabel, 'Samaritan Diaspora', p. 44.

cult at Mount Gerizim. It shows that the Samaritans were using the name
Israel to describe themselves as a religious community, just as Jews living all
over had done. However, they were specifying that their sacred temple was
not in Jerusalem, but at Mount Gerizim, thereby asserting the orthodoxy of
their Pentateuchal tradition over that of the Jewish community. The two
dedicatory inscriptions demonstrate that there were Samaritan 'diasporic'
settlements outside of Mount Gerizim even in the second half of the
Hellenistic period, when the temple existed.

Another important find that merits treatment is the fragmentary inscription
found near the columned street in Sebaste, explained and hypothetically
reconstructed by A.D. Tushingham.[164] It is assumed that the original text was
a dedicatory inscription to a king and had five lines. This fragmentary
inscription preserves only one word from each line, and line one is completely
lost. The only preserved words in the inscription are Σωτῆρα (line 2), Ἐγ
Βασιλέως (line 3), and Βασιλίσσης (line 4). Since the preserved letter in the
last line of the fragment starts with *Sigma*, and the inscription comes from
Samaria, it is assumed that this word may be Σαμαρεῖς, who is the donor of
this dedicatory inscription. Tushingham reconstructs the form of this
dedicatory text as starting with the name of the king who did the favours,
and dedicating it to him using the epithets Σωτῆρα, then the name of his father
and mother, then the reason for dedication and finally the name of a city,
group or a private person who expresses the appreciation. Since the word
Σωτῆρ is commonly applied to the Hellenistic rulers of Egypt, Syria, the
Lagids and Seleucids, Tushingham suggests that it is a reference to Ptolemy
IX Soter II, who, according to Josephus, helped Samaria by sending 6,000
troops to support Antiochus Cyzicenus while Samaria was under siege by the
sons of John Hyrcanus (*AJ*, XIII, 273-281). Therefore, he dates the inscription
before or during the destruction of Samaria in 108 BCE.

If Tushingham's reconstruction of the above inscription and its Samaritan
dedicators are right, then it would suggest that Samaritans lived in the
Gentile city of Samaria. If the inscription is to be dated to 108 BCE only on
the basis of the epithet Σωτῆρ, however, then it can also be dated to the
Roman period, for the word Σωτῆρ was also used for Roman rulers from
Julius Caesar to Hadrian and later emperors.[165] According to Jn 4:42, the
Samaritans hailed Jesus and welcomed him as the 'Σωτῆρ of the world'.
Therefore, on the basis of the provenance of the inscription in Sebaste, and
the use of the title Σωτῆρ, the find could be dated to the Greek or Roman

164. Tushingham, 'A Hellenistic Inscription from Samaria-Sebaste', *PEQ* 104 (1972), pp. 59–63.

165. Josephus reports that Vespasian was hailed as Σωτῆρ – *BJ*, III, 459; VII, 70-71; and later this title was given to Titus– *BJ*, IV, 112-113; VII, 100-103, 119. For a list of emperors to whom the title Σωτῆρ was given, see C.R. Koester, 'The Saviour of the World (John 4:42)', *JBL* 109/4 (1990), pp. 665–80.

period. Whether it has anything to do with a Samaritan community in Sebaste, however, is unknown. One difficulty in distinguishing the Samaritan settlements from Jewish ones needs to be noted. Crown mentions that 'the Samaritans can be identified only because of their affinity for Mount Gerizim but not because they are distinguished by the name Samaritan', and that they called themselves Israelites.[166] It can also be true of Samaria where one would find difficulty in identifying the genuine Samaritans from its Greek colonists, if the only identifying factor was the name Samaria.[167] Since the tendency is to link the identity of the Samaritans to their religious centre on Mount Gerizim or to the city of Shechem, those Samaritans who live in or nearby the city of Sebaste, in turn, should not be categorized as the Gentile inhabitants of the city.

3. There is no evidence to suggest that 'the Samaritans replaced Shechem with Sychar', but merely a speculation.

Both Hengel and Crown think that Sychar clearly replaced Shechem after the destruction of the latter by Hyrcanus. Hengel's argument is that Sychar is 'the nearest substantial place to Gerizim' and that 'its significance is attested by Jewish and Samaritan sources'.[168] Though Crown states that 'of all the towns available to the Samaritans we do not know why Sychar was seen as the logical substitute for Shechem', he still assumes that because Sychar is associated with the Samaritan sacred sites and has a reasonable water supply, it would have become a religious centre of the Samaritans.[169]

It must be noted that no Jewish or Samaritan sources name Sychar either as 'the city of Samaria' or as 'the Samaritan capital'. Josephus, the main Jewish author who widely treats the history of the Samaritans and the state of their religious and national identity, never states or implies that the Samaritans replaced Shechem with Sychar. And, there is no evidence that between the destruction of Shechem and the founding of Neapolis, Sychar had become the religious centre of the Samaritans. Even Neapolis, which was at first a Roman city, only became a Samaritan religious centre later on. Most of the sources on which Hengel's assumption is based must date from the late third century CE onwards, which would rather reflect the significance of Sychar, if there is any, in the post-New Testament period.

4. It is not necessary that a religious centre must provide a suitable milieu for the mission in Acts.

Hengel's argument that 'any one who wanted to address the Samaritans as a religious group had to seek them out at their religious centre on Mount Gerizim'[170] is very clumsy. Then, based on this dubiety, his identification of

---

166. Crown, 'Samaritan Diaspora', n.34, p. 202.
167. Crown, 'Samaritan Diaspora', n.35, p. 202.
168. Hengel, 'Geography', pp. 74–5.
169. Crown, 'Redating', p. 30.
170. Hengel, 'Geography', p. 74.

the city in Acts 8:5a as Sychar because 'it was the nearest substantial place to Gerizim'[171] is merely a speculation. According to the Fourth Gospel, neither Jesus nor the Samaritans had to seek out one another and meet together on Mount Gerizim when many of them gathered to hear him outside the town of Sychar, beside Jacob's well; instead, the Samaritans 'came out of the town and made their way toward him', while Jesus still remained outside the town (Jn 4:30). Philip went to Samaria not to proclaim himself as the Samaritan eschatological *Taheb* or to persuade the Samaritans to go with him to Gerizim, like the prophet who promised to show them the sacred vessels which Moses had hidden there (*AJ*, XVIII, 85-89), but to preach the Christ, which would not have demanded a gathering on Gerizim. This is further evidenced by the fact that Peter and John, on their return to Jerusalem, preached the gospel not on Gerizim, but in many Samaritan villages (Acts 8:25). Further, Hengel's statement that the religious centre of the Samaritans was not a city but Mount Gerizim would again suggest that Philip did not go to their religious centre but to 'the *city* of Samaria'. The Gerizim temple was destroyed in 128 BCE and it would not have existed in the first century CE in its splendour.

5. Luke must have thought that the Samaritan mission should start from the centre of socio-religious-political and economic oppression.

It is only in a religious sense that Mount Gerizim and Shechem were as significant to the Samaritans as the Jerusalem Temple and its city were to the Jews. But for Luke and his audience, Sebaste would probably have been the main city where the Samaritans in the main severely suffered from socio-religious-political and economic oppression. It was the centre for Roman domination in Samaria until it shifted to the newly founded city of Flavia Neapolis in 72 CE. The presence of Roman troops in Samaria-Sebaste would have been well-known to Luke, for as a historian, he was very much aware of the political situation of first-century Roman Palestine. Strabo (64 BCE-20 CE) mentions only Sebaste among the cities of Samaria. Pliny the Elder (23-79 CE) mentions Mount Gerizim, Sebaste and Neapolis as the main features of Samaria. It is only later, probably from the end of the first or the beginning of the second century CE that Neapolis began to grow as a Samaritan centre and Sebaste became less important. This would explain why Eusebius (*ca.* 260–340 CE), in his *Onomasticon*, designates Sebaste a 'small city'[172] and Ammianus Marcellinus (*ca.* 330–395 CE) mentions Neapolis, not Sebaste, among the prominent towns of Palestine.[173]

---

171. Hengel, 'Geography', p. 74.

172. Eusebius, *Onomasticon* (ed. Klostermann), p. 154.

173. The reference in Ammianus is XIV 8, 11. See Schürer, *History* II, pp. 163–4; M. Stern, *Greek and Latin Authors on Jews and Judaism* II (Jerusalem: Israel Academy of Sciences and Humanities, 1980), p. 604; Pummer, 'Samaritan Material', pp. 159–60.

6. Luke or his source must be employing the traditional name of the Old Testament city of Samaria.

That Acts 7:16 clearly mentions the name of Shechem suggests that Luke or his source is not ignorant of its significance. In this single verse, the name 'Shechem' appears twice, but if Luke's readers were able to relate or link Shechem to 'the city of Samaria', he would have used it synonymously rather than explicitly mentioning the name 'Shechem'.[174] If Luke really meant Shechem or Sychar in Acts 8:5, he could have explicitly named either site instead of using the imprecise phrase 'the city of Samaria'. Instead, he uses the very traditional name of the ancient Israelite city to describe the Samaritan mission, 'the city of Samaria', which is the birthplace of the Samaritans. Also, one must not assume that the city name Samaria had gone out of use.[175] This was the capital of Israel, conquered by the Assyrians and other forces, captured by Alexander the Great, destroyed by Hyrcanus and finally rebuilt as Sebaste by Herod the Great. As Barrett says, 'Luke, it may be, had in mind Sebaste, *the* city of the district of Samaria; copyists saw the difficulty in this and made the simplest possible change'.[176]

7. In light of the further portrayal of Philip in Acts, it is evident that Luke has Philip the Hellenist starting his ministry from a Hellenistic city and a political centre (Sebaste), and ending in another city of a similar nature (Caesarea).

A further indication that 'the city of Samaria' in Acts 8:5 refers to Sebaste becomes clear in light of the further travels of Philip in the rest of the chapter. Starting from the Gentile city of Sebaste, he then goes to the road leading to the Gentile city of Gaza and then to Azotus, another Gentile city, and finally ends up in the Gentile city of Caesarea. His activity begins in Sebaste, a political centre, and ends likewise in Caesarea, another political centre, which are the two main cities of Palestine built by Herod the Great. Though Philip is portrayed here as visiting only the Gentile cities and preaching the gospel there, Luke claims that the ministry was conducted among the Jewish or semi-Jewish population of the cities, not the Gentile groups. This is evident when Luke says that those who had been scattered by the persecution in connection with Stephen preached the message only to Jews (Acts 11:19). If it is applied also to the ministry of Philip in the city of Samaria, then Shechem or Sychar, which were entirely Samaritan centres, do not provide a proper milieu for a Jewish audience, since Jews and the Samaritans are distinctively separate groups in Luke. Even if one assumes with Hengel[177] that Philip was also a missionary to the Gentiles, it would make sense in the case

174. Spencer, *Portrait*, p. 85, comments that the link between the city in Acts 8:5 and the city of Shechem in 7:16 would have been obvious to Luke's readers. It is unlikely because the context is different and also for other reasons mentioned in the text above.

175. Hemer, *Acts*, pp. 225–6.

176. Barrett, *Acts* I, p. 402.

177. Hengel, 'Geography', p. 58.

of the Samaritan mission if the location were the Gentile city of Sebaste rather than a Samaritan capital like Sychar. When Hengel himself admits that 'in the end Luke, the Greek city-dweller, transfers the activity of the first missionary (Philip) to be depicted in detail to "hellenistic" cities',[178] it is, then, probable that in 8:5 Luke meant the Gentile city of Sebaste. In an investigation of the Lukan presentation of Paul's status and social location in Acts, J.H. Neyrey argues that Luke rhetorically presents Paul's location in urban centres and portrays him as travelling to and residing in the provincial capitals.[179] Similarly, it can be suggested that Luke also presents the activity of the Hellenist Philip in the capital cities.

8. It is likely that Luke is shaping the Samaritan mission in Acts 8:5 by interweaving its historical details into the framework of the Old Testament city of Samaria.

Most scholars agree that Luke has used Old Testament quotations, language, themes and models to shape his ideological viewpoint in various passages in Luke-Acts.[180] According to T.L. Brodie, as a Greco-Roman writer, Luke employs the ancient literary technique of *imitatio* and uses the skeletal framework of the Elijah/Elisha narratives in the LXX to rework his materials. Brodie suggests that in describing Simon and the Ethiopian eunuch in Acts 8:9-40, Luke has 'modelled largely' on the essence of the Elisha-Naaman narrative in 2 Kings 5.[181] Here, the dealings of Elisha with Naaman are analogous to the encounter of Philip with the eunuch,[182] and those with Gehazi are analogous to that of Peter with Simon. Though 2 Kings 5 does not provide an adequate parallelism for every detail in Acts 8:9-40, Brodie's thesis enhances the idea that Luke made use of Old Testament incidents to shape his story of the mission in Samaria.[183] In light of the process of inter-

---

178. Hengel, 'Geography', p. 57.

179. Neyrey's investigation includes four cities in Acts – Tarsus, Antioch, Ephesus and Corinth. See *idem*, 'Luke's Social Location of Paul: Cultural Anthropology and the Status of Paul in Acts', in Witherington (ed.), *History*, pp. 251–79.

180. J.A. Fitzmyer, 'The Use of the Old Testament in Luke-Acts', *SBLSP 1992* (ed. E.H. Lovering, Jr.; Atlanta: Scholars Press, 1992); C.A. Evans, 'Luke's Use of the Elijah/Elisha Narratives and the Ethics of Election', *JBL* 106 (1987), pp. 75–83; R.E. Brown, *The Birth of the Messiah* (Garden City, NY: 1977), pp. 235–499; E. Richard, *Acts 6:1-8:4: The Author's Method of Composition* (SBLDS 41; Missoula, 1978), p. 145; T.L. Brodie, 'Towards Unravelling Luke's Use of the Old Testament: Luke 7:11-17 as an *Imitatio* of 1 Kings 17:17-24, *NTS* 32 (1986), pp. 247–67; *idem*, 'Luke-Acts as an Imitation and Emulation of the Elijah-Elisha Narrative', in E. Richard (ed.), *New Views on Luke and Acts* (Collegeville, MN, 1990), pp. 78–85, 172–4; *idem*, 'Towards Unravelling the Rhetorical Imitation of Sources in Acts: 2 Kings 5 as One Component of Acts 8, 9-40', *Bib* 67 (1986), pp. 41–67; Spencer, *Portrait*, pp. 135–87; B.T. Arnold, 'Luke's Characterising Use of the Old Testament in the Book of Acts', in Witherington (ed.), *History*, pp. 300–23.

181. Brodie, '2 Kings 5', pp. 41–2.

182. See also Spencer, *Portrait*, pp. 139–40.

183. Luke specifically cited the Naaman incident in Lk. 4:27, and later refers to the cleansing of a Samaritan leper in 17:11-19. Also in the story of the Samaritan rejection of Jesus and his

nalisation and imitation of the Old Testament texts in the portrait of the Samaritan mission in Luke-Acts, it is likely that the ancient capital city of Samaria would provide an adequate milieu for Luke. This is not to say that as a theologian, Luke has distorted the historical details of the stories he writes to fit the Old Testament texts into his theological purpose; rather, it must be considered that the use of the Old Testament 'reveals not only the missionary purpose of the apostolic speeches historically, but also the polemical and theological purpose of the book of Acts literarily'.[184]

9. According to internal evidence in Acts, the Holy Spirit descended not merely in the religious centres, but in the main capital cities, which had more than a religious significance.

According to Acts 2, the Holy Spirit was poured out on Pentecost, not in the Temple of Jerusalem, but on the community of believers who gathered in the name of Jesus Christ. Likewise, the political city of Caesarea witnessed the outpouring of the Spirit in the case of the Gentile or God-fearer Cornelius (Acts 10). Similarly, Ephesus was the capital city of the province (Acts 19) where the Holy Spirit descended on the Ephesian Christians. In Acts 8:5, the most probable city where Philip preached and later on the Holy Spirit descended was also the capital city of Samaria-Sebaste, which fits well with the Lukan portrait of mission in urban capitals.

To summarize the foregoing discussion on the city of Samaria, Luke may be referring in Acts 8:5 to the traditional city of Samaria, which in his day was called Sebaste, where the Samaritans had originally lost their national identity. He may be trying to show that the gospel of Christ found its way into such a city and that the Samaritans' acceptance of Christ provided for them a new identity approved by the Holy Spirit.

3.9. Conclusion

The Samaritans, up to and including the New Testament period, were a people who struggled to find their status and lost identity as a nation in the midst of colonial, political and religious oppression. From a Jewish point of view, they were outcasts, syncretists, apostates and idolaters, and the legitimacy of their socio-ethnic and religious status was in question. The available sources are often ambiguous and ambivalent in their portrayal of the Samaritans' socio-religious and ethnic identity in the society. Though their Jewishness is obvious at certain levels, they were often treated as a rival sect outside Judaism. There existed animosity between the Samaritans and Jews in the New Testament period. The Judaeo-Samaritan hostility could have

---

disciples in Samaria (9:51-56), the Old Testament incident of Elijah calling down fire in Samaria is incorporated.

184. Arnold, 'Luke's Characterising', p. 323.

begun from when the Samaritans built their own temple on Mount Gerizim. It is probable that the enmity reached its climax with the destruction of this temple and the civic centre in Shechem, which forced the Samaritans to legitimize their separate identity as an independent religion.[185] Though they were monotheists like the Jews, some of them adopted foreign religious ideas. Early Samaritanism is not viewed as orthodox or monolithic, but a complex religious system.[186] It must be studied not merely against the background of Judaism but in terms of the social dynamics of the Samaritans themselves. In view of the ambiguous and ambivalent status and ethnic identity of the Samaritans, the questionable legitimacy of their rival centre on Gerizim and their alleged acceptance of paganization, any unplanned or unauthorized mission of the church, from a Jewish-Christian point of view, may possibly cast doubts on the legitimacy of Samaritan Christianity as well as on the mission itself. The Lukan Jesus makes contact with this ill-treated group of people with an anticipation to bring them within his Kingdom (Lk. 9:51-56; cf. 10:30-37; 17:11-19) and the ministry of Philip in Acts 8 accomplishes what Jesus began. As we shall see, it is in this scheme of anticipation-legitimation that the Samaritan references in Luke-Acts make best sense, especially the legitimation of the Samaritan mission and Samaritan Christianity in Acts 8:4-25.

185. Mor, 'Samaritans', p. 21.
186. Purvis, 'Samaritans and Judaism', p. 81.

Chapter 4

SAMARITANS IN THE GOSPEL OF LUKE

4.1. Introduction

In our review of the Samaritans up to and including the first century CE, we have demonstrated the tendency of Jewish sources to portray the Samaritans' identity in ambiguous and ambivalent terms and to depict their socio-religious dynamics as illegitimate. The present chapter explores the literary and theological significance of the Lukan narratives of Jesus' treatment of the Samaritans in light of their historical situation in the first century CE and the significance of his own interest in this people for the programmatic development of Christian mission. What does the Lukan portrait of the Samaritans in the Gospel convey in terms of their place in the historical mission of Jesus? Some of the discussions in this study may seem relevant also to the Gentile interest of Luke, but no attempt is made here to discuss the question of a Gentile mission or the extensive material of the fourth evangelist on Jesus and the Samaritans.

4.2. Samaritans in the Gospel of Luke

There are three incidents which deal with Jesus and the Samaritans in the Gospel of Luke: the Samaritan rejection of Jesus and his disciples (9:51-56), the parable of the Good Samaritan (10:30-37) and the healing of the Samaritan leper (17:11-19). All the three incidents occur in 9:51-18:14/19:44, a section variously called 'the Central Section', 'the Travel Narrative', or 'the Great Interpolation'.[1] According to the other Synoptics, after Jesus had finished his ministry in Galilee, he goes to Jerusalem turning eastwards

---

1.   For some work on this section, see J. Drury, *Tradition and Design in Luke's Gospel* (Atlanta: John Knox Press, 1976), pp. 138–64; G. Ogg, 'The Central Section of the Gospel according to St. Luke', *NTS* 18 (1971–72), pp. 39–53; D.P. Moessner, 'Luke 9:1-50: Luke's Preview of the Journey of the Prophet like Moses of Deuteronomy', *JBL* 102 (1983), pp. 575–605; J.L. Resseguie, 'Interpretation of Luke's Central Section (Luke 9:51-19:44) since 1856', *SBT* 5 (1975), pp. 3–36; J.W. Wenham, 'Synoptic Independence and the Origin of Luke's Travel Narrative', *NTS* 27 (1980–81), pp. 507–15.

through Perea (Mt. 19:1-2; Mk 10:1), whereas the Lukan Jesus moves from Galilee to Jerusalem directly southward through Samaria. There is a constant reminder in the narrative (9:51-19:44) that Jesus is on a journey and that Jerusalem is the place of his rejection, death and resurrection.[2]

There are differing views on Jesus' journey through Samaria and the Samaritan material in the central section of Luke. Some scholars suggest that there lies a journey motif in this section, but they assume that Luke does not say that Jesus journeyed through Samaria. For example, Conzelmann thinks that Luke wishes to convey a journey motif here and that Jesus in 9:56 once and for all left Samaria.[3] Likewise, Wilson is of the opinion that the Samaritan material in Luke, especially Lk. 9:51-56, does not have any significance for Luke: 'It may be simpler and ... more faithful to the facts to abandon the notion of a journey through Samaria altogether.... Even so, we might still ask whether despite the fact that we cannot speak of a Samaritan journey or of Jesus preaching to the Samaritans these pericopes have any significance'.[4] There are others who think that the Samaritan material in Luke intends to signify a Samaritan journey of Jesus.[5] C.C. McCown goes further to suggest that Jesus had a Samaritan mission in the Gospel of Luke, for 'the central section records a supposed mission in Samaria'.[6] Likewise, Creed suggests that Luke is 'probably desirous of including a Samaritan mission as prefiguring the universal expansion of the church'.[7] Fitzmyer considers the Samaritan references in the travel section (9:51-19:27) as only a journey through Samaria to Jerusalem and not as a Samaritan mission of Jesus.[8]

A major proponent of the view that the Samaritan material in the Gospel of Luke is Luke's own creation is Morton S. Enslin. He designates the central section of Luke 'the Samaritan Ministry', which according to him is not a detailed travel section, but 'a section of Lukan artistry deliberately intended to indicate Jesus' anticipation and blessing of the gentile mission'.[9] He strongly, though not persuasively, argues that all the Samaritan incidents in Luke are fragile and artificial, and Luke deliberately constructed them from other stories taken from Mark and its parallels.[10] He claims that the historical

---

2.   9:51, 53; 12:49-50; 13:22, 33-34; 16:31; 17:11, 25; 18:31-33; 19:11, 14, 28.

3.   Conzelmann, *Luke*, pp. 53, 60–65.

4.   Wilson, *Gentiles*, pp. 43, 45.

5.   Caird, *Luke*, p. 139; E. Lohse, 'Missionarisches Handeln Jesu nach dem Evangelium des Lukas', *TZ* 10 (1954), pp. 1–11.

6.   McCown, 'The Geography of Luke's Central Section', *JBL* 57 (1938), pp. 56–66, 63; *idem*, 'Gospel Geography; Fiction, Fact and Truth', *JBL* 60 (1941), pp. 1–25.

7.   J.M. Creed, *The Gospel According to St. Luke* (London: Macmillan Co. Ltd, 1953), p. 140. Against this view, see E. Franklin, *Christ the Lord: A Study in the Purpose and Theology of Luke-Acts* (London: SPCK, 1975), p. 141, who states that Luke's introduction of the Samaritans is not meant primarily to emphasize the later universality of the Gospel.

8.   Fitzmyer, *Luke* I, p. 166.

9.   Enslin, 'The Samaritan Ministry and Mission', *HUCA* 51 (1980), pp. 29–38, 31.

10.   Enslin, 'Luke and the Samaritans', *HTR* 36 (1943), pp. 277–97.

Jesus never had any contacts with the Samaritans or Gentiles. The travel section is Luke's own composition and is intended as 'a deliberate and conscious answer to Mt. 10:5'. Luke places the story of the Samaritan rejection at the beginning of this section, as 'a conscious and deliberate parallel to the rejection at Nazareth' in the beginning of the 'Galilean ministry'. Enslin considers the sending out of the Seventy an artificial section, composed freely by Luke from Mk 6:6-13, 30 and the Matthaean parallel as 'a deliberate counterfoil to the sending out of the twelve in Galilee' (9:1-6).[11] Likewise, the parable of the Good Samaritan and the healing of the Samaritan leper are not historical, but Luke himself has framed and produced them from other stories taken from Mk 12:28-34 and 1:40-45 respectively.

Before evaluating the above claim of Enslin, the tradition seemingly common to the Gospel of Luke and John is to be noted here. Of a few stories where both Luke and John offer parallel traditions, the account of Jesus' contact with the Samaritans in John 4 will throw further light on the possible origin and availability of the Samaritan traditions in Luke-Acts. J.A. Bailey considers that all the Samaritan material in the Gospel is pre-Lukan and goes back to Jesus himself.[12] He argues that both Luke and John encountered the Samaritan traditions, not in Samaria but in Jerusalem.[13] This is because all the traditions common in Luke and John concern events occurring in or near Jerusalem. Also, the Samaritan traditions in Luke focus on Samaria from a Jerusalem point of view, and were preserved in Jerusalem.[14] Bailey's view is based on the fact that both the Gospel of Luke and John are in their structure oriented towards Jerusalem.[15] Bailey further suggests how these related but independent traditions on the Samaritans, which originated in Jerusalem, came to Luke. Assuming that Luke being the companion of Paul gathered these traditions while he was with Paul in Jerusalem and Caesarea (Acts 21:8-18),[16] Philip and his daughters would have served as the main source of infor-

---

11. Enslin, 'Luke', p. 282.

12. Bailey, *The Traditions Common to the Gospels of Luke and John* (NovTSup.7; Leiden: E.J. Brill, 1963), p. 104; Hahn, *Mission*, p. 30.

13. Bailey, *Traditions*, pp. 109-11.

14. Bailey, *Traditions*, p. 109, refers to the mention of priests in Lk. 17:11-19 as evidence for a Jerusalem origin. Also, the tradition of Jesus' rejection in Samaria in Lk. 9:51-56 was preserved in Jerusalem, 'for such a story was hardly likely to have been treasured by Samaritan Christians' (p. 109). However, Bailey fails to explain the story of the Good Samaritan in Lk. 10:25-37, as this tradition was hardly likely to have been preserved and treasured in Jerusalem.

15. Bailey, *Traditions*, pp. 109-10: the traditions of the anointing of Jesus, of the last supper and last discourse, of the hearing before Annas, of the charge against Jesus that he claimed to be the king, of the two disciples going to the grave, of Jesus' resurrection appearances to the eleven in Jerusalem, and the geographical scheme of the gospels as moving towards Jerusalem suggest their general orientation towards Jerusalem.

16. Bailey, *Traditions*, p. 111, does not rule out the possibility that the traditions may have been transmitted to Luke by Silas of Jerusalem as they travelled together for a while (Acts 15:22-18:17).

mation. Philip's traditions originated in Jerusalem and came with him via Samaria to Caesarea. Bailey goes further to suggest that these traditions, before they reached Luke, had been 'written down for catechetical or liturgical purposes, and no one would have been more likely to possess such than a missionary like Philip'.[17] Bailey's suggestion of the possible Jerusalem origin of the Philip story is questionable as the missionary success of the Hellenists like Philip could hardly have been preserved in Jerusalem, given their expulsion from the city and the clash with the Jewish Christians (Acts 8:1). However, this does not rule out his claim for the availability of a possible tradition for Luke on the Samaritan mission of Acts as well as on the Samaritan material in the Gospel of Luke.

The views of Enslin and Bailey on the origin of the Samaritan material in the Gospel contradict each other. It could be that both Jesus' journey through Samaria and the Samaritan material may be pre-Lukan rather than a Lukan construction and that Luke might have used this traditional Samaritan material which was available to him rather than producing new stories.[18] Luke could be employing traditional materials on the Samaritans and reworking them to show that the Samaritans must become part of the *Heilsgeschichte* of God. Also, it is not merely a journey that brings Jesus to Samaria, but rather the theological concern of Luke and his special materials on Samaria and the Samaritans, either traditional or redactional or both, that Jesus is in Samaria. When Luke deviates from other Synoptics in bringing Jesus through Samaria, instead of Perea, the Samaritan references are not incidental, but deliberate and with a significance. The intention of Luke, as will be argued below, is to legitimize the Samaritans and to show that Jesus anticipated a mission to the hostile land of Samaria and that his mission transcends the ethnico-religious boundaries. Just as the mission of the Seventy symbolizes a world-wide mission, the Samaritan references would indicate the anticipation of a Samaritan mission. Now, we will turn to the Samaritan references in the Gospel of Luke.

4.2.1. *Jesus and the Samaritan Rejection (9:51-56)*
The beginning of Jesus' journey to Jerusalem (v.51) is marked with his rejection by a Samaritan village, which resembles his rejection at Nazareth at the beginning of his Galilean ministry (4:16-30 cf. 9:22).[19] The phrase 'set his face' (τὸ πρόσωπον ἐστήρισεν, v. 51 cf. v. 53) echoes the LXX usage: 'Hazael set his face to go up to Jerusalem' (2 Kgs 12:17); 'I have set my face

17. Bailey, *Traditions*, p. 111.
18. Bailey, *Traditions*, p. 104; against this view, see R. Bultmann, *The History of the Synoptic Tradition* (New York: Harper & Row, 1963), pp. 25–6.
19. A. Plummer, *A Critical and Exegetical Commentary on the Gospel According to St. Luke* (ICC; 4th edn.; Edinburgh: T. & T. Clark, 1913), pp. 261–2; Tannehill, *Luke-Acts* I, p. 230; Fitzmyer, *Luke* I, p. 827; Böhm, *Samarien*, p. 214.

like a flint' (Isa. 50:7); 'Son of Man, set your face towards Jerusalem' (Ezek. 21:2). C.A. Evans has taken this phrase to mean Jesus hinting at the impending judgement upon Jerusalem.[20] This is because he thinks that this phrase in the Old Testament often connotes a sense of judgement, especially as it is frequently found in Ezekiel, 'the most likely source from which Luke derived this language'.[21] Also, since Luke makes use of Ezekiel in other passages to depict Jerusalem's fate, says Evans, the expression in Lk. 9:51 could not only owe its form to Ezekiel, but also contribute to the passage a sense of the ominous. Further, Jesus' favourite self-designation 'Son of Man' which appears at Lk. 9:44 is also the most common designation for Ezekiel.[22] Therefore, according to Evans, the expression 'he set his face' is most likely a hint at Jerusalem's impending judgement. But C.H. Giblin, who thinks that Jesus does not explicitly pronounce judgement on Jerusalem until Lk. 19:41-45, claims that Lk. 9:51 does not have a sense of judgement on Jerusalem, rather it only depicts Jesus' intention to go to Jerusalem.[23] If Jesus intended to pronounce judgement on Jerusalem, says Giblin, it would be strange for Luke to mention that the Samaritans opposed Jesus for this intention (v.53).

If the expression at Lk. 9:51 is intended to hint at a judgement upon Jerusalem, then it does not explain why the Samaritans opposed Jesus knowing that he is going to pronounce judgement upon their rival city, as both Evans and Giblin rightly agree. It is ambiguous whether Luke intended to convey at Lk. 9:51 a sense of judgement upon Jerusalem. What is clear from the passage is the disciples' intention to pronounce judgement, not upon Jerusalem, but upon the Samaritans. Taking the text as a whole, it is not only Ezekiel who is alluded to here but also Elijah who took vengeance upon Samaria (v.54; cf. 2 Kgs 1:9-14). Also, the context suggests Jesus' dealing with his rejection by the Samaritans, not by Jerusalem. Luke's intention here is to show that the Samaritans are spared from judgement for their rejection of Jesus. It stands contrary to the instruction given in the mission of the Seventy that rejection of Jesus' messengers will result in condemnation (Lk. 10:12-15). If the expression 'he set his face' reflected prophetic hostility or doom,[24] then it would signify Jesus' prophetic warning of judgement upon Jerusalem

---

20.   C.A. Evans, '"He Set His Face": A Note on Luke 9,51', *Bib* 63 (1982), pp. 545–8; *idem*, '"He Set His Face": Luke 9,51 Once Again', *Bib* 68 (1987), pp. 80–4.

21.   C.A. Evans, 'Luke 9,51 Once Again', p. 81. For Luke's use of Ezekiel, compare Lk. 19:41-44; 21:20-24 with Ezek. 4:1-3; 21:6-12, 22; Lk. 23:31 with Ezek. 20:45-21:7. Evans thinks that the most likely passage that Luke has in mind for the expression in Lk. 9:5 is Ezek. 21:2-6.

22.   For example, Ezek. 4:1; 8:17; 20:45; 21:2, 6, 12.

23.   C.H. Giblin, *Destruction of Jerusalem according to Luke's Gospel: A Historical-Typological Model* (AnBib 107; Rome: Pontifical Institute, 1985), p. 32; also, Marshall, *Luke*, p. 405.

24.   So also Drury, *Tradition*, p. 67.

over against the Samaritans. The phrase could also imply 'fixedness of purpose' in time of difficulty or danger,[25] thus signifying Jesus' determination to go to Jerusalem through Samaria that symbolizes animosity and rivalry.

Jesus sent messengers on ahead of him (ἀπέστειλεν ἀγγέλους πρὸ προσώπου αὐτοῦ, v. 52a). This expression may allude to Mal. 3:1 (cf. Mal. 3:23) and the ministry of John the Baptist, in their ministry of going ahead and preparing for Jesus (ἑτοιμάσαι αὐτῷ, v. 52b). That the messengers went to a Samaritan village (καὶ πορευθέντες εἰσῆλθον εἰς κώμην Σαμαριτῶν, v. 52b) stands contrary to Jesus' saying in Mt. 10:5b (καὶ εἰς πόλιν Σαμαριτῶν μὴ εἰσέλθητε) and therefore could be seen as a deliberate counterpart to the prohibition to enter any town of the Samaritans. Luke says that the Samaritans did not receive Jesus (οὐκ ἐδέξαντο αὐτόν) because 'his face was set toward Jerusalem' (τὸ πρόσωπον αὐτοῦ ἦν πορευόμενον εἰς Ἰερουσαλήμ, v. 53). Here, the rejection of Jesus by the Samaritans is directly linked with his being on his way to Jerusalem. On a literary level, the rejection points to the failure of the Samaritans to act in accordance with the divine purpose of God to be accomplished in Jesus. But on a historical level, the hostility of the Samaritans towards the disciples fits what we know of their continuing opposition towards the Jews and the Jerusalem Temple in the first century CE and would also recall the story of Josephus of the incident in 51 CE at Ginae, a village on the border between Galilee and Samaria (*BJ*, II, 232-235, cf. *AJ*, XX, 118-123). The rhetoric for Luke is that the Samaritans, who are most often characterized negatively in some Jewish circles, are worthy of sparing from judgement, and are legitimate candidates for the reception of salvation and that Jesus anticipates a mission to them.

When the Samaritans rejected Jesus, his disciples James and John, surnamed the 'sons of thunder' (Mk 3:17), ask Jesus whether he would like them to call down fire from heaven to destroy the Samaritans (ἀναλῶσαι αὐτούς, 9:54b). Some manuscripts add the gloss 'even as Elijah did'[26] to v. 54, which probably evokes the incidents in 2 Kgs 1:9-14 where Elijah called down fire from heaven on certain groups of people in Samaria. The word ἀναλῶσαι means, 'to do away with something completely by using up', and it refers to destruction or annihilation.[27] Jesus reverses the attitude of the disciples and refuses to act as Elijah acted on Samaria. Also, Jesus does not allow them to act like Elijah or John the Baptist in pronouncing judgement (Lk. 3:9, 17; cf. 12:49-53; 17:29), though their ministry resembled that of the latter in preparing for him. It seemed legitimate to the disciples that Samaritans should be destroyed for refusing to accept Jesus and the messengers. The

---

25. Plummer, *Luke*, p. 263.

26. A, C, D, K, W, X. The gloss is absent in P45, P75, ℵ, B, and other major Alexandrian witnesses.

27. F.W. Danker (ed.), *A Greek-English Lexicon of the New Testament and other Early Christian Literature*, 3rd edn. (Chicago: The University of Chicago Press, 2000), p. 67.

action of Elijah who is also mentioned earlier in Lk. 9 gives them a scriptural sanction for their motif.[28] As mentioned above, Jesus tells the Seventy that those who reject his messengers will be condemned (Lk. 10:12-15). What is important to note is that Jesus does not show any resentment or feelings of revenge against the Samaritans, rather he rebukes the disciples. For him, the Samaritans do not become objects of destruction, rather his contact with Samaria conveys their legitimacy to become part of his divine plan and his anticipation of a mission to them. According to some witnesses,[29] Jesus says, 'You do not know what kind of spirit you are of, for the Son of man did not come to destroy people's lives, but to save them' (vv. 55–56). Verse 56 seems to be a variant of Lk. 19:10.

Scholars have observed the influence of the Elijah story of the Old Testament (2 Kgs 1:1-2:6) on the narrative of Lk. 9:51-56. T.L. Brodie, for example, has done an analysis of both the passages and suggested that Luke in 9:51-56 employed the literary procedure of rhetorical imitation of Elijah's departure for Jordan.[30] Luke, says Brodie, intending to provide a deliberate literary explanation that Jesus surpasses the Old Testament Elijah, adapted and emulated the Elijah text and integrated basic traditional or historical elements about Jesus. Brodie's analysis of the above passage is useful for understanding Luke as an ancient writer with literary techniques and rhetorical devices, but it does not succeed in suggesting a picture of Jesus in the context of the Lukan narrative. The literary ability of Luke in 9:51-56 is not merely an attempt to portray Jesus surpassing the Old Testament Elijah as Brodie concludes, but is rather preparing the ground for the yet to come mission in Acts 8:4-25, as is shown later in this chapter.

Four relevant points of contact between 9:51-56 and the Elijah story for our purpose are to be noted here. (1) The ἀναλήμψις (assumption) in 9:51 referring to Jesus' ascension is also an allusion to Elijah's assumption into heaven.[31] (2) Jesus goes to Jerusalem through Jordan to be finally taken up into heaven as Elijah in his last journey passed Jordan to be finally taken up

---

28. Tannehill, *Luke-Acts* I, p. 230; Green, *Luke*, p. 406.

29. For example, D, F, K, M. The additions in Lk. 9:55-56 are absent from such early witnesses as P45, P75, ℵ, A, B, C, L, W, Δ, X, Ψ and suggest that they are glosses derived from extraneous sources. The statement in v. 56 echoes 19:10. See B.M. Metzger, *A Textual Commentary on the Greek New Testament* (London: United Bible Societies, 1971), p. 148.

30. Brodie, 'The Departure for Jerusalem (Luke 9,51-56) as a Rhetorical Imitation of Elijah's Departure for the Jordan (2 Kings 1,1-2,6)', *Bib* 70 (1989), pp. 96–109; Evans, 'Elijah/Elisha Narratives', pp. 80–2.

31. The verb ἀναλαμβανεσθαι is used in 2 Kgs 2:9-11; Sir. 48:9, and 1 Macc. 2:58 to refer to the assumption of Elijah and in Sir. 49:14 to that of Enoch. C.F. Evans, 'Central Section', pp. 37–53, suggests that Luke's usage of ἀναλήμψις in 9:51 is an indication of his knowledge of the apocalyptic literature, *The Assumption of Moses*. Based on his knowledge and usage of the Old Testament, especially the frequent references and allusion to Elijah, it is more likely to say that Luke has the LXX reference to the ἀναλήμψις in his mind. So A. Denaux, 'Old Testament Models for the Lukan Travel Narrative: A Critcal Survey', in C.M. Tuckett (ed.), *The Scriptures*

into heaven. But the difference for Luke is that unlike the other Synoptics, the last journey of Jesus is to be fulfilled not through Jordan, but through Samaria (and then Jericho). (3) The indignation of James and John, wishing to call down fire from heaven upon the Samaritans, would recall the story of Elijah calling down fire from heaven to consume the captain and his fifty in 2 Kgs 1:9-14. (4) As the Elijah motif appears in the rejection story of the Galilean ministry (Lk. 4:16-30), it also reappears in the Samaritan rejection of Jesus (Lk. 9:54). Thus, in many ways, Elijah serves as a type of Jesus, but with regards to retaliation he is an antitype.

In Lk. 9:51-56, words like συμπληροῦσθαι, ἀναλήμψις, πορευόμαι, and Jerusalem have special significance for Luke. The word συμπληροῦσθαι means, 'to take place at the timely moment'.[32] As in Acts 2:1, it refers to a 'significant new beginning'.[33] It is the fulfilment of divine purpose to be carried out in Jerusalem. The term ἀναλήμψις can mean both ascension and death.[34] In the present context, it could refer to the various stages by which Jesus passed from the earthly to the heavenly realm, rather than to a single incident.[35] It refers to both Jesus' ascension to heaven (Acts 1:2, 11, 22) and the events of the passion and resurrection prior to his taking up. If the Elijah story had influenced the Lukan narrative in Lk. 9:51-56, then it is likely that the reference to ἀναλήμψις is an allusion to Elijah's assumption into heaven.[36] The word πορευόμαι indicates Jesus' movement towards the goal, which is

---

in the Gospels (Louvain: Leuven University Press, 1997), pp. 271–305, who says that Luke relates more to the LXX than to a remote non-biblical text (p.277); see also, *Test. Levi* 18; *Ps. Sol.* 4:20; 4 Esr.VI:26; VIII:20; XIV:49.

32.   Danker (ed.), *Greek-English Lexicon*, p. 959.

33.   Goulder, *Luke: A New Paradigm*, 2 vols. (JSNTSup.30; Sheffield: JSOT Press, 1989), vol. II, p. 460. The verb occurs in the New Testament only at Lk. 8:23; 9:51 and Acts 2:1.

34.   Danker (ed.), *Greek-English Lexicon*, p. 67.

35.   J.M. Creed, *The Gospel According to St. Luke* (London: Macmillan Co. Ltd, 1953), p. 141. Scholars are variously divided as to what ἀναλήμψις actually means in Lk. 9:51, whether it refers to the ascension or the death of Jesus or both. M. Miyoshi, *Der Anfang des Reiseberichts Lk. 9:51-10:24: Eine Redaktionsgeschichtliche Untersuchung* (AnBib 60; Rome: Biblical Institute, 1974), pp. 8–9, regards the word as referring primarily to Jesus' ascension, and then also to the events of passion and resurrection. Marshall, *Luke*, p. 405, suggests that it refers primarily to the 'death of Jesus' and alludes also to Jesus being 'taken up' to God in the ascension. G. Friedrich, 'Lukas 9:51 und die Entrückungschristologie des Lukas', in P. Hoffmann, *et al.* (eds) *Orientierung an Jesu: Festschrift für J. Schmid* (Freiburg: Herder, 1973), p. 52, claims that the word refers not to the ascension, but to Jesus' death. There are others, like Creed, who argue that ἀναλήμψις in Lk. 9:51 means not only death or ascension, but Jesus' entire transit to the Father via burial, resurrection, and exaltation; so Fitzmyer, *Luke* I, p. 828; R. Maddox, *The Purpose of Luke-Acts*, ed. J. Riches (Edinburgh: T. & T. Clark, 1982), p. 156; C.F. Evans, *Saint Luke*, pp. 435–6; Kingsbury, *Conflict in Luke: Jesus, Authorities, Disciples* (Minneapolis: Fortress Press, 1991), p. 55; Johnson, *Luke*, p. 162; Parsons, *Departure*, pp. 130–3; Tannehill, *Luke-Acts* I, p. 229; Green, *Luke*, p. 403.

36.   Cf. 2 Kings 2:9-11; Sir. 48:9; 1 Macc. 2:58.

Jerusalem.[37] In the present context, it has the connotation of 'proceeding towards death'.[38] That the word πορεύομαι has the sense of going to one's death is seen from Lk. 22:22.[39] In 18:31-33 Jesus tells his disciples that his journey to Jerusalem is a journey towards his death. Jerusalem in Luke is the city of Jesus' destiny – the place of his death and the post-resurrection appearances.[40]

In light of the above, it is reasonable to say that for Luke the ἀνάλημψις of Jesus is to be fulfilled also through his contact with the Samaritans, symbolizing an anticipation of a mission to them. As it was often thought, it is not after his resurrection that Jesus finds a mission to Samaria significant (Acts 1:8), rather Luke includes Samaria as part and parcel of the fulfilment of Jesus' mission before he reaches Jerusalem (Lk. 9:51-56). As mentioned above, the theme of Jesus' passion, resurrection, and ascension is interwoven into the reference to Samaria and the Samaritans. It is highly probable that Luke deliberately shaped his traditional materials in Lk. 9:51-56 to provide a coherent picture of Jesus' anticipation of a successful Samaritan mission in Acts 8:4-25. These two episodes project like a deliberate literary activity conveying a main theme that the hostile Samaritans would become the subjects of receiving the promise of the heavenly fire of the Holy Spirit rather than becoming the objects of the consuming fire of destruction and death. As Jesus' sending of messengers εἰς κώμην Σαμαριτῶν (Lk. 9:52) symbolizes the anticipation of the Samaritan mission, the Jerusalem apostles' sending of Peter and John to ἡ Σαμάρεια (Acts 8:14), as shown later in our study, functions as a legitimation of the Samaritan mission.

4.2.2. *Jesus and the Good Samaritan (10:29-37)*
The Good Samaritan story, which follows the mission of the Seventy, is portrayed as an answer given by Jesus to the lawyer's question of who his neighbour was.[41] It appears that Luke unskilfully combines two different

---

37.   Lk. 4:30; 13:22, 33; 17:11; 19:28; 22:22.

38.   J.H. Davies, 'The Purpose of the Central Section of St.Luke's Gospel', in F.L. Cross (ed.), *SE* 2 (TU 87; Berlin, 1964), pp. 164–73, 166.

39.   Danker (ed.), *Greek-English Lexicon*, p. 853; See M. Black, *An Aramaic Approach to the Gospels and Acts* (Oxford, 1967), p. 302.

40.   See Lk. 9:22, 31, 44, 51; 18:31-34; J.A. Weatherly, *Jewish Responsibility*, p. 55, refers to Jerusalem as the site and agent of Jesus' death (Lk. 13:31-35); J. Gnilka, *Die Verstockung Israels: Isaias 6, 9-10 in der Theologie der Synoptiker* (SANT 3; Munich: Kösel, 1961), pp. 132–40, considers Jerusalem as 'the point of departure of salvation' rather than 'the central point', because the last opportunity for Israel to repent, which the very ministry of Jesus represented, closes at the walls of the city as Jesus goes to Jerusalem to die. Parsons thinks that Jesus' journey to Jerusalem is couched in a promise-fulfilment schema. Though his journey is finished, neither his ἀνάλημψις nor his ἔχοδος has been fulfilled.

41.   For various interpretations of this story, see G. Sellin, 'Lukas als Gleichniserzähler: Die Erzählung vom barmherzigen Samariter (Lk. 10:25-37)', *ZNW* 65 (1974), pp. 166–89; *ZNW*

accounts in 10:25-37: that of the scribe (vv. 25-28) found in Mk 12:28 and Mt. 22:35, and the parable of the good Samaritan (vv. 30-37). But this entire story may be considered as authentic, and belonging to the special Lukan source.[42] (1) There is no proof that the scribe in Luke is the same as that of Mark and Matthew. Was there only one scribe in Israel who could enter into discussion with Jesus on such matters?[43] (2) In Mark and Matthew, the incident happens in Jerusalem, and in the days preceding the passion. (3) The content is different: the scribe in Mark and Matthew asks Jesus which is the greatest commandment and it is a theological question. The scribe in Luke asks Jesus what he should do to inherit eternal life and it is a practical question.[44] To this we can add another difference: in Mark and Matthew, it is Jesus who answers the question, but in Luke, it is the lawyer who answers by the summation of the Law of loving God and loving one's neighbour.

That it is a Samaritan, the enemy of the Jews, that Jesus uses in his parable, further introduces his interest in the Samaritans and their works of love within the salvific plan of God. Jesus agrees with the lawyer that the double love commandments that 'you shall love God' (Dt. 6:5) and 'you shall love your neighbour as yourself' (Lev. 19:18) are important for inheriting eternal life.[45]

The traveller from Jerusalem that Jesus refers to is introduced as 'a certain man' (ἄνθρωπός τις, v. 30),[46] and can possibly be a Jew.[47] In his journey to Jericho, he fell in with robbers and was stripped, beaten up, abandoned and left half dead.[48] The first man in the triad is the priest, and his action, in that he saw the wounded man and passed by on the opposite side of the road (καὶ ἰδὼν αὐτὸν ἀντιπαρῆλθεν, v. 31), speaks of his unwillingness to help the

---

66 (1975), pp. 19–60; J.D.M. Derrett, 'Law in the New Testament: Fresh Light on the Parable of the Good Samaritan', *NTS* 10 (1964–65), pp. 22–37; D.E. Oakman, 'Was Jesus A Peasant? Implications for Reading the Samaritan Story (Lk. 10:30-35)', *BTB* 22 (3, 1992), pp. 117–25; P.F. Esler, 'Jesus and the Reduction of Intergroup Conflict: The Parable of the Good Samaritan in the Light of Social Identity Theory', *BI* 8 (4, 2000), pp. 325–57.

42.   Godet, *Luke* II, p. 37; Marshall, *Luke*, pp. 440–1. Fitzmyer, *Luke* II, p. 877 considers it to be part of Luke's special source.

43.   Godet, *Luke* II, pp. 37–8.

44.   So C.F. Evans, *Saint Luke*, p. 463.

45.   See the discussion in E.P. Sanders, *Judaism*, pp. 195–6.

46.   See ἄνθρωπός τις in Lk. 12:16; 14:2, 16; 15:11; 16:1; 19:12; 20:9; Acts 9:33; ἀνὴρ (δέ) τις in Lk. 8:27; Acts 5:1; 8:9; 10:1; 13:6; 16:9; 17:5; 25:14.

47.   However, neither Jesus nor Luke gives any hint on identifying the ethnic-religious identity of the wounded man. It is rhetorically kept anonymous so that the hearers are challenged to act as neighbours to those in need irrespective of ethnic-religious questions. It is possible that a Jewish audience would assume the injured man to be a Jew, since he is not described otherwise (Tannehill, *Luke*, p. 184). So Plummer, *Luke*, p. 286.

48.   For a description of the road to Jericho, see *BJ*, IV, 474; II, 228-30; Strabo, *Geography*, XVI, 2.41.

wounded man and show love to people of his own race.[49] His action could find justification for the fear of defiling himself by contact with a dead body (Lev. 21:1-3; Num. 5:2c; 19:11-13, 16).[50] Likewise, the Levite came upon that place ([γενόμενος] κατὰ τὸν τόπον ἐλθών, v. 32) and passed by on the other side.[51] It should be noted here that the priests were a separate class in Jewish society and therefore they were counted legitimate people.[52] The priests and the Levites were part of the Temple cult and had a privileged status in Jewish society. However, they fail to keep the commandment to 'love your neighbour as yourself'.[53]

Over against the priest and the Levite, Jesus uses a Samaritan (Σαμαρίτης) as the third one in the triad.[54] Placing the Σαμαρίτης at the beginning of the sentence (v.33) emphatically makes the contrast between him and his Jewish counterparts. It could also provide a contrast between the allegedly religious 'apostate' and the 'law-abiding' clerics. The Samaritan's compassion towards the injured man speaks through his actions. He came to where the man was (ἦλθεν κατ' αὐτόν, v. 33a), saw him (ἰδών, v. 33b), had compassion (ἐσπλαγχνίσθη, v. 33c),[55] went to him (προσελθών, 34a), bandaged his

49.   The priest was going down the road (κατέβαινεν, v. 31), possibly leaving Jerusalem after performing his religious duties in the Temple. The two prepositions, παρά = 'alongside of', and ἀντί = 'on the other side', signify the action of the priest (and the Levite) in keeping away as far as possible from the injured man.

50.   The action of the priest could be seen in various ways. For example, he must have passed by for fear of the robbers. The fear of defilement and its consequences could justify his action (Fitzmyer, *Luke* II, p. 887). Derrett, 'Good Samaritan', pp. 24–9, is of the opinion that had the priest wished to help the wounded man, he could have found justification for defiling himself. So Tannehill, *Luke*, p. 183. See the reference to exceptions to ritual defilement in *m. Nazir* 7:1.

51.   Some MSS have γενόμενος in the beginning of the clause (p45, A, C, D, E). For Luke's use of γενόμενος κατά, see Acts 27:7, meaning, 'being present at'.

52.   Böhm, *Samarien*, p. 252; Lev. 21:16-24; 1QS.1:8-9; 5:1-4; Jeremias, *Jerusalem*, pp. 207–8.

53.   Cf. D. Wenham, *The Parables of Jesus: Pictures of Revolution* (London: Hodder & Stoughton, 1989), p. 158.

54.   In 1882 Halevy, *Revue des Etudes juives*, IV, (1882), pp. 249–58 (quoted in Creed, *Luke*, p. 152) argued that it is unlikely that Jesus singled out a Samaritan as a model of a good deed for his behaviour is incompatible with his relationship to the Jews in the first century. Therefore, the contrast is not with a 'Samaritan', but with an 'Israelite' (layman). The conversion of 'Israelite' into a 'Samaritan' is because of the universalism of the Gospel of Luke. So also Creed, *Luke*, p. 152; C.G. Montefiore, *The Synoptic Gospels*, vol. 2 (New York: Ktav, 1968), p. 467. This speculation of scholars rules out both the meaning and significance of the parable for Luke's readers. As in Lk. 9:51-56, the parable should be understood against the historical situation of the relationship between Jews and the Samaritans. Also, as Marshall, *Luke*, p. 446, suggests, the story provides a Palestinian local colour that points towards a historical context.

55.   Danker (ed.), *Greek-English Lexicon*, p. 938, uses this to mean, 'have pity, feel sympathy'. The noun form is σπλάγχνον, meaning 'the inward parts of a body', and refers to 'the bowels' which are the seat and source of love, sympathy and mercy. Cf. Mt. 9:36; 14:14; 18:27; 20:34; Mk 1:41; 6:34; 8:2; 9:22; Lk. 7:13; 15:20. Johnson, *Luke*, p. 173, makes the note that this is the emotion attributed to Jesus in Lk. 7:13. Also, M.J.J. Menken, 'The Position of σπλαγξνίζεσθαι and σπλάγξνα in the Gospel of Luke', *NovT* 30 (1988), pp. 107–14.

wounds (κατέδησεν τὰ τραύματα αὐτοῦ, v. 34b), poured on oil and wine (ἐπιχέων ἔλαιον καὶ οἶνον, v. 34c), mounted him on his donkey (ἐπιβιβάσας δὲ αὐτὸν ἐπὶ τὸ ἴδιον κτῆνος, v. 34d), took him to an inn (ἤγαγεν αὐτὸν εἰς πανδοχεῖον, v. 34e), took care of him (ἐπεμελήθη αὐτου, v. 34f), paid his costs (ἔδωκεν δύο δηνάρια, v. 35a), and was willing to reimburse extra expenses (προσδαπανήσῃς, v. 35b).[56] The Samaritan, who has no religious privilege before the eyes of the Jewish community, stands out in contrast to the Jewish religious leaders of his day as a representative of showing compassion and of keeping the law that transcends the socio-religious and ethnic boundaries.[57] The lawyer's answer, 'he that showed the act of mercy upon him' (ὁ ποιήσας τὸ ἔλεος μετ' αὐτου, v. 37a) is worth noting, as he avoids using the name Σαμαρίτης. His description, instead of using the name, could reflect the ethnic and religious hatred of some Jews towards the despised Samaritan.[58] It may also highlight that the act of compassion that the Samaritan showed towards the needy, is what determines what it means to be a neighbour.[59]

It is not certain whether Jesus is trying to show the Samaritans as the 'guardians of the Law' as they claim their name שׁמרים means. But it is obvious that Jesus links the inheritance of eternal life with the act of mercy shown by the Samaritan, and marks him out as a 'paradigm for Christian conduct'.[60] The expression, πορεύου καὶ σὺ ποίει ὁμοίως (v.37) is a command to follow the Samaritan who is the 'moral exemplar',[61] thereby Jesus approves the Samaritan's action and his sharing of the ultimate blessings of God's kingdom. Thus, over against the Jerusalem priesthood and its

---

56. A few scholars have noticed the striking similarities of the parable with 2 Chr. 28:15. J.M. Furness, 'Fresh Light on Luke 10:25-37', *ExpTim* 80 (1968–69), p. 182, draws attention to Lampe's suggestion that the Lukan parable of the Good Samaritan contains 'curious verbal echoes of 2 Chr. 28:15'; Derrett, 'Good Samaritan', pp. 22–3. According to Furness, the 'similarities can hardly be accidental' and Jesus draws on a well-known ancient episode of Jewish history and turns it to his purpose (p.182). Based on this striking parallelism between 2 Chr. 28:15 and Lk. 10:25-37, Furness claims that 'it is now impossible to believe with Halevy that Jesus could hardly have made a Samaritan the hero of His tale' (p. 182). The parable is by way of an *argumentum ad hominem*. The scribe is answered by reference to a story, which he already knew very well and he is left to think that, 'the answer to his question is to be found in the texts on which he is supposed to be an authority' (p. 182). Furness may be right that the lawyer already knew the story, as the lawyer asked Jesus the question of who his neighbour was in order to justify himself.

57. Fitzmyer, *Luke* II, p. 884; Marshall, *Luke*, pp. 445–6; Also A.J. Hultgren, *The Parables of Jesus: A Commentary* (Grand Rapids: Wm.B. Eerdmans Publishing Co., 2000), p. 98.

58. Cf. Sir. 50:26; 2 Macc. 6:2; Plummer, *Luke*, p. 289; Jeremias, *Parables*, p. 205; *contra*, Arndt, *St. Luke*, pp. 291–92; Nolland, *Luke* II, p. 596.

59. Brad H. Young, *The Parables: Jewish Tradition and Christian Interpretation* (Peabody, MA: Hendrickson Publishers, 1998), pp. 117–18; Hultgren, *Parables*, p. 99.

60. Fitzmyer, *Luke* II, pp. 883–4.

61. Johnson, *Luke*, p. 173; Marshall, *Luke*, p. 445; Hultgren, *Parables*, p. 94. Fitzmyer, *Luke* II, p. 883, makes the comment that the parable 'supplies a practical model for Christian conduct with radical demands and the approval/rejection of certain modes of action' and thus

cultic and religious system, Jesus approves the works of the hated and despised Samaritan who became a neighbour to the needy one, and presents him as the one who inherits eternal life.[62] The parable is in harmony with the general teaching of the Gospel that 'righteousness and salvation are not the exclusive privilege of the Jews'.[63] The Samaritan who is an outsider becomes the subject of showing compassion by being a neighbour to the needy.[64] It undoubtedly portrays the legitimacy of the Samaritan's action and in general the anticipation of their acceptance of the gospel.

4.2.3. *Jesus and the Grateful Samaritan (17:11-19)*

The story of the Grateful Samaritan begins with the Lukan note that Jesus is travelling to Jerusalem.[65] Luke mentioned earlier in 9:51-52 Jesus' contact with and his rejection by the Samaritans, but in 17:11, he is apparently still on the border between Galilee and Samaria.[66] In this story of the healing, the ten lepers call Jesus 'Master' (ἐπιστάτης) and they cry for 'mercy' (v.13).[67]

considers the story as an 'example'. There are, however, scholars who raise objections to treating this parable as an 'example' story for various reasons. For these different views, see Nolland, *Luke* II, pp. 590–1. (1) The christological interpretation of the parable implies: that Christ is the wounded man (Danielou; Gollwitzer, Binder); the link between the words 'neighbour' and 'shepherd' implies Jesus as the Good Shepherd (Gerhardsson). (2) The attempt to emphasize the kingdom of God as the main concern of the parable (Funk, Crossan). (3) The claim that the story is told from the perspective of the needs of the wounded man rather than from the perspective of the Samaritan, Nolland, *Luke* II, pp. 590–1, 594–5. All the above views fail to take into account the important presence of the Samaritan in the parable and Luke's special interest in the Samaritans. Also, in the light of the expression, πορεύου καὶ σὺ ποίει ὁμοίως (v. 37), it seems likely that Jesus asks the lawyer to go and practise just the way the Samaritan acted.

62.　J.M. Arlandson, *Women, Class and Society in Early Christianity: Models from Luke-Acts* (Peabody: Hendrickson Publishers, 1997), p. 177: 'Jesus exalts a man from the unclean and degraded class at the expense of men from among the religionists'.

63.　Plummer, *Luke*, p. 285.

64.　G.W. Forbes, *The God of Old: The Role of the Lukan Parables in the Purpose of Luke's Gospel* (JSNTSup.198; Sheffield: Sheffield Academic Press, 2000), pp. 69–70.

65.　Many scholars consider this story as a Lukan creation. For example, Enslin, 'Luke', p. 293; H.D. Betz, 'The Cleansing of the Ten Lepers (Luke 17:11-19)', *JBL* 90 (1971), pp. 314–28; W. Bruners, *Die Reinigung der zehn Aussaetzigen und die Heilung des Samariters Lk 17,11-19* (Stuttgart: Katholisches Bibelwerk, 1977), pp. 297–306. But Bultmann, *Synoptic Tradition*, p. 33, maintains that the story is a hellenised version of the story of the healing of a leper in Lk. 5:12-14 produced by the early church, and that the story is pre-Lukan, though v. 19b ('your faith has saved you') is a Lukan addition. Also R. Pesch, *Jesu ureigene Taten?* (Freiburg: Herder, 1970), pp. 130–1; Bailey, *Traditions*, p. 104, takes the story to be pre-Lukan and v. 19b as a Lukan addition. As Marshall rightly says, the Samaritan reference is a significant feature of the Lukan special source, and it cannot be doubted as a different version of another story (*Luke*, p. 649).

66.　See the discussion of διὰ μέσον Σαμαρείας καὶ Γαλιλαίας (v.11) in Marshall, *Luke*, p. 650; Fitzmyer, *Luke* II, pp. 1149–51.

67.　The christological title, 'Master' (ἐπιστάτης) attributed to Jesus by the lepers occurs only in Luke's Gospel (5:5; 8:24, 45; 9:33, 49; 17:13). So it may seem redactional. But in all other instances where this title occurs, it is used only by Jesus' disciples to address him.

Jesus' command to show themselves to the priests is reminiscent of the story of the leper in Mk 1:40-44; Mt. 8:1-4 and Lk. 5:12-14. If Jesus meant when he sent the lepers to show themselves to the priests that they would officially get their place in society,[68] then he is not only concerned about their personal physical healing, but their social status in the community as well. Like the compassionate Samaritan in the parable, Jesus singles out a grateful Samaritan in this story of healing. It appears in the outset that the Samaritan neglects the requirements set out in Lev. 13 and comes to Jesus bypassing the legal procedures, which were to be carried out by the clerics. Though his action seems to contradict the claim of the Samaritans that they are the keepers of the Law, Jesus accepts his action as legitimate. More than the legal observances, which were to be conducted by the clerics, Jesus focuses on what the Samaritan did himself to acknowledge his healing.

The effect of the healing of the Samaritan that he came back to Jesus, praising God in a loud voice (ὑπέστρεψεν μετὰ φωνῆς μεγάλης δοξάζων τὸν θεόν, v. 15) resembles the effect of the healing ministry of Philip that (πνεύματα ἀκάθαρτα βοῶντα φωνῇ μεγάλῃ ἐξήρχοντο, Acts 8:7a) the evil spirits came out of many with a loud voice. In both instances, the Samaritans experienced wholeness of life, forgiveness of sins and fullness of faith. Their acceptance of Jesus brought them to restoration and enabled them to participate in the blessings of the Kingdom. The expression that 'he fell on his face at his feet and thanked him' (καὶ ἔπεσεν ἐπὶ πρόσωπον παρὰ τοὺς πόδας αὐτοῦ εὐχαριστῶν αὐτῷ, v. 16) signifies the Samaritan's acknowledgement of Jesus' authority expressed through his actions, and not merely addressing him as ἐπιστάτης like the other nine did.

That the Samaritan praised God for his healing suggests that he was not a pagan but someone who knew God.[69] As Evans has noted, the central point is 'Jesus' commendation, not of faith as such, nor of thanksgiving in general, but of the genuine piety of a non-Israelite manifesting itself in gratitude'.[70] Jesus marks out a Samaritan from the Jews whose faith and act of worship brought him to the experience of salvation, which is beyond the merely physical cure.[71] Here, as Bailey suggests, Luke underlines that Jesus' attitude

68. Marshall, *Luke*, p. 651. Ravens, *Restoration*, p. 86, considers the possible influence of Isa. 56:6-7 on Luke's use of the term ἀλλογενής on the lips of Jesus and then suggests that 'the Samaritan glorifies God, not only for his healing, but also because he has been acknowledged as a member of Israel by Jesus the Jew'. This view seems unlikely because there is no indication in the text that the Samaritan leper went to the Jerusalem Temple. His immediate need was not to get an acknowledgement from a Jew and become a member of Israel, but to be healed of leprosy, which would in turn give him a status in the society.

69. Böhm, *Samarien*, p. 268.

70. C.F. Evans, *Saint Luke*, p. 623; Also Marshall, *Luke*, pp. 649, 652; Fitzmyer, *Luke* II, p. 1151. But Johnson, *Luke*, p. 260, takes it to mean the positive example of the Samaritan leper's faith.

71. Marshall, *Luke*, p. 649; Betz, 'Cleansing', p. 315; Tannehill, *Luke-Acts* I, p. 119.

towards the Samaritans was not different from his attitude towards the Jews, and that as the saving power of Jesus healed the Samaritan physically and also granted him forgiveness, a Samaritan is at no disadvantage as over against Jews.[72] In this story there seems to be a 'double dismissal' of the Samaritan by Jesus and a pattern of 'two-stage soteriology'.[73] The Samaritan leper is dismissed already with the other nine lepers (v. 14) and he is again dismissed after his return (v. 19). The first dismissal is of those lepers who were healed in body only, but the second is of the Samaritan who was converted to the Christian faith.

Scholars have noted that this narrative has implicit reference to the Temple. For example, according to Green, 'Luke's Christology reaches impressive heights as he presents Jesus in the role of the temple'.[74] The description of what the leper received is a metaphor for redemption.[75] Going to the priests and offering sacrifices clearly involves journeying to a temple. The act of giving praise to God also invokes images of the Temple cult.[76] Dennis Hamm takes the narrative to mean that the Samaritan finds the presence of Jesus as the proper place to worship.[77] The word 'foreigner' is also understood in the context of worship in the Jerusalem Temple where it was found on the inscriptions forbidding outsiders from entry into the Temple area of Jews.[78] The longstanding rift between Jews and Samaritans on the question of the place of worship, as Jerusalem Temple versus Mount Gerizim, is broken down as the Samaritan found a worship place at the feet of Jesus.

4.3. Theological Significance of the Lukan Narratives

In all the three narratives discussed above, it becomes clear that Luke intends to show Jesus as anticipating a Samaritan mission and legitimizing the Samaritans over against their counterparts. Luke presents Jesus' contact with the Samaritans as a necessary agenda in his last journey to Jerusalem, anticipating a Samaritan mission. In the narrative of the Samaritan rejection, the sending out of the messengers symbolizes the role of Elijah and John the Baptist in preparing for the eschatological salvation foretold in the Old Testament. Here, Jesus finds it important to include the Samaritans in his plan of death, resurrection and ascension. Though the Samaritans reject Jesus, the

---

72. Bailey, *Traditions*, pp. 104–5.
73. Betz, 'Cleansing', p. 315.
74. Green, *Luke*, p. 626.
75. Nolland, *Luke* II, p. 847; Green, *Luke*, p. 627.
76. Green, *Luke*, p. 621.
77. Dennis Hamm, 'What the Samaritan Leper Sees: The Narrative Christology of Luke 17:11-19', *CBQ* 56 (1994), pp. 273–87.
78. *BJ*, II, 417.

action of James and John in pronouncing judgement upon the Samaritans is condemned. In the last two narratives, the ethnicity of the Samaritans is highlighted at the end and thus, it surprises the hearers and overturns the popular prejudice against the Samaritans. In both the stories, a Samaritan is singled out for legitimate action over against the 'law-abiding' Jews. Both the compassionate Samaritan and the grateful Samaritan go against the piety of the clerics and obey what the Law requires of them. The former fulfils the demands of the Law by becoming a neighbour to the wounded and surpassing the socio-religious and ethnic boundaries; the latter fulfils the demands of the Law by loving God, praising and giving him thanks. This portrait of the Samaritans neutralizes their earlier refusal of Jesus in Lk. 9:53. Over against their counterparts, Jesus legitimizes the action of the Samaritans.

Two words need to be given special attention: neighbour (πλησίον, 10:29, 36), and foreigner (ἀλλογενής, 17:18). πλησίον in the LXX means 'one who has dealings with someone' and is used primarily to refer to a fellow Israelite (Lev. 19:18).[79] The term also means 'one who is near or close by'.[80] By using a Samaritan in the role of a neighbour, Jesus transcends the racial and religious boundaries and puts both the Jews and the Samaritans together as fellow Israelites. In doing so, he overturns the prejudices of the first-century Jews towards the Samaritans and calls for a radical change that the Jews should treat the Samaritans as their own people. As to ἀλλογενής, it is evident from various Jewish texts that the foreigner was excluded from the Israelites and was not given any socio-religious privileges with the people of God.[81] The Samaritan who is a religious outcast experiences the healing and salvation promised to the Jews. In the light of the Old Testament commandment to love one's neighbour and to extend the love even to foreigners (Dt. 10:19 cf. Mt. 5:43-48), the Samaritans in Luke are found obedient to the Law.[82] Probably Luke had in mind their claim that they are the 'keepers of the Law'. In all the above incidents relating to the Samaritans, their religiosity as well as their ethnicity is undoubtedly identified and highlighted. Luke shows that the Samaritan becomes both a neighbour (πλησίον) by crossing the ethnic boundary and an insider, though previously

---

79.   G. Friedrich (ed.), *TDNT* VI, pp. 312–14; see Lev. 19:18, where the word רֵעַ (πλησίον), 'neighbour' refers to the fellow members of Israel, though the command to love is also extended towards the גֵּר (alien) in Dt. 10:19.

80.   Danker (ed.), *Greek-English Lexicon*, p. 830; see *BJ*, VII, 260; *Ps.Sol.* 8:10; Test.Iss. 5:1-2.

81.   Büchel, 'ἀλλογενής', *TDNT* I, pp. 266–7; Num. 1:51; 3:10; 18:7; 16:40; Lev. 22:10 cf. 1 Esd. 9:7-15. This term is found on the barrier in the Temple at Jerusalem to forbid foreigners entering beyond the court of the Gentiles: μηδένα ἀλλογενῆ εἰσπορεύεσθαι (see Schürer, *History* II, p. 272). Josephus does not employ this word, but uses only ἀλλόφυλος (*BJ*, V, 194; *AJ*, XI, 306), and ἀλλοεθνεῖς (*AJ*, IX, 291; XV, 417).

82.   Literally and theologically this view holds good, if the proposal of C.F. Evans that the 'Central Section' in the Gospel is based on Deuteronomy ('Central Section', pp. 37–42) is accepted.

an outsider (ἀλλογενής), by breaking the religious barrier. And, the Lukan stories do not share any antagonism against the Samaritans, instead they portray them positively and legitimize their behaviour. Thus, the legitimacy of ethnicity and religiosity of the Samaritans in the Lukan narratives stands in sharp contrast with that of the Jews.

It is highly significant to note that in all the references to Samaria and the Samaritans in Luke-Acts, Luke always tries to link them with 'Jerusalem'. In Lk. 9:51-53, Jerusalem is referred to as Jesus' destination; in 10:30, the Samaritan ministers to the Jew coming from Jerusalem, though Jericho was his destination; in 17:11, Jerusalem is again mentioned as the destination of Jesus; in Acts 1:8 and 9:31, Samaria is mentioned along with Jerusalem and Judaea; and in 8:4-25, Jerusalem and the Jerusalem apostles are connected with Samaria and the Samaritans. It is made clear again and again in the Gospel that the goal or destination of Jesus is Jerusalem. In achieving this goal, the Lukan Jesus found it necessary to pass through a hostile land of the Samaritans with the principle of 'no retaliation'. And he also presented a merciful and sacrificial Samaritan traveller who broke the socio-religious boundaries of the Jewish-Samaritan relationship. Finally, he healed a Samaritan leper who is a 'religious alien' and a grateful one and made him whole. Here Luke is probably intending to show that Jesus is not only breaking the existing hostility between Samaria and Jerusalem and ameliorating the gap between them, but also preparing the ground for the yet to come Samaritan mission. In other words, Jesus is legitimizing the Samaritans and anticipating a Samaritan mission.

It is also significant that Luke never uses the word 'Gerizim' over against 'Jerusalem'. The fact that Samaria, not Gerizim, stands in sharp contrast with Jerusalem in the above-mentioned references would probably suggest that the activity of the Lukan Jesus and the early church is intended to break, not merely the religious antagonism between the Jews and the Samaritans, but the long-standing socio-political hostility between them. In this sense, as argued in the previous chapter, the Samaritan mission is to start from the ancient, Old Testament city of Samaria (Acts 8:5), a place where the Samaritans originally lost their socio-political and ethnic-religious identity as a people of God.

Another point to note here is the suggestion of Ravens, who says that for Luke the Samaritans play a vital role in the restoration of the unity of Israel which would reunite both the northern and the southern kingdoms as one nation, a unity that had once existed under King David.[83] He goes further

---

83. Ravens, *Restoration*, pp. 72–106. The idea of the reunification of the northern and southern kingdoms has already been suggested by John Bowman in his interpretation of 'other sheep' (Jn 10:16) based on Ezek. 37:22-24 that as the two sticks marked 'Ephraim' and 'Judah' are to be tied together as one stick, the Samaritans as the descendants of Ephraim (other sheep) are to be reunited with the Jews (Bowman, *Samaritan Problem*, p. 61). Also see the discussion by Bauckham, 'The Restoration of Israel in Luke-Acts', in J.M. Scott (ed.), *Restoration: Old*

to say that it was Luke's 'concern for Israel's restoration that made the Samaritans vital to his thesis'.[84] However, this concern of Luke does not exclude first of all his intention to portray Jesus' anticipation of a mission to the Samaritans. In other words, Luke has the Samaritans not only for some theological reasons such as the restoration of Israel, but also for literary and historical reasons that even as a hostile group in relation to Jerusalem, they are a legitimate people to come into the program of the promised salvation. Ravens stretches the evidence too far to find allusive associations in the Gospel with Samaritan theology. It is probable that Luke had known the Samaritan claim of their northern descendants, but it is unlikely that he wrote the Gospel with Samaritan perspectives. It may be that Luke is trying to unite the Samaritans with the Jews, but in light of his overall portrait of the Samaritans, he considers the Samaritans as they are, who would act in obedience to the Law and have a legitimate place in the history of God's plan of salvation.

To summarize the arguments thus far, there is no Samaritan mission as such in the Gospel of Luke, as neither Jesus nor the disciples have a mission to the Samaritans, but rather only a preparation for or an anticipation of the yet to come Samaritan mission of Acts 8:4-25. Jesus did not send the messengers to Samaria to conduct a Samaritan mission. Even when the apostles received the mission charge from the risen Lord to go to Samaria (Acts 1:8), Peter and John finally ended up there not to preach initially but to pray for the converts. For Luke, the historical Jesus *anticipates* a Samaritan and Gentile mission while the risen Jesus authorizes it. In his Gospel, Luke is trying to portray the anticipation of a Samaritan mission before that of the Gentile mission. This sequence in his Gospel may not be an anachronistic portrayal of what is presented in Acts.

4.4. *The Theme of Preparation and the Promise of Salvation.*

There are many instances in Luke's Gospel where the theme of salvation is closely associated with a divine summons to prepare for Jesus' coming or with a divine act of preparation, which further illuminates Jesus' intention to send his messengers to Samaria to prepare for him (Lk. 9:51-52). Firstly, Lk. 1:17: 'And he will go on before him (προελεύσεται ἐνώπιον αὐτοῦ) to turn the hearts of the fathers to their children ... *to make ready* for the Lord a people *prepared* (ἐτοιμάσαι κυρίῳ λαὸν κατεσκευασμένον)'. This is a prophecy of Gabriel to Zechariah about John's role to go before the Lord as inspired by

---

Testament, Jewish, and Christian Perspectives (JSJSup.72; Leiden: Brill, 2001), pp. 435–87, 470–71.

84. Ravens, *Restoration*, p. 99.

the same power as Elijah was.[85] It seems that here different texts are woven together by Luke.[86] The two verbs ἑτοιμάζω and κατασκευάζω, used to mean 'prepare', appear together here in 1:17, whereas they are used separately in 3:4 and 7:27. Κατασκευάζω means 'to form' or 'to fashion'. The task of John is to prepare a remnant that would respond to God.[87] The idea of a 'prepared people' would probably have come from Isa. 43:7 and 2 Sam. 7:24 which convey the restoration of Israel based on Davidic Messianic expectations. In light of this Davidic messianism which is made explicit in Lk. 1:32-35 (cf. Acts 1:6), Luke shows from the beginning of his Gospel the fulfilment of the eschatological expectation of the salvation and redemption of Israel.

Secondly, Lk. 1:76-77: '... *for you will go on before the Lord to prepare his ways* (προπορεύσῃ γὰρ ἐνώπιον κυρίου ἑτοιμάσαι ὁδοὺς αὐτοῦ, v. 76), to give his people the knowledge of *salvation* (γνῶσιν σωτηρίας τῷ λαῷ αὐτοῦ, v. 77a) through the forgiveness of their sins (ἐν ἀφέσει ἁμαρτιῶν αὐτῶν, v. 77b)'. This text is the second part of the 'Benedictus' (1:68-79) of Zechariah sung on the birth of his son John which describes the role of John as the forerunner of the Messiah and the messianic activity of Jesus.[88] The language and the content of this text echoes Mal. 3:1 (τὸν ἄγγελόν μου καὶ ἐπιβλέψεται ὁδὸν πρὸ προσώπου μου) and Isa. 40:3 (ἑτοιμάσατε τὴν ὁδὸν κυρίου).[89] John's activity 'to go before the Lord to prepare his way' conveys a messianic and salvific hope in the context of the first century BCE and CE,[90] but this role appears to have been ascribed to the Elijah figure.[91] The terms 'knowledge of salvation' and 'forgiveness of sins' together indicate that the inward experience of salvation is possible only through the forgiveness of people's sin,[92] and that the real enemy is not the aggressive neighbour but the sins of the people.[93]

Thirdly, Lk. 2:30-32: 'For my eyes have seen your *salvation which you have prepared* (τὸ σωτήριόν σου ὃ ἡτοίμασας) in the sight of all people, a light for revelation to the Gentiles and for glory to your people Israel'. These verses are the praises of Simeon, often called 'Nunc Dimittis', which shows the fulfilment of the promise that he would see the Messiah before his death. It is in the Jerusalem Temple that he holds the baby Jesus and proclaims God's

---

85. Marshall, *Luke*, p. 59.
86. Mal. 3:1, 23-24; Sir. 48:10. See Brown, *Birth*, p. 277; Marshall, *Luke*, pp. 58–9.
87. Bock, *Luke* I, p. 91.
88. See the discussion on the form and structure of the text in S. Farris, *Hymns of Luke's Infancy Narratives* (JSNTSup.9; Sheffield: JSOT Press, 1985), pp. 127–32. Marshall, *Luke*, p. 87, regards the hymn as a unitary composition.
89. See also 1 QS.8:13-14; 9:19-20.
90. Ford, *Enemy*, p. 27.
91. See Mal. 2:7, 3:1; 4:5-6.
92. Marshall, *Luke*, p. 93.
93. M. Coleridge, *Birth of the Lukan Narrative* (JSNTSup.88; Sheffield: JSOT Press, 1993), p. 121.

design of salvation for both Jews and Gentiles. Here the word 'prepare' is
used of God and thus it means God has 'ordained' blessings[94] or established
Jesus for salvation. If this text is taken against the background of the Old
Testament prophecies,[95] the salvation which God brought in Jesus transcends
the socio-religious and ethnic boundaries of Israel, and therefore carries a
universal significance.[96] The neuter form σωτήριον, which would mean both
salvation and the one who brings salvation,[97] occurs only three times in Luke-
Acts (Lk. 2:30; 3:6; Acts 28:28), all in the context of the universal mission
of Jesus. It is significant to note that the reference to the universal revelation
of God's σωτήριον at the end of the Lukan narrative in Acts 28:28 reminds
the reader of the proclamation of σωτήριον in the beginning of the Gospel
in 2:30.[98] The phrase 'light for revelation to the Gentiles' echoes Isa. 49:6 and
is significant for the mission of Paul in Acts 13:47. It should also be noted
that in Acts 26:17-18, Paul defines his mission in terms of the mission of Jesus
as presented in Lk. 4:18-19. Likewise, as Jesus' ministry brought release or
forgiveness (ἀφέσις) as mentioned in the beginning and end of the Gospel of
Luke (4:18; 24:47, cf. Isa.58:6), Peter brings the same message of release or
forgiveness (ἀφίημι) and repentance to Simon Magus in the narrative of the
Samaritan mission in Acts (8:22-24).

Luke says that Simeon has been looking for the 'consolation' (παράκλησιν,
2:25) of Israel. If the term παράκλησιν refers back to its usage in Jer. 38:9,
where God promises to lead Ephraim back, then Simeon's oracle could
probably indicate that the salvation of God is extended to bring back
Ephraim, from whom the Samaritans claimed to originate.[99] Simeon's oracle

---

94.   Plummer, *Luke*, p. 68.

95.   Isaiah 40:5; 42:6; 46:13; 49:6; 52:10; 55:5; 60:5; 61:9.

96.   The plural λαῶν in Lk. 2:31 can probably refer to both the Jewish and Gentile racial
groups, and thus is a universal reference. See Marshall, *Luke*, p. 120; Farris, *Hymns*, p. 148;
Brown, *Birth*, pp. 439–40; Fitzmyer, *Luke* I, p. 428; Tannehill, *Luke-Acts* I, p. 42; Nolland, *Luke*,
p. 120. According to C.F. Evans, *Saint Luke*, p. 217, v. 31 need not mean the Gentiles' participation in the salvation, but only that they will behold it. G.D. Kilpatrick, 'Laoi at Lk. 2:31 and
Acts 4:25, 27', *JTS* 16 (1965), p. 127, also denies the idea that the Gentiles would experience
the salvation and says that the plural λαῶν in v. 31, like the singular in Acts 4:25, 27, does not
refer to Gentiles, but to 'all the tribes of Israel'. However, it is obvious that the reference to ἐθνῶν
in v. 32 does not preclude the idea of a Gentile participation in salvation (for 'seeing God's
salvation', cf. Isa. 40:5; 52:10; Ps.98:2; Lk. 3:6; I QH.5:12 identifies salvation with a person).
Also, the term 'all mankind' (all flesh) in 3:6 emphasizes the universalism of the Gospel. In the
light of other texts under discussion and the Elijah-Elisha references in 4:25-27, it is clear that
the salvation is extended beyond Israel and the Gentiles will receive its blessings.

97.   Marshall, *Luke*, p. 120.

98.   See Isa. 40:5; cf. Ps. 67:2; J. Dupont, 'The Salvation of the Gentiles and the Theological
Significance of Acts', in *The Salvation of the Gentiles* (New York: Paulist, 1979), pp. 14–16,
thinks the use of σωτήριόν in Acts 28:28 is a deliberate inclusion that reflects its use in Lk. 2:30.
Cf. L.C.A. Alexander, 'Reading Luke-Acts from Back to Front', in J. Verheyden (ed.), *Luke-Acts*,
pp. 419–46, 435–6.

99.   Ravens, *Restoration*, p. 45.

states that the Gentile mission is fundamental to Luke's view of God's relationship to Israel,[100] and that the salvation of God is a public disclosure and the Gentiles will participate in it. However, in the context of Ephraim, the Samaritans make legitimate candidates for the anticipation of this salvation.

Fourthly, Lk. 3:4-6: '*Prepare* the way of the Lord (ἑτοιμάσατε τὴν ὁδὸν κυρίου, v. 4). ... And all mankind (flesh) will see God's *salvation*' (καὶ ὄψεται πᾶσα σὰρξ τὸ σωτήριον τοῦ θεου, v. 6). Here Luke, unlike Mark, has a lengthy quotation from Isa. 40:5 to include the verse 'all mankind will see God's *salvation*'. It emphasizes what Simeon refers to in 2:30-32 of seeing God's salvation. Here the phrase 'all mankind' (flesh), like the term 'all people' in 2:31, conveys the idea that both the Jews and the Gentiles must participate in salvation in order to fulfil the Isaianic prophecy (40:5). Here John has to play a significant role towards its fulfilment. It also throws light on the significance of πᾶσα σάρξ in the quotation from Joel 2:28 in Acts 2:17. It is worth noting that the Gentile mission in Luke is not a supplement to the promises to Israel as Franklin thinks,[101] rather it is the central message of the eschatological expectation which is promised in the Old Testament and brought in through the person and work of Jesus such that 'all flesh' will see God's salvation.

Fifthly, Lk. 7:27: 'I will send my messenger ahead of you, who will *prepare* your way before you' ('Ἰδοὺ ἀποστέλλω τὸν ἄγγελόν μου πρὸ προσώπου σου, ὃς κατασκευάσει τὴν ὁδόν σου ἔμπροσθέν σου). In light of what Jesus responded to the crowd concerning John the Baptist by quoting Mal. 3:1,[102] it is obvious that in Luke, John plays the role of Elijah *redivivus* and becomes the precursor of Jesus.[103] For Luke, Jesus in his Galilean ministry ascribes to John the function of preparing the way for him (cf. Acts 13:24). This role

---

100. Tiede, 'Glory to Thy People Israel', *SBL 1986 SP*, (ed. Kent H. Richards; Atlanta: Scholars Press, 1986), pp. 148–51.

101. Franklin, *Christ*, pp. 212–13, n.48, says that there is in fact little interest in the Gentiles for their own sake, and that it is part of Luke's interest in the fulfilment of the promises made to Israel. It is obvious that trying to keep the special status given to the Jews, Franklin undermines the universalism of the Gospel and the Lukan interest in the Samaritans and Gentiles.

102. Luke uses the second person pronoun 'you' in the citation of Mal. 3:1, instead of 'me'. According to Fitzmyer, *Luke* I, p. 674, this shift is the result of an adaptation of the Old Testament text to the gospel tradition. Johnson, *Luke*, p. 123, considers the text to be a mixed citation from LXX Ex. 23:20 and Mal. 3:1. Cf. Mk 1:2; Mt. 11:10.

103. Fitzmyer, *Luke the Theologian*, pp. 107–10; also Tannehill, *Luke-Acts* I, p. 24. C.T. Ruddick, 'Behold, I Send My Messenger', *JBL* 88 (1969), pp. 381–417, while arguing for the Pentateuchal background of Mark's Gospel, emphasizes the literary dependence of the theme of 'sending messengers ahead to prepare the way' in Mk 1:1-8 on the narrative of Jacob sending messengers ahead to his meeting with Esau in Gen. 31-32. However, it is not certain whether Mark and the other evangelists are formulating a parallel event from the Genesis story of Jacob, but the evangelists are narrating an event which Jesus and early Christianity regarded as the fulfilment of the Old Testament prophecy (Mal. 3:1).

of preparing the way seems to shift from John to the disciples as Luke begins his Samaritan episode in 9:51 as shown below.

The texts discussed above would convey that 'to go before the Lord to prepare the way' speaks of God visiting (ἐπισκέπτομαι, 1:78) his people with the long-expected eschatological salvation which was now inaugurated in Jesus, whose way culminates in the final destiny of ἔξοδος and ἀναλήμψις in Jerusalem.[104] The act of preparation and salvation which is to be extended beyond the people of Israel first takes its explicit step in the account of Jesus sending messengers ahead of him to Samaria (Lk. 9:51-56). Jesus, in this salvific visitation of God, anticipates Samaria and the Samaritans as part and parcel of God's eschatological fulfilment of salvation. Comparing the association between the themes of salvation and the divine summons of preparing for Jesus' coming with the Samaritan episode in 9:51-56 – he sent messengers ahead of him ... *to prepare* for him (ἀπέστειλεν ἀγγέλους πρὸ προσώπου αὐτοῦ. Καὶ πορευθέντες εἰσῆλθον εἰς κώμην Σαμαριτῶν ὡς ἑτοιμάσαι αὐτῷ) – would indicate that the preparation for which Jesus sent his disciples on ahead to Samaria carries the theme of salvation reaching the Samaritans. They are not sent to Samaria in order to make preparations for Jesus' 'hospitality' as Marshall thinks.[105] This theme can be further supported by the phrase that introduces the mission of the Seventy in 10:1 – 'the Lord sent them on ahead of him' – conveying the reality that the disciples are in a mission which brings the salvation of God prophesied in the Old Testament. In 9:51, 'the sending of messengers ahead' is not introduced by a prophetic quotation, but becomes part of the narrative. Further more, the use of the word ἀγγέλους in 9:52 to refer to human beings is unusual in Luke-Acts, being otherwise employed only at 7:24, 27 with reference to Jesus' discourse about John.[106] In both 9:51-53 and 10:1, Jesus sends his disciples, as God sent John the Baptist, to prepare the way for the yet to come mission that extends the boundaries of Judaism. Therefore, the Samaritan episode in 9:51-56 very well portrays that the eschatological expectation has reached the Samaritans and a mission to them would bring the salvation of God. This mission is anticipated in the Gospel, which is to be fulfilled in Acts 8:4-25. Therefore, the statement of Franklin that Luke's introduction of the Samaritans is not meant primarily to emphasize the later universality of the Gospel stands invalid.[107]

---

104. Lk. 19:41-44; cf. 1:68, 78; 7:16. A. Denaux, 'Old Testament Models', pp. 271-99, links the theme of ἔξοδος (Lk. 9:31) with the ὁδός of Jesus (1:76, 3:4; 7:27).

105. Marshall, *Luke*, p. 406.

106. Tannehill, *Luke-Acts* I, p. 229.

107. Franklin, *Christ*, p. 141.

4.5. Conclusion

To summarize the thrust of this chapter: (1) The Lukan Jesus neither engages in nor sends his disciples on a Samaritan mission, but only anticipates it. (2) In his Gospel, Luke has Jesus anticipating the salvation and healing of outsiders crossing social, religious, geographical and ethnic boundaries. (3) In all the three Samaritan episodes in the Gospel, Jesus was breaking the then existent hostility between Samaria and Jerusalem, and overturning the prejudices against the Samaritans, which were prevalent in some Jewish circles. (4) Luke tries to show that Jesus himself portrayed the Samaritans as legitimate candidates worthy of receiving salvation and restoration, thus paving the way for the church's acceptance of the Samaritans. (5) Since Luke presents the Samaritans favourably and has Jesus treat them positively, it is plausible that partly Luke is engaging in polemic against the Matthaean prohibition of the mission to the Samaritans (Mt. 10:5b) and that partly he is preparing the ground for the yet to come Samaritan mission in Acts 8. (6) When Luke begins the first Samaritan episode by saying that Jesus 'sent messengers ahead of him … to prepare for him' (9:52), it would probably mean that the long-expected eschatological salvation inaugurated in the coming of Jesus must have reached the Samaritans also and that they will participate in the messianic salvation of God.

Part III

THE PORTRAIT OF THE SAMARITAN MISSION IN ACTS

Chapter 5

STRUCTURAL ANALYSIS OF ACTS 8:4-25

5.1. Introduction

In the previous parts of our study, we have argued that Luke's stories of Jesus' contact and affinity with the Samaritans function as a device to show the anticipation of a Samaritan mission and to legitimate their identity and role in the context of first-century Jewish-Samaritan relationships. The subsequent chapters of the book explore the portrait of the Samaritan mission through structural and textual analyses of Acts 8:4-25. This chapter will attempt literary and structural analyses of two narratives: the Samaritan Rejection of Jesus (Lk. 9:51-56), and the Samaritan Mission of Philip and the apostles (Acts 8:4-25), including a syntagmatic and paradigmatic reading of the texts and integrating the approach of Barthes and the actantial analysis of Greimas. This study will reveal that Luke is employing a literary and rhetorical strategy of *Structural-Functional reversalism* in order to present the successful mission to the Samaritans narrated in Acts 8:4-25. This will help us to discover the significance for the theology and narrative of Luke of the method of *reversalism* he employs in these accounts.

5.2. Analysis of Luke 9:51-56

5.2.1. Sequential Analysis

The episode in Lk. 9:51-56 comprises a combination of both story or narrative (vv. 51-53, 55-56) and discourse or direct speech (v.54), where the direct speech may be seen as a fairly discrete enclave within the narrative. The narrative starts with the story of Jesus sending messengers to Samaria and then it changes to a direct speech as the intended performance of James and John is introduced. The story and the discourse are combined with a connecting link: 'when the disciples James and John *saw* this, they asked' (v.54a). The story does not have a meaning by itself, but only within the system of relationships with other elements in the text. Therefore, the narrative structure of Lk. 9:51-56 will be treated as a whole.

The narration starts with a chronological reference in v. 51a: 'as the time approached for him to be taken up to heaven'. It denotes the *symbolic code* of Jesus' ascension and exaltation, which is an upward movement.[1] It has a structural significance since at the close of the narrative (v.54) James and John wish to call fire down from heaven, which is a downward movement. At the surface level, the word 'fire' (πῦρ) with the association of the verb 'to destroy' (ἀναλῶσαι) in v. 54, signifies a destructive force as also is the case in Lk. 17:29 where the destruction of Sodom is mentioned (Gen. 19:15-29) and also as in 2 Kgs 1:10,12, where Elijah calls down fire on the men of King Ahaziah in Samaria. But, in the event of Lk. 9:54, this is not realized but appears to function as a *symbolic* code for the descent of the Holy Spirit upon the Samaritans which is yet to be administered later by the Jerusalem-based disciples.[2] Against this upward and downward movement (vertical), the forward journey of Jesus through Samaria (horizontal) is set in perspective. The upward movement of Jesus is in tension with the disciples' intention to bring down fire from heaven, and the forward movement of Jesus is in tension with the Samaritans' opposition to him. And, thus the upward movement and the downward movement in the narrative are *symbolic codes* and function antithetically in the text.

The geographical references and their sequences given in the narrative are significant: Jerusalem (v.51b) – a village of the Samaritans (v.52) – Jerusalem (v.53) – another village (v.56). It creates a significant opposition between Jerusalem and Samaria and corresponds to temporal, socio-religious, and cultural barriers. To go to Jerusalem, Jesus intended to go through Samaria and pass through the village of the Samaritans, thereby bridging the gap of relationship between the two places.

The text explicitly mentions the reason for the Samaritans' refusal of Jesus: 'He was heading towards Jerusalem' (v.53). If this information were not given in the text, one would think of the action of the Samaritans as a direct attack on Jesus and his disciples. It also implies certain knowledge on the part of the reader of the attitude of the Samaritans towards Jerusalem,

---

1.   According to Barthes, *S/Z: An Essay*, trans. Richard Miller (Oxford: Basil Blackwell, 1974), pp. 18–20, every narrative is interwoven with multiple codes and he outlines five such codes. (1) *The hermeneutic code*: it refers to any term in a story that is not explained and, therefore, exists as an enigma for the reader only to be disclosed at the end of the story. (2) *The proairectic code*: it refers to any action that creates interest or suspense on the part of a reader or viewer. This is a code of sequence that implies a further narrative action. (3) *The semic code*: it refers to any element in a text that points to a special meaning by way of connotation (e.g. femininity, age). (4) *The symbolic code*: it refers to the code that structures the text and organizes semantic meanings by way of antitheses or by way of mediations between antithetical terms. (5) *The cultural code*: it refers to any element in a text that points to shared knowledge and common sense.

2.   Luke often uses the term 'fire' in order to symbolize the Holy Spirit. See for example, Lk. 3:16-17; Acts 2:1-4. F.W. Danker, *Jesus and the New Age: A Commentary on St. Luke's Gospel* (Philadelphia: Fortress Press, 1988), p. 209, comments that the 'fire' of Jesus is of a different order (cf. Lk. 12:49).

and thus functions as the *cultural code*.[3] This additional information, which is according to Barthes a 'counter text',[4] indicates the legitimacy of the Samaritans' opposition, which in turn reflects their long-standing socio-religious, cultural and political rivalry towards the Jews and their Temple in Jerusalem.

The association of certain words and phrases in the narrative anticipates (symbolizes) significant events which are to take place in Acts. For example, as noted above, the ascension of Jesus takes place in Acts 1:11, where the words ἀναλημφθείς and πορεύομαι used for the action of Jesus correspond to those in Lk. 9:51. The expression ἐν τῷ συμπληροῦσθαι τὰς ἡμέρας in v. 51 is again used in Acts 2:1 in connection with the day of Pentecost. This is further identified by its association with other words like 'fire' (πῦρ), and 'from heaven' (ἀπὸ τοῦ οὐρανοῦ) in both Lk. 9:54 and Acts 2:2-3. In all the three narratives (Lk. 9:51-56; Acts 1:11 and 2:1-4) Jerusalem is set in focus. Therefore, various elements in Lk. 9:51-56 symbolize the ascension of Jesus, the day of Pentecost and the coming of the Holy Spirit, which all takes place in Acts 1-2.

5.2.2. Actantial Analysis

For this analysis I shall employ a form of structuralist exegesis using Greimas' actantial analysis. In Greimas' approach, as we already noted in Chapter 1, each narrative structure includes six distinct elements: sequence, syntagm, statement, actantial model, function, and actant.[5] They are explained as follows.

(1) Sequence: a narrative structure is made up of a series of sequences (narrative programmes). Each sequence consists of correlated sequences (initial and final sequences), topical sequences and sub-sequences. Initial correlated sequences involve the carrying out of a social order (contract or mandate) which is disrupted for any reason. Then topical sequences are intro-duced to re-establish the original contract by providing the hero with the necessary helper by which he is able to carry out the disrupted sequence. The sub-sequence is that which caused the disruption of the initial sequence, which is also called 'the villainy'. (2) Syntagms: each sequence consists of three syntagms (a succession of smaller narrative elements). They are the contract syntagms (expressing the establishment of the contract either in the initial sequence or in the topical sequence), the disjunction/conjunction syntagms (expressing the movements of those who receive a contract) and the performance syntagms (expressing the carrying out of the contract). (3) Narrative statements: each syntagm is made up of narrative statements,

---

3.   See n. 1 above for explanation.
4.   Barthes, 'Acts X-XI', p. 117.
5.   See Patte, *Structural Exegesis?*, pp. 37–52; Greimas, *Structural Semantics, passim.*

which are structural units, and each structural unit is a combination of 'functions' and 'actants' (other elements of the structure). (4) Functions: they are the various verbs of action (predicates of the class of 'doing') and present themselves in binary oppositions (Arrival – Departure; Conjunction – Disjunction; Mandating – Acceptance/Refusal; Confrontation/Affrontment; Domination – Submission; Communication – Reception; Attribution – Deprivation. (5) Actants: actants are not actors of the manifestation, but a role or status whose quality is to be the subject of, or participant in, a constant action.[6] (6) Actantial model: an actantial model displays the function of each actant in the narrative. In Greimas' method of actantial analysis, the actants are divided into three opposing pairs: (1) SUBJECT versus OBJECT, (2) SENDER (*Destinateur*) versus RECEIVER (*Destinataire*), and (3) HELPER (*Adjuvant*) versus OPPONENT (*Opposant*). They are portrayed diagrammatically as shown below.

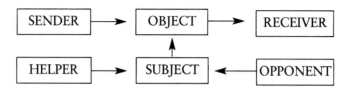

We will now place Lk. 9:51-56 into the opposing pairs of the actantial model. In the narrative structure of the story, the initial correlated sequence is manifested in the account of Jesus sending messengers ahead of him to Samaria to prepare for him. This sequence of the disciples is interrupted by the Samaritans, as they oppose the disciples. The hostility and the refusal of the Samaritans constitute 'the villainy', a sub-sequence, which explains how the sequence of the disciples has been interrupted. Thus the initial sequence is 'suspended', but the actants in the positions of SENDER (Jesus), OBJECT (Reception of Jesus) and RECEIVER (Samaritans) remain as potential actants.

To re-establish the possibility of fulfilling the original initial sequence, a topical sequence is introduced in the rest of the narrative. This is to provide an adequate HELPER for the actors of the initial sequence. This topical sequence, which according to Propp is the 'main test',[7] expresses how a hero is mandated to fulfil the topical contract which would help him to re-

---

6.   An *actant* is one of the two components of a statement; the other component is *function*. Dan O. Via, Jr, 'Parable and Example Story: A Literary-Structuralist Approach', *Bib* 1 (1974), pp. 105–33, says that the 'actant is perhaps usually a personal character, but it may be an object, institution, feeling, disposition, condition etc. Grammatically, it corresponds to the present participle' (p.107).

7.   See F. Jameson, *The Prison House of Language: A Critical Account of Structuralism and Russian Formalism* (Princeton: Princeton University Press, 1972), pp. 64–9; Patte, *Structural Exegesis?*, p. 38.

establish the initial sequence. The sub-sequence, which according to Propp is the 'qualifying test' and 'glorifying test',[8] describes how the hero acquires some help, for instance, a magical object, with which he is able to solve the interruption. In our narrative, we have one topical sequence: 'When the disciples James and John saw this, they asked' (v.54a). Seeing the hostility and refusal of the Samaritans, James and John felt they were mandated to do something to neutralize the hostility. The contract syntagm is manifested in the words, 'when the disciples James and John saw this'. The acceptance of this contract is expressed by the phrase, 'they asked'. When a contract is accepted by an actor, he takes the actantial position of the SUBJECT. Thus James and John are instituted into the actantial position of SUBJECT and are invested with a modality of *volition* to carry out a specific mandate. However, they are prevented from receiving their HELPER: 'Jesus turned and rebuked them' (v.55). This means they are not invested with other modalities of *power* and *cognition* to carry out the mandate. There is no disjunction/conjunction syntagm, which expresses their movements to carry out their contract.

James and John also knew how they could carry out their contract, which is the performance syntagm. This is manifested in the rest of the disciples' performance: 'Lord, do you want us to call fire down from heaven to destroy them?' (v.54b). They attempted to carry out the contract with the help of 'fire from heaven', but they became unsuccessful in solving the problem brought about by the villainy of the Samaritans. Their 'qualifying test' (bringing fire down from heaven) did not make them successful in their 'glorifying test' (manifestation as successful heroes). Thus, the topical sequence is interrupted once and for all and becomes unsuccessful. No other topical sequence is introduced and thus the final correlated sequence is not actualized. The text clearly says that they 'went to another village' (v.56). The sequence of the messengers, the sub-sequence of the Samaritans and the topical sequence of the disciples can be shown as follows.

Diagram 1

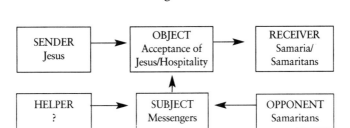

Sequence #1: Initial correlated Sequence (sequence interrupted)

8.   Jameson, *Prison House*, pp. 64–9.

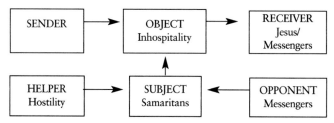

Sequence #2: Sub-sequence of the Samaritan opposition (confrontation, domination and deprivation

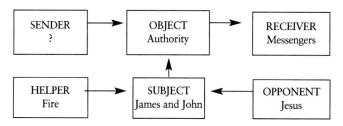

Sequence #3: Topical sequence of the disciples (volition established, power and cognition not received, movement not completed and sequence interrupted)

5.3. Analysis of Acts 8:4-25

Acts 8:4-25 comprises two narrative structures or sequences: vv. 4-13 and vv. 14-25. This is clear from the following observations:

1. In the narrative of Acts 8:4-13, Philip the evangelist, following the persecution after Stephen's martyrdom, separates himself from Jerusalem (disjunction) and arrives in the city of Samaria (conjunction) to carry out the contract of preaching the gospel (performance syntagm). The changes of place, time, and the departure and arrival of the character introduce a new sequence in vv. 4-13. However, the text does not mention the disappearance of Philip until v. 26.

2. That Acts 8:14-25 forms another sequence is evident from the text. Verse 14 indicates a change of time (when the apostles in Jerusalem heard that Samaria had accepted the word of God they sent Peter and John to them). It also indicates a change of characters, Peter and John, who arrive in Samaria from Jerusalem in v. 15 and return back to Jerusalem only in v. 25. In this narrative structure, the action of the apostles in Jerusalem in sending Peter and John to Samaria introduces a new contract whereby they propose to communicate the mandate, which is the Holy Spirit, upon the Samaritans. Thus, the change of time, change of characters, and the mandating of a new contract affirm a new sequence. It is to be noted here that the whole narrative

structure in Acts 8:14-25 comprises a combination of *story* or narrative (vv. 14-17, 25) and *discourse* or direct speech (vv. 18-24). The *discourse* is seen as a fairly discrete enclave within the whole *story* of vv. 14-25. The story is attached to the discourse with a connecting link: 'when Simon *saw...*' (v.18). This pattern exactly resembles the structure of Lk. 9:51-56, as shown above.

Despite their distinct sequences, the two narrative structures may be seen as a single cohesive literary unit. (1) The pattern in vv. 4-5 and 25, which according to Talbert exhibits an *inclusio* technique, suggests the literary unity of Acts 8:4-25.[9] The common elements in this pattern include: (a) beginning vv. 4 and 25 with οἱ μὲν οὐᾶν, where μὲν οὐᾶν is a device to indicate the transition to a new section or the close of a previous section or both (cf. Acts 1:6),[10] (b) reference to preaching the gospel (εὐαγγελιζόμαι) and proclaiming the word (τὸν λόγον), (c) the locality of Samaria. (2) The recipients in the two sequences are the same: the Samaria/Samaritans who accepted Christ through the ministry of Philip are the same participants who received the Holy Spirit through the ministry of Peter and John. (3) Simon Magus is introduced in both the narratives. (4) Philip who appears in Samaria in v. 5 does not disappear until v. 26 (though absent in the second narrative), thereby implying that Acts 8:4-25 is a literary whole. (5) There are common themes and features within the entire unit: reference to baptism (βαπτίζω) in vv. 12, 13, 16; proclaiming the good news (εὐαγγελιζόμαι) in vv. 4,12, 25; word (λόγος) in vv. 4, 14, 21, 25; Simon Magus is portrayed as the one who follows Philip, 'seeing' (θεωρῶν) the signs and mighty wonders he performed and also as he who offers money to Peter and John after 'seeing' (ἰδὼν) the Holy Spirit being given to the Samaritans. The presence of all these various elements observed in the narrative suggests that Acts 8:4-25 is a single literary unit.

5.3.1. *Analysis of Acts 8:4-13: The Samaritan Mission of Philip*
5.3.1.1. Sequential Analysis
The narrative starts with the progress of preaching the good news (εὐαγγελιζόμενοι τὸν λόγον, v. 4) by those who were scattered due to the persecution at Jerusalem. This provides the clue that though the apostles, who were to engage in the ministry of prayer and word (Acts 6:4) remained in

9. Talbert, *Reading Luke*, pp. 37, 44; also Spencer, *Portrait*, pp. 26–7.

10. F. Blass and A. Debrunner, *A Greek Grammar of the New Testament and Other Early Christian Literature* (trans. and ed. Robert W. Funk; Chicago: The University of Chicago Press, 1961), § 451(1) mentions that μὲν οὐᾶν is sometimes used to state further events, and sometimes to summarize the previous narrative in order to form a transition to a new subject (see Acts 1:6; 2:41; 9:31; Lk. 3:18); C.F.D. Moule, *An Idiom-Book of New Testament Greek* (2nd edn.; Cambridge: Cambridge University Press, 1960), p. 162. Barrett, *Acts* I, pp. 400, 418; Spencer, *Portrait*, p. 27; Haenchen, *Acts*, pp. 301, 305; Johnson, *Acts*, p. 45; John T. Squires, 'The Function of Acts 8:4-12:25', *NTS* 44 (1998), pp. 608–17, 609, all agree that v. 4 is a transitional verse and makes a change of scene with v. 25.

Jerusalem, the ministry of proclaiming the word was not at stake, rather, it was continued by those who were not originally chosen to do so. This contrast is further sharpened by the introduction of Philip who was chosen to 'serve tables' but went to the city of Samaria proclaiming Christ (ἐκήρυσσεν αὐτοῖς τὸν Χριστόν, v. 5). Thus, Philip plays a role different from what is originally ascribed to him. The text does not give any information about Philip, but implies certain knowledge of him on the part of the readers.

In v. 5, the geographical reference, 'the city of Samaria', is a *topographical code* as well as a *cultural code*. It has a narrative functionality, as this place becomes the location of Simon's activity later in the narrative (ἐν τῇ πόλει, v. 9) and also as the place where there was great joy after the ministry of Philip (ἐν τῇ πόλει ἐκείνῃ, v. 8). It also functions in the narrative of the arrival of Peter and John as the place of their ministry (ἡ Σαμάρεια, v. 14). It may also have a function of inter-textuality with other narratives in Acts (1:8; 8:1; 9:31; 15:3). The *cultural code* implies some knowledge on the part of the readers of this narrative of the socio-religious and ethnic situation of Samaria and the Samaritans in the first century CE. The downward movement of Philip (κατελθών) in v. 5 is symmetrical to the arrival of Peter and John to Samaria (καταβάντες) in v. 15. There are two *actional codes (proairetic codes)*[11] in v. 5: that Philip 'went down' (κατελθών) to Samaria and 'proclaimed to them Christ' (ἐκήρυσσεν αὐτοῖς τὸν Χριστόν). The result of Philip's action in terms of the Samaritans' acceptance of Christ is suspended until v. 12. There is a logical progression of the content and result of his message: Christ (v.5), Kingdom of God and the name of Jesus Christ (v.12); the result is: people paid attention (v.6), believed and were baptized (v.12). It implies that Philip starts with the messianic concept of the Samaritans[12] and then presents Jesus as the fulfilment of their hope. In contrast to this approach, he directly preaches Jesus (τὸν Ἰησοῦν) to the Ethiopian eunuch in v. 35 starting with a messianic concept based on Isa.53.

The crowd paid attention (προσεῖχον) with one accord (ὁμοθυμαδόν)[13] to what Philip had said, hearing and seeing (ἐν τῷ ἀκούειν αὐτοὺς καὶ βλέπειν) the miracles (τὰ σημεῖα) which he did (v.6). This initial response preceded their faith, as the Samaritans believed and were baptized (v.12). Verses 7–8 is a summary of Philip's ministry, especially of the signs of exorcism and healing he performs, which is a manifestation of the arrival of the kingdom of God.[14] There is a parallelism in these verses with the word, 'many'

---

11.   See n. 1 above for explanation.

12.   Their expectation is the coming of a 'prophet like Moses', who is called '*Taheb*' ('Returning One' or 'Restorer'); cf. Jn 4:25. See J. Macdonald, *The Theology of the Samaritans* (London: SCM Press, 1964), pp. 362–71.

13.   With the exception of one reference (Rom. 15:6), the word (ὁμοθυμαδόν) occurs only in Acts (1:14; 2:46; 4:24; 5:12; 7:57; 8:6; 12:20; 15:25; 18:12; 19:29).

14.   See for example, Lk. 5:17-26; 7:22; 9:1-2, 6, 11; 13:11-17; 14:13,21; Acts 3:1-10; 5:15-16.

(πολλοί): '*many*, who had unclean spirits, came out crying with a loud voice' (v.7);[15] *many* paralytics and lame were healed (v.7); and there was *great* (πολλή) joy in that city (v.8). This narrative of Philip is interrupted, as a new sequence on Simon Magus is introduced in v. 9.

The story of Simon Magus marks a new sequence in the narrative (v.9) as it begins with the expression, 'But there was a certain man named Simon' ('Ἀνὴρ δέ τις ὀνόματι Σίμων).[16] The proper name, Simon, is an *onomastic code* and he is introduced into the story as the one who was active in the same city (ἐν τῇ πόλει) before (προϋπῆρχεν, cf. Lk. 23:12) Philip went, and was practising sorcery (μαγεύων) and amazing (ἐξιστάνων) the people of Samaria. The information given here manifests a *topographical code* in which there is neither an opposition nor a temporal distance between the locations of Simon and Philip's activities, as they both work in the same city of Samaria (vv. 5, 8, 9). There is also a *chronological code* since Simon's bewitching activities preceded the ministry of Philip. His acts of sorcery and bewitchment are the *semic code*, which is the ensemble of the signified, not of the signifier, and refers to the character of Simon. This *semic code* can be read both anagogically and psychologically. If it is anagogical, where the text itself gives forth the meaning, the activity of Simon only refers to the general practice of all other magicians, and hence the connotation is structural. If it is read psychologically, it refers to the psychological character of Simon, and hence indicates his temperament signified. Taking together the word μαγεύων in v. 9, which occurs only here in the New Testament, and the claim of Simon in v. 10 as somebody 'Great' (μέγας), the *semic code* points towards a psychological reading of the text as well.

Verse 10, 'to whom they all gave heed', is linked to v. 11 by using the catchword, προσεῖχον, and by providing the reason for the people's close attention to Simon: because for a long time he had amazed them with sorceries (ταῖς μαγείαις ἐξεστακέναι αὐτούς). Earlier in the narrative of Philip, the people of Samaria paid attention (προσεῖχον) to Philip's words (v.6), but here they paid attention to Simon (vv. 10, 11). The cause and effect of people's close attention to Simon is contrasted with that of their attention to Philip: the sorcery of Simon and his amazement of the people on the one hand, the gospel message of Philip, which includes healings and exorcisms, and the faith and baptism of the people on the other. The ministry of preaching Christ and the Kingdom of God confronts and defeats the magical powers of Simon and the Samaritans' fascination by him. The rest of v. 10,

---

15.   Haenchen, *Acts*, p. 302; Johnson, *Acts*, p. 146; Barrett, *Acts* II, p. 404, consider v. 7 as an *anacolouthic*, since the verb 'came out' (ἐξήρχοντο), refers not to the 'unclean spirits', but to the 'many' (πολλοί). However, it can be best understood as producing a structural parallelism with 'many' in v. 7b and 8.

16.   Barthes, 'Acts X-XI', p. 123, says that the formula, 'there was', refers culturally to a code, called *narrative code*, and it marks the beginning of every narrative.

'from the least to the greatest, (ἀπὸ μικροῦ ἕως μεγάλου), saying, "This man is the great power of God'" (ἡ δύναμις τοῦ θεοῦ ἡ καλουμένη Μεγάλη), manifests a striking structural parallelism with vv. 12-13, as shown below.

1. The designation of Simon is also used for what he himself sees in the ministry of Philip (δυνάμεις μεγάλας, v. 13).

2. The pair, 'both men and women' (ἄνδρες τε καὶ γυναῖκες), who believed and were baptized by the ministry of Philip in v. 12, stands in contrast to those 'from the least to the greatest' (ἀπὸ μικροῦ ἕως μεγάλου), who gave heed to Simon. This distinction is significant as it explicitly mentions the category of people who can respond to the gospel in faith and baptism. This is further evident from the immediate context of Acts 8:3 (cf. 22:4), where Saul is said to have made havoc of the church, putting 'men and women' (ἄνδρας τε καὶ γυναῖκας) in prison. Still further, the believers who were added to the Lord in the context of the Jerusalem mission (Acts 5:14) are said to be 'both of men and women' (ἀνδρῶν τε καὶ γυναικῶν). On the one hand, the result of Philip's ministry resembles that of the apostles in Jerusalem, and on the other it is distinctive from that of Simon.

Verse 13 reverses the ongoing successful magical activity of Simon, as he believed (ἐπίστευσεν), was baptized (βαπτιζθείς), continued with Philip (προσκαρτερῶν), seeing (θεωρῶν) the great signs and miracles, and was amazed (ἐξίστατο). These are the *actional* codes, which change the present situation of Simon. His new situation corresponds to the genuine experience of those in the early church who believed and were baptized and continued in prayer and fellowship.[17] But the use of the word, θεωρῶν for seeing the miracles stands in opposition to the genuineness of his belief.[18]

The narrative manifests an inter-textual relationship between the activity of Philip and that of Simon Magus through the usage of similar words.

1.   The word προσεῖχον is used once in relation to the crowd's response to Philip's words (v.6), and twice in reference to their attention to Simon himself (vv. 10,11). But the addition of ὁμοθυμαδόν in their response to Philip denotes a radical difference from their response to Simon.

---

17.   The words πιστεύω and βαπτίζω, occur together only in Mk 16:16; Acts 8:12, 13; 18:8; 19:4. The use of προσκαρτερῶν may refer back to Acts 1:14; 2:42, 46; 6:4, in all of which it is used in the context of prayer and fellowship.

18.   Except for the present reference in 8:13, Luke never uses the word θεωρῶν for seeing the signs and miracles. The only other instances in the New Testament are Jn 2:23 and 6:2, where the former reflects a negative response in its context and the latter is set in contrast to a positive response (ἰδόντες) of the same crowd in 6:14. The word θεωρῶν signifies seeing as a 'spectator', whereas ἰδών means seeing with discernment or perception. G. Abbott-Smith, *A Manual Greek Lexicon of the New Testament* (3rd edn., Edinburgh: T. & T. Clark, 1973), pp. 206, 321; Danker (ed.), *Greek-English Lexicon*, p. 454; Michaelis, 'ὁράω', 'θεωρέω', in G. Friedrich (ed.), *TDNT* V, pp. 346–66.

2. The word ἐξίστημι is used twice for the crowd's amazement by Simon (vv. 9,11) and once for Simon's amazement by the ministry of Philip (v.13). Nowhere is this word used about Philip amazing the crowd: through his ministry, they believed (ἐπίστευσαν) and were baptized (ἐβαπτίζοντο), but were not amazed.

3. The adjective μέγας/μεγάλη is used twice in the context of Philip's ministry (vv. 7, 13) and thrice in reference to Simon himself and his activities (vv. 9,10). The greatness of Philip is his ministry of proclamation and miracles, whereas for Simon it is himself.

4. Likewise, the word δύναμις is used once for the miracles performed by Philip (v.13) and once for Simon himself (v.10). It is clear that in the context of Philip these words describe the nature of his ministry, whereas for Simon they are ascribed to himself.

5. Verse 13 reverses the picture of Simon where the words μέγας, δύναμις, and ἐξίστημι are used together for the success of Philip over Simon. The narrative on Simon (v.9) starts with his act of sorcery by which he amazes (ἐξιστάνων) the people of Samaria, but it ends with a reversal where Simon himself is amazed (ἐξίστατο) seeing the great signs and miracles of Philip (v.13). In other words, his initial victory is opposed to his final defeat.

5.3.1.2. Actantial Analysis

Now, before passing on to the actantial analysis of the narrative, a brief comment is to be made about the reader of Acts who, based on the narration in Acts 1:8, would probably look forward to the actualization of the Samaritan mission with a fixed model in their mind. According to this model, one may expect that the apostles (SUBJECT), who received the commission from the risen Lord (SENDER), would go to Samaria to proclaim the word (OBJECT) to the Samaritans (RECEIVER). They may do this with the help of the *dunamis* they received when the Holy Spirit came upon them on the day of Pentecost (HELPER). This can be represented as in Diagram 2.

Diagram 2

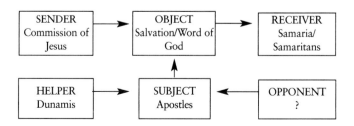

SENDER Commission of Jesus	OBJECT Salvation/Word of God	RECEIVER Samaria/ Samaritans
HELPER Dunamis	SUBJECT Apostles	OPPONENT ?

However, the actualization of this actantial model did not take place. This is because the sequence, which needs to begin with a contractual syntagm, is aborted as the contract is refused. In this case, the apostles who are supposed to undertake the contract and to take their position as SUBJECT remained in Jerusalem (Acts 8:1b, 14). The narrative in Acts 8:4-25 expresses the attempt to re-establish the original contract of the evangelization of Samaria, as Philip undertakes the actantial position of the SUBJECT.

The sequence in v. 4 starts with a disjunction-conjunction syntagm, in which all the scattered people, due to the persecution in Jerusalem, make a movement to other places (διῆλθον) and proclaim the word (εὐαγγελιζόμενοι). This refers back to the situation in Acts 8:1b, where all except the apostles were scattered (διεσπάρησαν). Verse 5 manifests the disjunction and conjunction syntagm of Philip, who leaves Jerusalem and goes down (κατελθών) to the city of Samaria. The statement, 'Philip went down to the city of Samaria and proclaimed Christ to them', functions as the mandating and acceptance of the contract syntagm. The rest of Philip's activities in the narrative function as the performance syntagm in order to actualize the initial correlated sequence of preaching Christ and so to bring salvation to the Samaritans. There is no explicit opposition from the Samaritans against the ministry of Philip, but he confronts the hostile spirit or evil forces working in the people, as his activities include casting out evil spirits as well. The success of Philip's ministry and the mention of having 'great joy' in the city of Samaria explicitly refer to the final actualization of the correlated sequence.

Diagram 3

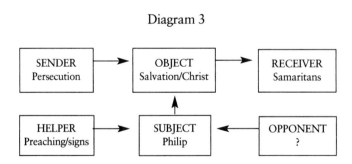

5.3.2. *Analysis of Acts 8:14-25: The Ministry of Peter and John*
5.3.2.1. Sequential Analysis
The *topographical codes* in v. 14, Jerusalem and Samaria, are again put in perspective with each other. The Samaritan mission of the apostles in Jerusalem starts only after they heard that Samaria had accepted the word of God (δέδεκται ἡ Σαμάρεια τὸν λόγον τοῦ θεοῦ, v. 14). This information serves as a *chronological code*, as it functions to justify the time at which the ministry of the apostles starts in the narrative. The 'lack' mentioned in Lk. 9:53, that the Samaritans did not receive Jesus (καὶ οὐκ ἐδέξαντο αὐτόν) is

already overcome now. But the arrival of Peter and John in Samaria and their prayer for the Samaritans indicate another 'lack', which is the reception of the Holy Spirit. The narrative provides additional information as to why Peter and John had to pray for the Samaritans: 'because the Holy Spirit had not yet come upon any of them; they had simply been baptized into the name of the Lord Jesus' (v.16). This information, on the one hand, does not provide the exact reason for the delay, rather it emphasizes the lack and refers only to a stage in the process of the Samaritans' inclusion in the family of God. On the other hand, if this information were not in the text, one would think that the delay of the Holy Spirit is due to the 'defective' ministry of Philip, or the 'superficial' nature of the Samaritans' conversion. This information in the 'counter text' conveys that neither Philip nor the Samaritans were responsible for the delay of the Spirit. It also conveys that for the Samaritans, the baptism of the Holy Spirit and the water-baptism can be two different experiences altogether. The absence of the Holy Spirit before the arrival of Peter and John and the descent of the Holy Spirit after their arrival thus bring significant meanings to the text.

The word καταβῆναι used by the disciples in the discourse of Lk. 9:54 for bringing down fire, is employed for their arrival (καταβάντες) in Samaria in the narrative of Acts 8:15. Since the ascension of Jesus has already taken place at this stage, the upward movement of the *symbolic code* in Lk. 9:51 is now realized. The forward journey of Jesus is also realised as Samaria has accepted (δέδεκται) the word of God through the ministry of Philip. However, in order to actualize the downward movement of the *symbolic code* in Lk. 9:54, the apostles need to be present in the ministry to the Samaritans. Since they remained in Jerusalem it did not come to pass. Their arrival (καταβάντες) signifies the actualization of the reception (ἐλάμβανον) of the Holy Spirit by the Samaritans. Thus what is anticipated in Lk. 9:51-56 is positively and creatively actualized in Acts 8:14-15.

The t*opographical codes*, Jerusalem and Samaria, which were opposed to each other like two poles hitherto, find unity for the first time only after Samaria accepted the word of God, and when Peter and John arrived in Samaria. This is obvious from a comparison of the *topographical code* in Acts 8:14-25 with Lk. 9:51-56. The geographical references and their sequences in Acts 8:14-25, Jerusalem-Samaria-Jerusalem-many Samaritan villages, is similar to those of Lk. 9:51-56, but with a great difference. In Lk. 9:51-56, it starts with Jerusalem but ends in a non-Samaritan village, whereas in Acts 8:14-25, it starts with Jerusalem but ends in many Samaritan villages. This means that the place of exit in the former becomes the place of entry in the latter. It paves the way for the outsider and the insider to mutually communicate to each other. Now, the socio-religious and ethnic barriers between the two places are no more evident in the narrative. It appears that the hostility is absent here because the apostles' movement is now *towards* Samaria, not *towards* Jerusalem (εἰς Ἰερουσαλήμ) unlike Lk. 9:53. But Acts 8:25 suggests otherwise: 'Peter and John returned to Jerusalem (εἰς Ἱεροσόλυμα) preaching the gospel in many Samaritan villages'. Though they were going *towards* Jerusalem through many Samaritan villages, no element of hostility was said to be present at this stage. The reason for this reversal is two-fold: the acceptance of the word of God by the Samaritans and the acceptance of the Samaritans by the disciples. It is at this stage of unity that the Holy Spirit often descended upon various communities in Acts. It is evident from the narrative that the ministry of the word and the ministry of the Holy Spirit transcend ethnic, religious and cultural barriers, break down rivalries between communities and unite them together, even the marginalized.

The narrative suddenly changes into a discourse in a 'direct style', where Peter and Simon Magus directly intervene in the plot of the story (vv. 18-24). The focus is changed from the Spirit-filled Samaritans to the power-seeking individual. Two *actional codes* (*proairetic codes*), *saw* and *offered*, turn the whole narrative into the discourse: when Simon *saw* (ἰδών) that through laying on of the apostles' hands the Holy Spirit was given, he *offered* them money (προσήνεγκεν αὐτοῖς χρήματα, v. 18). The expression, '*offered them money*' is the *symbolic code*, the signifying of bringing sacrifice to the Lord (cf. Acts 7:42; 21:26). 'Give me also this power' (δότε κἀμοὶ τὴν ἐξουσίαν ταύτην) does not refer to the Holy Spirit which the Samaritans received, but to the ability with which Peter and John conveyed the Holy Spirit. In this respect Simon appears to wish to take upon himself the role of a Spirit-imparting missionary, having an authority bought with money.[19] The word ἐξουσία used here, instead of δύναμις, is significant. Simon himself was associated with δύναμις and he saw Philip's miracles also as δύναμις; whereas Simon perceived the conferring of the Holy Spirit as an act of authority (ἐξουσία) more appealing than his own magic and that of the healing miracles of Philip. This gives the clue that he did not want to purchase the δύναμις which he saw in the miracles performed by Philip, but the ἐξουσία from Peter, the apostolic authority which the magician could not possess before.

Peter's answer, 'May your money (ἀργύριον) perish with you' (v.20), is a confrontation with the demand of Simon and shows a signified of connotation of Peter's authority. Here ἀργύριόν and χρήματα are used synonymously for 'money', and often they have a negative connotation in Luke-Acts.[20] The reason for Peter's curse upon Simon is explicitly mentioned in the text: 'because you thought you could buy the gift of God (τὴν δωρεὰν τοῦ θεοῦ) with money'. This information is *anagogical*, as the text clearly manifests its meaning: riches could not purchase the divine authority, which is a free gift of God.[21] The encounter between Simon and Peter leads to the

---

19.   According to Luke, Jesus gave the disciples both power and authority (δύναμις καὶ ἐχουσία) when he sent them for mission (Lk. 9:1). In the context of exorcism, authority takes precedence or is singled out (Lk. 4:36; 10:19 cf. Mt. 10:1; Mk 6:7). And the source of authority is Jesus himself and authority cannot be exchanged for money as Simon thought.

20.   See Lk. 9:3; 18:24; 22:5; Acts 3:6; 8:20; 20:33; 24:26.

21.   See Jn 4:10; Acts 11:17.

consummation of the exposure of Simon's wicked heart and the need for his repentance and prayer (vv. 21-23).

There are multiple oppositions in the text. (1) The nature of perception: Simon *sees* (ἰδών) the outward miracle-working manifestation of the Spirit (v.18); the description of what Peter *sees* (ὁρῶ) in Simon is the metaphor for condemnation, as he exposes the inward wicked nature of the heart of Simon (v.21-23). (2) The lack of object: for Simon, it is the *ability* to induce the Spirit, whereas Peter senses Simon's need as to own a *right heart*. (3) The disposition of the Spirit: Simon wanted to *purchase* the power with money, but it is a *free gift* of God. (4) The prospect of mission: Simon offers money to purchase the power so that he can make further *prospect* out of his new 'magical' mission, but the opposite is predicted that his money may go with him to *perdition* and that he has no part or share in this ministry.[22]

5.3.2.2. Actantial Analysis

The initial correlated sequence of the narrative is manifested as the Jerusalem apostles initiate and give a mandate to Peter and John: 'When the apostles in Jerusalem heard that Samaria had accepted the word of God, they sent Peter and John to them' (v.14). The final correlated sequence is achieved and is mentioned explicitly in the text, as the Samaritans received the Holy Spirit (v.17) and as Peter and John returned to Jerusalem (v.25). The contract syntagm of Peter and John is manifested in the words 'when they arrived they prayed for them' (v.15). Since they accepted the contract (as it is expressed in the words, 'they prayed for them'), they are invested with a modality, which is the modality of *obligation*, as it was imposed upon them by the Jerusalem apostles. Since they knew that they could carry out the contract with the help of prayer and laying on of hands, and the fact that it enabled them to successfully communicate the Holy Spirit to the Samaritans, they are invested with other modalities of *power* and *cognition*. The disjunction/conjunction syntagm is manifested as Peter and John departed from Jerusalem and arrived in Samaria and also as they leave Samaria for Jerusalem after the completion of the contract. The performance syntagm is expressed in the statements, 'they prayed for them' (v.15) and 'they placed their hands on them' (v.17). Peter and John perform other canonical functions to fulfil the contract. (1) Confrontation: they confront the lack, which is the Holy Spirit the Samaritans need to receive. (2) Domination: they are successful through praying and laying on of hands. (3) Attribution: they facilitate the need and the Holy Spirit is given to the Samaritans. So the sequence of Peter and John is actualized and the Samaritans received the Holy Spirit. In this actantial model, the Jerusalem apostles function as the SENDER, Peter and John as the SUBJECT, and prayer and laying on of hands as the HELPER. The

---

22. See the parallel between the description about Simon and the fate of Judas mentioned in section 6.2.3 of this work.

OBJECT is the Holy Spirit and the RECEIVER is the Samaritans/Samaria. The OPPONENT that caused the lack is uncertain. The actantial model of this sequence can be represented as follows.

Diagram 4

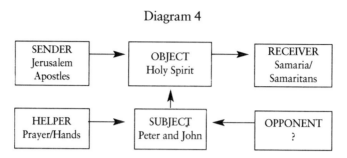

It is evident that Acts 8:14-17 can be best understood as a new correlated sequence which is not interrupted, but fully actualized in the narrative. However, it also appears to resemble the topical sequence of James and John in Lk. 9:55, in bringing down fire on the Samaritans. If Acts 8:14-17 can be taken in resemblance to Lk. 9:55, then what James and John proposed to communicate in Lk. 9:51-56 is actualized with a reversed effect in Acts 8:14-17. The constructive fire of the Spirit came upon the Samaritans as opposed to the destructive fire of God's wrath. In other words, the coming of Peter and John to Samaria, according to Acts 8:14-17, is two-fold. (1) The surface level of the text tells us that they came and prayed for the Samaritans to receive the Holy Spirit. (2) The deep structure of the text echoes the fulfilment of a contract, which James and John could not carry out before in Lk. 9:55, but which is now actualized in a more positive and reversed way by Peter and John.

Now, Simon's sequence begins: that he 'saw' and 'offered them money' signifies the acceptance of his contract of buying from Peter and John the authority (ἐξουσία) to induce the Spirit on others. In this actantial model, the SENDER is unknown, but one could expect it as the hidden financial motive in Simon. The OBJECT is purchasing the authority and the RECEIVER is Simon himself. Simon functions as the SUBJECT and his money the HELPER. The OPPONENT who confronts and dominates is Peter and John. This model can be represented as follows.

Diagram 5

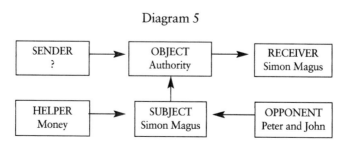

It is important to note that Acts 8:25 functions as the actualization of the Samaritan mission expected from Acts 1:8 (but earlier interrupted; see Diagram 2): 'When they had testified and proclaimed the word of the Lord, Peter and John returned to Jerusalem, preaching the gospel in many Samaritan villages'. Thus, the coming of Peter and John to Samaria fulfils another correlated sequence, to be witnesses in Samaria, which was proposed to communicate in Acts 1:8. This sequence can be shown in the following diagram, which also resembles Diagram 2.

Diagram 6

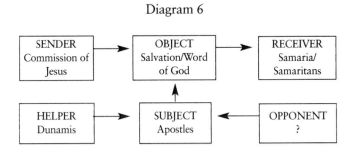

5.4. A Synthesis of the Narratives

The structural analyses of the above narratives reveal the following:

1. Two unsuccessful contracts of the disciples – the correlated sequence of the messengers of Jesus in Lk. 9:52 and that of the Jerusalem apostles in Acts 1:8 (cf. 8:4) – are actualized in Acts 8:14-17 and Acts 8:25 respectively. It shows their mission to Samaria and the Samaritans as finally successful.
2. The purpose of the coming of the Jerusalem apostles, Peter and John, to Samaria is three-fold. (a) To pray for the Samaritans that they would receive the Holy Spirit. (b) To actualize the final correlated sequence of the messengers which was interrupted in Lk. 9:51-56. (c) To actualize what was proposed to communicate (being witnesses in Samaria) in Acts 1:8.
3. The hostility of the Samaritans manifested in the sub-sequence of Lk. 9:53 is no longer evident in the Acts narrative. When the topical sequence of James and John was prevented by not providing them the adequate HELPER (fire or authority to bring down fire), it seems that the hostility existed in the level of the Gospel narrative. But it disappears in the Acts narrative.
4. The ministry of Philip in Acts 8:4-13 appears to serve as a bridge between Lk. 9:51-56 and Acts 8:14-25.

A comparison of the narrative structures of Lk. 9:51-56 and Acts 8:14-25 reveals that there exist striking parallelisms between them.

1. Both narrative structures comprise a combination of *story* and *discourse*, where the *discourse* is seen as a fairly discrete enclave within the *story*.

Levels	Luke	Acts
Story	9:51-53	8:14-17
Discourse	9:54	8:18-24
Story	9:55-56	8:25

2. In both the narratives, the *story* is linked to the *discourse* with the same word, 'seeing' (ἰδόντες/ ἰδών).
3. In each narrative it is in the *discourse* level that the failure or the non-actualization of the contract is manifested.
4. The topical sequence of the unfulfilled contract of James and John in the first narrative is similar to that of Simon Magus in the last. (1) In both cases, they (SUBJECT) accept the contract. This is clearly expressed in the text: 'When the disciples, James and John saw this, they asked' (Lk. 9:54); 'When Simon saw that ... he offered them' (Acts 8:18). (2) In both the narratives, it is their 'seeing' that led them to accept the contract. (3) Both want to carry out a specific mandate, and they are invested with a modality of *volition*. (4) In both cases they are prevented from receiving their HELPER: in the first case, it is fire or the authority to bring down fire from heaven – 'Jesus turned and rebuked them' (Lk. 9:55); in the second case, it is money to purchase the ability to induce the Spirit – 'May your money perish with you ...' (Acts 8:20). (5) In both cases, they are not invested with modalities of *power* and *cognition* to carry out their specific mandate. (6) In both, the 'qualifying test' and the 'glorifying test' fail and both James and John, and Simon Magus are portrayed as unsuccessful heroes. This comparison reveals that the contract cannot be actualized with an improper and inappropriate HELPER. In other words, abuse of authority and improper method does not fulfil the divine role.
5. The mandating of James and John in Lk. 9:54 is similar to the mandating of Peter and John in Acts 8:14-17. In both cases they accept the contract to carry out a specific function, to fulfil the lack. The former is in the topical sequence of the narrative and the latter is in the correlated sequence, if not in the topical sequence.
6. In the end of both narratives, Jesus the SENDER and his apostles take the actantial position of the OPPONENT. It is not the Samaritans any longer, but Jesus himself who is the OPPONENT against James and John in the former, and Peter and John against Simon Magus in the

latter. Divine agents oppose both improper and inappropriate HELPERS and those SUBJECTS who seek them.

5.5. The Function of 'seeing' in the Samaritan Episodes

A close look at the Samaritan episodes in Luke-Acts reveals that Luke is employing a literary and rhetorical strategy whereby the events in each narrative make a new turn on the action of 'seeing' by various characters in the narratives. This element of 'seeing' is significant in the Lukan portrait of the Samaritans, in which it runs throughout like a connecting thread. The literary structure of the various narratives on the Samaritans in Luke-Acts will make this clear.

Lk. 9:54	ἰδόντες δὲ οἱ μαθηταὶ ᾽Ιάκωβος καὶ ᾽Ιωάννης
10:31	... ἱερεύς ... καὶ ἰδὼν αὐτὸν ἀντιπαρῆλθεν
10:32	... καὶ Λευίτης ... καὶ ἰδὼν ἀντιπαρῆλθεν
10:33	Σαμαρίτης δέ ... καὶ ἰδὼν ἐσπλαγχνίσθη
17:14	καὶ ἰδὼν εἶπεν αὐτοῖς
17:15	ἰδὼν ὅτι ἰάθη ... 17:16 ... καὶ αὐτὸς ἦν Σαμαρίτης
Acts 8:6	οἱ ὄχλοι ... ἐν τῷ ἀκούειν αὐτοὺς καὶ βλέπειν τὰ σημεῖα
8:13	ὁ δὲ Σίμων ... θεωρῶν
8:18	ἰδὼν δὲ ὁ Σίμων ...
8:20-23	Πέτρος δε ... ὁρῶ

As mentioned elsewhere in this study, the act of 'seeing' serves as a unique and significant feature in the Samaritan references in Luke-Acts.[23] Why did Luke or his sources find this theme important in the overall understanding of the Samaritans in the first-century context? What is the effect that brings on the respective characters in the story and how does this affect the readers of Luke-Acts?

In all the Samaritan references, it is the function of 'seeing' on which the events in the narratives turn to a new direction. In Lk. 9:51-56, we have noted the *inappropriate act* of the disciples when they faced hostility from the Samaritans. Jesus refused to sanction their request and also rebuked them (v. 55). When Jesus commissioned his disciples for mission he instructed them to act in a certain way in times of rejection and inhospitality (Lk. 9:5). This instruction is given in addition to what they have already received in the Sermon on the Plain (6:17-49). When they faced rejection from the

---

23.   This is not to overlook the numerous other references to the word 'seeing' in Luke-Acts, rather it is an attempt to see the significance of various usages of the term in the Samaritan references where the act of 'seeing' determines what follows next in each narrative.

Samaritans, they were expected to act according to what they had heard and been taught. In Lk. 9:51-56, Luke is trying to portray behaviour which is contrary to what is expected of them: (1) James and John failed to obey the commandment of Jesus to '*love* their enemies'. *Hatred* overpowered them. (2) Their desire was to bring down fire upon the Samaritans. It was not to *bless* them but to *curse* and destroy them. (3) When the Samaritans resisted them, James and John thought that they could exercise their power just like Elijah brought fire on Samaria (2 Kings 1:1-16), thus 'their proposed action against the Samaritans would seem to have had scriptural sanction'.[24] (4) It is to be noted that both James and John were with Jesus in his transfiguration and had known the divine necessity of rejection. Their proposal clashes with the divine will of Jesus. He rebuked (ἐπετίμησεν) them, 'as if they were representatives of a diabolic mission'.[25] (5) They *turned away* to another village, presumably not to a Samaritan village.

In the first and the last references to 'seeing', it is the disciples (James and John/Peter and John) who see the hostility of the Samaritans and the wicked heart of Simon respectively. And in both instances, it leads to the same action of confrontation, but they succeed not with the Samaritans, but with Simon, as their action was appropriate in the latter case. In the former, the problem is a socio-religious and ethnic one, whereas in the latter it is moral and ethical. James and John fail to see the inclusion of the Samaritans in the salvific plan of Jesus and to keep the mission mandate given to them by Jesus.

In the parable of the Good Samaritan (Lk. 10:25-37), the central issue is the appropriate moral behaviour that transcends ethnic boundaries.[26] This behaviour or action, motivated by compassion, is the praxis of God's word.[27] The repeated occurrence of the verb 'to do' (vv. 25, 28, 37) is related to the practice of what is appropriate. (1) The expert in the law is asked to do (obey) the law by loving God and loving his neighbour in order to inherit eternal life. (2) The priest and the Levite, who are associated with the Temple and the law, do not fulfil appropriately what the law requires of them in loving their neighbour. (3) An individual Samaritan is singled out to portray the characteristics of a person who 'loves the enemy' and 'shows mercy', thereby fulfilling what the law requires of being a neighbour. (4) He offers service and money not for selfish desires or to gain power, but to help the needy. This

---

24. Green, *Luke*, p. 406.

25. Green, *Luke*, p. 406.

26. Esler, 'Intergroup Conflict', pp. 325–57, extensively discusses the issue in the light of Social Identity theory and proposes a new approach to moral behaviour. Also see, Derrett, 'Good Samaritan', pp. 22–37; Fitzmyer, *Luke* II, p. 883.

27. Marshall, *Luke*, pp. 444–5, 449, refers to the 'practical compassion' and action for helping the man in need. See also Green, *Luke*, p. 425; Danker, *Jesus*, p. 224; Tannehill, *Luke*, p. 184. Johnson, *Luke*, pp. 173, 175, gives attention to the various actions of the Samaritan, for example, 'approaching', 'seeing', 'having compassion', 'coming closer', etc.

also reflects the right use of material possessions. (5) The final answer of the expert – 'the one who showed him mercy' – and the response of Jesus – 'go and do likewise' – summarizes that it is not hearing or philosophically discussing the law that leads to eternal life but practical living of the law.[28]

The priest and the Levite see the same wounded man as does the Samaritan, but it is the appropriate action of the Samaritan that transcends the socio-religious and ethnic barriers and thus from being an 'enemy' he becomes a 'neighbour'. The Samaritan sees in the wounded man a place for fulfilling what the Law demands, whereas the priest and the Levite fail to see the man as the object of their 'mission'.

In the story of the Good Samaritan, the Samaritan 'showed mercy' and acted appropriately, whereas in the story of the Samaritan leper, the Samaritan received 'mercy' and also acted appropriately by returning to Jesus, praising God, falling at Jesus' feet and thanking him. The Samaritan leper, in contrast to the other nine, perceives his healing and his appropriate action transforms him from being a 'foreigner' to an 'insider', who finds a place of worship at the feet of Jesus. The nine remain superficial in the most momentous experience of healing without realizing its meaning, but the Samaritan alone 'sees' that he is healed; he 'understands that his cure represents only the foreground of the deepest significance of divine salvation'.[29] However, the story can be better understood as a contrast between the ingratitude of the other nine and the gratitude shown by the Samaritan who was a foreigner.[30] The term 'seeing', which is used in relation to 'seeing the salvation of God' in the oracles of Simeon (εἶδον, Lk. 2:30) and the lengthy quotation from Isaiah in Lk. 3:6 (ὄψεται, cf. Isa. 40:5), is used of the Samaritan leper 'seeing' his healing (ἰδών, v. 15) with the eyes of faith.[31] The healing also recalls the fulfilling of Jesus' ministry started in Lk. 4:18-19, 27. The Samaritan who is an ἀλλογενής, 'a religious alien',[32] an outsider with no social, ethnic and religious status in the society, experiences the salvation promised in the Old Testament and inaugurated in the person and work of Jesus. This is certainly an anticipation of those who are not of 'the house of Israel', who on account of their faith in and gratitude to Jesus will become the objects of God's love and salvation.

---

28. S.G. Wilson, *Luke and the Law* (SNTSMS 50; Cambridge: Cambridge University Press, 1983), pp. 14–15.
29. Betz, 'Cleansing', p. 315.
30. Fitzmyer, *Luke* II, p. 1151; Tannehill, *Luke*, pp. 256–7.
31. Also Mk 2:10, 12; Lk. 7:10; Acts 9:35 cf. Lk. 11:16, 29; 12:54-56.
32. C.F. Evans, *Saint Luke*, p. 625.

Ref.	Character A	Word	Object B	Action of A	Reaction to A	Transformation in A/B
Lk. 9:54	James & John	Ἰδόντες	Opposed Samaritans	Hostile & destructive	Jesus rebukes	Acceptance to refusal
10:31-32	Priests & Levites	Ἰδών	Wounded man	Passed by	Passed by	Neutral
10:33	Samaritan	Ἰδών	Wounded man	Compassion	Jesus praises	Enemy to a neighbour
17:15	Samaritan Leper	Ἰδών	His healing	Returns to worship	Jesus praises	Outsider to an insider
Acts 8:6	Samaritans	Βλέπειν	Signs	Paid attention	Great joy	Refusal to acceptance
8:13	Simon	Θεωρῶν	Signs and miracles	Faith & baptism	Amazement	Outsider to insider
8:18	Simon	Ἰδών	Giving of the Holy Spirit	Offers money for authority	Peter rebukes	Acceptance to refusal
8:23	Peter	Ὁρῶ	Wicked heart of Simon	Confrontation	Submission	Simon as an outsider

The Samaritans in Acts see the signs of the kingdom and appropriately respond to it by believing the word and being baptized. What they really see is the breaking-in of the eschatological salvation inaugurated by Jesus. As in the case of Simeon (Lk. 2:30) and 'all flesh' of Isa. 40:4 (cf. Lk. 3:6), the Samaritans see the salvation of God with spiritual eyesight and experience it.[33] In their acceptance of the gospel, the marginalised and the socially outcast Samaritans become part of the kingdom. Though Simon is initially a 'spectator' of the signs of the kingdom and later on perceives the 'magical' art of conferring the Spirit, his inappropriate and unethical act of offering money to purchase the gift of the Spirit causes him to become a 'foreigner', an 'enemy' and an 'outsider', having no part or share in the inheritance of the kingdom. Thus, it is more than clear that it is not the socio-religious and ethnic differences that make somebody a 'foreigner' or an 'enemy' or an 'outsider' of the kingdom, rather his/her improper, inappropriate and unethical behaviour. Entering the kingdom is not a guarantee of remaining in the kingdom unless there follows action appropriate to the kingdom (cf. Mt. 25:31-46). All the Samaritan references emphasize the fact that those who

---

33. As noted in Chapter 4, the reference to 'seeing' (εἶδον) of salvation from Simeon (Lk. 2:30) could be linked to Paul's final statement in Acts 28:26-28 taken from Isaiah 6:9-10, where Israel fail to 'see' (ἰδών) the salvation of God. Cf. Alexander, 'Reading Luke-Acts', pp. 435–6.

'see' the mandates of the kingdom and respond to them properly, will transcend socio-religious and ethnic distinctions and will become the partakers of the inheritance, and that the inappropriate and unethical behaviour of those who are already in the kingdom, will disqualify them from remaining as an 'insider' unless they repent.

5.6. *The Lukan Strategy of Structural-Functional Reversalism*

The literary and structural analyses of the narratives in Lk. 9:51-56 and Acts 8:4-25 clearly manifest a method of *reversalism* as shown below.

1. The disciples of Jesus, who are rebuked (Lk. 9:54-55) for their abuse of authority, now rebuke Simon Magus (Acts 8:18-24) for the same cause.[34] The unsuccessful disciples (James and John) in the former narrative become successful heroes (Peter and John) in the latter: (a) in their mission to the Samaritans (vv. 14-17) and (b) in their confrontation with Simon Magus. The successful hero Simon Magus in Acts 8:9-11 becomes a defeated villain in Acts 8:18-24.
2. In Lk. 9:51-53, Jesus sends his messengers to Samaria to make Samaria/the Samaritans *accept* him. In the narrative of Acts 8:14-25 the Jerusalem apostles send Peter and John to Samaria only after they heard that Samaria had *accepted* the word of God. The Samaritans' acceptance of the word precedes the apostles' arrival. In both the narratives, the verb δέχομαι is used and Jesus is the object in the former and the word of God in the latter.
3. The disciples' HELPER, the fire, in the first narrative is replaced by prayer and laying on of hands in the second. They witness to the fire of the Holy Spirit in Samaria, as it was in the case of Acts 2:1-4 (cf. Lk. 3:16-17).
4. Neither the messengers in the narrative level nor the disciples in the direct speech level in Lk. 9:51-56 become successful in their alleged mission to the Samaritans. But, Peter and John are successful both in the narrative level and in the direct speech level in Acts 8:14-25. The initial failure of the Jerusalem-based disciples in Samaria is reversed now and they go back to Jerusalem having accomplished their mission to the Samaritans.
5. The literary technique in Acts 8:14-25 produces a *reversalism* in structure and function against Lk. 9:51-56 and thus leads to a

---

34. For an interesting discussion of the reversal of vindication and rebuke in the gospel stories, see L.C.A. Alexander, 'Sisters in Adversity: Retelling Martha's Story', in George J. Brooke (ed.), *Women in the Biblical Tradition* (SWR 31; Lampeter: The Edwin Mellen Press, 1992), pp. 167–86.

climactic and positive portrayal of the Samaritan mission. The structural reversal is evident from the following.

Lk. 9:51-56

1. πορεύεσθαι εἰς Ἰερουσαλήμ
2. ἀπέστειλεν ἀγγέλους
3. εἰς κώμην Σαμαριτῶν
4. καὶ οὐκ ἐδέξαντο αὐτόν
5. ἰδόντες δὲ οἱ μαθηταὶ Ἰάκωβος καὶ Ἰωάννης

Function: καταβῆναι ἀπὸ τοῦ οὐρανοῦ καὶ ἀναλῶσαι αὐτούς

Acts 8:14-25

5. Ἀκούσαντες δὲ οἱ ἐν Ἰεροσολύμοις ἀπόστολοι
4. δέδεκται ... τὸν λόγον τοῦ θεοῦ
3. ἡ Σαμάρεια
2. ἀπέστειλαν πρὸς αὐτοὺς Πέτρον καὶ Ἰωάννην
1. ὑπέστρεφον εἰς Ἰεροσόλυμα

Function: καταβάντες προσηύξαντο περὶ αὐτῶν ... λάβωσιν πνεῦμα ἅγιον

A comparison of the functions of the apostles in Acts 8:4-25 with those in Lk. 9:51-56, as listed elsewhere in this study, clearly brings a reversal. (1) The enmity of the Jerusalem apostles is no longer evident; love and the commission of Jesus motivate them to accept the Samaritans. (2) Now they have arrived to pray for them, not to destroy them but to bless them with the gift of the Holy Spirit. This prayer motif of blessing is doubly portrayed as Simon Magus asks Peter to engage in prayer so that curse and destruction will not fall on him. In doing so, the Jerusalem apostles are reminded of a reversal of their previous attitudes to the Samaritans. (3) The apostles return to Jerusalem, but passing through other Samaritan villages preaching the Word of God. (4) Simon Magus is singled out to portray the nature of a selfish person with wrong motifs. (5) He offers money not to serve others, but to gain power for himself. (6) The story leads to the question of how one could fall into the trap of eternal condemnation.

6. Luke's method of employing a structural-functional *reversalism* is also evident when we compare certain features of the Samaritan mission with the Jerusalem and Judean mission narrated in the first part of Acts.

(a) In the Jerusalem and Judean mission, it is the mission after Pentecost that leads to persecution, but in Samaria, it is the mission after the persecution that leads to the Samaritan Pentecost.

$$\text{Pentecost} \quad \xrightarrow{} \quad \text{Mission} \quad \xrightarrow{} \quad \text{Persecution}$$
$$\xleftarrow{} \qquad\qquad \xleftarrow{}$$

(b) In the Judean mission, it is the reception of the Spirit by the apostles that leads to mission, but in the case of the Samaritan mission, the mission of the apostles leads to the reception of the Spirit by the Samaritan converts.

(c) In Judea, the preaching of the apostles follows the Spirit's reception on the day of Pentecost, but in Samaria, the Spirit's reception follows the preaching of Philip.

(d) In the context of the Judean mission, money is demanded of the apostles and is never given (Acts 3), but in the story of the Samaritan mission, money is offered to the apostles, but is never accepted.

(e) From the Judean point of view, the mission of Peter and John is centrifugal, but from the Samaritan point of view, it is centripetal.

(f) The Judean mission leads to riot, revolt and disturbances, but the Samaritan mission brings 'great joy' in the city.

5.7. Conclusion

The various narratives on the Samaritans in Luke-Acts reveal a gradation of positive and creative portraits where the 'enemies' and the 'foreigners' are transformed into 'neighbours' and 'participants' by fulfilling what is appropriate to the standard of the kingdom. The nature of their perception and the corresponding appropriate function transcends the set boundaries of the time and enables them to be recipients of salvation anticipated by Jesus. The symbolic elements in Lk. 9:51-56 of ascension, Pentecost, reception (of Jesus), the descending of the 'fire' from heaven, and confrontation (with the Samaritans) are actualized in the mission to the Samaritans in Acts 8:4-25 in a different but reversed manner. James and John, the priests and the Levites, the nine lepers, and Simon Magus, all stand in contrast to the 'Samaritan(s)', who are 'religious aliens' but move from outside to inside to be part of the salvific blessings of the kingdom. They all fail to see what the Samaritan(s) do see, and fail to act appropriately in contrast to the appropriate behaviour of the Samaritan(s). Luke is employing a literary and rhetorical strategy of *reversalism* in order to legitimate and present the successful mission to the Samaritans narrated in Acts 8:4-25. This strategy, which he begins from the first reference to the Samaritans in Lk. 9:51-56, is employed also in the parable of the Good Samaritan (Lk. 10:25-37) and the healing of the Samaritan leper (Lk. 17:11-19), and comes to its climax in Acts 8:4-25. Features of all the Samaritan references in the Gospel are clustered together in Acts 8:4-25 to produce a climactic and reverse effect on the popular prejudices against the Samaritans. Here, motifs, attitudes, roles and sequences of events in the previous narratives are structurally and functionally reversed in Acts 8:4-25, thus breaking down the longstanding socio-religious and ethnic boundaries and achieving a climactic and successful mission to the Samaritans. The readers of the narratives are challenged to make a decision to 'see' the Samaritans, the 'marginalized' and the 'outcasts' of the day, as part and parcel of the salvific plan of God and then to 'act' appropriately to be partakers of the kingdom. Thus, the mission anticipated in Lk. 9:51-56 is also legitimized in Acts 8:4-25.

Chapter 6

Textual Analysis of Acts 8:4-25

6.1. Introduction

In the previous chapter, we have explored a literary and rhetorical strategy that Luke is employing in order to portray the success and legitimacy of the Samaritan mission. In this chapter, we will engage in an exegetical study of the text in Acts 8:4-25 and hence the approach is both literary and theological. What is the redactional motive of the author and how does his literary creativity enable him to achieve in this narrative a positive and successful portrait of the Samaritan mission? Since the figure of Simon appears in both vv. 4-13 and 14-25 and there exists a strong Simon Magus tradition outside Acts 8, a brief discussion on Simon will also be included in this study in order to draw out the significance of his portrait for the theology of Luke.

6.2. Textual Analysis of Acts 8:4-25

6.2.1. Setting and Structure

The account in Acts 8:4-25 is the first full dramatic episode where a mission is carried out beyond the borders of Jerusalem and Judaea, and by people other than the Twelve.[1] Undoubtedly, this helps Luke to fulfil the new and advanced stage in mission which is in accordance with his programmatic scheme set out in Acts 1:8. Luke mentions in Acts 8:1 the great persecution

---

1.   Philip, who ministers in Samaria, is taken to be one among the Seven (Acts 6:5) and is later on called the 'evangelist' (21:8) and must be distinct from the apostle Philip who is in the list of the Twelve (Lk. 6:14; Acts 1:13). So Pesch, *Apostelgeschichte* I, p. 272; Jervell, *Apostelgeschichte*, p. 259; Marshall, *Acts*, p. 154; Fitzmyer, *Acts*, p. 400; Witherington, *Acts*, p. 279; Barrett, *Acts* I, p. 401; Kollmann, 'Philippus', pp. 552–3. For a discussion on two Philips, see A.M. Johnson, 'Philip', pp. 49–72. For an extensive study on the identity of Philip, see Matthews, *Philip*, who argues that the two Philips were one and the same, and the confusion of the 'two Philips' has its origin with Luke himself. 'Since Luke obviously connected the Philip stories in Acts 8 with the person of the same name mentioned in Acts 6:5, and since he undoubtedly judged the list of the Twelve to be prior to that of the Seven (in terms of status, as well as temporally), he was led to conclude that the Philip mentioned in the latter list was someone other than the apostle of the same name' (p. 19).

against the church at Jerusalem which followed Stephen's martyrdom and its consequence that all except the apostles were scattered (διεσπάρησαν) throughout the regions of Judaea and Samaria.[2] The dispersed are portrayed as those who went about from place to place proclaiming the word (οἱ μὲν οὖν διασπαρέντες διῆλθον εὐαγγελιζόμενοι τὸν λόγον, v. 4; cf. 2:41; 4:4).[3] Thus, persecution becomes a catalyst for mission. And Philip goes to 'the city of Samaria' proclaiming Christ (v.5). By placing the narration of the Samaritan mission in the context of the dispersed, Luke shows that (1) Philip is one among the scattered who flees from Jerusalem and goes to the city of Samaria; (2) the Samaritan mission is to be seen as the direct consequence of persecution; and (3) though the Twelve remained in Jerusalem, the mission to the Samaritans was carried out to actualize their inclusion in God's plan of salvation.

Before we go into the text, a brief discussion on the identity of the Hellenists will help us to set the context of their mission in perspective. Regarding the question of the Hellenist-Hebrew dichotomy in Acts 6:1–8:4, it has been commonly maintained that the Hellenists and the Hebrews were two distinct parties within the earliest church in Jerusalem, distinct in language and culture.[4] The Hellenists were Greek-speaking Jews of the Diaspora who had been converted to Christianity, whereas the Hebrews were Aramaic-speaking Christians of Palestinian origin.[5] However, in contrast to this linguistic distinction, some scholars argue for an ideological difference between the two groups where the Hellenists represented a more liberal, anti-legalistic view, in contrast to the conservative legalistic view of the Hebrews. That means, the liberal views of Stephen and his group, in contrast to the conservative Jewish legalism of the Hebrews, resulted in a selective persecution of the Hellenists. That there existed such a distinction and division between these groups is based on the assumption of scholars that Luke attempts to portray

2.   Luke employs the term, 'scatter' (διασπείρω) three times in Acts 8:1, 4; 11:19 and it is found only here in the New Testament. Cf. Jer. 30:21; *AJ*, VII, 244; XII, 278.

3.   The construction, οἱ μὲν οὖν διασπαρέντες διῆλθον, as used in 8:4 introduces also the story of the Antiochene mission in 11:19. Luke tells us that the scattered group preached the word only to the Jews and some very exceptionally to the Gentiles (11:19-20). Thus he links the Hellenist mission, which was accomplished in 11:20 back to 8:4. For the use of οἱ μὲν οὖν, see Blass and Debrunner, *Greek Grammar* § 451(1); Moule, *Idiom-Book*, p. 162.

4.   C.F.D. Moule, 'Once More, Who Were the Hellenists?', *ExpTim* 70 (1958–59), pp. 100–2; Hengel, *Between Jesus and Paul*, pp. 8–11; *idem*, *The 'Hellenization' of Judaea in the First Century after Christ* (London: SCM Press, 1989); D.A. Fiensy, 'The Composition of the Jerusalem Church', in Bauckham (ed.), *The Book of Acts in Its Palestinian Setting*, pp. 213–36, 235; Craig C. Hill, *Hellenists and Hebrews: Reappraising Division within the Earliest Church* (Minneapolis: Fortress Press, 1992), pp. 22–4. Also see G. Schneider, 'Stephanus, die Hellenisten und Samaria', in Kremer (ed.), *Les Actes des Apôtres*, pp. 215–40.

5.   N.H. Taylor, 'Stephen, the Temple, and Early Christian Eschatology', *RB* 110/1 (2003), pp. 62–85; Esler, *Community*, pp. 137–9.

the early Christian community as free of factions and therefore he conceals any differences among them, but only refers to the problem of the daily distribution of food.[6]

Marcel Simon makes a distinction between the Christian Hellenists who are the disciples of Stephen and those Hellenists who are the non-Christian Jews.[7] The latter group of Hellenists are the ones who wanted to kill Paul in Jerusalem after his conversion (Acts 9:29) and are the same group as Stephen's adversaries. That the disciples of Stephen were Christians, and that they did not remain in Jerusalem but were scattered abroad, and that they were least likely to argue and disagree with Paul about the Lord Jesus make the point that the Hellenists of Acts 6 and 9:29 are different from each other. Therefore, Simon claims, 'the term Hellenists, as used by Luke, includes all Greek-speaking Jews, whether already converted, as in the case of the Seven, or still opposing the Christian message'.[8]

It is disputed whether there is anything in the account of the persecution in Acts 8:1-4 to claim distinctiveness in the ideology of the Hebrews and the Hellenists. For example, Hill argues that if the persecution was selective and the Hellenist Christians were persecuted by their fellow Hellenists, then nothing can be deduced from the persecution about the relationship between the Hellenists and the Hebrew Christians.[9] If the Hellenists were persecuted by the chief priests, then they were opposed by those who on other occasions also opposed the Hebrews. If the persecution was not selective, then it would serve to unite, rather than to divide the Hellenists and the Hebrews.[10] Thus Hill rules out the possibility of any ethnic or ideological distinction between the two groups. Taylor argues along different lines based on the presupposition that the early Christian communities of Jerusalem including the original disciples of Jesus stand in continuity with Jesus himself in their condemnation of the Temple. That means there is no essential difference between the ideology of the Hellenists and that of the Hebrews. However, this view does not explain why only the Hebrews remained.

It is not clear whether the persecution was directed against only the Hellenists or the whole Christian community in Jerusalem. Whether the persecution is directly linked to the ideological difference between the Hebrews and the Hellenists or between two different factions within the Hellenists themselves, what is significant is that there was some kind of dichotomy between the Hebrews and the Hellenists, and it seems to be primarily linguistic. It should also be noted that the most important

---

6.   Conzelmann, *Acts*, p. 44; Haenchen, *Acts*, pp. 264–8.

7.   Marcel Simon, *St Stephen and the Hellenists in the Primitive Church* (London: Longmans, Green and Co., 1958), pp. 14–15.

8.   Simon, *Stephen*, p. 15.

9.   Hill, *Hellenists*, p. 40.

10.   Hill, *Hellenists*, p. 40.

missionary field for the Hellenists was Samaria. The Samaritans would probably welcome and protect those who had been cast out from Jerusalem and by the Jerusalem authorities. That this was the case is attested in Josephus, who says that the Jewish apostates would find refuge among the Samaritans (*AJ*, XI, 346-347). If the Hellenists shared the same views as those reflected in the speech of their leader Stephen, especially their opposition to the Jerusalem Temple which led to their persecution, it was easier for the Samaritans to accept a message which denounced their rival Temple at Jerusalem.[11] However, it is not certain whether the Hellenists were significantly influenced by the Samaritan theology or the Samaritans as a group were influenced by the ideas from the Hellenists.[12] It may be that the ideology of the Hellenists could have found sufficient common ground to win the sympathy of the Samaritans.

6.2.2. Philip and the Characterization of the Samaritan Mission
Now we will focus on the way in which Luke portrays the ministry of Philip in the city of Samaria. First of all, Philip's movement is introduced by the expression, κατελθὼν εἰς (v.5) which is often used in Acts of going down from a place with a specific goal.[13] It may be that he is shown to have gone down from Jerusalem to the city of Samaria with an evangelistic purpose in mind, in contrast to the depiction of the term, διῆλθον used for the general movement of the scattered from place to place.[14] Unlike his role as a charity worker in Jerusalem (6:5), Philip appears in Samaria with his new activity as an evangelist and later on he is explicitly designated 'the evangelist' (ὁ εὐαγγελιστής, 21:8).

---

11. So O. Cullmann, 'Samaria and the Origins of the Christian Mission', in *idem, The Early Church* (London: SCM Press, 1956), pp. 185–92, 191; Simon, *Stephen*, p. 35.

12. For the Samaritan influence on Hellenism, see Scobie, 'Source Material', pp. 399–421; Simon, *Stephen*, p. 38, gives the contrary view that it was the Samaritans who were influenced by the Hellenists. What is clear is that there seems to be an ideology common to the Hellenist group of Stephen, and to the Samaritans and that it could have emerged from the dependence of one on the other or been developed independently of each other drawing from a common tradition.

13. Danker (ed.), *Greek-English Lexicon*, p. 531; see Acts 11:27; 12:19; 13:4; 15:30; 19:1; Cf. Lk. 4:31; *AJ*, VIII, 106.

14. Rick Strelan, 'The Running Prophet (Acts 8:30)', *NovT* 43 (1, 2001), pp. 31–8, draws attention to the movement of Philip to the Ethiopian eunuch in 8:30, where he is said to have 'run' (προσδραμών). Mainly based on the use of this term in the Old Testament, Strelan argues that Luke is trying to show Philip as carrying out a sacred service, to fulfil a specific mission under the impulse of the Spirit just as the inspired and commissioned prophets, and of priests and others called to cultic service. This throws further light on Philip's movement in v. 5 such that it is likely to be evangelistic. The particular goal of Philip to go to Samaria stands in contrast to the movement of the generally scattered Christians which, as Marshall points out, 'is not attributed to any specific guidance from the Spirit', but is a natural opportunity for them to preach the gospel (*Acts*, p. 154).

Secondly, Philip is said to have proclaimed Christ (ἐκήρυσσεν αὐτοῖς τὸν Χριστόν, v. 5). The use of ἐκήρυσσεν in the imperfect implies the continuous activity of Philip in proclaiming Christ to the inhabitants of the city. Philip, and others who were scattered preached the word (εὐαγγελιζόμενοι τὸν λόγον, vv. 4, 14). Theoretically, the ministry of the word was reserved for the apostles (6:2-4). The combination of κηρύσσω (v.5) and εὐαγγελίζομαι (vv. 4, 12) signifies the kerygmatic and pneumatic nature of the gospel proclaimed by Philip and these terms were used previously of the ministry of Jesus and the apostles.[15] Philip's preaching of Christ (τὸν Χριστόν) stands in contrast to his preaching of Jesus (τὸν Ἰησοῦν) to the Ethiopian eunuch later in v. 35 (cf. 9:20; 19:13). Bruce suggests that it need not be inferred that he used the term Christ.[16] It is not clear whether Philip starts with the messianic concept of the Samaritans and then presents Jesus as the fulfilment of their hope. The terminology, τὸν Χριστόν, employed by Luke in the context of the Samaritan mission may mean that the Samaritans would have understood Philip's proclamation of Christ as the fulfilment of their own messianic hope.[17] Two points are to be noted here. (1) Philip's ministry of preaching is portrayed in the same terms as that of Jesus and the apostles.[18] (2) Jesus, whom Luke depicts explicitly as Christ, the anointed one in the 'Nazareth Manifesto' (Lk. 4:18), is preached to the Samaritans thus making available to them the anticipated liberation announced in the beginning of his ministry at Galilee (cf. Isa. 58:6; 61:1). These characteristics in the narration may probably point to the kerygmatic legitimacy of the mission in Samaria.

The nature of Philip's ministry is further depicted as proclaiming the kingdom of God and the name of Jesus Christ (v.12). The phrase, 'kingdom of God' means 'the royal reign of God', anticipated in the Old Testament and taught by Jesus.[19] The name of Jesus refers to 'the active power of Jesus,

---

15.   κηρύσσω: Lk. 4:18, 19, 44; 8:1 (Jesus); 9:2 (apostles); 24:47 (church); Acts 9:20; 19:13; 20:25; 28:31 (Paul). εὐαγγελίζομαι: Lk. 4:18, 43; 9:6; Acts 5:42; 8:25; 11:20; 13:32; 14:7, 15, 21; 15:35; 16:10; 17:18. W.J. Larkin Jr., 'Mission in Acts', in W.J. Larkin Jr. and J. F. Williams (eds), *Mission in the New Testament: An Evangelical Approach* (ASMS 27; Maryknoll, NY: Orbis Books, 1998), pp. 170–86, 178.

16.   Bruce, *Acts: Greek Text*, p. 217.

17.   The Samaritans only believed in the coming of a 'prophet like Moses' of Dt. 18:15-19 whom they later called the *Taheb* or 'Restorer' or 'Returning One'. They did not share a messianic expectation with the Jews. The Samaritan woman in Jn 4:25 probably shared the view of a 'prophet like Moses' when she said, 'when he comes, he will show us all things'. See Macdonald, *Theology*, pp. 362–371; Bruce, *Book of Acts*, p. 164; Marshall, *Acts*, p. 154; Barrett, *Acts* I, p. 403. The use of the term Χριστόν *simpliciter* in Philip's preaching is unusual for Acts, as it does not directly tie in to Jesus unlike other instances, see Spencer, *Portrait*, p. 38; cf. Acts 2:31-32, 36; 3:20; 5:42; 9:22; 17:2-3; 18:5, 28 cf. 26:23.

18.   Tannehill, *Luke-Acts* II, p. 104; Spencer, *Portrait*, p. 53; Matthews, *Philip*, p. 48.

19.   Danker (ed.), *Greek-English Lexicon*, p. 168; Mi. 4:7, 8; Ps. 102:19; 144:11-13; Dan. 3:54; 4:3; Mt. 6:33; 12:28; 21:31, 43; Mk. 1:15; 4:11, 26, 30; Lk. 4:43; 6:20; 7:28; 8:1. See the discussion on the significance of the phrase, βασιλεία τοῦ θεοῦ in the following section of this study.

visibly at work in the healing of disease and in spiritual healing also' (Acts 3:6, 16).[20] For Luke, the name of Jesus is linked with forgiveness of sins, resurrection and salvation (Acts 4:10-12).[21] In essence, the message of Philip was about release from Satan's authority and it was reinforced through the miracles of healing and exorcism (cf. Lk. 10:9, 17-20).[22]

Thirdly, the result of Philip's ministry is that the crowd paid attention (προσεῖχον) with one accord (ὁμοθυμαδόν) to what he had said, hearing and seeing (ἐν τῷ ἀκούειν αὐτοὺς καὶ βλέπειν) the miracles (τὰ σημεῖα) which he did (v.6).[23] This initial response preceded their faith, as the Samaritans believed and were baptized (v.12). The phrase, τὰ σημεῖα ἃ ἐποίει, indicates that Philip's miracles were not merely 'wonders' or 'marvels', but 'signs' generated as obedient and unselfish acts in the power of Jesus.[24] It also signifies that Philip has been performing miracles just like the apostles did (4:30; 5:12; cf. 6:8).[25] The combination of the terms, σημεῖα (v.6) and δυνάμεις μεγάλας (v.13) employed here to refer to the ministry of Philip further signifies the christological and kerygmatic nature of his miracles. The exorcisms and healing of the paralysed or lame in the ministry of Philip (v.7) are the manifestations of the arrival of the kingdom of God[26] and the fulfilment of the messianic hope (Isa. 35:3, 6) and served as a confirmation of his message.[27] The term, πνεύματα ἀκάθαρτα, is another indication of Philip, a non-apostle who does exorcisms just like the apostles do (5:16).[28]

---

20.   Barrett, *Acts* I, p. 408.

21.   Jervell, *Apostelgeschichte*, p. 262.

22.   Garrett, *Demise*, p. 65.

23.   The articular infinitive, ἐν τῷ ἀκούειν αὐτοὺς καὶ βλέπειν, has a temporal sense which indicates the time at which the crowd paid attention to Philip (cf. 2:1); Blass and Debrunner, *Greek Grammar*, § 404 (1). Johnson, *Acts*, p. 145, thinks that προσεῖχον in v. 6 means 'mental attentiveness' whereas a 'commitment of heart' is implied in vv. 10-11. However, there seems to be no good reason for this distinction.

24.   Rengstorf, 'σημεῖον', *TDNT* VII, p. 240. See Acts 4:16, 22; 19:11.

25.   Tannehill, *Luke-Acts* II, p. 104; Spencer, *Portrait*, pp. 45–6; Pesch, *Apostelgeschichte* I, p. 273; Marshall, *Acts*, p. 154; Matthews, *Philip*, p. 45.

26.   Johnson, *Acts*, p. 146; Compare Lk. 5:17-26; 7:22; 9:1, 2, 6, 11; 13:11-17; 14:13, 21; Acts 3:1-10; 5:15-16.

27.   Marshall, *Acts*, p. 154; Bruce, *Book of Acts*, p. 165.

28.   Many commentators consider v. 7 as an *anacolouthic*, since the verb 'came out' (ἐξήρχοντο), refers not to the 'unclean spirits', but to the 'many' (πολλοί). For discussion, see Metzger, *Textual Commentary*, pp. 356–7. Haenchen, *Acts*, p. 302, says, 'the identification of the sick with their devils is in conflict with the distinction between them (the sick man has the unclean spirit)'; Johnson, *Acts*, p. 146; Barrett, *Acts* I, p. 404; But Fitzmyer, *Acts*, p. 403, maintains that the construction in v. 7 can be understood as a Lukan way of speaking about mental illness. Lake and Cadbury, *Beginnings* I.4, p. 90, take the construction to mean a 'mental telescoping'. It is likely that it was the 'unclean spirits' that came out, not those who were possessed by them. However, as shown in Chapter 5 of our study, it can be best understood as to produce a structural parallelism with the word, 'many' (πολλοί) in v. 7b and 8: '*many* (πολλοί), who had the unclean spirits, came out crying with a loud voice' (v.7); *many* (πολλοί) paralytics and lame were healed (v.7); and there was *great* (πολλή) joy in that city (v.8).

The phrase, βοῶντα φωνῇ μεγάλῃ, reflects the gospel stories where exorcisms are mentioned.[29] The significance of the mention of exorcism is that like Jesus and the apostles, Philip also possesses power and authority over the spiritual enemies of humankind and that his ministry reiterates the familiar patterns of redemption envisioned in Jewish scripture.[30] The mention of πολλοὶ δὲ παραλελυμένοι καὶ χωλοὶ ἐθεραπεύθησαν reflects other healing miracles performed by apostles (3:2; 9:33; 14:8). Thus, just like his ministry of preaching, Philip's healing miracles and exorcisms are also portrayed as similar to the ministry of Jesus and the apostles. This may intend to provide a pneumatic legitimacy to the Samaritan mission and the faith of Samaritan Christianity, as part of Luke's response to some controversies raised against this new community in Samaria.

Fourthly, Luke mentions that there was great joy in the city of Samaria (ἐγένετο δὲ πολλὴ χαρὰ ἐν τῇ πόλει ἐκείνῃ, v. 8). According to Pesch, the joy (χαρά) could not be the result of the faith of the Samaritans.[31] Barrett suggests that 'Luke has not yet spoken explicitly of the conversion of the Samaritans (v.12)' and therefore it is unlikely that the joy can be a sign of conversion.[32] On the contrary, Jervell suggests that as always in Luke, the χαρά is the joy of salvation brought by the Holy Spirit (cf. Lk. 2:10; 24:52; Acts 13:52; 15:3).[33] It is true that in the context of the Samaritan mission, the joy is associated with various healing miracles and exorcisms performed by Philip.[34] But it could also be on account of Philip's preaching of Jesus as the Messiah[35] with the signs and miracles accompanying to confirm his message. That it could have been originated from the faith of the Samaritans is clear from v. 12, though it is reserved to be mentioned later as Luke wanted to introduce the story of Simon before he talks about the faith of the Samaritans. Though the faith of the Samaritans is not yet related explicitly in v. 8, it is unclear that Luke intends to separate their experience of joy from their faith. Also, there is nothing in the account to suggest that the Samaritans believed and got baptized on a later occasion in the ministry of Philip different from that which is mentioned in vv. 5-8. If Luke had purposely detached the faith of the Samaritans in v. 12 from the mention of the miraculous signs in vv. 6-8, it may have been to show that their faith is directly

29. Mk 1:26; Lk. 4:35, 41; 8:33; 9:42; 11:14. For a discussion on the significance of the phrase φωνῇ μεγάλῃ in both Graeco-Roman texts and in Jewish literature, see Rick Strelan, 'Recognizing the Gods (Acts 14:8-10)', *NTS* 46 (2000), pp. 488–503.

30. T.E. Klutz, *With Authority and Power: A Socio-Stylistic Investigation of Exorcisms in Luke-Acts* (PhD Thesis; Sheffield: University of Sheffield, 1995), pp. 407, 409.

31. Pesch, *Apostelgeschichte* I, p. 273.

32. Barrett, *Acts* I, p. 404; also Witherington, *Acts*, p. 283, n.17.

33. Jervell, *Apostelgeschichte*, p. 260.

34. Haenchen, *Acts*, p. 302; Marshall, *Acts*, p. 154; Barrett, *Acts* I, p. 404; Witherington, *Acts*, p. 283, n.17.

35. Fitzmyer, *Acts*, p. 403; Witherington, *Acts*, p. 283.

linked to Philip's preaching. That in the following story of Philip's mission, the Ethiopian eunuch went on his journey rejoicing (χαίρω, v. 39) after his baptism suggests that his joy was not because of the miracles, if there were any, but because of his acceptance of Jesus (cf. Lk. 8:13). The point here is that the ministry of Philip, according to Luke, brought into Samaria the joy of salvation anticipated by the people of God in the coming of the saviour Jesus (cf. Lk. 2:10), and experienced on account of accepting him.

Now Luke introduces Simon in vv. 9-11 as someone who was 'practising magic' (μαγεύων, v. 9; cf. v. 11) and 'amazing' (ἐξιστάνων) the people of Samaria in the same city (ἐν τῇ πόλει) before (προϋπῆρχεν, cf. Lk. 23:12) Philip went, and thus vv. 9-11 can be seen as a 'flashback' in the story. It is interesting to note that Luke does not use the word μάγος for Simon, instead he uses the participle μαγεύων (practising as a magus, v. 9) and the phrase ταῖς μαγείαις (the works of a magus, v. 11).[36] Luke uses neither of these words elsewhere, even when he describes the Jewish false prophet Elymas as a μάγος (13:6-8).[37] Also, the word μαγεύων in v. 9 occurs only here in the New Testament. It has been suggested that the word μέγας (great) in v. 9 should be read as μάγος (magician).[38] This is because of the emendation μάγον for μέγαν in Lucian's reference to Christ in *De morte peregrini* 11. But this suggestion is unlikely because (a) Luke uses this again in v. 10 as a title. (b) Simon's claim that he is μέγας meant that he was more than a magician, and for Luke magi are the magicians. (c) By this title Luke may be linking Simon with the tragic destiny of Theudas, who also made a similar claim to that of Simon (λέγων εἶναί τινα ἑαυτόν, 5:36; cf. λέγων εἶναί τινα ἑαυτὸν μέγαν, 8:9).

In v. 12 the story turns from the past to the present. The Samaritans 'believed' (ἐπίστευσαν) Philip not because of the miracles he did but because of his preaching of Christ, the kingdom of God and of the name of Jesus Christ.[39] The construction πιστεύω with the dative τῷ Φιλίππῳ in v. 12 is taken to mean by Dunn that Luke deliberately indicates the belief of the Samaritans as an assent of the mind directed towards the evangelist Philip, rather than to Christ himself, and shows therefore, that their faith and response was defective.[40] However, there seems to be no good reason for such a view. (1) Luke uses the aorist, ἐπίστευσαν in v. 12 for the Samaritans' final

36. So E.M. Yamauchi, *Pre-Christian Gnosticism: A Survey of the Proposed Evidences* (London: Tyndale Press, 1973), p. 58. See the discussion in Haar, *Simon Magus*, pp. 174–5.

37. Barrett, 'Light', p. 286. For a discussion of the term μάγος, see A.D. Nock, 'Paul and the Magus', in Jackson and Lake (eds), *Beginnings* I.5, pp. 164–88.

38. C.S.C. Williams, *The Acts of the Apostles* (BNTC; London: A. & C. Black, 1957), p. 115; Lake and Cadbury, *Beginnings* I.4, p. 90.

39. Barrett, *Acts* I, p. 403; Jervell, *Apostelgeschichte*, p. 262.

40. Dunn, *Baptism*, pp. 63–8; idem, *Acts*, p. 110.

response to Philip, whereas he uses the imperfect, προσεῖχον in vv. 6, 10 and 11 for their response to Simon and for their initial response to Philip.[41] The cause and effect of people's close attention to Simon is contrasted with that of their attention to Philip: they paid attention to Simon and followed him because of their fascination with him, not their belief. But the people followed Philip because they believed. (2) In v. 12, Luke offers another contrast between the sorcery of Simon and his amazement of the people on the one hand, the gospel message of Philip and the faith and baptism of the people on the other. (3) That the Samaritans' conversion was genuine is evident from Acts 2:41 and 11:1, 18 where Luke employs the same language as in 8:12 and echoes the result of the first Christian Pentecost in Jerusalem where the Jews believed and got baptized at the preaching of Peter.[42] (4) The report which the Jerusalem apostles heard was that 'Samaria had received the Word of God' (v.14) and there is no indication that they misunderstood the Samaritans' acceptance of God's Word. (5) Dunn's claim that the Samaritans' belief was only a mental assent rather than an authentic Christian faith, and that it was directed to Philip (ἐπίστευσαν τῷ Φιλίππῳ), not to Christ, does not bear weight in the light of the conversion of Lydia who gives heed to *what was spoken by Paul* (προσέχειν τοῖς λαλουμένοις ὑπὸ τοῦ Παύλου, 16:14, 34; cf. 18:8). In his account of the mission of the Seventy (-two) Luke has Jesus say, 'Whoever hears you, hears me' (ὁ ἀκούων ὑμῶν ἐμοῦ ἀκούει, Lk. 10:16a). To believe Philip means to hear the God who speaks through him.[43] (6) Luke portrays Philip as a successful missionary whose preaching and performing of miraculous deeds are similar to those of Jesus and the disciples.[44] The cumulative effects of the terms such as κηρύσσω, Χριστόν, εὐαγγελίζομαι, βασιλεία τοῦ θεοῦ, σημεῖα καὶ δυνάμις, θεραπεύω, πιστεύω καὶ βαπτίζω all suggest the message and miracles of Philip as no less effective than those of the other early Christian missionaries. Therefore, Dunn's suggestion is unlikely given Luke's positive portrayal of the experience of the Samaritans, the missionary success of Philip and especially his success over Simon and his followers. It may be that in this non-Lukan expression, πιστεύω with the dative τῷ Φιλίππῳ, Luke is reflecting a source or tradition, which attributed the conversion of the Samaritans to Philip saying that they believed Philip now instead of Simon.[45]

---

41. Haenchen, *Acts*, p. 303.
42. Fitzmyer, *Acts*, p. 406; Turner, *Power*, p. 365.
43. Marshall, *Acts*, p. 156; Turner, *Power*, p. 365.
44. Pesch, *Apostelgeschichte* I, p. 273; Marshall, *Acts*, p. 154; Tannehill, *Luke-Acts* II, p. 104; Johnson, *Acts*, p. 151; Spencer, *Portrait*, p. 53, says that the 'Samaritan ministry of Philip the evangelist in Acts 8:4-13 clearly reflects the principal hallmarks of authentic mission activity disclosed throughout Luke-Acts'.
45. Dickerson, 'Sources', p. 229.

Luke says in v. 13 that Simon believed (ἐπίστευσεν), was baptized (βαπτιζθείς), continued with Philip (προσκαρτερῶν), seeing (θεωρῶν) the great signs and miracles, and was amazed (ἐξίστατο). Luke uses the words μέγας, δύναμις, and ἐξίστημι together for the success of Philip over Simon (v.13). Earlier by his act of sorcery, Simon amazes (ἐξιστάνων) the people of Samaria, but later he himself was amazed (ἐξίστατο) seeing the great signs and miracles of Philip. Simon is now seen as a Christian.[46] His new situation appears to correspond to the genuine experience of those in the early church who believed and were baptized and continued in prayer and fellowship.[47] But the use of the word, θεωρῶν for seeing the miracles stands in opposition to the genuineness of his belief and thus makes him a spectator.[48] His situation could well be summarized in Klauck's words: 'Simon's conversion and faith are indeed generated by a subjectively honest attitude, but his faith is not yet so firm as it ought to be. Simon's previous activities have left their mark on him in the form of a deficit: he bases his faith too exclusively on miracles, too little on the word'.[49] Here Luke shows that the ministry of preaching Christ and the kingdom of God confronts and defeats the magical powers of Simon and the Samaritans' fascination by him. It is a Lukan intention to portray the superiority of Philip over Simon[50] or to differentiate Christianity from magic and paganizm.[51] Luke's apologetic interest is evident in this portrayal of Philip and Simon.[52]

Conzelmann considers the narrative in v. 13 as 'not historical'.[53] He says that the astonishment of Simon after he has already been converted 'arises from Luke's desire, in making the transition to the following episode, to establish some connection with the events in vv. 18-24, and from his concern to illustrate the superiority of Christian power over magic'.[54] Barrett thinks v. 13 is probably an 'editorial supplement', and therefore he claims that there

---

46.   Haar, *Simon Magus*, p. 180; Pesch, *Apostelgeschichte* I, p. 275; Fitzmyer, *Acts*, p. 405; Jervell, *Apostelgeschichte*, p. 264; Johnson, *Acts*, p. 148; Barrett, *Acts* I, p. 409, says that there is nothing in v. 13 to suggest that Simon was 'less sincere or in any way a less satisfactory convert than the other Samaritans'. For a discussion on the contrary view of Witherington (*Acts*, p. 288) that Simon was never converted at all, see section 2.4 of the study.

47.   The words πιστεύω and βαπτίζω, occur together only in Mk 16:16; Acts 8:12, 13; 18:8; 19:4. The use of προσκαρτερῶν may refer back to Acts 1:14; 2:42, 46; 6:4, in all of which it is used in the context of prayer and fellowship.

48.   As mentioned in Chapter 5, Luke never uses the word θεωρῶν for seeing the signs and miracles. The only other instances in the New Testament are Jn 2:23 and 6:2, where the former reflects a negative response in its context and the latter is set in contrast to a positive response (ἰδόντες) of the same crowd in 6:14.

49.   Klauck, *Magic*, p. 18

50.   Klauck, *Magic*, p. 18.

51.   Garrett, *Demise*, p. 76; Williams, *Acts*, p. 116.

52.   Johnson, *Acts*, p. 148; Smith, 'Account', p. 736, considers the entire episode as a 'piece of Christian propaganda against the followers of Simon'.

53.   Conzelmann, *Acts*, p. 64.

54.   Conzelmann, *Acts*, p. 64.

was no original connection between Philip and Simon. For him, v. 13 is 'the only verse that brings Philip and Simon together, and if we are right in taking it to be redactional we must conclude that the pre-Lucan tradition did not connect these two figures'.[55] Thus v. 13 poses apparent historical, literary and theological discrepancies.

It should be noted that the narrative manifests a striking similarity or an inter-textual relationship between the activity of Philip and that of Simon Magus in 8:4-13. Karlmann Beyschlag has drawn a comparison as follows:[56]

Philip	Simon
1. came to the city (v.5)	1. was already in the city (v.9)
2. proclaimed Christ (vv. 5, 12)	2. designated himself a great power (v.9)
3. did great acts of power (vv. 6f, 13)	3. did magic (vv. 9f)
4. the people followed him (vv. 6, 12)	4. the people followed him (vv. 9, 11)
5. There was great joy, faith and the baptism of all (vv. 8, 12)	5. Simon saw Philip's mighty acts of power and was beside himself (v.13)

It is noted by Beyschlag that the major elements in the account of Philip (8:5-8) are also found in the account of Simon (8:9-13).[57] According to Lüdemann, the comparison emerges only when redactional features in the text are ignored. He thinks that the tradition about Simon underlying vv. 9-13 is 'part of a written or oral tradition from the Hellenist circles which reported the clash between the supporters of Simonian and Christian religion'.[58] He further suggests that this 'Hellenist tradition would have contained not only an account of the successful mission to the Gentiles in Samaria but also an account of the victory over the god of the Simonians'.[59] Though Lüdemann sees the section as thoroughly Lukan in language, he identifies the designation Δύναμις Μεγάλη for Simon as part of the tradition. That both the Lukan account and the early Christian sources report that Simon had a significant number of followers in Samaria affirms a tradition about Simon.

55. Barrett, 'Light', pp. 283–4; *idem*, *Acts* I, p. 409.
56. Beyschlag, *Simon Magus*, p. 101.
57. Beyschlag, *Simon Magus*, p. 101.
58. Lüdemann, *Traditions*, p. 98.
59. Lüdemann, *Traditions*, pp. 98–9.

6.2.3. *The Jerusalem Apostles, Samaritan Christians and Simon*

When the apostles who remained in Jerusalem (cf.8:1) heard that Samaria had accepted the word of God, they sent (ἀπέστειλαν) Peter and John to Samaria, as their emissaries. The use of ἀπέστειλαν implies an official mission just as Jesus sent the Twelve and the Seventy (Lk. 9:2; 10:1). Peter and John act together here in Samaria as in 3:1–4:22. When they arrived they prayed for the Samaritans that they might receive the Holy Spirit (v.15). 'The Holy Spirit had not yet come upon any of them; they had simply been baptized into the name of the Lord Jesus' (v.16). When they laid their hands on them, the Samaritan Christians received the Holy Spirit (v.17). The laying on of hands, in general, could signify transfer of blessing, 'life-force', the Spirit and Charismata.[60] The double action of the apostles is mentioned in vv. 15 and 17 – prayer and imposition of hands. The same double action is mentioned in 6:6 for the commissioning of the Seven (προσευξάμενοι ἐπέθηκαν αὐτοῖς τὰς χεῖρας). This action now legitimizes the faith of the Samaritan Christians.

The story again turns from the new experience of the Samaritan Christians to the intention of Simon who attempted to buy the authority (ἐξουσία) of dispensing the Holy Spirit with money (ἀργύριον, v. 18). Simon would have thought of the bestowal of the Spirit as a valuable magic and that the authority of the apostles was worth purchasing to make profit in the future.[61] It is interesting to note a parallel here to Lk. 9:1, where Jesus gave the disciples both power and authority (δύναμις καὶ ἐξουσία) when he sent them for mission. In the context of exorcism, authority (ἐξουσία) takes precedence or is singled out (Lk. 4:36; 10:19; cf. Mt. 10:1; Mk 6:7). The source of authority is Jesus himself and authority cannot be exchanged for money as Simon thought. Similarly, in the same context of the mission of the Twelve, Jesus specifically prohibits the disciples to carry money (ἀργύριον, Lk. 9:3).[62] In other words, humanity cannot and should not manipulate ἐξουσία and ἀργύριον for selfish purposes, and ἐξουσία has nothing to do with ἀργύριον as Simon thought. It stands against the characteristics of the leadership and lifestyle of Jesus and his apostles.[63] Though Simon's faith appears to be genuine in v. 13, Luke now depicts him as 'lapsing' into the old pattern of behaviour.[64]

---

60.   J.P. Tipei, *The Laying on of Hands in the New Testament* (PhD Thesis; Sheffield: University of Sheffield, 2000), p. 275.

61.   Tannehill, *Luke-Acts* II, p. 107; Klauck, *Magic*, p. 20; Barrett, 'Light', p. 288.

62.   Thomas E. Schmidt, *Hostility to Wealth in the Synoptic Gospels* (JSNTSup.15; Sheffield: Sheffield Academic Press, 1987), p. 144.

63.   Steve Walton, *Leadership and Lifestyle: The Portrait of Paul in the Miletus Speech and 1 Thessalonians* (Cambridge: Cambridge University Press, 2000), p. 136.

64.   Klauck, *Magic*, p. 21.

Next, we will analyse Peter's response to Simon and its rhetorical and theological significance for the portrayal of the Samaritan mission. Peter's answer is, 'May your money perish with you' (τὸ ἀργύριόν σου σὺν σοὶ εἴη εἰς ἀπώλειαν, v. 20a), the literal rendering of which is, 'Your money be with you to perdition'. The phrase, εἴη εἰς ἀπώλειαν can be compared with εἰς ἀπώλειαν ἔσεσθε in Dan. 2:5c (Theodotion) and εἰς ἀπώλειαν ἔσονται in Dan. 3:96 (MT 29) (Theodotion) and it refers to the destruction that one experiences.[65] The word ἀπώλεια appears also in the magical papyri in the context of driving out demons: 'Come out, daimon, since I bind you with unbreakable adamantine fetters, and I deliver you into the black chaos in perdition (ἐν ταῖς ἀπώλειαις)'.[66] In the New Testament, the term is used for eternal destruction and signifies 'an everlasting state of torment and death'.[67] The one who becomes a victim to perdition, as in the case of Judas, is designated ὁ υἱὸς τῆς ἀπωλειας (Jn 17:2; cf. 2 Thess. 2:3). The force of the term in Acts signifies the seriousness of the sin of Simon and the inescapable consequence of his action. The reason for Peter's curse upon Simon is explicitly mentioned in the text: 'because you thought you could buy the gift of God with money' (ὅτι τὴν δωρεὰν τοῦ θεοῦ ἐνόμισας διὰ χρημάτων κτᾶσθαι, 20b). B. Lindars notes that in both classical and biblical Greek, the term δωρεά is not used of the presents given by men but it is reserved for expressing divine bounty.[68] In Acts, the term is used to refer to the Holy Spirit (2:38; 10:45; 11:17). In Jn 4:10, it could possibly mean the divine activity of God or the Holy Spirit.[69] If Acts 8:20 shares the meaning of Jn 4:10, then the term 'gift of God' fits very well with the context of Simon trying to purchase the authority to bestow the Holy Spirit on others. Here ἀργύριον and χρήματα are used synonymously for 'money', and often they have a negative connotation in Luke-Acts.[70] Simon's request, 'whomever I lay hands on' (ᾧ ἐὰν ἐπιθῶ τὰς χεῖρας, v. 19) indicates his intention to make use of God's Spirit for his own selfish purposes and to make a profit out of it. It unmasks the falsehood of pagan magic.[71] The text clearly manifests its meaning: riches could not purchase the divine authority, which is a free gift of God.[72] Or, the manifestations of the Spirit are not saleable and it cannot be dispensed for rewards.[73]

---

65. Danker (ed.), *Greek-English Lexicon*, p. 127; Job 26:6; 28:22; Prov. 15:11; *AJ*, XV, 62; *Test. Dan.* 4:5.

66. *PGM*, IV.1247-48. The text is from H. D. Betz (ed.), *The Greek Magical Papyri in Translation* (Chicago: The University of Chicago Press, 1986), p. 62.

67. Oepke, 'ἀπώλεια', *TDNT* I, p. 397; See Mt. 7:13; Rom. 9:22; Phil. 1:28; 3:19; 1 Tim. 6:9; Heb. 10:39; 2 Pet. 2:1, 3; 3:7, 16; Rev. 17:8, 11.

68. Lindars, *John*, pp. 181-2.

69. Barrett, *John*, p. 233, thinks that the word 'gift' here may not mean Jesus himself.

70. See Lk. 9:3; 18:24; 22:5; Acts 3:6; 8:20; 20:33; 24:26.

71. Jervell, *Apostelgeschichte*, p. 264.

72. Cf. Acts 2:38; 11:17; Jn 4:10.

73. Barrett, 'Light', pp. 291-2.

The encounter between Simon and Peter leads to the consummation of Simon's wicked heart being exposed and the need for his repentance and prayer (vv. 21–23). Peter's words, 'you can have no part or share in this matter' (οὐκ ἔστιν σοι μερὶς οὐδὲ κλῆρος ἐν τῷ λόγῳ τούτῳ, v. 21a) echoes Dt. 12:12 – ὅτι οὐκ ἔστιν αὐτῷ μερὶς οὐδὲ κλῆρος μεθ' ὑμῶν.[74] This expression is again used in Dt.14:27 – ὅτι οὐκ ἔστιν αὐτῷ μερὶς οὐδὲ κλῆρος μετὰ σοῦ and it signifies excommunication.[75] A similar expression is found in *m.Sanh.*10:1-4, which refers to various people as 'having no portion in the age to come'. The word κλῆρος is used in Acts 1:17, 26 in the recounting of Judas' fate and the election of Matthias. The phrase, ἐν τῷ λόγῳ τούτῳ (in this 'word' or 'matter') may refer to the apostolic ministry (cf. 6:4) in which Simon wanted to participate, rather than to membership in the people.[76] This again could reflect the destiny of Judas who lost his share in the apostolic ministry (τὸν κλῆρον τῆς διακονίας ταύτης, 1:17), and the participation of Matthias who took over this share (τῆς διακονίας ταύτης καὶ ἀποστολῆς, 1:25).[77] In Simon's case, it means he has no part in the apostolic ministry and could also imply excommunication from the Samaritan Christian community.[78] In Simon, one could see a prototype of the enemy of God and the enemy of Christ's church.[79]

The reason for Simon's exclusion is further expressed in Peter's words, 'for your heart is not right before God' (v.21b). A similar expression is found in Ps. 78 (LXX 77):37. Peter asks Simon to repent (μετανόησον) and pray (δεήθητι) that, if possible, the thought of his heart may be forgiven him (ἡ ἐπίνοια τῆς καρδίας σου, v. 22).[80] The terms, μετανοέω and ἀφίημι used in Peter's response here are also used at the conclusion of his speech at Pentecost (2:38). The construction is conditional. εἰ with the future subjunctive,

74. Danker (ed.), *Greek-English Lexicon*, p. 633.
75. Fitzmyer, *Acts*, p. 407; Barrett, *Acts* I, p. 414.
76. Haar, *Simon Magus*, p. 184; Johnson, *Acts*, p. 149.
77. Schuyler Brown, *Apostasy and Perseverance in the Theology of Luke* (Rome: Pontifical Biblical Institute, 1969), pp. 82–97.
78. Haenchen, *Acts*, p. 305; Barrett, *Acts* I, p. 414; Jervell, *Apostelgeschichte*, p. 265; Klauck, *Magic*, p. 22. *Contra* Haar, *Simon Magus*, p. 185, who denies the idea of excommunication and points to Lev. 19:17 where one ought to rebuke his 'neighbour' who either sins or is about to commit sin.
79. Pesch, *Apostelgeschichte* I, p. 278.
80. The word ἐπίνοια which means a thought or intention, is used only here in the New Testament. It could be used in the sense of wicked intention as in Wis. 9:14; 14:12; 15:4. In the present context in v. 22, the term is used to refer to Simon's heart or thought. The term is also a title used for Simon's female partner, Helen. Justin, *I Apology* 26.3 uses the word ἔννοια; Hippolytus, *Ref.* 6.19, ἐπίνοια. Lüdemann, *Traditions*, pp. 100–1, thinks that the pre-Lukan tradition contained a reference to Simon's consort, Helen, but Luke altered the tradition to make Peter ironically refer to her. It is not certain whether Luke is aware of Helen and that he is making an allusion to her. But it is significant that he is retaining the term, which he probably found in his source referring to Simon's intention or to his female partner or to both.

ἀφεθήσεταί indicates a possibility of Simon being forgiven, and the use of ἄρα strengthens the doubt of Peter's intended verdict.[81] The expression, μετανόησον οὖν ἀπό (v.22) where μετανόειν introduced with ἀπό is a unique construction and it means to repent from a particular sin as in Jer. 8:6 and 1 Clem. 8:3.[82] Therefore, it may be that Simon needs to repent from the recently committed sin of attempting to buy the Holy Spirit with money.[83] Simon's request for prayer may show that he wants to avoid the threatened curse by the apostles but not to come out of his magical activities.[84] His request indicates the powerlessness of magic before the one who bears the Spirit.[85] The Bezan text of Acts adds in v. 24, ὃς πολλὰ κλαίων οὐ διελίμπανεν, 'who did not stop weeping copiously'.[86] This addition suggests that 'Simon's tears are of remorse and perhaps of repentance'.[87] But, it is not clear whether Simon repented and that Luke ends Simon's story on a favourable note.[88]

In Acts we have various stories where the offenders of God were given immediate death penalties or given time to repent that they might be forgiven and possibly escape the punishment. Ananias and Sapphira (5:1-11), and Herod Agrippa I (12:20-23) die immediately, whereas Simon is given time to repent (8:22). There are Jewish parallels to the kind of crime and punishment Luke narrates in his Simon story.[89] For example, Brodie points out a parallelism between the story of Gehazi's avarice in 2 Kings 5:20-27 and the story of Simon.[90] Both Gehazi and Simon wanted to make a profit from the demonstration of God's power, but the former received Naaman's leprosy, and the latter a rebuke and warning to repent of the wicked thought. Though this story only partially resembles the Simon episode, the theme of money and its improper handling and the possible consequences are

---

81.	The combination of εἰ with ἄρα is used in expressions of expectation. See Blass, Debrunner and Funk, *Greek Grammar* § 375.

82.	See also 1 QS 5.1; CD 15.7.

83.	Jervell, *Apostelgeschichte*, p. 265.

84.	So Pesch, *Apostelgeschichte* I, p. 277.

85.	Conzelmann, *Acts*, p. 66.

86.	D cop[G67] Sy[hmg] Tert[anima 34] Ephr[cat (p409)]; Metzger, *Textual Commentary*, pp. 358–9. For a detailed study on the Bezan Text of Acts, see Jenny Read-Heimerdinger, *The Bezan Text of Acts: A Contribution of Discourse Analysis to Textual Criticism* (JSNTSup.236; Sheffield: Sheffield Academic Press, 2002).

87.	Metzger, *Textual Commentary*, p. 359.

88.	*Contra*, Fitzmyer, *Acts*, p. 407.

89.	Also, there are Hellenistic parallels to the kind of stories which Acts narrates regarding the divine punishment that the trespassers must undergo, but for our Simon story, Jewish parallels are more convincing. For a useful discussion of different Hellenistic parallels to such stories in Acts, see Henriette Havelaar, 'Hellenistic Parallels to Acts 5:1-11 and the Problem of Conflicting Interpretations', *JSNT* 67 (1997), pp. 63–82.

90.	Brodie, '2 Kings 5', pp. 41–67; *idem*, 'Elijah-Elisha Narrative', pp. 78–85.

highlighted in each. On the basis of his use of the Septuagint,[91] it is possible that Luke may be employing here a rhetorical imitation of 2 Kings 5.[92] That he is aware of Naaman's story is clear from his use of it in his Gospel (Lk. 4:27).

In Qumran, offenders in relation to money or property are excluded from the community life and are given time to repent: 'If one of them has lied deliberately in matters of property, he shall be excluded from the pure Meal of the Congregation for one year and shall do penance with respect to one quarter of his blood' (1QS 6.25). This rule of excommunication and repentance in relation to the theme of money resembles Peter's response to Simon. These parallels, especially where excommunication and repentance are involved in the punishment, suggest that Luke's readers of the Simon story may very well have been familiar with the sort of punishment that offenders had to undergo in their own day and therefore will find sanction for Peter's strong rebuke of Simon. Their familiarity with similar possible events, based on their wider experience of the world and their experience of other texts will provide the readers with a feel of the factual event in Luke's narrative of the Peter-Simon encounter.

As mentioned in the previous chapter, the nature of the 'seeing' of Simon and Peter is significant in the text. Earlier Simon was portrayed as the one who follows Philip, 'seeing' (θεωρῶν, v. 13) the signs and mighty wonders he performed and thus Simon is depicted as a 'spectator'.[93] In the context of the apostles' ministry, he offers money to Peter and John after 'seeing' (ἰδὼν, v. 18) the Holy Spirit being given to the Samaritans. In contrast to this, Peter 'sees' (ὁρῶ, v. 23) the wickedness of Simon and this could refer to the prophetic insight of Peter (Lk. 5:22; 7:39; 9:47; 24:38; Acts 5:2). Four points should be noted here.

(1) Simon probably saw some manifestations of the Holy Spirit after the imposition of the apostles' hands and thought it was more appealing and so worth purchasing by paying money. In other words, Simon would have seen

---

91.   D.L. Bock, *Proclamation from Prophecy and Pattern: Lukan Old Testament Christology* (Sheffield: JSOT Press, 1987); W.K.L. Clarke, 'The Use of the Septuagint in Acts', in F.J. Jackson and K. Lake (eds), *The Beginnings of Christianity: Part 1. The Acts of the Apostles, vol. V* (London: Macmillan, 1922), pp. 80–4; Fitzmyer, 'Old Testament', pp. 525–6; Arnold, 'Luke's Characterizing', pp. 300–23; Brodie, 'Luke 7:11-17', pp. 247–67; C.A. Evans, 'Elijah/Elisha Narratives', pp. 75–83; H. Ringgren, 'Luke's Use of the Old Testament', *HTR* 79 (1986), pp. 227–35; David Peterson, 'The Motif of Fulfilment and the Purpose of Luke-Acts', in B.W. Winter and A.D. Clarke (eds), *The Book of Acts in Its First Century Setting I. The Book of Acts in Its Ancient Literary Setting*, pp. 83–104.

92.   Brodie, '2 Kings 5', pp. 41–67, makes the point that 'whatever be the extent of Luke's information about the historical Simon, his final picture of the magician, as now found in the text of Acts, includes a careful reworking of the text of 2 Kgs 5' (p. 50).

93.   Danker (ed.), *Greek-English Lexicon*, p. 454; Abbott-Smith, *Greek Lexicon*, p. 206; Michaelis, 'ὁράω', 'θεωρέω', in G. Friedrich (ed.), *TDNT* V, pp. 346–66.

the laying on of hands and the conferment of the Spirit as 'an outstanding piece of magic'.[94] And he wanted to have the ἐξουσία from Peter, instead of δύναμις. Simon himself was or associated with δύναμις and he saw Philip's miracles also as δύναμις; whereas Simon perceived the conferring of the Holy Spirit as an act of authority more appealing than his own magic and that of the healing miracles of Philip. In other words, Simon claimed to be δύναμις μεγάλη, without having the real ἐξουσία. This gives the clue that he did not want to purchase the δύναμις which he saw in the miracles performed by Philip, but the ἐξουσία from Peter, an authority which the magician could not possess before.[95] In this respect, the claim of Conzelmann that the story originally was about Simon seeking to buy the power to do the miracles, not to impart the Spirit and that Luke appears to have changed this is unjustifiable.[96]

(2) In contrast to what is said of Simon in v. 13, we have a different picture of him in vv. 18-24. That means, Luke gives us two portraits of Simon: he was practising magic but when he believed the message of Philip, he was baptized and became an 'insider'; in a later stage he is found guilty of misconduct and is treated as an 'outsider'. The Simon whom Peter confronts in vv. 18-24 is different in character from the one whom Philip confronted in vv. 9-11. In vv. 18-24, Peter speaks to Simon of the 'gift of God', of having 'no part or share' in the ministry, that 'his heart is not right before God', of the need for him to 'repent' and 'pray', and of the possibility of receiving 'forgiveness' of his sins. This suggests that in vv. 18-24, Luke portrays Simon who was already an 'insider' unlike his portrait of him in vv. 9-11, where he is an 'outsider'. Peter's prophetic insight reveals Simon's wicked condition, and excludes him from the newly formed community of Samaritan Christianity. Thus, Luke makes a distinction between the authentic faith of the Samaritan Christians and the wicked intention of Simon. In other words, portraying Simon as an 'apostate', Luke legitimizes the Samaritan Christians and subverts the Jewish charge of them being 'apostates'.

(3) In light of what he has Peter perceive in Simon and through the portrayal of Simon's exclusion, Luke further defends the purity of Samaritan Christianity. The expression, 'bond of iniquity' (σύνδεσμον ἀδικίας, 8:23) figuratively means 'fetter that consists in unrighteousness'.[97] It may allude metaphorically to Isa. 58:6, which Luke makes use of in Lk. 4:18-19.[98] In Philip's message of preaching Christ, the anointed one (Acts 8:5), the antic-

---

94. Casey, 'Simon Magus', p. 151; Barrett, 'Light', p. 292; Pesch, *Apostelgeschichte* I, p. 276; Jervell, *Apostelgeschichte*, p. 264.

95. Berger, 'Propaganda', p. 315.

96. Conzelmann, *Acts*, p. 66.

97. Danker (ed.), *Greek-English Lexicon*, p. 966.

98. *Contra* Fitzer, 'σύνδεσμος', *TDNT* VII, p. 858, assumes an expression like 'epitome of shame' (1 QH 1:22), instead of Isa. 58:6.

ipated result of liberation proclaimed at Nazareth is extended to the Samaritans, which also includes loosening the bond of wickedness. However, in contrast to the Samaritans' experience of freedom, Peter sees Simon being still in a bond of iniquity.[99]

(4) It is likely that other than magic and hypocrisy, Luke is also condemning the sin of idolatry in his portrayal of Simon. The expression, 'gall of bitterness' (χολὴν πικρίας, v. 23) in Peter's response to Simon refers to the latter's predicament in a state of sin[100] and echoes Dt. 29:17-18 (ἐν χολῇ καὶ πικρια) where it refers to the condition of the idolatrous.[101] Similarly, the claim that Simon made before his conversion that he was somebody (λέγων εἶναί τινα ἑαυτὸν μέγαν, v. 9), equals him with Theudas who also made the same claim (λέγων εἶναί τινα ἑαυτόν, 5:36)[102] and with king Herod who 'did not give God the glory' (12:23; cf. 10:25-26; 14:12-17). For Luke, the self-deification of these men brings a tragic destiny. In his claim that he is the 'power of God', Simon exalts himself as a god and commits the same sin that the devil had once committed in the wilderness (Lk. 4:6-7).[103] The request he made after his conversion, 'give me this authority', which he wanted to buy with money, is a devilish one and could again refer to Lk. 4:6, where idolatry is condemned.[104] In this respect, the connection that Jervell makes between Simon's attempt to buy the gift of God with money for profit and the condemnation of the sin of Israel by Stephen in making the golden calf (Acts 7:39-41) is remarkable. Regarding the profit-making pagan magic, Jervell says, 'Sie ist für Lukas so etwas wie die Ursünde, die Verneinung Gottes als Gott und Schöpfer, die Idolatrie, wie sie schon von dem Fall des Goldenen Kalbes her bekannt ist, 7:39ff'. (Luke sees this as the original sin, the denial of God as God and creator. This is the kind of idolatry seen in the case of the golden calf).[105] The significance is that just as Stephen condemned the idolatry of Jerusalem-bound Jews, Luke shows through his portrayal of Simon that idolatry is prohibited in the Samaritan Church and that there is no place for such a charge in the new Samaritan Christian community. This becomes of further significance in light of the Jewish portrait of the Samaritans in general, as shown earlier in Chapter 3, that they were idolaters, in that Luke reverses the charge of idolatry to the Jews through the words

99. Garrett, *Demise*, p. 72.
100. Danker (ed.), *Greek-English Lexicon*, p. 1086. See also Heb.12:15; Lam. 3:19; 1QS 2.11-12.
101. Haar, *Simon Magus*, p. 190; Barrett, *Acts* I, p. 417; Johnson, *Acts*, p. 149.
102. For a useful discussion on Theudas and other leaders of popular movements in first century Palestine, see Rebecca Gray, *Prophetic Figures in the Late Second Temple Jewish Palestine: The Evidence from Josephus* (Oxford: Oxford University Press, 1993), especially pp. 114–16 on Theudas.
103. Garrett, *Demise*, p. 67.
104. Pesch, *Apostelgeschichte* I, p. 276.
105. Jervell, *Apostelgeschichte*, p. 265.

of Stephen and thus legitimizes the new Samaritan Christian community. Also, relating the charge of idolatry to Simon, Luke portrays the legitimacy of Samaritan Christians and defends their purity in contrast to the popular Jewish view of the Samaritans as idolaters.

6.3. *The Lukan Themes in Acts 8:4-25*

The narrative in Acts 8:4-25 combines a number of themes that are significant in Acts and manifests the redactional interest of the author. For example, the Lukan traits of the proclamation of the word of God, the kingdom of God, faith, baptism, the reception of the Holy Spirit, the role of the Jerusalem apostles, the use of possessions, and the defeat of magic, all are linked together in the story of the Samaritan mission.

6.3.1. *The 'Kingdom of God' as the Content of Philip's Preaching*
It is striking to note that Philip is the first one mentioned in Acts as preaching the kingdom of God (βασιλεία τοῦ θεοῦ, 8:12). Both at the beginning and end of the narrative in Acts, the subject of the Christian kerygma is referred to as the 'kingdom of God' (1:3; 28:23, 31).[106] In the first reference the risen Jesus speaks of the 'kingdom of God' to his followers and in the last reference Paul proclaims the 'kingdom of God'. These references are among the most 'Lukan' sections of Acts. The only other reference in Acts, apart from those referring to Jesus and Paul, to proclaiming the 'kingdom of God' occurs in the ministry of Philip himself (8:12).[107] Nowhere in the ministry of the Twelve in Acts, is the term βασιλεία τοῦ θεοῦ employed to refer to their proclamation. The phrase 'kingdom of God' never appears in the kerygma of either the Pauline letters or the early speeches in Acts which seem to contain kerygmatic elements.[108] Since the basic preaching of the kingdom of God is diversely attested in the synoptic gospels it has to be traced to the historical ministry of Jesus himself.[109] This is significant in the light of other observations mentioned below.

The content of Jesus' message in Luke is summed up in Jesus' own words at Nazareth: 'I must proclaim the good news of the kingdom of God to the other cities also' (Lk. 4:43). Unlike in Matthew (3:2), John the Baptist in Luke does not proclaim the kingdom of God. Unlike in Mark (6:12), Jesus in Luke sends his disciples explicitly 'to proclaim the kingdom of God' (9:2). Luke

---

106. See, Alexander, 'Reading Luke-Acts', p. 430; A. Del Agua, 'The Lucan Narrative of the "Evangelization of the Kingdom of God": A Contribution to the Unity of Luke-Acts', in Verheyden (ed.), *Luke-Acts*, pp. 639–61.

107. It is to be noted that Barnabas is mentioned along with Paul in Acts 14:22. Other references to Paul proclaiming the kingdom of God are 19:8; 20:25.

108. Fitzmyer, *Luke* I, p. 156.

109. Fitzmyer, *Luke* I, p. 156.

repeatedly mentions the 'kingdom of God', as the subject of Jesus' proclamation in Lk. 8:1 and 9:11. This content of proclamation is also given in the
commission to the other disciples (9:60, 62; 10:9, 11). In Acts 1:3, the risen
Jesus continues the same message which he himself started to proclaim at
Nazareth in his earthly ministry and which he sent his disciples also to
proclaim. This message of the kingdom of God spoken by the risen Jesus to
the disciples just before Pentecost is the same message proclaimed by Philip
to the Samaritans, thus linking the message of the 'kingdom of God' with the
Samaritan Pentecost. This message of the kingdom inaugurated as spoken
of in Is. 61:1-2, that included the poor, the blind, the lame, the captives, the
sinners and tax collectors, the marginalized and the outcasts, finally found
the Samaritans through the proclamation of Philip. Thus, for Luke, the
expression βασιλεία τοῦ θεοῦ is significant because it portrays the Samaritan
mission of Philip on an equal footing with the ministry of Jesus and the
apostles and thereby Luke defends the divine origin and legitimacy of
Samaritan Christianity.

6.3.2. *Faith, Baptism and the Reception of the Holy Spirit*
The themes of faith, baptism and Spirit-reception are embedded in the
narrative of Acts 8:4-25. Especially vv. 14-17 has become an important
section in the historical-critical discussions on the portrait of the Samaritan
mission, and it needs to be given special attention here. What is this section
doing in the narrative of Acts 8:4-25? Is vv. 14-17 entirely a Lukan composition to connect the two independent stories about Philip and Peter or does
it reflect a possible source? The majority opinion is that Luke wants to
incorporate the Samaritan church into the Jerusalem community and he does
so with the redactional bridge of vv. 14-17. Also these verses are thoroughly
Lukan in language and themes. Thus the issues seem both literary and
theological. However, if vv. 14-17 is meant only to join two sources, then it
fails to take into consideration why Luke insists that the Spirit had not yet
fallen on any of the Samaritan Christians. A case can equally be made that
Luke was not giving his own opinion here but the opinion of his sources with
a view to achieving the same objective of uniting the communities together
or to have a different purpose altogether.[110] In any case, one cannot
completely rule out the redactional activities for the sake of Luke's use of
sources or vice-versa. Since it is intended here only to find the significance
of the above themes, especially in vv. 14-17, no extensive discussion will be
made here to unravel Luke's theology of water-baptism or Spirit-reception.

---

110. Hull, *Holy Spirit*, p. 106, however, comments that 'to seek to explain the discrepancies
in Acts by appealing to sources is to reduce its author to a mere recorder of the views of others.
A study of Acts does not suggest that Luke either had no opinions of his own or was afraid to
express them'.

As discussed earlier in Chapter 2, scholars suggest various reasons for the delay in Spirit-reception by the Samaritans in 8:17.[111] For example, Dunn argues that the delay happened because the Samaritans' faith was inadequate.[112] According to Beasley-Murray, the Samaritans had already received the Spirit at their baptism, but what was lacking in 8:17 was the spiritual gifts.[113] But while Dunn may be right that one cannot have the Spirit if one's faith is defective, there is little reason to believe that this was the case with the Samaritans. As shown earlier, there are clear evidences in the text to strongly suggest that the activity of Philip and the faith of the Samaritans are valid and genuine. Likewise, according to 2:38, it is the conversion of the people, not preaching or prayer or baptism administered by the apostles that will result in the reception of the Spirit. But in the case of the Samaritans, it is not the failure in their conversion that caused the delay in their reception of the Spirit.[114] It appears at the outset that the delay is to do with the absence of the apostles in Samaria, not with the Samaritans' faith. Also there is no indication that when the apostles came to Samaria, they started undoing or redoing the activities of Philip and then started all over again from scratch.[115] Again, that what the Samaritans lacked was the Spirit, not the spiritual gifts is clear from v. 16a that the Spirit was not *fallen* on any of them (οὐδέπω γὰρ ἦν ἐπ' οὐδενὶ αὐτῶν ἐπιπεπτωκός). When Luke uses the word ἐπιπίπτειν in the same context elsewhere in Acts, it refers not to the spiritual gifts, but to the Spirit himself.[116] In the case of the Samaritans, what is promised in 2:38 is fulfilled in 8:17, and not at their baptism.[117] According to Luke, 8:17 is the Samaritans' first reception of the promise of the Spirit. Therefore, the claims of both Dunn and Beasley-Murray find very little support in the text. And, it is to be emphasized that there is no linguistic and contextual evidence to suggest that either the ministry of Philip or the faith of the Samaritans and/or Simon is defective. Therefore other factors need to be discussed for the delay of the Holy Spirit on the Samaritans.

Another explanation for the delay of the Holy Spirit is that Luke is presenting two historically distinct baptismal paradigms in Acts 8. For example, Michel Quesnel[118] attempts to show that there was one rite of

---

111. For a useful summary of various views, see Turner, *Power*, pp. 360–75.

112. Dunn, *Baptism*, p. 65.

113. Beasley-Murray, *Baptism*, pp. 118–19.

114. Bultmann, *Theology* I, p. 139, thinks that the Samaritans had received 'no proper baptism'; in contrast to this view, see Pesch, *Apostelgeschichte* I, p. 276, who says that the baptism mentioned in the text cannot be viewed as defective, and that God is not bound by any norm (2:38; 10:48).

115. So Witherington, *Acts*, p. 286.

116. See Acts 10:44; 11:15.

117. Turner, *Power*, p. 369.

118. Quesnel, *Baptisés dans l'Esprit: Baptême et Esprit Saint dans les Actes des Apôtres* (Paris: Cerf, 1985), pp. 48–53, 92–98, quoted in Turner, *Power*, pp. 369–70 and Dickerson, 'Sources', p. 228.

baptism 'in the name of Jesus Christ' (ἐν τῷ ὀνόματι ᾽Ιησοῦ Χριστοῦ) which was for the forgiveness of sins. This is the baptism referred to in 2:38 and 10:48 and was associated with Spirit-reception. But there was also another Hellenistic-Pauline rite of baptism 'into the name of the Lord Jesus' (εἰς τὸ ὄνομα τοῦ κυρίου ᾽Ιησοῦ) which meant to signify 'into union with' the death of Jesus. The Hellenists developed this initiation that deferred the Spirit from baptism. This is the baptism that Luke preserves in 8:16 and 19:5-6, which was not associated with the bestowal of the Spirit. Thus in Quesnel's view, Luke is faithfully reflecting the Hellenistic-Pauline type of initiation in 8:12-17.

It seems anachronistic to read the Pauline theology of baptism into 8:17 signifying the believer's union with the death of Jesus. There is no reason to believe that Philip, being a man full of the Spirit, practised a baptism quite different from that mentioned in 2:38 and that he deferred the Spirit from his baptismal rite. The very episode of Simon teaches that people cannot buy or control the bestowal of the Spirit as they wish, but it is the 'gift of God' and it is ultimately he who gives it. It also raises the question whether Luke knew such a distinction between the two baptismal rites, if they really existed. Thus the view of Quesnel also finds very little support in the text.

Is Luke aware of the difference between the two forms or modes of baptism, which is 'in the name of Jesus Christ' and 'into the name of the Lord Jesus'? Dickerson tries to show that Luke had two sources, one in v. 12 that said Philip baptized 'in the name of Jesus Christ', and another in v. 16 which said that the Samaritans were baptized 'into the name of the Lord Jesus'.[119] Since Luke could not combine the two sources without smoothing over the differences in the baptismal formula, he has altered the source of v. 12 to obscure the phrase, 'in the name of Jesus Christ'. According to Dickerson, the text in v. 12 as it stands now is odd because of the combination of the phrases, 'preaching about the kingdom of God' and 'about the name of Jesus Christ'.[120] Preaching in the name is Lukan, but preaching 'about' the name is unusual in Luke. Therefore, in Dickerson's view, the original source of v. 12 said, 'When they believed Philip, in the name of Jesus Christ they were baptized, both men and women'.[121]

Dickerson's arguments imply that Luke found in the source of v. 12 a simple and straightforward text, but to reconcile it with v. 16 he created an unusual and problematic usage. If Dickerson is right then the inconsistencies, non-Lukan expressions and unusual phraseologies reflect not the sources, but Luke's redactional activities. The reverse, however, may well be the case. The problematic phrase, 'preaching *about the name*' (v.12b), may well have come to him from a pre-Lukan tradition. Since the following v. 13 is about Simon and his conversion, it is possible that the pre-Lukan tradition meant

119. Dickerson, 'Sources', pp. 227–31.
120. Dickerson, 'Sources', p. 229.
121. Dickerson, 'Sources', p. 231.

to portray the sovereign name of Jesus Christ over the claim of Simon about whose name his followers proclaimed before. Luke shows that Simon and his followers acclaimed *about the name* 'Great power', but when they heard Philip proclaiming *about the name* of Jesus Christ, they believed and were baptized. If this is right, then the source in v. 12 serves to make a contrast between the significance of the name of Jesus Christ and the apparent claim of Simon and his followers, which Luke could have fully understood. If v. 12 originally said 'in the name of Jesus Christ' as Dickerson claims, it was easy for Luke to reconcile his sources by making the redactional change in v. 16 ('in the name' instead of 'into the name') without complicating the text in v. 12. Also there is no indication of Philip baptizing with the specific formula 'in the name of Jesus Christ'. Further, it is uncertain whether Luke uses the prepositions ἐν and εἰς deliberately or interchangeably. Turner thinks that Luke uses the phrase 'into the name of the Lord Jesus' simply as a stylistic variant for the form 'in the name of Jesus Christ', without any awareness of differences of origin.[122] If it is so, then nothing can be deduced from the difference in the usage of the baptismal formula. This is not to deny the possibility that there existed one source for what Luke narrates in v. 12 and another one for v. 16. As mentioned earlier, the unusual expressions like ἐπίστευσαν τῷ Φιλίππῳ, preaching *about the name* (εὐαγγελιζομένῳ περὶ ... ὀνόματος Ἰησοῦ Χριστοῦ), also the rare usage of the phrase the *Kingdom of God* (βασιλεία τοῦ θεοῦ) as the object of Philip's preaching, all occurring in v. 12 point towards Luke employing a source here.

It must be noted that vv. 14-17 is an essential part of the whole narrative without which the following story of Peter and Simon in vv. 18-24 does not make sense. Simon's desire to buy the ability to confer the Spirit and his offer of money to Peter only fits well in the context of him having *seen* the Spirit falling on the Samaritans by the laying on of the apostles' hands. It means that the event of Spirit-reception paves the way for the confrontation between Peter and Simon where the latter presupposes and depends on the former. If vv. 14-17 is merely a redactional bridge to conflate two independent sources Luke could have achieved it without mentioning Peter's bestowal of the Spirit on the Samaritan Christians.

How did Luke's readers understand the separation of Spirit-reception from water-baptism, if it is seemingly an anomaly or enigma? Luke wants Theophilus to understand that in the case of the Samaritans, 'For as yet the Spirit had not come upon any of them; they had only been baptized in the name of the Lord Jesus' (v.16). This intends to show a possible break with the apparent norm the reader might expect from Acts 2:38. It must be noted that water-baptism and Spirit-reception are linked in Acts but there seems no

---

122. Turner, *Power*, p. 370; Bruce, *Acts: Greek Text*, p. 221, suggests that the expression, 'into the name' is common in a commercial context and means 'into someone's account' and thus implies, 'someone's property'.

set paradigm in this link. For example, Peter's instruction in 2:38 is 'Repent, and be baptized every one of you in the name of Jesus Christ so that your sins may be forgiven; and you will receive the gift of the Holy Spirit'. There are apparent exceptions to this rule in the accounts of 8:14-17; 10:44-48 and 19:1-7. Joel B. Green makes the point that in Acts when Spirit-baptism occurs in instances temporally distant from water-baptism, the community of God's people which is not always prepared to accept the newly formed Christians is convinced of a need on their part for a metamorphosis to recognize the divine acceptance of persons and incorporate them into the community.[123] This is the case both in 8:14-17 and 10:44-48.

Though it was the Christian baptism administered 'in the name of the Lord Jesus' (8:16) that the Samaritans underwent, the Holy Spirit did not come upon them until the arrival of Peter and John. In the case of the Cornelius story, the sequence is reversed: first Spirit-reception takes place and then the water-baptism. The Ephesian disciples, who earlier underwent John's baptism, were re-baptized in the way of Christian baptism, but it is only the laying on of hands of Paul that led to their Spirit-reception. That means, in the case of both the Samaritans and the Ephesian Christians, baptism did not merely confer the Spirit unlike instructed in 2:38. Here, the laying on of hands is linked to Spirit-reception rather than to baptism. In the case of the Cornelius incident, Spirit-reception preceded water-baptism but it is not clear whether laying on of hands was essential at all in baptism or Spirit-reception. Also, in the case of Paul himself, he received the Spirit first through the laying on of hands and later he was baptized by Ananias of Damascus. From this it is clear that water-baptism, Spirit-reception and laying on of hands are correlated in Acts, but their correlation is not to be seen in terms of priority of order. Also there are no links given between the laying on of hands and baptism in the Didache and Justin.[124] Implicit here is the important point that Spirit-reception either precedes or follows water-baptism. Therefore, the claim of Haenchen that in the Samaritan episode Luke divides 'one indissoluble whole' event among Philip and the apostles in order to bring Peter and Simon together is very scanty.

The ministry of the Jerusalem apostles in Samaria, and their presence in the Samaritans' reception of the Holy Spirit should also be understood in the socio-religious historical context of the relationship between the Samaritans and Jews. That a Christian mission, which was beyond the Jewish territory, could raise issues is evident from Acts 10-11 and 19. In addition to the non-Jewish factor, a mission to the Samaritans whom the Jews consider as an

---

123. Green, 'From "John's Baptism" to "Baptism in the Name of the Lord Jesus": The Significance of Baptism in Luke-Acts', in S.E. Porter and A.R. Cross (eds), *Baptism, the New Testament and the Church*, Historical and Contemporary Studies in Honour of R.E.O. White (JSNTSup.171; Sheffield: Sheffield Academic Press, 1999), pp. 157–72, 172.

124. *Didache* 7:1-4; *I Apology* 61:2-3.

illegitimate group and identify with idolaters and heretics could raise further issues on the legitimacy of the Samaritan Church. Because of the long-standing hostility between the Jews and the Samaritans, the Jerusalem Church would need the confirmation of the Samaritans' conversion and it could be done as the Samaritans receive the Holy Spirit by the ministry of the apostles.[125] In this context, for Luke, the descent of the Holy Spirit upon the Samaritan Christians after the arrival of the apostles is significant. (1) While it is said in Lk. 9:53 that the Samaritans did not receive Jesus (καὶ οὐκ ἐδέξαντο αὐτόν), now in Acts 8:14, Samaria accepted the word of God (δέδεκται ἡ Σαμάρεια τὸν λόγον τοῦ θεοῦ). (2) In Luke 9:53, the disciples could not go to Samaria, but in Acts 8:14, Peter and John arrived in Samaria. (3) The word καταβῆναι used by James and John in Lk. 9:54 for bringing down fire on the Samaritans corresponds to the arrival (καταβάντες) of Peter and John in Samaria at v. 15. The Samaritans received the Holy Spirit (ἐλάμβανον, v. 17) and the prayer and laying on of hands of the apostles were legitimized, in contrast to their earlier wish to destroy them in Lk. 9:54. What is anticipated in Lk. 9:51-56 is positively actualized in Acts 8:14-15. That the Samaritans accepted the word of God, welcomed the Jerusalem apostles and received the Holy Spirit enables Luke to legitimize both the mission started by Philip and the origin of the Samaritan Christian community. Thus, the suggestion of Conzelmann that the Samaritan church is legitimate if it has been sanctioned by Jerusalem is highly likely.[126]

6.3.3. *The Role of the Twelve*
In the story of the Samaritan mission, Philip serves as a bridge between the ministry of Jesus and the mission of the church represented by the Twelve. Originally that the Twelve themselves had to play this role is clear from Acts 1:8 (cf. Lk. 24:45-49). It was they who should have served as a bridge between the ministry of Jesus and the mission of the church.[127] Peter, James and John represent the inner core of the Twelve in Luke's Gospel (8:51; 9:28), whereas in the early section of Acts, Peter and John are the representatives and Peter is the spokesman (2:14, 16-37; 3:1, 3-4, 11; 4:13, 19; 5:29; 8:14, cf. Lk. 22:8). The Twelve remained in Jerusalem and their mission was to the Jews. In the case of the Samaritan mission, Peter and John perform their representative role only in the sense of visiting the already evangelized city of Samaria. Their primary visit was not to preach the word, but Luke in his redactional verse at Acts 8:25 shows that they finally ended up doing so on their return trip to Jerusalem. In this sense it is apt to say of the role of the

---

125. Witherington, *Acts*, p. 289.

126. Conzelmann, *Acts*, p. 65.

127. So Nolland, *Luke (1-9:20)*, p. 268; A. Clark, 'The Role of the Apostles', in Marshall and Peterson (eds), *Witness*, pp. 169-90.

apostles as Clark points out that 'the apostles are closely associated with a stationary role in Jerusalem rather than a missionary one',[128] or as Jervell says that they perform 'a prophetic role'.[129] If the Twelve symbolize for Luke the restoration of Israel in Christ and the new Christian community's continuity with her, then the presence of the Jerusalem-based apostles in Samaria should also be seen in this sense. The city of Samaria that represents the lost Northern Kingdom of Israel has to be included in this restoration and the role of Peter and John symbolizes its fulfilment. In other words, the presence of Peter and John in Samaria enables Luke to achieve both the authentication of the new Samaritan Christian community[130] and the incorporation of them into the restoration of Israel. Now, in spite of their diversity, the Samaritans and Jews are seen as one in Christ. No controversies are raised regarding the socio-ethnic and religious situations concerning the Samaritans.

Another significant achievement of Luke is the reversal of the apostolic antagonism against the Samaritans. From Luke's first Samaritan references in Lk. 9:51-56, one can observe the negative attitude of the apostles towards the Samaritans. The apostles remained in Jerusalem when a mission to the Samaritans was breaking through (Acts 8:1b, 14). They failed to understand the affinity and the positive attitude Jesus showed towards the Samaritans in his treatment of them in Lk. 9:51-56, in the Good Samaritan story in Lk. 10:25-37 and the healing of the Samaritan leper in Lk. 17:11-19. In light of the incident in Lk. 9:51-56, they also failed to keep the commandment of Jesus to love their enemies. In this respect, the Samaritan traveller in Lk. 10:25-37 is portrayed as better than the apostles who hated the Samaritans for no reason. This is reversed in Acts as Peter and John are now present in the scene. Luke portrays the Samaritan mission and the delay of the Spirit in such a way as to communicate a greater truth, which the apostles Peter (and John) are to learn for their ongoing missionary activities. It was James and John who expressed their desire to call down fire from heaven to destroy the Samaritans (Lk. 9:54). But Jesus did not grant their desire, but rebuked them. The Spirit is delayed in Samaria so that the Jerusalem apostles or their representatives, Peter and John should be brought to Samaria with a purpose of praying for the heavenly fire of the Spirit to fall upon the Samaritans. And this prayer is granted and the Samaritan Christians received the Spirit. The transformation needed to happen not in the Samaritans, but in the Jerusalem-based apostles. It may be that the Pentecost experience transformed them to go to Samaria when the Samaritans received the Word of God. John, who

---

128. Clark, 'Role of the Apostles', p. 180. This is not to overlook the missionary journey of Peter to Caesarea in Acts 10, as Clark rightly mentions, but here Peter is taken by surprise on his visit (10:29).

129. Jervell, *Luke*, p. 93.

130. So Pesch, *Apostelgeschichte* I, p. 275; Tannehill, *Luke-Acts* II, pp. 102-3; Johnson, *Acts*, p. 148; Spencer, *Portrait*, pp. 220–41; Witherington, *Acts*, p. 287.

was present in Lk. 9:54, is brought in again in Acts 8:14-17. Likewise, Peter is brought into the scene with a view that this incident should prepare him for the forthcoming Gentile mission. This is further portrayed through his vision of the large sheet containing impure and unclean creatures and his hesitance to eat them (10:9-23). Both Peter and John needed to understand that the Samaritans (and the Gentiles) are part of God's plan of salvation and that the apostles should love their hostile neighbours enough to engage in mission to them.

Further, Luke links the Samaritans' experience to that of the Jerusalem-based Christians at Pentecost: they believed, were baptized, and received the Spirit.[131] Again, the rival locations, Samaria and Jerusalem, which hitherto stood as opposite poles, are rejoined as the Samaritan mission is accomplished. And still further, Luke is able to rejoin the representative of the Seven and the Twelve, the Hellenists and the Jewish Christians, though persecution caused them separation. Now the Seven and the Twelve in spite of their diversity are brought together in their mission to Samaria, and both the groups have a part to play in the inclusion of the Samaritans into the kingdom. Luke refers to the act of preaching the gospel (εὐαγγελιζόμαι) and proclaiming the word (τὸν λόγον) both in v. 4 and v. 25. In v. 5 Philip proclaims the gospel in Samaria and in v. 25 the Jerusalem apostles continue the preaching on their return. Besides this reunion, Luke is also able to show that Philip's ministry is in continuity with that of Jesus and the apostles: preaching, healing, exorcism, and the manifestation of the kingdom of God in Samaria.

6.3.4. *Magic, Sorcery and Hypocrisy*

It is evident from Acts that in his portrayal of significant progress of mission, Luke has a general tendency to expose magic, hypocrisy and paganizm, and to show the defeat of false gods and magicians.[132] For example, Luke mentions the practice and fate of Bar-Jesus (Elymas) the magician and the false prophet (13:6), the deliverance of the Philippian sorceress (16:16) from demon possession, and the defeat of the Ephesian Jewish exorcists and sorcerers (19:13-20). Luke exposes false gods and goddesses as he has Paul refer to an inscription to the unknown god at Athens (17:23), Demetrius and the town clerk affirm the deity of Ephesian Artemis (19:26-27, 37), the Lycaonians address Barnabas as Zeus and Paul as Hermes (14:12), and in Malta, the people claimed that the just vengeance of the gods (ἡ δίκη)

---

131. Klauck, *Magic*, p. 20.

132. There are references in the early Christian literatures prohibiting Christians to become magicians. See Didache 2:2; 5;1; 3:4; Barnabas 20:1; Justin, *I Apology* 1:14. Cf. Philo, *Spec. Leg.* 3.100f; Lucian, *Asinus* 4, *Alexander* 5, 6, 17, 25, 43; Philostratus, *Life of Apollonius* 8.7, cf. 7.39; Celsus compares the gospel miracles with works of magicians, see Origen, *Contra Celsum* I.68; Acts of Thomas 20, cf. 101, 152.

brought punishment upon Paul, and later on they regard Paul himself as a god (28:4, 6). Likewise, he exposes the hypocrisy and fate of apparently prominent figures: for example, the wickedness and destruction of Judas (1:18 cf. Lk. 22:3-6), the evil hearts of Ananias and Sapphira (Acts 5:3-9) and their death, the false claims of Theudas, and Judas the Galilean and their destruction (5:36-37), and the self-admiration and death of Herod (12:22-23).

In view of his general interest in exposing magic, sorcery, hypocrisy, and false gods, Luke is able to emphasize that magic and forces of evil cannot have a place in a Spirit-filled community of Christians. Also Luke builds on the theme of the Holy Spirit that no one can use or control the authority and power of God for selfish purposes. Luke has Jesus equate apostasy with blasphemy against the Holy Spirit (Lk. 12:12). Resisting the Holy Spirit brings punishment. The inner motivation of Ananias and Sapphira is discerned as they lied to the Holy Spirit. Further Luke is able to show the fate of those who try to use the gift of the Holy Spirit as a means of making profit. The improper use of handling possessions by those inside the kingdom, as in the case of Ananias and Sapphira, can cause them to become outsiders.[133] Luke has a special interest in portraying the use and misuse of money and possessions.[134] He condemns economic, commercial and profit-making dealings either with the false and demonic powers of magic or with the genuine and true possession of the gift of the Spirit.[135] Simon was financially motivated in attempting to buy authority and the consequence of such motivation is destruction (ἀπώλεια).

So, to summarize significant features in Luke's account of the Samaritan mission:

(1) Luke sets the Samaritan mission in the context of persecution. (2) Philip performs a ministry of preaching and healing equal to that of Jesus and the apostles, and thus indicates the kerygmatic and pneumatic legitimacy of the Samaritan mission. (3) The experience of the new Samaritan Christian community is similar to that of the new community in Jerusalem – acceptance of God's word, faith, baptism, reception of the Holy Spirit and joy. (4) The physical presence of the Jerusalem apostles in Samaria and the outpouring of the Spirit upon the Samaritans together affirm the validity of the newly formed community and their continuity with the Jerusalem-based Christians. (5) The coming of the apostles to Samaria also serves to portray a reversal of the apparent popular socio-religious antagonism shared and expressed previously by the disciples (Lk. 9:54) and is a symbol of the restoration and

---

133. Brawley, *Centering*, p. 199.

134. Cadbury, *Luke-Acts*, pp. 260–3; Johnson, *Possessions, passim*; Pilgrim, *Good News*, pp. 103–46; J. Dupont, 'Community of Goods in the Early Church', in *Salvation of the Gentiles*, pp. 85–102; T.E. Phillips, 'Reading Recent Readings of Issues of Wealth and Poverty in Luke and Acts', *CBR* 1 (2, 2003), pp. 231–69.

135. Barrett, 'Light', pp. 288–91.

reunion of Israel. (6) Sorcery, hypocrisy, idolatry and improper handling of possessions are condemned in the same way as they were dealt with within the early Christian community of Jerusalem and thus Luke legitimises the purity of Samaritan Christianity. (7) By a distinct portrayal of Simon as an outsider, apostate, and idolater, which were the accusations and charges directed against the Samaritans by some Jews, as shown in Chapter 3, Luke singles out the Samaritan Christians as a legitimate people.

6.4. Simon Magus Traditions outside Acts 8

The purpose of this section is to explore (1) the possible ethnic identity of Simon, (2) the possibility of Luke's awareness of the existence of Simon's followers when writing his account of Acts 8, which in turn serves for him as another impetus to portray the legitimacy of Samaritan Christianity as opposed to that of Simon's followers. There is a strong consensus among scholars regarding the existence of a Simon tradition in Acts 8.[136] Since there are sources, apart from Acts 8, that will help us, to a certain extent, to explore the nature and influence of a tradition that vividly portrayed the identity of Simon, they are worth mentioning here. The main sources are the Apocryphal Acts of Peter, Patristic sources including the Pseudo-Clementines, and the Samaritan tradition of Abu'l Fath. First of all we will start with a text in Josephus.

Josephus describes an incident which occurred towards the end of the period (26-36 CE) when Pontius Pilate was the governor of Judea, when a certain man persuaded the Samaritans to accompany him to Mount Gerizim:

> For a man who made light of mendacity and in all his designs catered to the mob, rallied them bidding them go in a body with him to Mount Gerizim, which in their belief is the most sacred of mountains. He assured them that on their arrival he would show them the sacred vessels which were buried there, where Moses had deposited them. His hearers, viewing this tale as plausible, appeared in arms. They posted themselves in a certain village named Tirathana, and, as they planned to climb the mountain in a great multitude, they welcomed to their ranks the new arrivals who kept coming. But before they could ascend, Pilate blocked their projected route up the mountain with a detachment of cavalry and a heavy-armed infantry, who in an encounter with the first comers in the village slew some in a pitched battle and put the others to flight. Many prisoners were taken, of whom Pilate put to death the principal leaders and those who were most influential among the fugitives (*AJ*, XVIII, 85-89).

This story of Josephus has led a few scholars to suggest the appearance of a messianic claimant among the Samaritans and to identify him probably as

---

136. See Lüdemann, *Traditions*, p. 98; Barrett, *Acts* I, pp. 404–5; Alberto Ferreiro, 'Simon Magus: The Patristic-Medieval Traditions and Historiography', *Apocrypha* 7 (1996), pp. 147–65.

Simon Magus of Acts 8.[137] But Bruce Hall raises objections to such a view and attempts to refute the ethnic identity and activity of Simon as portrayed by the author of Acts, so as to identify him as the arch-heretic of Gnosticism.[138] His argument is not mainly focused on the messianic claimant of Josephus' story, as we shall see below. According to Hall, the above Josephan passage neither states nor implies that before or after the incident which it describes, messianic expectation existed among the Samaritans. However, one could argue contrary to Hall's view. If the tradition in the fourth gospel is accurate, the statement of the Samaritan woman – 'I know that Messiah is coming' – and the recognition of Jesus as the Messiah in a Samaritan village very explicitly and strongly suggests that messianic belief existed among the Samaritans early in the second quarter of the first century CE.[139] Further, one should not expect or look for an explicit evidence in the passage for the messianic belief of the Samaritans, because it is not intended to describe their theological belief. The passage rather seems to demonstrate that Roman justice was not merely an instrument of oppression, but that it fairly dealt with the offences committed by its own officials.[140] The very fact of the tumult, which Pilate repressed at the foot of Mount Gerizim, would nonetheless reflect that he felt threatened by a Samaritan political movement. That the Samaritans were looking forward to a life of liberation becomes very clear from their appeal to Vitellius when they said that they had assembled not to rebel against Rome but to escape from Pilate's tyrannical rule. It may also indicate the intensification of their expectation of a political Messiah. Again, the claim of Simon and his followers in Acts 8:9-10 would confirm the fact that a 'movement' among the Samaritans as early as the first half of the first century CE was not impossible. Though it is uncertain from the passage in Josephus that the man who promised to show the sacred vessels was Simon of Acts 8, there is no evidence to suggest a case against Simon.[141]

---

137. Gaster, *Samaritans*, p. 91; Macdonald, *Theology*, p. 361; Bowman, 'History', pp. 101–15; Bowman suggests that the messianic claimant may have been Simon Magus (p.107).

138. Hall, 'From John Hyrcanus to Baba Rabbah', in Crown (ed.), *Samaritans*, pp. 32–54, 39.

139. Jn 4:25-26, 29, 42. Macdonald, *Theology*, p. 361 says that the story of the Samaritan woman in Jn 4 'reflects actual knowledge of Samaritan theology'. See also W. Munro, 'The Pharisee and the Samaritan in John: Polar or Parallel?', *CBQ* 57/4 (1995), pp. 710–28, who insists that the Samaritan woman 'serves as an able exponent of Samaritan theology in opposition to the Judaism based in Jerusalem' (p. 723). Even if John had put the title *Messiah* in the mouth of the Samaritan woman as Meeks believes, he intended to show that Jesus fulfilled the Samaritan expectation of the one who is to come: see *idem, The Prophet-King: Moses Traditions and the Johannine Christology* (NovTsup.14; Leiden: E.J. Brill, 1967), p. 318.

140. Coggins, 'Samaritans in Josephus', p. 268. He also says that both in this incident and the Cumanus story (*AJ*, XX, 118-136; *BJ*, II, 233-46), the disputes with the Samaritans are almost incidental, and the main point is concerned with Jewish grievances under Roman rule (pp. 268–9).

141. Commenting on the various movements reported in Josephus, Rebecca Gray, *Prophetic Figures*, pp. 164–5, says, 'From Josephus' spare and hostile accounts, we can determine that

Now the question is: was Simon a Samaritan? Was his activity located among the pagan population of Samaria or among the Samaritans? Casey, Haenchen, Stanton and others think that Simon belonged to and addressed the pagan population of Samaria.[142] Following this line of thought, Bruce Hall argues that the author of Acts was wrong when he represented Simon as winning converts among the members of the Samaritan ethnic group in Samaria.[143] According to Hall, Simon was active and he won followers, not among the Samaritans, but among the Gentiles living in Samaria. His several arguments can be summed up as follows:

(1) Acts 8 neither states nor implies that Simon was a Samaritan. (2) When Justin Martyr speaks of Simon as a 'Samaritan', he uses the term in the sense of 'an inhabitant' of Samaria. (3) The Simonian movement of the second and third centuries CE was almost an exclusively Gentile movement and there is no evidence in the Christian writings of this period apart from those of Justin Martyr that Simonianism was strong, or even existed among the Samaritans. (4) On the basis of his doctrines which Irenaeus ascribed to Simon, he would not have won a significant following among the Samaritan ethnic group, for it is evident from Jn 4:21-22 and *AJ*, IX, 290 that 'in the first century AD at least the vast majority of Samaritans worshipped the same God as the Jews worshipped, and worshipped this God as their sole God'. (5) Neither Mishnah nor Memar Marqah nor the early Samaritan amulets refer to Simonianism as existing among the Samaritans.

Hall builds his hypothesis mainly on the basis of the link between Simon of Acts 8 and the Gnostic Simonianism of second and third century Christian writings, an evidence which cannot easily be used, or preferred to the early tradition of Acts 8 for the portrait of first century Samaritan mission. His arguments do not prove that Simon and his followers were not Samaritans, rather they make inferences from the later evidences that Simonianism was a Gentile movement.[144]

A case for Simon's Samaritan identity and Samaritan followers can be made:

(1) As mentioned earlier in Chapter 2, for Luke the activity of both Philip and Simon probably took place in the same 'city of Samaria'. And Luke does

Theudas, the Egyptian, and the other sign prophets were leaders of large popular movements; that they claimed to be prophets; that they announced to their followers that God was about to act to deliver them in some dramatic way; and that they promised to perform miracles that would either constitute that deliverance itself (in the case of Theudas and the Egyptian) or confirm that they were God's messengers and that what they said was true'.

142. Casey, 'Simon Magus', p. 152; Haenchen, *Acts*, p. 307; G. Stanton, 'Samaritan Incarnational Christology?' in M. Goulder, *Incarnation and Myth: The Debate Continued* (London: SCM Press Ltd., 1979), pp. 243–6.

143. Hall, 'John Hyrcanus', pp. 40–41.

144. The discussion of the relationship of the later Gnostic system to Simon of Acts 8 is beyond the scope of our present study.

not make a distinction between the Gentile inhabitants and the religious Samaritans. Even if Philip's ministry was limited only to the Samaritans, there is no reason to think that Simon also limited his activity only to the Gentiles. As a magician, Simon would have amazed people irrespective of their ethnic and religious convictions. If Simon the magician was most probably a Samaritan, in all probability he would have come across Philip and his ministry among the Samaritans. This becomes clear when Luke says that after Simon's conversion, 'he followed Philip everywhere, astonished by the great signs and miracles he saw' (Acts 8:13). Again, had there not been an association in the original tradition between the activity of Philip and Simon's conversion, it would have enabled Luke to bring Peter straight away into confrontation with Simon instead of separating a Philip-Simon tradition (vv. 5-13) from a Peter-Simon tradition (vv. 18-25). In other words, if there existed an earlier tradition that attributed the conversion of Simon the magician to Peter's ministry, then Luke would hardly have substituted a lesser figure for Peter.[145]

(2) Luke is building up the Church's mission of Acts 1:8 starting from Jerusalem to Judaea, Samaria and to the uttermost parts of the earth. When the expansion of Christianity and the successive events follow this program, it appears that Luke wants his audience to understand this progression without further explicitness. For instance, neither he nor his source explicitly mentions that Theudas (Acts 5:36) who claimed himself to be somebody and won many followers was a Jew, but it is thus understood in the context of the Jerusalem mission. Similar is the case of Simon in the context of the Samaritan mission. When it is not so, Luke explicitly states the case.[146] And it should also be noted that Peter's vision of the large sheet full of creatures (Acts 10:9-16) comes only after the Samaritan mission and that the Gentile mission started only with the conversion of Cornelius in Acts 10. The Jerusalem Council ratified the decision that the gospel should be preached to the pagan population after it had been made independently by Peter (chs.10-11), Paul (chs.13-14) and certain unnamed travellers (11:20). Samaria was evangelized (cf. 9:31; 15:3) before the Gentile mission started. Even Peter was not opposed to the mission at Samaria nor did Luke consider the Samaritans as Gentiles.[147]

145. Haenchen, 'Simon Magus in der Apostelgeschichte' in K.W. Tröger (ed.), *Gnosis und Neues Testament* (Gütersloh: Mohn, 1973), pp. 267–79, 277.

146. A Jewish sorcerer and false prophet named Bar-Jesus (Acts 13:6) at Paphos; seven sons of Sceva, a Jewish chief priest at Ephesus (19:14).

147. For this latter point on the identity of the Samaritans in Luke-Acts, see the discussion in section 7.2 of the book. Goulder in his brief response to Graham Stanton on the question of the Samaritan hypothesis assumes that 'all converts before Cornelius are circumcised, Jews, Samaritans or proselytes, including the Ethiopian eunuch and Simon in Acts 8'. Goulder, 'The Samaritan Hypothesis', Appendix (ii), in *idem* (ed.), *Incarnation*, pp. 247–50, 248.

(3) Even if Acts had explicitly said that Simon was a Samaritan, those who try to identify Simon on the basis of the later Simonianism would not have been convinced by the Lukan account, for they even assume the term 'Samaritans' to mean 'the inhabitants of Samaria' as supposed to be the case in the explicit reference to the 'Samaritan' by Justin Martyr. If Simon was a Gentile, it would not make sense for Justin who himself was a native of Samaria to contradict his view that Simon was a Samaritan from the village of Gitta.[148]

(4) It is highly implausible to cast Simon as a Gentile, whose *Gentile* identity is responsible for the exclusiveness of a third century *Gentile* movement. It is possible that Simonianism incorporated ideas from the Jewish and/or Hellenistic environment and flourished as a Gentile movement, which later could have paved the way for Gnosticism proper.

Luke's description of Simon as the 'Great Power' may provide a further clue to set Simon's identity in Jewish or Samaritan context. Simon's acclamation that he is the 'power of God called Great' may be a Jewish description and could be seen, as Pesch points out, 'als Selbstprädikation benutzte und sich als Inkarnation des höchsten Gottes vorstellte'.[149] Jervell suggests that the use of τοῦ θεοῦ and δύναμις by Luke in the designation of Simon would suggest that Simon was a Jew.[150] Though one cannot make a clear distinction as to whether Simon was a Jew or a Samaritan, what is likely is that he was not a Gentile. Also, if his title, the 'Great Power' is considered as a Samaritan designation for the supreme deity, and that there is an Aramaic original behind the title Μεγάλη, as Wellhausen and Torrey postulate, then it is unlikely that Simon could be seen as a Gentile. Further, it is possible that there were Samaritans who considered Simon to be a deity, just as there were Jews who acclaimed Herod to be divine (Acts 12:22).[151]

(5) It is true that the Samaritans worshipped the same God as the Jews worshipped: they were monotheistic, but not monolithic in the New Testament period. Acts 8 does not say that Simon's followers worshipped him as God, but that they paid *attention* (προσεῖχον) to him as they later paid close *attention* (προσεῖχον) to Philip's preaching. If Philip's converts were 'Samaritans', it is highly probable that Simon's followers would also have consisted of some Samaritans. Further, from the account of Josephus' description of an incident in which a certain man persuaded a number of Samaritans to accompany him to Mount Gerizim, it is evident that the Samaritans, though they were monotheistic, did not hesitate to follow a certain man who gave them a promise. When Josephus and Acts clearly

---

148. Justin, *I Apology* 26.3.
149. Pesch, *Apostelgeschichte* I, p. 274; Dt. 9:26; Mk 14:62; Lk. 22:69; Philo, *Vita Mos* I, 111.
150. Jervell, *Apostelgeschichte*, p. 262.
151. M. Edwards, 'Simon Magus, the Bad Samaritan', in M. Edwards and S. Swain (eds), *Portraits: Biographical Representation in the Greek and Latin Literature of the Roman Empire* (Oxford: Clarendon Press, 1997), pp. 69–91, 73.

mention that in the first century CE, many cult leaders and messianic pretenders won followers from within Judaism, it would not have been impossible for Simon to get Samaritan followers.[152] Jesus, who was called a Samaritan by the Jews (Jn 8:48), portrayed as a magician, revolutionary, false prophet and the like, gathered around himself people of every sort.

(6) The absence of Simonianism in Mishnah, Memar Marqah or early Samaritan amulets does not in any way disprove the Samaritan identity of Simon and his followers of Acts 8. It may very well be the case that these sources would not have found a necessary relationship of Simon with the Gnostic Simonianism. That Abu'l Fath contains a tradition of Simon as a magician but no reference to Simonianism would seem to imply that the link between Simon and Simonianism is not a Samaritan tradition, but a later Christian speculation.

Thus, in all probability the author of Acts was not wrong when he represented Simon as winning converts from the Samaritan ethnic group in Samaria. Simon was most probably a Samaritan and the majority of his followers too were Samaritans. It is plausible that Simon was a forerunner of Gnosticism. But the absence of Gnostic Simonianism among the Samaritan community may imply that it was a later phenomenon developed among the Gentiles.

The references to Simon traditions outside of the Canonical Acts will further illumine our point. In the Apocryphal Acts of Peter (APt), as in Acts 8, Simon is portrayed as a miracle-worker who claimed to be the 'great power of God (APt 4)', who practised magic, exercised mass appeal, and persuaded many by his incantations (APt 4, 6, 12, 16, 23, 31, 32). The patristic texts,[153] especially those of Justin who himself comes from Samaria, might at least be evidence for the existence of Simon's followers which could at least provide independent support for some kind of Samaritan sect such as Luke describes (*I Apology* 26.3; 56). Justin says that Simon was an active magician from Samaria who performed magical deeds in Rome and that the Roman people honoured Simon as a god. The Pseudo-Clementine *Homilies* and *Recognitions* contain stories of controversies between Peter and Simon Magus and a description of Simon's biography, ideology and the claim of his greatness. The tradition inherent in the Pseudo-Clementines portrays Simon as a Samaritan and as a successful magician.[154] According to these traditions

---

152. *AJ*, XX, 97-98; *BJ*, II, 258-60, cf. *AJ*, XX, 167-68; *BJ*, II, 261-63, cf. *AJ*, XX, 169-72; *BJ*, VI, 283-87; *BJ*, VII, 437-41; cf. Acts 5:36.

153. See discussion in Edwards, 'Bad Samaritan', pp. 69–91; Ferreiro, 'Simon Magus', pp. 147–65; Casey, 'Simon Magus', pp. 151–63; R. Bergmeier, 'Gestalt des Simon Magus', pp. 238–46; Lüdemann, 'Beginnings', pp. 420–6; P.M. Palmer and R.P. More, *The Sources of the Faust Tradition: From Simon Magus to Lessing* (New York: Octagon Books Inc., 1996), pp. 9–41.

154. *Hom.* II. 22-25; *Rec.* II. 7-12.

Simon considered Gerizim holy and claimed himself to be the 'Standing One'.[155] Both in the Acts of Peter and in the Clementines, Simon and Peter confront each other in Rome. Thus the account of Justin shows coherence with these writings. Also the additional information in Justin about Simon's birthplace Gitta, his visit to Rome during the reign of Claudius, his Phoenician partner named Helen, and her importance in his theology are clearly not derived from Acts, but from some independent sources. Irenaeus speaks of Simon as the one from whom all heresies originated (*Adversus Haereses* 1.23.1-4). In his account, Simon is portrayed as the Samaritan magician who with his magical competence wanted to become famous and persuaded the crowd to marvel at his magic. Like Justin, Irenaeus also refers to the people's veneration of Simon as a god, and to Simon's female partner Helen. Origen speaks about Simon as the Samaritan magician and includes him in the category of messianic claimants along with Theudas and Judas (*Contra Celsum* VI.11). He associates him with Dositheus, and says that he claimed to be the Great Power of God and that the Simonian sect was very few in number during his time.

The Samaritan tradition of Abu'l Fath has references to Simon, but they are mentioned not particularly in the interest of describing Simon himself.[156]

> He and the disciples of the Messiah opposed each other with magic and he got the better of them. He found a Jewish Philosopher called Philo, from Alexandria. He (Simon) said to him, "Help me, and I will wipe out the religion of the Messiah". Philo replied to him, "Be at peace. For if this thing comes from God, then no one will be able to wipe it out". So Simon returned and came to Beit 'Alin where he died. He was buried in the Valley which faces the house of the disciple who first bore witness to the Messiah, who was called Stephen.[157]

The use of the term, 'the Messiah' in reference to Jesus, could possibly betray a Hebrew source.[158] The description of Philo as 'Jewish', as opposed to 'Samaritan', may betray the use of an independent Samaritan tradition. The mention of Stephen and the proximity of his burial site with that of Simon could plausibly reflect the association of these figures in the tradition, and this is reflected also in Acts where Simon is introduced into the story of Philip, one of the members of the Stephen group. It is possible, therefore, that Abu'l Fath is reflecting an independent Samaritan tradition which relates the activity of Simon who lived at the same time as that of the disciples of Jesus, and Philo and which is also aware of the death of Stephen who was active

---

155. *Hom.* II.22; cf. *Rec.*II.7.

156. The Chronicle of Abu'l Fath is the fourteenth century CE Samaritan document compiled by Abu'l Fath, who was a Samaritan, at the command of the High Priest Phinehas in 1352.

157. Stenhouse (trans.), *Abu'l-Fath*, lines 1030-32, p. 222.

158. In Chronicle Adler the term, 'Jesus son of Mary, of Nazareth' is used instead of 'Messiah'.

as a Hellenist. It is clear from the above story that the tradition it describes considered Simon as 'the wizard' who practised exorcism and charged fees for his magical activities. He was the opponent of the disciples of Jesus (cf. *Chronicle Adler*, 67) and he bested them with his magic.

Though one could doubt the historical reliability of the Simon episode, the reference to Simon's connection with Philo cannot easily be dismissed. It would seem to suggest that the activity of Simon as a magician had found a place in the Samaritan tradition.[159] To mention the comment of Montgomery who says, 'the Samaritan version of the Simon legend is very scanty, being based on the Christian romance, and yet embracing some independent details drawn probably from a Palestinian form of the story'.[160]

The prominent place ascribed to Simon in different traditions makes it historically plausible that he came into conflict with Christian missionaries.[161] As Edwards puts it: 'No doubt there were many Simons in the region, and more than one who boasted of his miracles; but the Simon of Hippolytus and Justin has no traits that are inconceivable in the Simon of the Acts'.[162] However, how much of the later Simonian doctrines goes back to Simon himself is difficult to decide, though one could say that various traditions found him to be a possible target and at the same time an influential figure to set in rivalry with early Christian leaders. Alternatively, his portrait of the victory of Peter over Simon in Acts 8:18-24 may reflect that Luke possibly knew some form of Simon's movement in his day and that he wanted to legitimate the new Samaritan Christian community.[163]

The strong presence of various traditions of Simon outside Acts 8 will nevertheless suggest that Luke is dealing with a historical figure and that the information he gives in Acts 8:4-25 on Simon has a historical kernel of truth. These traditions, associating Simon with Peter/the Samaritans in the early Christian and non-Christian sources, in Coggins' judgement, are 'notoriously difficult to evaluate, but must certainly be taken seriously'.[164] It is to be noted that Luke speaks of Simon as the 'power of God which is called great' (ουᾶτός ἐστιν ἡ δύναμις τοῦ θεοῦ ἡ καλουμένη Μεγάλη, Acts 8:10b).

---

159. Fossum, 'Samaritan Sects and Movements', in Crown (ed.), *Samaritans*, pp. 293–389, 357 says: 'It is clear that this story has very little or no historical value'. In his earlier work, *The Name of God*, Fossum relates the first and the last part of the story to a 'peculiar Samaritan tradition' (p. 170).

160. Montgomery, *Samaritans*, p. 267.

161. Klauck, *Magic*, p. 17.

162. Edwards, 'Bad Samaritan', p. 75.

163. Smith, 'Account', p. 736, suggests that the account of the Samaritan mission in Acts 8:4-25 is 'a piece of Christian propaganda against the followers of Simon' in order to show that the cult of Simon was inferior to that of Jesus and the apostles; Barrett, 'Light', p. 293, casts doubt on this when he says that Luke has given us no hint that he is aware of the Simonians. Though one cannot deduce the existence of a Simonian gnosis in the middle of the first century from Acts 8, it is possible that there were followers of Simon around that period.

164. Coggins, 'Samaritans and Acts', p. 429.

However, Luke does not use the title Δύναμις Μεγάλη as a designation for Simon. But that Δύναμις Μεγάλη is a designation for Simon is confirmed in various early Christian and non-Christian writings. This title has been considered to be distinctively Samaritan as it is attested as a divine designation in Samaritan traditions. Though the portrayal of Simon varies in different sources, it seems clear that here Acts is working with traditions of a historical figure.

Now, based on the various traditions embedded in the non-canonical literatures, Patristic sources, and the Samaritan tradition of Abu'l Fath the following information can be derived regarding the person and activities of Simon. (1) Simon was probably a Samaritan and was inclined to the holy Mount Gerizim rather than to Jerusalem. (2) He was active among the Samaritans and in Rome, and probably had a significant number of followers during the later part of the first century CE. (3) He practised magic and persuaded people with his magical prowess. (4) He claimed himself to be the 'Great Power of God', and the 'Standing One'. (5) He wanted to do the same as Jesus did in order to get power over people. (6) He often craved for leadership and had been in confrontation with prominent early Christian leaders like Peter. (7) It is possible that Luke knew of the existence of Simon's movement in its earliest form. In brief, it is likely that Simon might have worked among the Samaritan populace where Philip worked and that Luke is making use of Simon's apostasy to defend the legitimacy of Samaritan Christianity.

6.5. Conclusion

The textual analysis shows that Luke is portraying the kerygmatic and pneumatic legitimacy of Philip's mission supported by the apostolic legitimacy of Jerusalem whereby he is defending the divine origin and legitimacy of both the mission and Samaritan Christianity. This portrait is to be seen in light of the first century CE depiction of the Samaritans in general and Luke's portrait of them in his Gospel in particular. The mission to the Samaritans anticipated by Jesus in the Gospel is legitimized in Acts 8:4-25 where the alleged apostates and the marginalized find a new identity and legitimacy through their acceptance of Christ. The enemies and the outsiders become the sharers of the Kingdom and the participants of the divine Spirit. This new development in Samaria is narrated in a way by which Luke validates the mission with that of the Jewish mission and defends the divine origin and legitimacy of Samaritan Christianity. Thus, the narrative of the Samaritan mission not only accomplishes Luke's purpose in conformity with his programme laid out in Acts 1:8, a mission which is the first of its kind beyond the borders of Jerusalem and Judaea and as fulfilling the commission of the risen Lord, but also serves as an apologetic purpose for Luke to legitimate it.

Chapter 7

THE SAMARITAN MISSION IN ACTS 8:4-25:
AN ANTICIPATION-LEGITIMATION DEVICE

7.1. Introduction

Putting the Samaritan references of Luke's Gospel into the context of the socio-political and religious situation of the Samaritans in the New Testament period, we argued earlier that Luke shows Jesus' affinity to and his positive treatment of the Samaritans as an anticipation of a Samaritan mission. While the Samaritan references in Luke's Gospel anticipate a Samaritan mission, the episode in Acts 8:4-25 portrays its fulfilment and also affirms the validity of the newly formed community of the people of God. In this chapter we argue the thesis that in his portrayal of the Samaritan mission in Acts 8:4-25, Luke tries to show that the mission to Samaria is equally valid with the Jewish mission and that he intends to defend the divine origin and legitimacy of Samaritan Christianity. This anticipation-legitimation device of Luke in the presentation of the Samaritan mission could have served for him an apologetic purpose for authenticating the ongoing mission of the early church to the non-Judaeo-centric community of his day.

7.2. The Legitimacy Question

The question of the legitimacy of the mission to Samaria and of the Samaritan Christian community becomes important in this new stage of the mission because of various factors. To understand its significance, we need to consider both the wider historical context of the Samaritans in the first century CE and Luke's own treatment of them in his Gospel, which we have discussed earlier in the study.

First of all, the wider context of the socio-political and ethnico-religious background of the Samaritans should be given prominence in understanding the issue of the legitimacy of the Samaritan mission.[1] Historically, as we mentioned earlier in our study, from a Jewish point of view, the Samaritans

---

1. See Chapter 3 of the book on the socio-political and religious situation of the Samaritans.

were considered as the 'Cutheans', 'the apostates from the Jewish nations', 'the foolish people that dwell in Shechem' or as 'the people that dwell in Gerizim'. They were regarded as illegitimate in race and religion. They were religiously hated and politically persecuted down through the centuries. They were treated by some Jews as socially outcasts and marginalized. Due to the longstanding historical hostile attitude of the Jews towards the Samaritans, it is possible that the Jews and the Jewish Christians of Luke's day accused Samaritan Christianity of being an illegitimate group.[2] Luke prepares his audience by overturning the alleged socio-political and ethnico-religious status of the Samaritans and by portraying them as a legitimate community of people equal to Jews.

Secondly, given the cumulative evidence for the existence of a Simon movement from the early second century CE onwards, it is possible that there were at least some followers of Simon in Luke's day who venerated Simon as a divine figure.[3] This factor could have raised a question of legitimacy for the Samaritan Christian community of which Simon was a member after his conversion. If Luke knew of this movement of Simon in its earliest form,[4] then it is probable that he included the Simon story in Acts 8:9-24 with the polemical purpose of refuting the claim of Simon's followers. In this light, the observation of Scobie that Luke had only very scanty information on the mission to Samaria and that the story of Simon and the visit of Peter and John occupy most of Acts 8:4-24, makes good sense.[5] Two factors may help us to understand this seemingly disparate account. (1) Luke makes a selection of materials on Simon from his possible available sources in order to fit his polemical purpose of refuting the claim of Simon's followers and that he is not intending to tell us every detail of it. (2) Luke gives most of the space in 8:4-25 to the activities of Simon and the Jerusalem apostles because they serve for him the purpose of defending the legitimacy of Samaritan Christianity, as will be shown later in this chapter.

Thirdly, it must be remembered that the Samaritan mission of Philip in Acts 8 might contradict the saying in Mt. 10:5b: 'Go nowhere among the Gentiles,

---

2.   Wilson, *Gentiles*, pp. 248–9, while mentioning Luke's emphasis on the Old Testament prophecies of the Gentile mission, makes the point that the Jewish contemporaries of Luke's Church could possibly have accused the Gentile Christian community of being an illegitimate offspring of Judaism, and in response to it Luke places the Gentile mission in the historical roots of the Old Testament. Given the alleged illegitimate origin of the Samaritans and the longstanding hostility of the Jews towards them, it is all the more likely that more than the Gentile Christian community, the new Samaritan Christian community had faced from their Jewish contemporaries a similar accusation.

3.   See section 6.4 of the book for a brief discussion on the Simon Magus traditions in early Christian and non-Christian literatures.

4.   Cf. section 6.4.

5.   Scobie, 'Origins', p. 390.

and enter no town of the Samaritans', at least for the early years of the early church.[6] The same might be true of Jesus' sending of the messengers into a Samaritan village in Lk. 9:52. Spencer rightly suggests in passing that possibly 'Luke was defending the legitimacy of Samaritan Christianity against advocates of a restrictive mission policy like that reflected in Mt. 10:5b'.[7] That this is the intention of Luke is clearly evident from our historical, literary and theological discussions on the relevant texts on the Samaritans. Here we must note that the incidents in both Lk. 9:51 and Acts 8:5 overturn the popular belief and attitude of the Jews or the Jewish Christians towards the Samaritans. This is not to overlook the universal nature of mission recorded in Mt. 28:19 that the disciples must 'make disciples of all nations' and in Acts 1:8 that they will be his 'witnesses in Jerusalem and in all Judaea and Samaria and to the end of the earth'.[8] As Cullmann notes, since Samaria was an important step in the preaching of the gospel beyond the Jewish people,

6.   It is possible that in the beginning of the early Christian history of missions, some Jewish Christians would still have maintained such a view on a mission to the Samaritans and Gentiles. On this point, Barrett, *Acts* I, p. 399, rightly says, 'It would hardly however have stood in the gospel if there had not been some Christians who took it to be a command of perpetual obligation upon the church'. Coggins, 'Samaritans and Acts', p. 432, thinks that Mt. 10:5b 'may allude to the rejection of the very idea of Samaritan Christianity'. If this were the case, then it may be the reason why a special divine intervention was necessary for Peter to launch a new mission to Cornelius. For the view that the mission to Samaria contrasts with the saying in Mt. 10:5b, see Barrett, *Acts* I, p. 399; Spencer, *Portrait*, p. 86; M. Hengel, *Earliest Christianity* (London: SCM Press, 1986), p. 78.

7.   Spencer, *Portrait*, p. 86.

8.   The authenticity of the Great Commission in Mt. 28:16-20 is disputed as the text raises linguistic, genre and provenance problems as well as the question on the date of its underlying tradition. It also raises the theological issue whether the Great Commission is exclusively directed to the Gentiles or inclusive of the Jews. This is because of the expression, πάντα τὰ ἔθνη in v. 19, which could mean either 'all Gentiles' excluding the Jews or 'all nations' including both Gentiles and Jews. For a detailed discussion on this text, see Jostein Adna and Hans Kvalbein (eds), *The Mission of the Early Church to Jews and Gentiles* (WUNT 127; Tübingen: Mohr Siebeck, 2000). For our purpose, the missionary-historical relevance of Mt. 28:16-20 seems important. Because of the Matthaean terminology, many scholars consider this text as purely a Matthaean redactional construction. For example, J.D. Kingsbury, *Matthew: Structure, Christology and Kingdom* (Philadelphia: Fortress Press, 1975), pp. 75–6; Ulrich Luz, *The Theology of the Gospel of Matthew* (Cambridge: Cambridge University Press, 1995), pp. 139–40; However, there are other scholars who think that there is a tradition behind Mt. 28:16-20 and it goes back to the beginning of the early Christian history of missions. For example, R.H. Gundry, *Matthew: A Commentary on His Literary and Theological Art* (Michigan: Wm.B. Eerdmans Publishing Co., 1982), p. 596; P. Stuhlmacher, 'Matt 28:16-20 and the Course of Mission in the Apostolic and Post-apostolic Age', in Adna and Kvalbein (eds), *Mission*, pp. 17–43, thinks that the text is not a late tradition of a particular Galilean Christendom or a Matthaean redactional work, but 'a very old Jewish-Christian tradition' which Matthew took up, 'which had been provided and transmitted faithfully in Jerusalem because this old missionary Commission was still important to him' (p. 43). Stuhlmacher suggests that Matthew summarized this tradition which was upheld in Jerusalem by the apostles reputed to be pillars and which formed the basis for the decisions of the apostolic council.

it was important for the first Christians who went to Samaria to be certain that they were acting in accordance with the purpose of Christ.[9] Therefore, given that Samaria was the first place for the mission beyond the boundary of the Jews, as is outlined in Acts 1:8, it needed to be legitimized.

Fourthly, one must also take into account Luke's treatment of the Samaritans in his Gospel. In the Samaritan rejection (Lk. 9:51-56), there is no charge being made against the Samaritans' rejection of Jesus nor are they allowed to be the victims of the disciples' fire of destruction. They are treated favourably by Jesus in contrast to the criticism directed towards his disciples.[10] Luke, while mentioning the reason for their rejection of Jesus that 'he was going to Jerusalem', wants his readers to understand the legitimacy of their action and hence he seems to defend them.[11] Likewise, in the story of the Good Samaritan (10:25-37), Jesus commands the lawyer to be a neighbour (πλησίον) to anyone in need, just like the Samaritan who acted in compassion to encounter the wounded man and thus participated in the status of God's people.[12] If love of neighbour is to act beyond one's own religious and racial boundaries,[13] then Luke not only defends the action of the merciful Samaritan in contrast to the inaction of the priest and the Levite, but also the Samaritan's status as part of Israel in fulfilling the love command of the Law.[14] It may be that Luke intends to show that the Jews must learn from the action of their enemies, the Samaritans, what love of neighbours means[15] and that they must treat the Samaritans just like their fellow Jews and as their neighbours. In other words, the Samaritans are to be treated as a legitimate people worthy of receiving neighbourly love and the Jews must love them as their own without boundaries. Also, in the healing of the ten lepers (17:11-19), the Samaritan, though a foreigner (ἀλλογενής), becomes the sharer of true faith and worship,[16] and thereby

---

9.   Cullmann, 'Samaria', p. 186.

10.   Marshall, *Luke*, p. 403, draws the implication of the story that the 'Samaritans who reject the gospel are to be treated in the same way as Jews'.

11.   Arlandson, *Women, Class, and Society*, p. 176.

12.   As Johnson, *Luke*, p. 173, puts it, the identity of the neighbour is not one of 'legal obligation (who deserves my love)', but one of 'gift-giving (to whom can I show myself neighbour)'; Green, *Luke*, p. 431.

13.   Fitzmyer, *Luke* II, p. 884; C.F. Evans, *Saint Luke*, pp. 467, 471.

14.   *Contra* Nolland, *Luke* II, p. 594, who thinks that the 'Samaritan is not being presented specifically as one who loves his neighbour and thus keeps the law'. However, the very mention of the Samaritan identity of the person in the story and the description of his compassion and action in contrast to the law-oriented priest and the Levite require us to assume a positive picture of the Samaritans. According to Fitzmyer, *Luke* II, p. 884, the story suggests that even the Samaritan by showing true love of neighbour has found the way to eternal life.

15.   Tannehill, *Luke*, p. 184.

16.   Hamm, 'Samaritan Leper', while providing a Christological interpretation of the text, suggests that the Samaritan finds 'Jesus as the appropriate place to worship' (p. 286), and Jesus accepts 'the worshipful behaviour of the healed Samaritan as appropriate' (p. 284); Johnson,

Luke defends the action of the Samaritan and his new experience of salvation. In brief, all the Samaritan references in the Gospel seem to defend the legitimacy of the Samaritans and their action and also their status as part of Israel. Therefore, they function as apologetic for Luke's church, especially for the Samaritan Christians whose legitimacy and origin the Jews and the Jewish Christians could possibly have questioned. It is in this context that one must understand what Luke is intending to do in Acts 8:4-25.

Fifthly, the mission to the Samaritans was not initially an apostolic mission, but a Hellenistic mission. It was not started by any of the apostles, but by Philip, one of the Seven who was chosen to 'serve tables'. Though there were many others who were exiled with Philip, he was the 'first significant foreign missionary' beyond the borders of Judaea.[17] Philip might have shared the same views as those of the Hellenist Stephen that caused the latter's martyrdom and the outbreak of the persecution thereof. If only the apostles were untouched by the persecution, then there seems to be some ideological differences between them and the Hellenists and therefore the question of the legitimacy of the community formed by their ministry may possibly have arisen.[18] Also, if the visit of the apostles was necessary to 'sanction' the new development in Samaria and the work of Philip,[19] this might imply that a mission, which was started without the apostles, would not have been easily accepted as legitimate. In the case of the Gentile mission, it was Peter who took the initiative after it was ratified by his heavenly vision of a large sheet containing animals, reptiles and birds. In the case of the Samaritans, it was neither an apostle who started the work nor was there any heavenly or supernatural vision to ratify the mission. Therefore, it was necessary for Luke to show the origin and legitimacy of the mission in order to portray a positive picture of the Samaritan mission and to achieve his goal laid out in Acts 1:8.

Finally, the Samaritan mission took place without any human planning or control, as it was the result of the dispersion following the persecution in Jerusalem.[20] It was not so in the case of other missions, for example, the

---

Luke, p. 260, comments that here 'the Samaritan gives a positive example of faith'; C.F. Evans, *Saint Luke*, p. 623, mentions the main point of the story as the commendation of Jesus of 'the genuine piety of a non-Israelite manifesting itself in gratitude'; So also Marshall, *Luke*, pp. 648, 652; Green, *Luke*, p. 626; Fitzmyer, *Luke* II, p. 1151; Arndt, *Luke*, p. 372, sees in the Samaritan leper the elements of faith, salvation, forgiveness of sins and a place among God's children; Nolland, *Luke*, p. 848, suggests that this Samaritan 'in his dealings with Jesus experiences an encounter with God'; Tannehill, *Luke*, p. 258, makes the point that the Samaritan's response to the healing led him to have a powerful experience of God and thus Jesus makes him a model for others; Betz, 'Cleansing', p. 315, speaks of the Samaritan's Christian faith and salvation.

    17.   Kollmann, 'Philippus', pp. 551–65.

    18.   *Contra* Hill, *Hellenists*, p. 40.

    19.   While discussing the role of the apostles in Samaria, some commentators agree on the view that the apostles came to sanction the newly formed community or to confirm the work of Philip. See Conzelmann, *Acts*, p. 65; Tannehill, *Luke-Acts* II, p. 102.

    20.   Tannehill, *Luke-Acts* II, p. 103.

mission of Peter to Cornelius and Paul's mission to the Gentiles. As mentioned above, the heavenly vision of Peter and the heavenly vision of Cornelius together legitimate Peter's action in going to the Gentiles, other than his own status as a Jerusalem apostle. Peter's mission to Cornelius, therefore, did not happen accidentally, but with divine direction and human control. Likewise, the three accounts of Paul's conversion experience, referring to his supernatural encounter with the risen Lord and the specific commission he received from him to go to the Gentiles authenticate Paul's mission (Acts 9:1-20; 22:1-21; 26:2-23). Also the mission of Paul and Barnabas was planned and conducted with the approval of the church (Acts 13:1-3).

In short, the legitimacy question of the Samaritan Christianity is important because of (1) the longstanding religious hostility between the Samaritans and the Jews, and of the historical question of the identity of the Samaritans. (2) If there existed followers of Simon in Luke's day who still venerated their leader as a divine being and Luke knew about it, then in his account of Simon, he must both refute their claim and legitimate the Samaritan Christianity of which Simon was a member before. (3) Luke's theological intentions behind his positive treatment of the Samaritans in his Gospel could betray questions raised about their legitimacy. (4) If the anti-Samaritan motif still existed among some of the Jewish Christians (e.g. Mt. 10:5b) of Luke's day, then it is possible that they had brought accusations against the Samaritan mission and Samaritan Christianity. (5) The Samaritan mission was the first of its kind started by a non-apostle. The ideology and authenticity of the Hellenist Philip, who was a member of the scattered group after Stephen's death and also the founder of the new Samaritan Christian community had possibly raised issues of legitimacy. (6) The Samaritan mission did not originate either according to any human planning or control, or out of any supernatural heavenly vision of Philip or the Samaritans, but as a result of the scattering of the Hellenists. Thus, Luke intends to defend the identity of the new community by portraying the legitimacy of the Samaritans themselves, the authentic context of the origin of the Samaritan mission, and the authority of the person(s) involved in its mission, as will be argued below.

Before going into the discussion, we need to face two objections against our thesis that Luke's intention in Acts 8:4-25 is to show the validity of the Samaritan mission and to defend the divine origin and legitimacy of Samaritan Christianity. First, if one agrees with the view of Jervell who claims that the mission in Samaria was a Jewish mission and therefore no specific justification was needed for the mission to Samaria as was necessary in regard to Cornelius, then the question of legitimacy does not arise.[21]

---

21. Jervell, 'Lost Sheep', p. 124; Also Haenchen, *Acts*, pp. 307–8, who thinks that the Samaritans 'could be roughly classified as (from Jerusalem's point of view) Jews not wholly unexceptionable either racially or dogmatically speaking'; *contra* Enslin, 'Luke and the Samaritans', p. 281.

Second, it can be claimed that the inclusion of the Samaritans caused none of the problems for the church that were raised by the inclusion of the Gentiles and therefore the Samaritan mission was already found to be legitimate.

We will start with the second objection first, as it does not deserve much explanation. The inclusion of the Gentiles caused problems for the church because they were not circumcised and did not observe the Law. So the reason was ceremonial or ritualistic. In the case of the Samaritans, there was no such problem because they were circumcised on the eighth day and observed the Law. However, there was no antagonism between the Jews or the Jewish Christians and the Gentiles regarding matters of the Temple and of the city of Jerusalem, as there existed between the former and the Samaritans. The hostility towards the Samaritans was not due to their lack of observance of the Law, but rather to their veneration of Mount Gerizim and their allegiance to the city of Shechem. So the reason was more of a historical one – both political and religious. Luke told his readers earlier how Jesus behaved exactly opposite to his Jewish contemporaries in relating to the Samaritans (Lk. 9:51-56) and that the Samaritan was more of a neighbour to the Jew than were the priest and the Levite (Lk. 9:28-37), and that one Samaritan, though a 'foreigner', experienced what the other nine Jews could not (Lk. 17:11-19). In Acts 8, Luke begins to tell us of a mission to a nation of enemies who are particularly offensive to the Jews and that a mission to them is equally valid with the Jewish mission.

Now the question of whether Luke meant the Samaritan mission as a Jewish mission needs to be briefly discussed. The above-mentioned claim of Jervell is mainly based on his understanding that Luke regards the Samaritans not as Gentiles but as Jews.[22] We have argued earlier in Chapter 4 that the Samaritans cannot be designated Jews. Jervell's positive argument that the Samaritans are Jews is based on his understanding of the Samaritan rejection of Jesus (Lk. 9:51-56) in the beginning of the 'travel narrative' and the Samaritan mission of Philip in Acts 8:4-13. The Samaritan rejection of Jesus, according to Jervell, is due to 'Jesus' or the church's Jewish orthodoxy' that he was on the way to Jerusalem.[23] Jerusalem is theologically significant for Luke in that the messianic event in the life of Jesus must be concentrated

---

22. Jervell, 'Lost Sheep', pp. 117–18. He argues that the Samaritan mission is not a transition to the Gentile mission, for the entire book of Acts is concerned with the mission to the Jews and to the Jewish 'diaspora'. For Jervell, the actual Gentile mission first starts at Acts 28:28. He also claims that because Luke does not inform the readers in an illustrative way who the Samaritans really are, the Samaritan episodes in Luke are 'incomprehensible', 'unintelligible', 'less informative' and 'unusual' to the readers if the Samaritans are Gentiles. See also *idem*, 'The Mighty Minority', *ST* 34 (1980), pp. 13–38.

23. Jervell, 'Lost Sheep', p. 124.

around Jerusalem. Jervell claims that Gentiles are never said to reject Jesus or the apostles in Acts, and elsewhere in Luke-Acts the rejection motif appears only in connection with the Jews.[24] Also, the mission in Acts 8 is a Jewish mission because it is connected to the preceding materials where all the missionary activities occur in the Jewish territory and also because Samaria is mentioned along with Judaea and is distinguished from 'the ends of the earth'.[25]

One of the problems with Jervell's view is that it overlooks the historical situation of the Samaritans in the first century CE. In the story of the Samaritan rejection in Lk. 9:51-56 where Luke brings for the first time the Samaritans' contact with Jesus and his disciples and where he also mentions the city of Jerusalem as the reason for the Samaritans' hostility, one cannot avoid the first century historical context of the Jewish-Samaritan relationships in interpreting the text. Jerusalem is theologically significant for Luke, as Jervell rightly points out, but not so for the Samaritans. That Luke specifically mentions Jerusalem as the reason for their hostility towards the disciples means that he expects on the part of his readers some knowledge about the longstanding historical-religious and political animosity of the Samaritans towards Jerusalem and its Temple. Likewise, Luke does not make a norm that all who reject the gospel must be Jews. There is a similarity between the rejection of Jesus at Nazareth in Lk. 4:16-30 and the Samaritan rejection of him in Lk. 9:51-56, but they are distinct. The latter differs in its rationale and there is no charge directed towards the Samaritans.[26] If the Jerusalem destination of Jesus' journey through Samaria brought the Samaritans' initial rebuff and hostility to Jesus' disciples (Lk. 9:51-53), their reception of God's word and the Holy Spirit brought salvation to them in an unprecedented and uncontroversial way.

As to the connection of Acts 8 with the preceding materials, it could well be that Acts 8 is distinctive as it marks a new phase in mission to a new territory, Samaria, initiated by a new character, Philip. If one considers the first major transition in the Acts narrative as taking place at 6:1 or 8:4, this does not make the Samaritan mission a Jewish mission.[27] The only

---

24. Jervell, 'Lost Sheep', p. 121.
25. Jervell, 'Lost Sheep', pp. 122, 124.
26. Sanders, *Jews in Luke-Acts*, p. 149.
27. Based on the introduction of new characters like Stephen and his Hellenist group, and of the new expansion of mission beyond Jerusalem by the scattered Hellenists, some scholars locate the first structural transition in Acts at 6:1. See Lake and Cadbury, *Beginnings* I.4, p. 63; Marshall, *Acts*, p. 124; Dunn, *Acts*, p. 75. But other scholars consider Acts 8:4 as marking the first structural transition because it takes a new step in mission from Jerusalem and Judaea to Samaria and beyond: Johnson, *Acts*, p. 143; Squires, 'Function', pp. 608–17, argues that Acts 8:4–12:25 'comprises a discrete and cohesive section' in which Luke prepares for the 'turn to the Gentiles'.

connection of Stephen and the Hellenists in Acts 6-7 to that in Acts 8:1 is their previous location of ministry as Jerusalem and that was only until the persecution broke out. With Philip's mission to Samaria in Acts 8:5, the location changes and a new mission begins. The account of the Samaritan mission in Acts 8:4-25 could be seen as part of the section in Acts 8-12.[28] As Tyson points out, the section in Acts 8-12 points to the enlargement of both the geographical setting and the ethnic diversity of people.[29] Also, that the connection is made forward is clear as Luke links the persecution in Acts 8:1 as the immediate cause for the mission to Samaria (Acts 8:4-25) and to the ends of the earth (Acts 11:19).[30] The link between Judaea and Samaria does not make the Samaritan mission a Jewish mission, rather it indicates Luke's programmatic development of mission from one location to another. Also the mass conversion in Samaria does not prove that the Samaritans are considered Jews,[31] but shows that they are a distinct group who can easily accept the word of God and that it is a reversal of their behaviour in Lk. 9:53,[32] which may contribute to Luke for his device of authentication.

Another problem with Jervell's view is his claim of the alternative status of the Samaritans in Luke-Acts that since they cannot be Gentiles, they are Jews. Here also Jervell fails to take into account not only the distinctive position of the Samaritans in Luke-Acts as a group existing between the Jews and the Gentiles but also the marginality rendered to them from a Jewish point of view. It is true that Luke distinguishes the Samaritans from the Gentiles and they are not included under the broader category of Gentiles.[33] It is also true that for him the Gentile mission starts with the conversion of Cornelius. However, this does not mean that the Samaritans should be seen as Jews. In this respect, it is interesting to note the comment of Coggins when he says,

---

28.   Squires, 'Function', p. 611.

29.   J.B. Tyson, *Images of Judaism in Luke-Acts* (South Carolina: University of South Carolina Press, 1992), p. 116, says, 'Acts 8-12 is to a large extent a transitional section that stands between those parts of Acts that locate the Christian movement in Jerusalem and among Jews to those that focus attention on the spread of Christianity to diverse people in distant lands'.

30.   Wilson, *Gentiles*, p. 138; Also for the view that Acts 8:4 indicates a significant step forwards in the mission of the church, see Barrett, *Acts* I, p. 400; Marshall, *Acts*, p. 152; Dunn, *Acts*, p. 102; Tannehill, *Luke-Acts* II, p. 102.

31.   Sanders, *Jews in Luke-Acts*, p. 149, says that the 'volume of mass conversions is precisely what it should be for an intermediate group, large but not quite as large as that of the Jewish conversions during the "Jerusalem springtime", which ran to the "myriads" (Acts 21:20)'. Therefore, the volume of conversion in Samaria, according to Sanders, fits well with the Lukan oddity that, as the mission moves from the Jews to the Gentiles, the volume of conversion declines.

32.   The Samaritans' initial rejection of Jesus (καὶ οὐκ ἐδέξαντο αὐτόν, Lk. 9:53) is reversed as they later accepted the word of God (δέδεκται ἡ Σαμάρεια τὸν λόγον τοῦ θεοῦ, Acts 8:14).

33.   Coggins, 'Samaritans and Acts', p. 431, says that it is implicit in Luke-Acts that clearly, the Samaritans are not regarded simply as a Gentile race.

'all attempts to divide the Lucan world neatly into Jews and Gentiles must break down at this point'.[34] However, attempting to place the Samaritans in a separate group, Sanders thinks that the claim of the alternative status of the Samaritans in Luke-Acts, i.e., either Gentiles or Jews, is a false one. He claims that for Luke there are three divisions in the population: the Jews, the periphery about Judaism and the Gentiles; the Samaritans are in the periphery of Judaism along with outcasts and proselytes and God-fearers.[35] Sanders' inclusion of the Samaritans with proselytes and God-fearers does not do justice to the particular role Luke assigns for the Samaritans. Also, as Ravens mentions, the Samaritans did not want to be close to Judaism, as the other groups did.[36]

There are scholars, on the other extreme, who think that for Luke the Samaritans are on the Gentile side. For example, Bowman considers the mission to the Samaritans in Acts as the first step in the church's mission to the Gentiles. He claims that for the author of Luke-Acts, 'the Samaritans, who indeed do not belong to the rabbinic-Jewish community and who according to their own self-understanding do not belong to Israel, represent an essential part of the gentile world to which he wants to turn'.[37] Likewise, regarding the mission in Samaria, Cullmann says: 'For the first time the gospel entered a country which did not belong to the Jewish community'.[38] These statements of Bowman and Cullmann indicate that the Samaritans cannot be considered Jews at all, but Gentiles.

From the above discussions, it is clear that there are irreconcilable views regarding Luke's understanding of the status of the Samaritans in Luke-Acts. We have seen earlier in our study the ambiguous and ambivalent treatment of various sources on the question of the status of the Samaritans.[39] Based on the available evidence, we argued that it is not reasonable to portray them either as fully Jews or as fully Gentiles, rather as another tradition which is parallel to Jewish tradition within the Israelite religion. A better term to refer to them is 'Israel'.[40] Therefore, historically it is inappropriate to consider them

34. Coggins, 'Samaritans and Acts', p. 432.
35. Sanders, *Jews in Luke-Acts*, pp. 142–53; Tyson, *Images*, p. 116, also includes the Samaritans and the 'diaspora' Jews in the peripheral.
36. Ravens, *Restoration*, pp. 72–106, 84, n.54.
37. Bowman, *Samaritan Problem*, p. 70.
38. Cullmann, 'Samaria', p. 186.
39. See the ambiguous treatment of their status discussed in sections 3.3-3.7 of the study.
40. See Purvis, 'Samaritans and Judaism', pp. 90–5; it is reasonable to speak of the Samaritans as part of Israel rather than as part of the Jewish community which constitutes a Judaism that is centred on Jerusalem. According to Meier, 'The Historical Samaritans', pp. 216–17, who rules out the idea of a 'schism' between Judaism and Samaritanism, neither religion was derived from the other nor broke away from the other. Therefore, he thinks it is appropriate to use the term 'Israel' to refer to the Samaritans instead of the term 'Judaism' or as a sect within Judaism (p. 217, n.32). Coggins, 'Issues', pp. 75–6, also affirms the point that

as Jews or as a sect within Judaism or as Gentiles.[41] In Luke-Acts, it may well be that Luke does not share the popular feeling of the Judaism of his day towards the Samaritans. However, his treatment of the Samaritans makes good sense only if it is understood from a Jewish point of view.[42] Luke or the Lukan Jesus always portray them in a benign light and they are certainly to be distinguished from the Jerusalem-centred Judaism and the Gentiles. For him they are to be better understood as Israelites.

If one might define the term 'Jews' (Ἰουδαῖοι) in the first century CE in geographical, ethnic or religious terms, the Samaritans cannot be called Jews.[43] Geographically, the Jews are identified as people from Judaea and they differ from the Samaritans who were the inhabitants of the region called Samaria. Ethnically, they belong to the tribe of Judah and are centred on the territory called Judaea, whereas the Samaritans claimed to be the descendants

---

we cannot consider the Samaritans as Gentiles *tout court* or as Jews *tout court*, but as 'Israelites', a term the Samaritans would have used to describe themselves; also *idem*, 'Samaritans and Acts', p. 431. However, Coggins, 'Samaritans and Acts', p. 432, seems to include them within Judaism when he says that within the total spectrum of Judaism in its broader sense, the Samaritans will have represented a conservative element, perhaps most likely akin to the Sadducees.

41.   So Meier, 'Historical Samaritans', pp. 216–17.

42.   Coggins, 'Samaritans and Acts', p. 432.

43.   The meaning of the term Ἰουδαῖοι is variously understood as it can be rendered as 'Judeans' in a narrow ethno-geographical sense, designating the inhabitants of Judaea or as 'Jews' in a broader religio-cultural sense, for those who live according to a particular set of ancestral laws and customs. Danker (ed.), *Greek-English Lexicon*, pp. 478–9, prefers the meaning 'Judeans'. R.A. Horsley, *Galilee: History, Politics, People* (Valley Forge: Trinity Press International, 1995), takes the term to mean 'Judeans' in a geographical sense, so as to designate the Galileans 'Israelites', rather than 'Jews'. Shaye Cohen, 'Ioudaios: "Judean" and "Jew" in Susanna, First Maccabees, and Second Maccabees', in Hubert Cancik, Hermann Lichtenberger and Peter Schaefer (eds), *Geschichte-Tradition-Reflexion: Festschrift fuer Martin Hengel zum 70. Geburtstag*, vol. I (Tübingen: Mohr, 1996), pp. 211–19, thinks that the term Ἰουδαῖος took its religio-cultural meaning 'Jew' in the Maccabean period because of the need for Jewish self-definition (2 Macc. 2:21; 8:1; 14:38), as against its earlier narrow geographical referent 'Judean' (2 Macc. 6:1-11; 9:16-19); Sean Freyne, 'Behind the Names: Samaritans, *Ioudaioi*, Galileans', in S.G. Wilson and M. Desjardins (eds), *Text and Artefact in the Religions of Mediterranean Antiquity*, Essays in Honour of Peter Richardson (SCJ 9; Canada: Wilfrid Laurier University Press, 2000), pp. 389–401, in his brief discussion on the Samaritans' animosity to the Galilean pilgrims (*AJ*, XX,118, cf. Lk. 9:52-56, John 4:4), suggests that from the Hasmonean period the religio-cultural sense of the term Ἰουδαῖος became prominent and it referred to all who worshipped at Jerusalem rather than to the inhabitants of Judaea. 'This extended use of the term and the assumptions that it carried', says Freyne, 'are applicable to the Galileans also, thereby providing the explanation for the Samaritan/Galilean hostilities, similar to those that obtained between the Samaritans and the Judeans' (p. 398). The point is that the term Ἰουδαῖοι carries both ethno-geographical and religio-cultural meanings, referring to both the territory and the people (cf. *AJ*, XI, 173) who live according to the ancestral laws and customs which included worship at Jerusalem. However, the Samaritans are not. See also the discussion in S. Zeitlin, 'The Names Hebrew, Jew and Israel', *JQR* 43 (1952/53), pp. 365–79; R.S. Kraemer, 'On the Meaning of the term "Jew" in Greco-Roman Inscriptions', *HTR* 82 (1989), pp. 35–53.

of the tribes of Ephraim and Manasseh and belonged to the Northern Kingdom of Israel. Religiously, the Jews are the worshippers at the Jerusalem Temple, whereas the Samaritans venerated the sanctuary on Mount Gerizim and the holy city of Shechem and are, therefore, distinct from the Jerusalem-centred Judaism. Even if the geographical territory of Judaea is extended to include other Jews, who by birth or conversion are seen to be part of the Jerusalem-centred Judaism,[44] the Samaritans cannot be considered as Jews. Also, taking the treatment of the Samaritans in his Gospel, nowhere in Luke-Acts does the author explicitly or implicitly refer to the Samaritans as Jews ('Ιουδαῖοι). That does not mean that he did not consider them to be Israelites.[45] The term, 'Ιουδαῖοι, which is used to describe the members of Jerusalem-centred Palestinian Judaism, is never used in Luke-Acts to describe the Samaritans. The words, οἱ ὄχλοι are rendered in Acts 8:6 to refer to the people who paid attention to the ministry of Philip. For Luke, ὄχλος refers to either Jews or Gentiles, whereas λαός is used to refer to Jews or the people of Israel exclusively.[46] Also the reference to τὸ ἔθνος τῆς Σαμαρείας in Acts 8:9 seems to suggest a race of people different from the Jews.[47] Further, the terminology ὁ ἀλλογενής used for the healed Samaritan in Lk. 17:18 means a member of a distinct race and it suggests that Luke or the Lukan Jesus did not consider the Samaritans as belonging to Judaism. However, Jervell does not seem to give credit to this meaning of ἀλλογενής when he says, 'By itself this does not mean that they are non-Israelites in a purely ethnic sense, even though this is the usual use of the term in the Septuagint'.[48]

Further, even if Luke had considered the Samaritans as Jews and a mission to them as a Jewish mission, that does not mean that his readers also had necessarily meant the same and had legitimized such a mission. If Luke's audience were Jewish Christians, as Jervell himself claims, then it is possible

44.   Freyne, 'Behind the Names', p. 394, takes this point to prefer the broader religio-cultural sense of the term 'Ιουδαῖοι to its narrower geographical meaning. See also, J.D.G. Dunn, 'Judaism in the Land of Israel in the First Century', in J. Neusner (ed.), *Judaism in Late Antiquity, Part II: Historical Syntheses* (HOS; Leiden: E.J. Brill, 1995), pp. 229–61, 234.

45.   For the view that Luke considered the Samaritans to be Israelites, see Böhm, *Samarien, passim*.

46.   Liddell and Scott, *A Greek-English Lexicon*, with a revised supplement (Oxford: Clarendon Press, 1996), pp. 1029–30, note that in the LXX, the word λαός is used of the *people* as opposite to priests and Levites, and in the New Testament, of Jews and Christians as opposite to heathens; for its various usages in the early Christian literature, see Danker (ed.), *Greek-English Lexicon*, pp. 586–7.

47.   Danker (ed.), *Greek-English Lexicon*, p. 276: the word, ἔθνος means 'a body of people united by kinship, culture, and common traditions' and its specific link to Σαμαρείας in 8:6 distinguishes them from the Jews. Similarly, to denote exclusively the Jews, Luke uses the term, τοῦ ἔθνους τῶν 'Ιουδαίων (Acts 10:22).

48.   Jervell, 'Lost Sheep', p. 124.

that they had shared the common Jewish view of the Samaritans as not belonging to their race.[49] That the disciples of Jesus also shared this popular feeling of hostility and antagonism of Jews against the Samaritans is obvious from Luke's first reference to them in that the disciples wished to destroy them by fire. That the legitimacy of a mission to the Samaritans could be questioned is beyond any doubt. The significance of Samaria in Luke's mental map is that the alleged nation of apostates and idolaters from a Jewish point of view become the sharers of the Kingdom of God and find their legitimacy and identity as the people of God, overcoming the socio-ethnic and religious boundaries.

7.3. The Legitimating Devices in the Samaritan Mission Episodes

7.3.1. The Portrait of the Samaritans in the Gospel of Luke

To legitimate the mission to Samaria, first of all, Luke's objective, both theological and literary, is to portray the Samaritan mission as being in accordance with the divine plan of God, and rooted in the authority of Jesus. To explicate this we need to draw attention to the connection Luke makes in his first reference to the Samaritans with the resurrection and ascension of Jesus (Lk. 9:51) as well as his allusions to the Old Testament.[50] We have argued earlier that Jesus' sending of messengers into Samaria is an anticipation of a Samaritan mission and that Samaria is particularly found to be important in the event of Jesus' last journey to Jerusalem. In other words, though the Lukan Jesus did not have a mission proper to the Samaritans, they are to be included as part of the recipients of salvation brought through his death and resurrection. We have also noted that the expression, ἐν τῷ συμπληροῦσθαι τὰς ἡμέρας τῆς ἀναλήμψεως (Lk. 9:51), refers to the fulfilment of the divine plan. The themes of 'sending the messengers before

49. Jervell, 'Lost Sheep', p. 127.
50. We discussed earlier in our study the association Luke makes in Lk. 9:51-52 with the themes of Jesus' death, resurrection and ascension and also with the prophecy of 'sending the messengers before the face of the Lord' and 'preparing the way of the Lord' in Isa. 40:3 and Mal. 3:1. The other possible Old Testament allusions include the ascension of Enoch (Gen. 5:24) and Elijah (2 Kgs 2:11; 1 Macc. 2:58; Sir. 48:9), the rejection of the prophets of Israel, and perhaps Elijah's sending of fire on Samaria (2 Kgs 1:10-12). See Meier, 'Historical Samaritans', pp. 224–5; C.A. Evans, 'Luke 9,51 Once Again', pp. 80–4, *contra* Giblin, *Destruction*, argues that the expression, 'he set his face', in the Old Testament connotes a sense of judgement and is especially found in Ezekiel (6:2; 13:17; 20:45-21:7), the most likely source from which Luke may have derived this language. The point is that whether Luke intended the theme of judgement or not, Lk. 9:51 echoes Luke's use of the Old Testament in this section of his reference to the Samaritans. For a similar view that Lk. 9:51-56 contains Old Testament allusions, see Davies, 'The Purpose of the Central Section', pp. 164–9; Fitzmyer, *Luke* I, p. 828; Green, *Luke*, p. 403; Marshall, *Luke*, p. 405.

him' (ἀπέστειλεν ἀγγέλους πρὸ προσώπου αὐτοῦ, v. 52a) and 'to prepare for him' (ἑτοιμάσαι αὐτῷ, v. 52b) are to be seen in connection with Old Testament prophecy.[51] Likewise, the theme of rejection of the prophets in the Old Testament comes into play when Luke says that the Samaritans did not receive Jesus (καὶ οὐκ ἐδέξαντο αὐτόν, v. 53).[52] In other words, in his last journey to Jerusalem, Jesus' initial contact with the Samaritans is in accordance with the divine plan of God, and his anticipation of a future mission to them is therefore legitimate.

In the other references to Samaria and the Samaritans in his Gospel also, Luke portrays Jesus' treatment of the Samaritans in a benign light and also defends the legitimacy of their action. In the parable of the good Samaritan (Lk. 10:29-37), Luke makes the Samaritan 'a paradigm for Christian conduct'.[53] Contrary to the action of the priest and the Levite, the Samaritan is depicted making use of his material possessions such as oil, wine, mount and money.[54] In showing this act of 'mercy' (ἔλεος, v. 37) he becomes a 'neighbour' (πλησίον) to the wounded man which, in turn, would qualify him to inherit 'eternal life' (ζωή αἰώνιος). The command to love God and to love one's neighbour is the core of the Jewish law (Dt. 6:5; Lev. 19:18), and both the Jewish lawyer and Jesus agree on this.[55] In the eyes of the Jews, the Samaritan has been a schismatic and been excluded from the covenant fellowship of neighbours, but he, in contrast to the behaviour of the priest and the Levite, meets the requirements of the covenant.[56] If the lawyer's question is to do with sharing the ultimate blessings of God's kingdom,[57] then certainly the Samaritan has a part in it. Through the expression, πορεύου καὶ σὺ ποίει ὁμοίως (v.37) Jesus commands the lawyer to follow the Samaritan who is the 'moral exemplar',[58] and who through his action shares the ultimate blessings of God's kingdom. Jesus having placed the Samaritan in a Jewish context and depicted his action of neighbourliness rooted in the Old Testament law asks the lawyer to follow the Samaritan example. Here Luke intends to show that the rejection of Jesus by the Samaritans in the previous account (Lk. 9:53) is now reversed as the Samaritan moved with compassion, acted in generosity and extended neighbourly love to the Jewish unfortunate victim by crossing his ethnic and religious boundaries. That means, for Luke, the socio-religious and ethnic hostility of the Samaritans towards the Jews seems to have been reduced at some level, as the Samaritan is said to have shown compassion and behaved as a neighbour.

---

51. See the above footnote and the discussion of the text in section 4.4 of the work.
52. However, Jesus treats them in a benign light and seems to defend them against the desire of the disciples to punish them.
53. Fitzmyer, *Luke* II, p. 884; Marshall, *Luke*, pp. 445, 450.
54. Fitzmyer, *Luke* II, p. 888; Tannehill, *Luke*, p. 184.
55. C.F. Evans, *Saint Luke*, p. 465; Tannehill, *Luke*, p. 182.
56. Marshall, *Luke*, pp. 446, 449; C.F. Evans, *Saint Luke*, p. 469.
57. Tannehill, *Luke*, p. 181.
58. Johnson, *Luke*, p. 173; Marshall, *Luke*, p. 445; Fitzmyer, *Luke* II, p. 883.

Thus Luke achieves a progression in his legitimizing device as the Samaritans move from the outer boundary of hostility to the inner side of acceptance and neighbourliness.

In the healing of the ten lepers (Lk. 17:11-19), Jesus singles out the one Samaritan who is designated a 'foreigner' (ἀλλογενής) and contrasts his action with the other nine. The Samaritan leper's action is that he saw, returned, and glorified God, fell on Jesus' feet, and gave thanks. Returning and giving thanks to Jesus is identified as giving glory to God. The faith of the other nine was incomplete, as it did not come out of gratitude.[59] The Samaritan leper 'in his dealings with Jesus experiences an encounter with God'.[60] Here Jesus refers to the faith of the Samaritan that was authentic enough to lead him to salvation which Jesus himself brought. In doing so he challenges the response of the Jews.[61] The faith of the Samaritan leads him beyond physical cure and brings him 'full salvation, the forgiveness of sins, a place among God's children'.[62] He recognized the visitation of God in Jesus.[63] It is interesting to note that in the previous story of the good Samaritan (Lk. 10:29-37), the Samaritan showed mercy to the unfortunate victim (ἔλεος, v. 37), but here the Samaritan leper received both mercy (ἔλεος, v. 13) and salvation from God (ἡ πίστις σου σέσωκέν σε, v. 19). It may be that Luke intends his readers to see Jesus elevating the Samaritans over the Jews for the legitimacy of their dealings with men and their true worship of God. It is also likely that the text secures a 'foothold for the Samaritan mission'.[64] We may infer the same quality of faith in the healed Samaritan to the audience of Philip also in Samaria when they believed his message of the Kingdom of God. Here too Luke legitimizes not only the action of the Samaritan but also the quality of his faith expressed in gratitude that enabled him to experience the salvation which the other nine Jews were expected to experience more than the 'foreigner', but they did not. Luke is able to make further progression on his legitimizing device in that the inhospitable Samaritans move from rejection to acceptance, and now to the sharing of salvation and to the true worship of God.

One further point of contrast is necessary here: that is to do with Jesus' reaction or command to the Jewish counterparts in the above stories over against that to the Samaritans.[65] Jesus rebukes (ἐπετίμησεν, 9:55) James and

---

59.	Marshall, *Luke*, p. 652.
60.	Nolland, *Luke* II, p. 848.
61.	Nolland, *Luke* II, p. 847.
62.	Arndt, *Luke*, p. 372; also, Marshall, *Luke*, p. 649.
63.	Johnson, *Luke*, p. 260.
64.	Nolland, *Luke* II, p. 847.
65.	This is not to suggest or imply any anti-Semitic motif in these passages. They are to be better understood as part of Lukan apologetic devices rather than polemic against Jews. For the latter view, see S. Sandmel, *Anti-Semitism in the New Testament* (Philadelphia: Fortress Press, 1978). Fitzmyer, *Luke* II, p. 885, avoids any suggestion of anti-Semitic tendency and warns that,

John, as they *failed* to understand the purpose of his mission. The priest and the Levite could help the physically afflicted person, but they *failed* to perform any practical assistance for him.[66] In that instance, the Jewish lawyer is asked to go and do what the Samaritan did (πορεύου καὶ σὺ ποίει ὁμοίως, 10:37), which the representatives of the official Jewish priesthood *failed* to do. Likewise, the nine lepers *failed* to see what the Samaritan leper saw in Jesus. This is clear from the command of Jesus to him, ἀναστὰς πορεύου· ἡ πίστις σου σέσωκέν σε (17:19). In other words, all the Jewish counterparts in the stories, since they seemed to have lacked understanding and acted inappropriately, have not as yet reached the standard of the Samaritans who, in Jesus' sight, fulfilled the law and attained the demands of the Kingdom of God. The Samaritan becomes both a neighbour (πλησίον) by crossing the ethnic boundary and an insider, though previously an outsider (ἀλλογενής), by breaking the religious barrier. Being a neighbour to the wounded man, the Samaritan traveller fulfils the commandment in the Old Testament of loving his neighbour (Lev. 19:18), and, having acknowledged Jesus as God and worshipped him, falling at his feet, the Samaritan leper fulfils the commandment of loving God (Dt. 6:5) It is explicit, therefore, that Luke achieves a reversal of the Samaritans' status and thereby he intends his readers to see the legitimacy of the Samaritan community as part of God's people, an apologetic purpose which he very strongly signals throughout these stories.

Next, the commission of the risen Lord in Acts 1:8 – 'you shall be my witnesses in Jerusalem, in all Judaea and Samaria, and to the ends of the earth' – links back to the story in Lk. 9:51-56 and points forward to Acts 8:4-25. That means what happened in Acts 8:4-25 is in accordance with what is anticipated by Jesus in Lk. 9:51-56 and what is commissioned by the risen Christ in Acts 1:8. In other words, the Samaritan mission is to be linked to the resurrection, ascension and the commission of Jesus Christ. Whichever way one interprets Acts 1:8,[67] the commission of the risen Lord finds no real

---

'to read the Lucan Gospel in this way is to import into it anachronistic issues that were not really Luke's concern'.

66. Fitzmyer, *Luke* II, p. 884.

67. Acts 1:8b – 'you shall be my witnesses in Jerusalem and in all Judea and Samaria and to the end of the earth' – is generally understood as a command of Jesus referring to a universal mission inclusive of Gentiles. But there are scholars who claim that the command includes a mission only to the Jewish diaspora. For example, K.H. Rengstorf, 'The Election of Matthias', in W. Klassen and G.F. Snyder (eds), *Current Issues in New Testament Interpretation*, Essays in honour of O. Piper (London: SCM Press, 1962), pp. 178–87, thinks that a special vision to Peter was necessary to convince him of a mission to the Gentiles, because the command in 1:8 did not include preaching to the Gentiles. Apart from this question of whether the command included a mission only to the Jewish 'diaspora' or the Gentiles as well, Acts 1:8b also poses the problem of whether the command was a construction of the early Church to explain the Gentile mission. See the discussion in Wilson, *Gentiles*, pp. 90–6.

fulfilment in the later works of the Twelve but only in making their representatives affirm the missions conducted by others.[68] The commission of the
risen Lord to the apostles in Acts 1:8 to engage in a centrifugal mission out
from Jerusalem finds its fulfilment in the activity of Philip with regard to
Samaria, though the apostles remained inviolable in Jerusalem. Therefore,
in Acts 8:4-25, Luke is not only portraying the fulfilment of the mission, but
is also defending its divine origin and legitimacy by linking it to the
commission of the risen Christ.

7.3.2. *The Ministry of Philip in Samaria*

Apart from linking the Samaritan mission to the ascension, resurrection
and the commission of the Lord Jesus, Luke also associates it with the theme
of *persecution*. Since this is the immediate context in which Luke sets his
narrative, its significance needs to be taken into consideration. He shows
special interest in mentioning that it was the *persecution* following Stephen's
martyrdom that brought the Hellenist Philip into Samaria. It was neither
planned nor initiated by any of the twelve apostles, as they remained in
Jerusalem. Commenting on the response of the apostles to persecution that
they 'remained in Jerusalem', Fitzmyer says, 'Luke records a historical recol-
lection, and it gives his story the picture of unflinching apostolic reaction to
persecution, a characteristic that he gladly records: it is the way Christians
should react to persecution'.[69] Fitzmyer may be right in saying that Christians
should react to persecution by 'remaining', but this is not what Luke says of
the Hellenistic Christians. Had they remained in Jerusalem like the apostles
did, a mission outside of Jerusalem, especially that to Samaria, would not
have been accomplished in the way Luke narrates (cf. Lk. 9:1-9, 51-56).

The introductory remark in Acts 8:1 that the persecution in Jerusalem
resulted in a mission beyond Jerusalem reflects the events of Lk. 4:25-27
where the rejection of the gospel symbolises the extension of mission.[70] The

---

68.   Wilson, *Gentiles*, p. 240. It is true that Luke mentions Peter's dealings with Cornelius,
but in most cases they appear not to have been directly involved in the Church's mission
beyond Jerusalem. One exception is Luke's mention, in his redactional comment, of Peter and
John preaching in many Samaritan villages (8:25) on their return to Jerusalem after their visit
to the Samaritan Christians.

69.   Fitzmyer, *Acts*, p. 397.

70.   *Contra* Brawley, *Luke-Acts*, pp. 6–27, who objects that Lk. 4:16-30 does not
foreshadow 'the reciprocal irrevocable transfer of the gospel from the Jews to the gentiles' (p.6).
He claims that the references to Elijah and Elisha do not prefigure a gentile mission, rather 'Luke
attempts to show that Jesus, like Elijah and Elisha, is a prophet who is not acceptable in ἐν τῇ
πατρίδι αὐτοῦ (p.26). According to Brawley, Lk. 4:16-30 functions for Luke to epitomize the
identity of Jesus as the Spirit-anointed Messiah and prophet. Though Brawley may be right in
saying that in the Nazareth pericope, Luke intends to show who Jesus is and what he will do,
it is unconvincing that Luke does not envisage a gentile mission here. In the light of Luke's interest
in the gentiles and his portrayal of the spread of the gospel in the midst of rejection and persecution, Brawley's claim does not prove to be authentic. M. Prior, *Jesus the Liberator: Nazareth*

proclamation of Jesus' good news to the poor inaugurated in the Nazareth Manifesto has finally reached the Samaritans. The Samaritans' acceptance of God's word reversed their status and brought them inside the Kingdom and in relationship with the Jerusalem-based community. This reversal denotes not only their spiritual liberation but also the socio-religious liberation with regard to their relationship with the Jewish community. In order to achieve this end, persecution plays a part.

Two points are to be noted here. (1) It is obvious at the literary level that the mission to Samaria does not appear as a result of human calculation, but as 'the accidental by-product of persecution'.[71] In Acts 8:1 it is the persecution of the Hellenists that caused the extension of mission to Samaria which in turn serves Luke's literary strategy in Acts 1:8. (2) At the theological level, mission to Samaria highlights the salvation of the Samaritans anticipated in Lk. 9:51-56 which is now actualized as they accept Christ. Here the rejection of the Hellenists and of the gospel in Jerusalem resulted in their acceptance by the Samaritans. In other words, the scattering (διασπείρεσθαι, Acts 8:1,4) led to the gathering together of the scattered Samaritans.[72] It also fits with Luke's highlighting of the Jewish diaspora as a locus of salvation. Though the apostles remained in Jerusalem, the mission was in progress by the dispersed Hellenists. This new and advanced stage in mission is in accordance with Luke's programmatic scheme set out in Acts 1:8. Therefore in the episode on the Samaritan mission in Acts 8:4-25, Luke's ability to achieve both his literary and theological purposes is made obvious.

However, Luke's mention of the persecution as the direct cause for the spread of mission to Samaria carries a deeper theological significance. This becomes clear in the light of the role that persecution plays in Luke-Acts. Scott Cunningham, in his extensive study on persecution in Luke-Acts, identifies five prominent theological functions of the persecution theme in Acts. They are: persecution is part of the plan of God; it is the rejection of God's agents; the persecuted people of God stand in continuity with God's prophets; it is an integral consequence of following Jesus, and it is the occasion of divine triumph.[73] He also shows that the persecution of the disciples in Acts is a continuation of the persecution of Jesus in Luke's Gospel, and is seen as the

Liberation Theology (Luke 4:16-30) (Sheffield: Sheffield Academic Press, 1995), pp. 142–8, argues that the references in Lk. 4:25-27 does not imply a turning away from the Jews in favour of an exclusive mission to Gentiles, instead they indicate that the Gentiles also would receive the benefits of salvation. Also, C.M. Tuckett, *Luke* (NTG; Sheffield: Sheffield Academic Press, 1996), pp. 52, 54, interprets the Elijah-Elisha references as a prefiguration of the Gentile mission.

71.   Johnson, *Acts*, p. 150; Barrett, *Acts* II, p. cii.

72.   David Seccombe, 'The New People of God', in Marshall and Peterson (eds), *Witness*, pp. 349–72, 359.

73.   S. Cunningham, *'Through Many Tribulations': The Theology of Persecution in Luke-Acts* (JSNTSup.142; Sheffield: Sheffield Academic Press, 1997).

fulfilment of prophecy made by Jesus in the Gospel, particularly Lk. 21:12-19. For example, the Sanhedrin opposes the proclamation of Peter and John (Acts 4:1-22) and of the Twelve (Acts 5:17-41) which thereby demonstrates the validity of their message and legitimates them as worthy.[74] In the proclamation and rejection of Jesus at Nazareth (Lk. 4:16-30), the Lukan Jesus serves as a 'paradigm' for his followers who will also engage in a Spirit-empowered mission.[75]

For our purpose, two points need to be emphasized here. (1) The identification of the speech of Stephen with the words of Jesus in the Nazareth pericope: 'You stiff-necked people, uncircumcised in heart and ears, you are forever opposing the Holy Spirit, just as your ancestors used to do. Which of the prophets did your ancestors not persecute? They killed those who foretold the coming of the Righteous One, and now you have become his betrayers and murderers' (Acts 7:51-52). These words echo the response of Jesus in his rejection at Nazareth: 'Truly I tell you, no prophet is accepted in the prophet's hometown' (Lk. 4:24).[76] On the one hand, these words of Stephen and his very martyrdom 'ironically illustrate his prophetic nature'.[77] On the other, they reflect the legitimacy of a mission beyond the Jewish boundary, as in Jesus' case prefiguring a Gentile mission. Thus, Stephen, and his Hellenist group who were persecuted following his death, join the

---

74.   Cf. e.g. Brawley, *Luke-Acts*, pp. 24–5; B.R. Gaventa, 'Toward a Theology of Acts: Reading and Rereading', *Int* 42 (2, 1988), pp. 146–57.

75.   Drury, *Tradition*, p. 87, makes the comment: 'The whole scene at Nazareth is the prototype of similar scenes in Acts where Christians will preach the gospel and meet with a hostile, even violent response'; also Brawley, *Luke-Acts*, p. 24. There are various parallels between the events surrounding the passion of Jesus and those surrounding his followers. For example, the passion of Jesus and the martyrdom of Stephen (Acts 7), the death of James (Acts 12:1), the suffering of Paul (Acts 9:16; 14:19-20; 20:22-25; 21:30-32; 23:12-15; 25:3). For a detailed parallel list, see Talbert, *Reading Luke*, pp. 186–7; Cunningham, *Tribulations*, pp. 187–8, *passim*. Especially, for the view that Jesus' death is 'paradigmatic', see J.T. Carroll and J.B. Green, *The Death of Jesus in Early Christianity* (Peabody, MA: Hendrickson, 1995), p. 81.

76.   Some scholars have noted a correspondence between Jesus and Moses in Stephen's speech. The point is that Moses is seen as a type of Jesus who can be designated a prophet like Moses. Both Moses and Jesus were rejected by their people of Israel and Stephen stands in continuity with them. See, Johnson, *Acts*, p. 136; *idem*, *Possessions*, pp. 70–7; J.J. Kilgallen, 'The Function of Stephens's Speech (Acts 7:2-53)', *Bib* 70 (1989), pp. 173–93, 186. For a contrary view, see Wilson, *Gentiles*, p. 134.

77.   Brawley, *Luke-Acts*, p. 25. There are other striking parallels in the sayings of Stephen before his death to the sayings of Jesus in his passion: (1) Stephen's testimony before the Sanhedrin corresponds to that of Jesus: 'I see the heavens opened and the Son of Man standing at the right hand of God' (Acts 7:56). Cf. Lk. 22:69: 'But from now on the Son of Man will be seated at the right hand of the power of God'. (2) The prayers of both: 'Lord Jesus, receive my spirit' (Acts 7:59). Cf. Lk. 23:46: 'Father, into your hands I commend my spirit'. (3) Asking forgiveness for the persecutors: 'Lord, do not hold this sin against them' (Acts 7:60). Cf. Lk. 23:34: 'Father, forgive them; for they do not know what they are doing' (Witnesses such as p75 א B D W Θ 0124 1241 ita, d syrs copsa, bo Cyril omit this verse). According to Tannehill, *Luke-Acts* II, p. 99, these similar responses show that 'Stephen is a true follower of Jesus'.

rejection of God's servants such as the prophets of Israel, Jesus himself, Peter and John and the Twelve, and this indicates the authenticity of their mission.

(2) The association of the theme of the Holy Spirit with proclamation and rejection for both Jesus and the Stephen-Philip group. In the beginning of the Nazareth section, Luke describes Jesus as the one in the 'power of the Spirit' (ἐν τῇ δυνάμει τοῦ πνεύματος, Lk. 4:14; cf. 2:40, 52), having the 'Spirit of the Lord' (πνεῦμα κυρίου) and as the one whom God 'anointed' (ἔχρισὲν, Lk. 4:18). Stephen is described as a man 'full of Spirit and wisdom' (πλήρεις πνεύματος καὶ σοφίας, Acts 6:3), 'full of faith and of the Holy Spirit' (πλήρης πίστεως καὶ πνεύματος ἁγίου, Acts 6:5), and 'full of God's grace and power' (πλήρης χάριτος καὶ δυνάμεως, Acts 6.8). Philip and the rest of the Seven are also described with Stephen as men 'full of Spirit and wisdom' (πλήρεις πνεύματος καὶ σοφίας, Acts 6:3).[78] They were rejected just as Jesus was rejected. The association of the qualities like full of 'wisdom' and 'Spirit' with the theme of rejection in the ministry of the Stephen-Philip group creates a correspondence with that of Jesus himself and with the apostles who were also rejected during their Jewish mission (Acts 5:41). Thus, the description of the qualities of Stephen and Philip and the theme of rejection functions for Luke as a technique of legitimation.[79]

From the above, we can deduce that both the persecution of the Hellenists and the mission following it are legitimate as part of the plan of God and that the origin of the nascent Samaritan Christian community formed as a result of the work of the dispersed Philip is indeed authentic. Philip (along with Stephen) shares the qualifications of authentic characters in the Scriptures. Also, he stands in continuity with God's prophets and Jesus himself in his rejection and flight from Jerusalem, apart from his continuity with them in terms of the kind of ministry he performs. Here Luke uses the persecution and the rejection of the Hellenists as a legitimating device to validate the message of the dispersed, especially that of Philip and to legitimate him as worthy, exactly as he does with the apostles in Acts 5:41, and with Jesus himself.

In addition to the persecution, there is another factor that motivates the mission to Samaria. Philip or his Hellenist group went to Samaria and preached there though they knew exactly what the status of the Samaritans was. But they did not seem to share the popular hostility of the Jews towards

---

78. Tannehill, *Luke-Acts* II, p. 83, associates these qualifications of Stephen with those of the leading figures like Joseph and Moses and then suggests that Stephen 'shares qualities with God's most important messengers'. This is also true of Philip as he also shares in these qualities.

79. Tannehill, *Luke-Acts* II, p. 83, makes the point that since Stephen and Philip are new characters in the story, 'it is important to establish their credentials for the roles they are about to play'.

the Samaritans.[80] Though the Jerusalem-based apostles did receive a missionary commission to be witnesses in the hostile land of Samaria (Acts 1:8), none of them went to Samaria to evangelize the Samaritans. Apart from other reasons, whatever they may be, their enmity towards the land and the people of Samaria (cf. Lk. 9:54) would have probably stopped the apostles from being engaged in a proper mission to the Samaritans. Even the commission of the risen Lord and the event and experience of Pentecost did not transform them to contain the Samaritans in the plan of salvation. Here Luke is able to show the successful missionary achievement of the Hellenists and the apparent failure of the Twelve in not taking the first initiative step towards reaching Samaria. The account of the mission in Acts 8:4-25 portrays that it is not by specially commissioned apostles alone that the mission of the church and the saving plan of God could be accomplished, but by those who are 'full of the Spirit and wisdom' (Acts 6:3) and are prepared to carry out his commission. Philip's mission to Samaria implies an acceptance of the Samaritans as part of God's people.[81] Philip and his group may be acting in accordance with the prophetic hopes of Jeremiah, Ezekiel and Zechariah for a reunion of North and South.[82] This in turn reflects the positive attitude of Jesus towards the Samaritans as is evident from the Gospel of Luke, the anticipation of a mission to Samaria, and the fulfilment of the words of the risen Christ in Acts 1:8 regarding Samaria.

As mentioned above, the hope for a reunion and restoration of Israel in which the Samaritans are to play a part is rooted in the authority of the Old Testament scriptures.[83] This restoration is to be attained as the fulfilment of the divine oracles of God prophesied through the Old Testament prophets (Jer. 15:19; Mal. 3:22-23; Isa. 11:11-12 cf. Sir. 48:10). One specific text to mention is Ezek. 37:15-17, where Ezekiel is asked to tie the two sticks together marked with 'Judah' and 'Ephraim' and make them one stick, symbolizing the reunification of Israel and Judah, where the inhabitants of Northern Israel at Ezekiel's time were Samaritans.[84] Bowman relates this symbolism (cf. Ezek. 34:22-24) to the words of Jesus in Jn 10:16 that he has 'other sheep which are not of this fold', and thinks that Jesus is speaking about the Samaritans who are the inhabitants of Northern Israel.[85] Bowman's

80. Scobie, 'Origins', p. 399; Cullmann, 'Samaria', p. 191, thinks that the Hellenists went to Samaria because like them, the Samaritans also rejected the Temple worship of Jerusalem: 'What was more natural than that those who had been persecuted because of their hostility to the temple at Jerusalem should take refuge among those who for the same reason had long been separated from the Jews?'

81. Scobie, 'Origins', p. 399.

82. Scobie, 'Origins', p. 400.

83. Bauckham, 'Restoration', pp. 473–4; Jervell, 'Lost Sheep', pp. 113–32; Ravens, *Restoration*, pp. 72–106.

84. Bowman, *Samaritan Problem*, p. 61.

85. Bowman, *Samaritan Problem*, p. 61; Jn 4:40, cf.1:11.

interpretation is a likely hypothesis but it does not allow any space for the wider community other than the Samaritans in the 'other sheep' of Jesus. However, it is clear that any attempt to win the Samaritans to bring restoration is a divine act and is in accordance with the divine plan of God. This hope of restoration is brought to the fore in Acts as the apostles ask the risen Lord whether he will restore (ἀποκαθιστάνεις) the kingdom to Israel (Acts 1:6) at that time. In response to their inquiry, Jesus brings the theme of an empowered mission including one to Samaria too (1:8), thereby making a direct link between the theme of restoration and the Samaritan mission. Thus, Luke is able to show that the mission to Samaria is part of the fulfilment of the prophetic oracles for reunion and restoration of Israel, which, in turn, serves for him to defend the divine origin and legitimacy of Samaritan Christianity.

Regarding restoration, it is also important to note the connection Luke makes between the Samaritans and the characters from Northern Israel, especially Elijah and Elisha. The Elijah motif is strongly present in the account of the Samaritan rejection (Lk. 9:51-56) as the disciples wished to call down fire from heaven to destroy the Samaritans, thus reflecting the story in 2 Kings 1:9-16.[86] The same motif becomes explicit, if the textual addition in Lk. 9:54, ὡς καὶ Ἐλίας ἐποίησεν, is considered. Also, allusions to Elisha's healing of Naaman (2 Kings 5:9-19) appear in the healing of the ten lepers in Lk. 17:11-19, which is another Samaritan reference in Luke. Here only the Samaritan leper, like Naaman, returned to give thanks (2 Kings 5:15).[87] There may also be an allusion to the story of Naaman's servant, Gehazi, in the account of Simon Magus.[88] Luke had already mentioned both Elijah and Elisha in his account of Jesus' rejection in Nazareth (Lk. 4:25-27), the former with the widow of Sarepta and the latter with Naaman the Syrian, as he intended to show the extension of mission to outsiders. But now he brings them in the context of the Samaritans, thus linking the fulfilment of what was anticipated by Jesus with the Samaritan mission.

In light of Luke's intention to link the Samaritan mission with the restoration and reunion of Israel, and with the characters of the Northern Kingdom, it is important to see his mention of the 'city of Samaria' in Acts 8:5. We argued earlier that Luke seems to have associated 'the city of Samaria' with the main Samaritan city of the Old Testament thereby associating the Samaritan mission with the lost Northern Kingdom of the Old

---

86. The references to Elijah occur again in Lk. 9: in mentioning people's identification of Jesus with Elijah (v.8), in the account of Peter's confession of Christ (v.19), in the story of Jesus' transfiguration (vv. 30, 33), and as an allusion in the context of discipleship (vv. 57-62).

87. So Enslin, 'Samaritan Ministry', p. 33.

88. Brodie, '2 Kings 5', pp. 41–67, argues 2 Kgs 5 as one component of Acts 8:9-40 and that Luke is following the Greco-Roman rhetorical practice of *imitation*.

Testament and with the lost sheep of the house of Israel.[89] The significance is that the Samaritans find a new identity through their acceptance of the word of God, as the gospel reached the same place where they previously lost their socio-religious and political identity as a people of God. Luke shows that the power of the gospel transcends racial, social, ethnic and religious boundaries and liberates the unprivileged and the outcasts, and brings them into fellowship with the people of God.

Now we will turn to the ministry of Philip itself to see the theological intention of Luke. Initially Philip appears in Acts as a relatively minor figure (Acts 6:5). He is not chosen to be an evangelist, but as one to serve at table (6:2-3). However, like the apostles, he proclaimed the word and brings good news to Samaria. Later on in 21:8, he is called the evangelist (ὁ εὐαγγελιστής). Here Luke makes use of a minor figure, Philip, to carry out a major and difficult stage in preaching to the marginalized Samaritans and thus portrays Philip's success in the Samaritan mission and his victory over magic and evil forces. Three different aspects of Luke's mention of Philip need attention here. First, as mentioned above, Luke's introduction of Philip along with Stephen as the one 'full of Spirit and wisdom' (6:3) equates him with leading figures of Scripture. Second, as we have seen earlier from the study of the text, Luke portrays the ministry of Philip as being like the ministry of Jesus and the apostles. What is the significance for Luke of the similarity in the nature of Philip's ministry with that of Jesus and the apostles? In light of the significance of the Samaritan mission and of the ministry of Philip himself, Luke portrays Philip as one who continues the work of Jesus and of the apostles.[90] The ministry involves preaching, healing, exorcism, and the manifestation of the kingdom of God in Samaria. The miracles that Philip performed in Samaria (8:7) exactly resemble for Luke those performed by the apostles in Jerusalem in 5:16: '... bringing their sick and those tormented by evil spirits, who were all healed'. His mission and miracles serve as an apologetic purpose of Luke.[91] Third, Philip symbolizes the work of Jesus in that as the rejection of Jesus in Nazareth resulted in the extension of mission,

---

89. See the discussion in section 3.8 of the study.

90. Tannehill, *Luke-Acts* II, p. 104; Johnson, *Acts*, p. 151; Spencer, *Portrait*, p. 53. Based on the view of Moessner that Luke characterizes Peter, Stephen and Paul after a Mosaic model, Spencer goes further to suggest that Philip is portrayed as a 'prophet like Moses'. This is because Philip's ministry resembles that of Moses in preaching, performing signs and mighty deeds, and also in being rejected. For discussion, see Spencer, *Portrait*, pp. 104–15; Also, Moessner, 'Paul and the Pattern of the Prophet like Moses in Acts', in *SBLSP 1983* (ed. K.H. Richards; CA: Scholars Press, 1983), pp. 203–12; *idem*, '"The Christ Must Suffer": New Light on the Jesus-Peter, Stephen, Paul Parallels in Luke-Acts', *NovT* 28 (1986), pp. 220–56.

91. For a discussion on the apologetic motif of miracles and mission, see E.S. Fiorenza, 'Miracles, Mission, and Apologetics: An Introduction', in *eadem* (ed.), *Aspects of Religious Propaganda in Judaism and Early Christianity* (Notre Dame: University of Notre Dame Press, 1976), pp. 1–25.

the persecution of the Hellenists resulted in the acceptance of the gospel by the Samaritans. In this aspect of persecution, he also resembles the prophets of the Old Testament who were rejected and persecuted. Therefore, Philip stands in continuity with Jesus both as his ministry is set in the context of persecution and for the kind of ministry he performs. In brief, Luke wants to show that Philip is an authentic figure like other leading figures of Scripture, and that the Samaritan mission is legitimate and is no lesser in result than the ministry of Jesus and the Jerusalem mission conducted by the apostles.

To sum up the foregoing arguments, it is reasonable to suggest that in the portrayal of the Samaritan mission in Acts 8:4-25, Luke has an apologetic purpose and he intends to defend the divine origin and the legitimacy of Samaritan Christianity. He wants to show that the Samaritan mission did not take place illegitimately nor was it merely an accidental by-product of perse-cution. For him, (1) Jesus himself anticipates the mission to Samaria as he encounters the Samaritans and treats them in a favourable light. (2) The mission is rooted in the authority of Jesus as it is linked to his resurrection and ascension (Lk. 9:51), and is also commissioned by the risen Lord (Acts 1:8). (3) The context of the mission is persecution and so it is divinely ordained in that as the rejection of Jesus at Nazareth caused the extension of mission beyond Judaea, the persecution of the Hellenists brought the gospel to Samaria. This rejection also resembles that of the prominent figures in Scripture. (4) In the context of the persecution, Philip stands in continuity with Jesus and God's prophets, and his going into Samaria after the perse-cution is in the divine plan of God. (5) The activity of Philip in Samaria is to be understood in accordance with the divine prophetic oracles for a reunion of the North and South. (6) The qualifications of Philip and the nature of his ministry put him on the same footing as Jesus and the apostles. Thus, to achieve his purpose of authentication, Luke links the origin of Samaritan Christianity to the ministry of the earthly Jesus, the commission of the risen Lord, the divine context of persecution, the prophetic oracles of the restoration of Israel, and to the authentic ministry of prominent figures in the Scripture. Now, we need to explore Luke's purpose in his portrayal of Peter and John, and Simon.

7.3.3. The Role of Peter and John in Samaria
We have discussed earlier in the study various reasons that scholars suggest for the delay in the reception of the Holy Spirit by the Samaritans and for the presence of Peter and John in Samaria.[92] Regarding the coming of Peter and John, it has been suggested that they came 'to check the reports received',[93] or 'to examine the faith of the Samaritans for its

92. See Chapter 2, especially section 2.3, for a detailed survey of scholarly discussions.
93. Witherington, *Acts*, p. 285.

authenticity'[94] or because they 'conceived it as their responsibility to supervise the expansion of the faith'.[95] However, the arrival of Peter and John in Samaria may reflect, as Barrett suggests, some controversy caused by the Samaritan mission regarding the legitimacy of its development.[96] At the outset it appears that the Jerusalem apostles, Peter and John, come to Samaria to pray for the Samaritan Christians that they might receive the Holy Spirit (Acts 8:15). But why is it that they must come to share in the ministry of Philip's mission and how does this function for Luke to achieve his theological purpose?

As argued earlier in our synchronic study of the text,[97] it is reasonable to suggest that on a literary level the story of the arrival of Peter and John in Samaria functions for Luke as a reversal of their antagonism against the Samaritans as was reflected in Lk. 9:56. Luke links the coming of the apostles to Samaria and their prayer for the Samaritans in Acts 8:14-17 to Lk. 9:51-56 where the disciples James and John asked Jesus if they were allowed to bring down fire from heaven to destroy the Samaritans. Now, the apostles are in Samaria praying for the heavenly fire of the Holy Spirit to fall upon the Samaritans. Also, after the Samaritans' resistance in Lk. 9:56, James and John go to another village, which is most probably not a Samaritan village. On the contrary, after their prayer for the Samaritans in Acts 8, Peter and John on their journey back to Jerusalem then fulfil the mission charge of Jesus in Acts 1:8 as they witnessed in many Samaritan villages (8:25). Now they understand that the Samaritans are part of God's plan of salvation. This reversal of attitude in the apostles would seem to imply that they accepted the mission to the Samaritans as legitimate and fulfilling the commission of the risen Lord. Here Luke establishes the legitimacy of Samaritan Christianity both by integrating the ministry of authoritative and authentic figures, Peter and John and that of Philip, and by portraying the reception of the Spirit by the Samaritan Christians. Thus, both literarily and theologically, Luke is able to demonstrate the plot of 1:8 being fulfilled by the combined ministry of the Hellenists and the Twelve.

In the account of the coming of the apostles to Samaria, Luke may also be employing a reversal of the saying in Mt. 10:5b, just as he did with that of Philip (Acts 8:5). In effect, Luke has not only Philip who goes against this notion, but also the Jerusalem apostles who were once forbidden to go to any Samaritan city. Though the apostles could not originally fulfil the command in Acts 1:8 regarding Samaria, they act in reverse to the saying in Mt. 10:5b by going into Samaria and thus legitimating the Samaritan mission. In other

---

94. Bowman, *Samaritan Problem*, p. 58.
95. Bruce, *Acts*, p. 220.
96. Barrett, *Acts* I, p. 399.
97. See section 5.3.2 of the study.

words, if there were some Jewish Christians in Luke's day who still shared the same view as that stated in Mt. 10:5b, then the act of the Jerusalem apostles would have served as a legitimating factor to authenticate Samaritan Christianity.

The significance of two elements in the ministry of Peter and John – imposition of hands and prayer – needs to be mentioned here. Earlier in the commissioning of the Seven (Acts 6:6), the apostles laid on their hands and prayed for them but now they perform the same double action for the Samaritan Christians to convey the gift of the Spirit (8:15, 17).[98] Luke does not make it a norm that the imposition of hands is necessary for the reception of the Spirit (cf.10:44). Therefore, the double action of the apostles communicates more than merely conferring the Spirit.[99] It may be possible to see the Samaritan community being offered fellowship and solidarity with the Jerusalem Christian community.[100] Therefore, the action could indicate an assurance to the Samaritans that they are fellow members of the elect community of God.[101] However, it cannot be seen as a symbol of exercising the apostles' superiority over the Samaritan Christians.[102]

It may also be that the coming of the Jerusalem apostles to Samaria serves for Luke to unite the Samaritan Christian community to Jerusalem.[103] Just as the Seven and the Twelve share in the ministry to Samaria, the Samaritan Christians and the Jewish Christians are included together as is explicitly manifested in 9:31. The restoration of these communities takes place only when the representative leadership acknowledges and acts accordingly. The arrival of Peter and John, and their prayer and imposition of hands links the Samaritan community into fellowship and solidarity with the Jerusalem-based Christians, and the Holy Spirit functions as the restoration factor in uniting the rival communities. Thus Luke succeeds in bringing the Jewish and the Samaritan Christian communities into unity with each other and thus legitimates the Samaritan mission.

Also Luke links the Samaritans' experience of the new faith to that of the Jerusalem-based Christians at Pentecost: they believed, were baptized, and received the Spirit.[104] For Luke, the reception of the Holy Spirit is related to the eschatological hope of the People of God. This is clear as he makes Peter link the outpouring of the Holy Spirit at Pentecost (Acts 2:17-21) to Joel 2:28. Since the Samaritan Christians also received the Spirit after a special visit by

---

98. So Fitzmyer, *Acts*, p. 406.

99. See also, Tipei, *Laying on of Hands*, p. 275.

100. Lampe, *Seal*, p. 70.

101. Bruce, *Acts*, p. 221.

102. Ehrhardt, *Acts*, p. 48, says that the 'Samaritans had been brought into subjection instead of partnership by the apostles'.

103. Johnson, *Acts*, p. 151; Barrett, *Acts* I, p. 410; Klauck, *Magic*, p. 20.

104. Fitzmyer, *Acts*, p. 405.

Peter and John, just as the early church in Jerusalem received the Spirit after a period of waiting, it makes the point that the Samaritans are part and parcel of the church's mission.

Luke is also able to show the continuity between the Seven and the Twelve,[105] the representatives of the Hellenists and the Jewish Christians, though persecution caused them separation. The apostles remained but the Hellenists were driven out of Jerusalem. Now the Seven and the Twelve in spite of their diversity work co-operatively in the Samaritan mission.[106] Because Peter and John continued Philip's ministry in Samaria without redoing or undoing what he had done, they confirm or complete the previous work of Philip.[107] Since Luke has the apostles' co-operative effort in the mission to the Samaritans, their coming to Samaria functions for him as a technique of legitimation in defending Samaritan Christianity.

In brief, in his portrayal of the apostles' coming to and their ministry in Samaria, Luke succeeds in reversing the previous antagonism of the apostles against the Samaritans, in showing the harmonious relationship of the Jewish and Samaritan Christian communities and in the reunion of the Seven and the Twelve. Hence it functions as a legitimating device to defend the authentic birth of Samaritan Christianity.

7.3.4. *The Function of Simon in the Portrait of the Samaritan Mission*
We now proceed to another important question of why Simon Magus is introduced in Acts 8:4-25. This is important especially as Luke brings Simon in contact with both Philip and Peter separately in his report of the Samaritan mission. We have argued earlier that Simon was a Samaritan magician and that he became a Christian under the ministry of Philip. At the outset it appears that Simon is introduced into the story simply because the ministry of Philip and the magical activity of Simon both took place in the same vicinity of Samaria and therefore it was an event worth reporting due to the proximity of location. Also it seems that Simon is introduced into the story in order to portray the missionary success of Philip. It also appears that Simon is in the story because of Luke's general interest in the exposure of magic and sorcery. All these views, however, do not take into consideration the significance of Luke's treatment of the Samaritans in his Gospel and Acts. They all serve only as secondary purposes for Luke in the context of the Samaritan mission. A far more primary theological significance can be deduced based on the character of Simon himself and on Luke's treatment of the Samaritans as a whole, as we shall see below.

---

105. Johnson, *Acts*, p. 151; Barrett, *Acts* I, p. 399.
106. So also Barrett, *Acts* I, p. 412; Witherington, *Acts*, p. 287.
107. Tannehill, *Luke-Acts* II, pp. 102–3; Johnson, *Acts*, p. 148; Spencer, *Portrait*, pp. 220–41; Witherington, *Acts*, p. 287.

The introduction of Simon into the story of the mission to Samaria is to be demonstrated in the light of Luke's overall treatment of the Samaritans in his Gospel and Acts. In other words, Luke's interest lies more in the nature of the Samaritan mission than in Simon himself. The central argument here is that Luke uses Simon not to tell a story about him, but to portray the legitimacy of Samaritan Christianity and to show that it is a mission on a par with the Jewish mission. That means Simon is only a vehicle for Luke to authenticate Samaritan Christianity.

Now we need to briefly look at the character of Simon and then deduce what he represents in the story. Luke is particularly highlighting the two stages of Simon:

(1) Simon the 'outsider' before he came into contact with Philip: Luke depicts at various points in Acts the defeat of magicians in the realm of Christian mission. Besides the Simon story, he records the blindness which happened to a Jewish magician and false prophet, Bar Jesus as he tried to pervert the proclamation of God's word by Paul (13:4-12). The seven sons of Sceva, Jewish exorcists active in Ephesus, were stripped and flogged by a demon when they tried to exorcise in Jesus' name (19:11-20). Also Luke depicts the tragic destiny of those who claim self-deification. For example, Theudas, who claimed to be somebody (λέγων εἶναί τινα ἑαυτόν, Acts 5:36 cf. λέγων εἶναί τινα ἑαυτὸν μέγαν, 8:9), and also king Herod, who was smitten by an angel and was eaten by worms and died because he 'did not give God the glory' (Acts 12:23; cf. 10: 25-26; 14:12-17) are in this category. In view of his general interest in exposing magic, sorcery, hypocrisy, and false gods, Luke is able to emphasize with the character of Simon the defence of the gospel against magic and its victory over magicians.

The use of the terms, μαγεύων καὶ ἐξιστάνων, εἶναί τινα ἑαυτὸν μέγαν (v.9), ἡ δύναμις τοῦ θεοῦ ἡ καλουμένη Μεγάλη (v.10), and ταῖς μαγείαις ἐξεστακέναι αὐτούς (v.11) all refer to the practice and claim of Simon before he became a Christian. Scholars have suggested that for Luke, Simon the magician represents the demonic force that works against the kingdom of God.[108] According to Garrett, Simon's magic and his claim that he is the 'power of God' imply for Luke an association with the devil.[109] He exalts himself as a god and commits the same sin that the devil had once committed in the wilderness (Lk. 4:6-7) and thereby promotes idolatry.[110] Simon's initial victory and his fascination of others are contrasted with his own fascination at the ministry of Philip and defeat of his magical deeds.

As an 'outsider' Simon can be best compared to the messianic claimants, Theudas and Judas whose self-acclamation brought them to nothing. Earlier in the context of the Jerusalem mission, Luke wanted his readers to under-

---

108. Johnson, *Acts*, p. 152.
109. Garrett, *Demise*, p. 67.
110. Garrett, *Demise*, p. 67.

stand through the words of Gamaliel that the mission of the apostles was of divine origin and that the destruction that came upon Theudas and Judas proved their claim to be false (5:34-39). In the context of the Samaritan mission, Luke uses the description of Simon as an 'outsider' and his defeat by the power of the gospel preached in Samaria to show that the Samaritan mission is of divine origin and in no way lesser than the Jewish mission. Thus Simon's claim and activity before he became a Christian serves for Luke to portray the divine origin and the legitimacy of the Samaritan mission.

(2) Simon the 'insider' whom Peter confronted: it has become obvious from our earlier study of the text that the confrontation between Peter and Simon resembles Luke's recounting of the fate of Judas and Peter's confrontation of Ananias and Sapphira, who all were 'insiders'. This is clear from Luke's description of Simon in Peter's response to Simon. For example, 'you have no part or share in this matter' (v.21a) echoes the fate of Judas in Acts 1:17, 26.[111] Further, Peter's words, 'for your heart is not right before God' (8: 21b) also echoes the condition of Judas, and Ananias and Sapphira. Just as Satan entered the heart of Judas (Lk. 22:3), and Ananias and Sapphira also allowed Satan to enter their hearts, Simon's heart is exposed as being not right with God.[112] There are occasions where Luke links one's possessions with the heart (cf. Lk. 12:34). This becomes clearer when Luke has Peter say, 'Ananias, how is it that Satan has so filled your heart that you have lied to the Holy Spirit and have kept for yourself some of the money you received for the land?' (Acts 5:3). Simon's condition is further mentioned by the expressions, 'gall of bitterness' (χολὴν πικρίας) and 'bond of iniquity' (σύνδεσμος ἀδικίας). The term, 'gall of bitterness' may be an allusion to the Septuagint where it refers to the condition of the idolatrous (Dt. 29:17).[113] The expression, 'bond of iniquity' alludes to Isa. 58:6 which Luke uses with Isa. 61:1 while introducing the ministry of Jesus in the Nazareth Manifesto in Lk. 4:18-19.[114]

The theme of possessions plays a part in the story of Simon. Generally in Acts, Luke is interested in the proper and improper use of money in relation to holy things.[115] Possessions are symbolic terms that play on the antitheses: rejection and acceptance, death and life, outside and inside.[116] Just like Judas, their improper handling of possessions cuts Ananias and Sapphira off from the community. Both Judas, and Ananias and Sapphira were insiders, but their improper use of possessions caused them to become outsiders.[117] As the apostles dealt with Ananias and Sapphira (5:1-11) in the Jerusalem Church, Peter confronts the wicked intention of Simon. Simon used to make

---

111. Brown, *Apostasy*, pp. 82–97; Johnson, *Acts*, p. 149.
112. Brown, *Apostasy*, pp. 110–14; Johnson, *Acts*, p. 152.
113. Barrett, *Acts* I, p. 417; Johnson, *Acts*, p. 149.
114. Garrett, *Demise*, p. 71.
115. Barrett, 'Light', p. 288; Phillips, 'Recent Readings', pp. 231–69.
116. Johnson, *Possessions*, p. 37.
117. Brawley, *Centering*, p. 199.

money by his magical activities before he met Philip and followed him. After he became an insider of the Kingdom, he wanted to purchase with money the authority to induce the Holy Spirit, as he probably regarded it as a 'specially effective piece of magic'[118] and thought it worth purchasing for making a benefit.[119] The story shows the fate of those who try to use the gift of the Holy Spirit as a way of making profit. Luke also portrays the superiority of the Spirit-filled representatives of Christ over the magicians and over those who want to manipulate the activities of the Holy Spirit. The practice of magic is condemned (cf.13:6; 19:13-19) and there is no place for magic and the forces of evil in a Spirit-filled community of Christians.

For Luke, the way of handling possessions by a member of the Spirit-anointed community also speaks of the way in which that person treats the Holy Spirit or handles its gifts, as blasphemy against the Holy Spirit is a prominent theme for Luke.[120] For example, Peter and John do not possess silver or gold but the authority to heal the sick (Acts 3:6). The Holy Spirit or the authority to induce the Spirit on others is a free gift of God and should not be treated as an object of commercial transactions.[121] As it is also evident from the Samaritan incident in Lk. 9:55, neither the representatives of Jesus nor others like Simon in the community of Christians should use and control the authority and power of God for selfish purposes. Luke has Jesus equate apostasy with blasphemy against the Holy Spirit (Lk. 12:10). Resisting the Holy Spirit brings punishment. The sin and punishment of Ananias and Sapphira are to do with deceiving the Holy Spirit and lying to God (Acts 5: 3).

For Luke, what does Simon represent as an 'insider'? It is worth noting that the Simon whom Peter confronted in vv. 19-24 was not the same kind of Simon that Philip encountered. For Philip, Simon was initially an 'outsider' of the Kingdom, whereas Peter confronted Simon the 'insider'. For Peter, Simon was someone like Judas or Ananias and Sapphira who were the 'insiders' but were led to perdition because of their use of possessions.[122] Peter's confrontation with Simon and the pronouncement of a curse upon him reflects the fact that sin was treated just the same way in the church in Jerusalem. Also, Peter's response to Simon that he must repent in order to receive forgiveness (v.22) echoes the conclusion of the Pentecost speech (2:37, 38).[123] Here, the association of the words, 'repentance', 'forgiveness' and 'heart', has a striking similarity with Peter's Pentecost address. Thus, Luke

118. Haenchen, *Acts*, p. 304; Casey, 'Simon Magus', p. 151; Barrett, 'Light', p. 292.

119. Klauck, *Magic*, p. 20; Barrett, 'Light', p. 288.

120. Johnson, *Possessions*, p. 208.

121. Klauck, *Magic*, p. 22.

122. Klauck, *Magic*, p. 21, also makes the point that Simon Magus' faith was 'lapsing' and he will take his place in the ranks of Judas, Ananias and Sapphira because their faith was choked by wealth (cf. Lk. 8:13-14).

123. As Johnson, *Acts*, p. 149, comments, in the case of Simon, the offer is conditional.

intends to show that the Samaritan church is as equally legitimate and genuine as the Jerusalem church. The Samaritan mission is of divine origin and sin inside the church is confronted and rebuked, just as it was dealt with within the Jerusalem church. Therefore, Simon plays an important double role for Luke in that both as an outsider and as an insider he stands to portray the divine origin and the legitimacy of the Samaritan mission. In turn, the account of Simon may serve for him as polemic against the claims of Simon's followers of his day. That is, it serves to drive a wedge between Simonianism and Samaritan Christianity.

In the early chapters of Acts, Luke depicts the community of goods of the earliest Jerusalem church which had 'all things in common' (παντά or ἄπαντα κοινά, 2:44; 4:32) and was involved in selling property and possessions to meet the needs of its members.[124] He does not say anything about this practice among the Samaritan Christians. However, Philip, the founder of the Samaritan Church was a charity worker (Acts 6:1, 5). In the story of the Good Samaritan, the Samaritan traveller gave money (δηνάρια) for the wounded man and also showed his willingness to reimburse any charges incurred (Lk. 10:35-36). This could plausibly reflect the charity of the Samaritans. Likewise, in the mission charge of Jesus to the Twelve in Lk. 9:3, there is an explicit prohibition of money (ἀργύριον).[125] This could be compared to the response of Peter to the lame man at the gate of the Temple of Jerusalem in Acts 3:5, ἀργύριον καὶ χρυσίον οὐχ ὑπάρχει μοι. In both instances, their mission was a Jewish mission and they were not allowed to carry money nor did they give it.[126] Instead, their purpose was to fulfil the commission of preaching the gospel and exercising their divine authority over sickness and demons. The encounter between Peter and Simon in the account of the Samaritan mission has a striking similarity with the Jewish mission in that money is strictly prohibited in both. In brief, Luke may be intending to show that the misuse of money and possessions in the Samaritan Christian community was also confronted just as it was dealt with within the Jewish Christian community.

Now the main purpose of Luke in bringing Simon into the story of the Samaritan mission is obvious. Simon is introduced *not* merely because of the *proximity of location*, or to show the missionary success of Philip, or because of Luke's interest in the exposure of magic and sorcery, rather, it was to

---

124. For a discussion on the community of goods in the early Church at Jerusalem, see Brian Capper, 'The Palestinian Cultural Context of Earliest Christian Community of Goods', in R. Bauckham (ed.), *The Book of Acts in Its Palestinian Setting: The Book of Acts in Its First Century Setting*, vol. 4 (Michigan: Wm.B. Eerdmans Publishing Co., 1995), pp. 323–56; Johnson, *Possessions*; idem, *Sharing Possession: Mandate and Symbol of Faith* (Philadelphia: Fortress Press, 1981).

125. Schmidt, *Hostility*, p. 144.

126. This is not to underestimate the generosity of the apostles towards the poor (cf. Acts 11:28-30; 20:2-4, 35; 24:17; cf. Acts of Thomas 20). See also Walton, *Leadership*, pp. 124–5.

portray the divine origin and the legitimacy of the mission to the Samaritans. First of all, he wants to show that the Samaritan mission is legitimate and in no way inferior to the mission conducted in Jerusalem and Judaea by the apostles. Philip's ministry in Samaria is authenticated not only by the signs and miracles he performed (σημεῖα καὶ δυνάμις μεγάλη, Acts 8:6, 13), but also by the defeat of Simon who is the representative of the demonic realm in Samaria. Luke's apologetic purpose in portraying the authenticity of the Samaritan mission is further evident as he particularly emphasizes the effect of Philip's ministry upon Simon (v.13).[127] Again, the curse pronounced upon Simon by Peter is another indication that just as hypocrisy had found no place in the Jerusalem church, the Samaritan church is also genuine even in its early stage of growth. Also, Luke shows that the Samaritan church encountered the self-deification of human beings, improper use of money and blasphemy against the Holy Spirit, thus treating the new community on an equal footing with that of the Jerusalem church. The account also serves for Luke as polemic against the claims of Simon's followers. That Luke intended to legitimate the Samaritan mission is further attested by his final redactional comment (v.25). Since Peter and John are said to have continued preaching in many Samaritan villages, it shows their approval of a mission to Samaria. Thus Luke uses Simon to portray that the Samaritan mission is on a par with the Jewish mission and thus he defends the legitimacy of the origin and growth of Samaritan Christianity.

7.4. *The Significance of the Samaritan Mission in the Plot of Luke-Acts*

The narrative of the Samaritan mission accomplishes, in conformity with Luke's programme laid out in Acts 1:8, a mission which is the first of its kind beyond the borders of Jerusalem and Judaea. However, there is more to it and its relevance should be drawn now. Negatively, in the light of the antic-ipation-authentication technique which Luke employs to defend the legit-imacy of Samaritan Christianity, as argued here in the study, the opinions of scholars that Luke wanted to stigmatize the ministry of Philip or portray the defects of the Samaritans' conversion or that only the apostles are the custo-dians of the Holy Spirit seem unnecessary hypotheses. Also, based on what Luke is intending to achieve with the figure of Simon, the claim of scholars that Luke has downgraded Simon to a mere magician seems unlikely. It may either be that Luke was not interested in all the details of Simon or that he did not have more information on him. Further, Luke is not polemical against the Samaritans like 2 Kings 17, Josephus, Sir. 50:26 or some of the Rabbinic writings, rather he is pro-Samaritan and all the references in Luke-Acts portray the Samaritans positively over against their Jewish counterparts.

127. So, rightly, Johnson, *Acts*, p. 148.

The nature of the ministry of Philip, the involvement of the Jerusalem apostles, the delay of the Holy Spirit, and the role of Simon Magus all can be best and must be understood in the light of Luke's apologetic purpose of defending the legitimacy of Samaritan Christianity. Therefore, it could be considered more as an 'internal' apologetic within the early Jewish Christian community than as an 'external' one aimed at the Roman authorities or non-Jewish communities. It is 'internal' in the sense that it portrays a reversal of Mt. 10:5b and that it treats the new community on an equal footing with the Jewish Christians. This might further imply a re-examination of the overall purpose of Luke-Acts for casting the whole work into an exclusively political apologetic purpose.[128]

Positively, we must consider the significance of our study as it bears on the history of the beginnings of the Christian mission, especially the early church's early involvement with the Samaritans. Portrayed, from a Jewish point of view, as apostates, foreigners, a rival and marginalized community of people, the Samaritans in an unprecedented way become the object of God's salvation which is of the Jews. For Luke, the Samaritan mission is an integral part of the *Heilsgeschichte* which has its initial explicit root of antic-ipation in Lk. 9:51-56 and its final fruit of legitimation in Acts 8:4-25. In between Luke builds this anticipation-legitimation model through the parable of the Good Samaritan and the account of the healing of the Samaritan leper. This anticipation-legitimation portrait of the Samaritan mission seems to imply Luke's apologetic purpose of showing the authenticity of Samaritan Christianity and of convincing the Church to further its missionary activity into the Gentile world.[129] It may be that Luke has in mind a refutation of the claim of the subsequent followers of Simon in their veneration of him as a divine figure. Also, if some of the Jewish Christian communities still shared the view as stated in Mt. 10:5b, then Luke's picture of the anticipation-legit-imation of the mission to the Samaritans becomes more relevant as an apologetic. It is the Samaritan mission, not the Gentile mission, that primarily marks a decisive turning point in the development of the early Church, as the former paves the way for the latter. Though it is unorganized from a human point of view, it is rooted in the authority of Jesus, commissioned by the risen Lord, confirmed by the descent of the Holy Spirit and sanctioned by the apostolic involvement. It is portrayed as equally valid with the Jewish mission and is originated out of the divine context of persecution and as the fulfilment of the prophetic and eschatological hope of reunion and restoration. Luke's portrayal will also imply the need for the early Church to continue its

---

128. For the view of Luke's various apologetic purposes, see Alexander, 'Apologetic Text', pp. 15–43; Esler, *Community*, pp. 46–70; Maddox, *Luke-Acts*, pp. 91–3.

129. Bowman, *Samaritan Problem*, p. 58: 'It is entirely possible that the early Church did not lack voices which used the success of the mission to the Samaritans as proof for the world-wide relevance of the gospel.'

mission to other Samaritans who are not included in the list of the converted in Acts 8.[130] The Samaritan mission, which is initiated by Hellenistic Christianity, is the consequence of the persecution at Jerusalem and by linking it to the persecution Luke intends to show that the Hellenistic Christians are acting within the divine plan of God by fulfilling the anticipated mission of Jesus. The double rejection motif – the Samaritan rejection of Jesus in the beginning of the gospel narrative (Lk. 9:51-56) and the rejection of the Hellenists at Jerusalem in the beginning of the Acts narrative (Acts 8:4) – play a significant part in the portrait of the Samaritan mission. This, in turn, could be linked to the extension of mission after the rejection of Jesus at Nazareth, and to the rejected prophets of the Old Testament. The origin of Samaritan Christianity, which is to be seen in the light of this double rejection motif in Luke-Acts as well as in the light of the longstanding hostility of the Jews towards the Samaritans, appears to point towards the great success of the gospel in a hostile environment. It is only after the accomplishment of the Samaritan mission that Luke is able to say: 'Meanwhile the church throughout Judea, Galilee, and Samaria had peace and was built up; living in the fear of the Lord and in the comfort of the Holy Spirit, it increased in numbers' (Acts 9:31).

130. Bowman, *Samaritan Problem*, pp. 58, 59, thinks that when the Gospel of Luke was written the debate over the expansion of the mission was already over but not all the Samaritans were won. For example, he mentions the Dosithean Samaritans and the Samaritan-priestly orthodoxy, to the latter of which the author of the Gospel of Luke and the Acts of the Apostles addressed himself. Though one cannot explicitly identify the groups, which were yet to be reached by the gospel, it is reasonable to believe that there were other Samaritans like the Jews requiring a continued mission of the Church and that with Acts 8:25 a mission to them was not fully completed.

Chapter 8

CONCLUSION

The purpose of this research was to investigate the rhetorical and theological function of the Samaritan mission episode in Acts 8:4-25. The review of scholarly discussions on the text displayed the need for taking into consideration the historical context of the Samaritans in the first century CE as well as Luke's special interest in the Samaritans as depicted in his Gospel. As proposed in our study, the function of the narrative makes sense in this setting, and therefore, we have explored the relevant socio-political and religious background of the Samaritans in the New Testament period and the significance of the Samaritan episodes in the Gospel of Luke.

In the historical analysis of the Samaritans, up to and including the New Testament period, I have brought out their ethnic and religious ambiguity and the struggle to find their status and lost identity as a nation in the midst of colonial, political and religious oppression. In some Jewish circles, they had been given derogatory designations, were considered as outcasts, syncretists, apostates and idolaters, and, therefore, the legitimacy of their socio-ethnic and religious status was in question. There existed Judaeo-Samaritan hostility in the New Testament period, mainly on account of the rival places of worship. In view of the ambiguous and ambivalent status and ethnic identity of the Samaritans, and the questionable legitimacy of their rival centre on Gerizim, any unplanned or unauthorized mission of the church, from a Jewish-Christian point of view, might possibly cast doubts on the legitimacy of Samaritan Christianity as well as on the mission itself. In order to legitimate this ill-treated group of people, the Lukan Jesus makes contact and treats them in a benign light, with an anticipation of bringing them within his Kingdom, and the ministry of Philip in Acts 8 accomplishes this. Luke locates this mission as accomplished in the 'city of Samaria', probably in the capital city of Old Testament times, where the Samaritans originally lost their ethnic and religious identity but which later became the locus for their legitimacy.

I have also argued that all the Samaritan references in the Gospel of Luke serve to defend the legitimacy of the Samaritans and their action and also their status as part of Israel. Therefore, they function as apologetic for Luke's church, especially for the Samaritan Christians whose legitimacy and origin the Jews and the Jewish Christians could possibly have questioned. Though his ministry was confined to the Jews, the Lukan Jesus breaks the socio-religious and ethnico-geographical boundaries of his day and prepares the ground for and anticipates a mission to the Samaritans. Jesus did not engage in a historical Samaritan mission, rather he presented the Samaritans in a radical way that challenged the Jews in their historically longstanding hostile relationship with the former. Luke's literary ability brings in the Samaritan episodes within the framework of Jesus' ministry and his theological interest includes the Samaritans as recipients of the anticipated eschatological salvation inaugurated in the person and work of Jesus. Unlike the contemporary views, which were popular among some Jewish circles, Jesus portrays the Samaritans as legitimate people and shows that they are to be treated as fellow Israelites and that they have a place in the soteriological plan of God. From the very start of his ministry at Galilee Jesus anticipated a wider mission which in its immediate context includes the Samaritans. When 'he set his face to go to Jerusalem' (Lk. 9:51), the city of his death and destiny, the Lukan Jesus found it necessary to go through Samaria in anticipation that an allegedly despised and marginalized community also would experience the salvation and healing disclosed at the Galilean ministry (4:18-19).

Luke shows that in his last journey to Jerusalem, Jesus' initial contact with the Samaritans is in accordance with the divine plan of God, and his anticipation of a future mission to them is therefore legitimate. In his Gospel, the initial rejection of Jesus by the Samaritans (Lk. 9:53) is reversed as the Samaritan in the story of the compassionate Samaritan (10:29-37) moved with compassion, acts in generosity and extends neighbourly love to the Jewish unfortunate victim by crossing his ethnic and religious boundaries. The socio-religious and ethnic hostility of the Samaritans towards the Jews seems to have been reduced at some level, as the Samaritan is said to have shown compassion and behaved as a neighbour. Thus Luke achieves a progression in his legitimizing device as the Samaritans move from the outer boundary of hostility to the inner side of acceptance and neighbourliness. In the story of the compassionate Samaritan (10:29-37), the Samaritan shows mercy to the unfortunate victim (ἔλεος, v. 37), but in the story of the grateful Samaritan (17:11-19), the Samaritan receives both mercy (ἔλεος, v. 13) and salvation from God (ἡ πίστις σου σέσωκέν σε, v. 19). The Samaritan becomes both a neighbour (πλησίον) by crossing the ethnic boundary and an insider, though previously an outsider (ἀλλογενής), by breaking the religious barrier. Being a neighbour to the wounded man, the Samaritan traveller fulfils the commandment in the Old Testament of loving his neighbour, and having acknowledged Jesus as God and worshipped him falling at his feet, the Samaritan leper fulfils the commandment of loving God. It is explicit, therefore, that Luke's Gospel achieves a reversal of the Samaritans' status and thereby he intends his readers to see the legitimacy of the Samaritan community as part of God's people, an apologetic purpose which he very strongly signals throughout these stories.

On a literary level, various narratives on the Samaritans in Luke-Acts reveal a gradation of a positive and creative portrait where the 'enemies' and the 'foreigners' are transformed into 'neighbours' and 'participants' by fulfilling what is appropriate to the standard of the Kingdom. The nature of their perception and the corresponding appropriate function transcends the set boundaries of the time and enables them to be recipients of salvation anticipated by Jesus. The symbolic elements in Lk. 9:51-56 of ascension, Pentecost, reception (of Jesus), the descending of the 'fire' from heaven, and confrontation (with the Samaritans) are actualized in the mission to the Samaritans in Acts 8:4-25 in a different but reversed manner. James and John, the priests and the Levites, the nine lepers, and Simon Magus, all stand in contrast to the 'Samaritan(s)' who are 'religious aliens' but move from outside to inside to be part of the salvific blessings of the Kingdom. They all fail to see what the Samaritan(s) do see, and fail to act appropriately in contrast to the appropriate behaviour of the Samaritan(s). Luke is employing a literary and rhetorical strategy of *Reversalism* in order to legitimate and present the successful mission to the Samaritans narrated in Acts 8:4-25. This strategy, which he begins from the first reference to the Samaritans in Lk. 9:51-56, is employed also in the parable of the Good Samaritan (Lk. 10:25-37) and the healing of the Samaritan leper (Lk. 17:11-19), and comes to its climax in Acts 8:4-25. Features of all the Samaritan references in the Gospel are clustered together in Acts 8:4-25 to produce a climactic and reverse effect on the popular prejudices against the Samaritans. Here, motifs, attitudes, roles and sequences of events in the previous narratives are structurally and functionally reversed in Acts 8:4-25, thus breaking down the longstanding socio-religious and ethnic boundaries and achieving a climactic and successful mission to the Samaritans. The readers of the narratives are challenged to make a decision to 'see' the Samaritans, the 'marginalized' and the 'outcasts' of the day, as part and parcel of the salvific plan of God and then to 'act' appropriately to be partakers of the Kingdom. Thus, the mission anticipated in Lk. 9:51-56 is legitimized in Acts 8:4-25.

In the textual analysis of Acts 8:4-25, I have shown that Luke is portraying the kerygmatic and pneumatic legitimacy of Philip's mission as supported by the apostolic legitimacy of Jerusalem whereby he is defending the divine origin and legitimacy of both the mission and Samaritan Christianity. The mission to the Samaritans anticipated by Jesus in the Gospel is legitimized in Acts 8:4-25 where the alleged apostates and the marginalized find a new identity and legitimacy through their acceptance of Christ. The enemies and the outsiders become the sharers of the Kingdom and the participants of the divine Spirit. This new development in Samaria is narrated in a way by which Luke validates the mission with that of the Jewish mission and defends the divine origin and legitimacy of Samaritan Christianity. The narrative of the Samaritan mission also accomplishes Luke's purpose in conformity with his programme laid out in Acts 1:8, a mission which is the first of its kind beyond the borders of Jerusalem and Judaea and which fulfils the commission of the risen Lord.

Luke has Philip stand in continuity with Jesus and God's prophets, and has him minister in Samaria after the persecution as the divine plan of God. The activity of Philip is to be understood in accordance with the divine prophetic oracles for a reunion of the North and South. The qualifications of Philip and the nature of his ministry put him on the same footing as Jesus and the apostles. Thus, Luke links the origin of Samaritan Christianity to the ministry of the earthly Jesus, the commission of the risen Lord, the divine context of persecution, the prophetic oracles of the restoration of Israel, and to the authentic ministry of prominent figures in Scripture.

It has become evident that on a literary level the story of the arrival of Peter and John in Samaria functions for Luke as a reversal of their antagonism against the Samaritans as was reflected in Lk. 9:56. Here, Luke integrates the ministry of authoritative and authentic figures, Peter and John and that of Philip, and portrays the reception of the Spirit by the Samaritan Christians as part of his authenticating device. Though the apostles could not originally fulfil the command in Acts 1:8 regarding Samaria, they act in reverse to the saying in Mt. 10:5b by going into Samaria and thus legitimating the Samaritan mission. In other words, if there were some Jewish Christians in Luke's day who still had shared the same view as that stated in Mt. 10:5b, then the act of the Jerusalem apostles would have served as a legitimating factor to authenticate Samaritan Christianity. Also, the double action of the apostles – prayer and laying on of hands – communicates more than merely conferring the Spirit. It could be seen as the Samaritan community being offered fellowship and solidarity with the Jerusalem Christian community. Therefore, the action could indicate an assurance to the Samaritans that they are fellow members of the elect community of God. Again, Luke succeeds in bringing the Jewish and the Samaritan Christian communities into unity with each other and thus legitimates the Samaritan mission.

With the figure of Simon, Luke may be intending to show that the misuse of money and possessions in the Samaritan Christian community was also confronted as it was dealt with in the Jewish Christian community. That is, the Samaritan mission is legitimate and in no way inferior to the mission conducted in Jerusalem and Judaea by the apostles. Luke's apologetic purpose in portraying the authenticity of the Samaritan mission is evident as he particularly emphasizes the effect of Philip's ministry on Simon, who is the representative of the demonic realm in Samaria. Again, the curse pronounced upon Simon by Peter is another indication that just as hypocrisy had found no place in the Jerusalem church, the Samaritan church is also genuine even in its early stage of growth. Also, Luke shows that the Samaritan church encountered the self-deification of human beings, improper use of money and blasphemy against the Holy Spirit, thus treating the new community on an equal footing with that of the Jerusalem church. The account also serves for Luke as polemic against the claims of Simon's followers. Thus, Luke uses Simon to portray that the Samaritan mission is on a par with the Jewish mission and thus he defends the divine mission and legitimacy of Samaritan Christianity.

Now, the contribution of our research to the field of New Testament scholarship is to be noted here:

Negatively, in the light of the anticipation-legitimation device which Luke employs to defend the legitimacy of Samaritan Christianity, the opinions of scholars that Luke wanted to (1) stigmatize the ministry of Philip or (2) portray the defects of the Samaritans' conversion or that (3) only the apostles are the custodians of the Holy Spirit seem unnecessary hypotheses. Also, based on what Luke is intending to achieve with the figure of Simon, the claim of scholars that (4) Luke has downgraded Simon to a mere magician seems unlikely. It may either be that Luke was not interested in all the details of Simon or that he did not have more information on him. (5) Further, the apologetic purpose of Luke explains why he is not polemical against the Samaritans like 2 Kings 17, Josephus, Sir. 50:26 or some of the rabbinic writings, or even Mt. 10:5b, if it seems polemical. The fact that Luke is pro-Samaritan and that all the references in Luke-Acts portray the Samaritans positively against their Jewish counterparts makes sense in the light of this anticipation-legitimation device.

Positively, as emerged from the research, Luke employs in his Samaritan episodes an anticipation-legitimation device whereby he defends the divine origin of the Samaritan mission and the legitimacy of Samaritan Christianity. The rhetorical and theological function of Acts 8:4-25 and Luke's special interest in the Samaritans is that it portrays Samaritan Christianity on an equal footing with Jewish Christianity. From a Jewish point of view, the Samaritans were apostates, foreigners, a rival and marginalized community of people, but in an unprecedented way they have become the object of God's salvation which is of the Jews. The anticipation-legitimation portrait of the Samaritan mission seems to imply Luke's apologetic purpose of showing the authenticity of Samaritan Christianity and of convincing the Church for its further missionary activity into the Gentile world. It may also be that Luke has in mind a refutation of the claim of the subsequent followers of Simon in their veneration of him as a divine figure, and of the possibly accused identification of Samaritan Christianity with the followers of Simon. The nature of the ministry of Philip, the involvement of the Jerusalem apostles, the delay of the Holy Spirit, and the role of Simon Magus all can be best and must be understood in the light of Luke's apologetic purpose. Therefore, it could be considered more as an 'internal' apologetic within the early Jewish Christian community than as an 'external' one aimed at the Roman author-ities or non-Jewish communities. It is 'internal' in the sense that it portrays a reversal of Mt. 10:5b and that it treats the new community on an equal footing with the Jewish Christians. This might further imply a re-examination of the overall purpose of Luke-Acts for casting the whole work into an exclusively political apologetic purpose.

The portrait of the mission in Acts 8:4-25 also has a bearing on the history of the beginnings of the Christian mission, especially the early church's early involvement with the Samaritans. Luke is also able to show the successful missionary achievement of the Hellenists and the apparent failure of the Twelve in not having the first initiative step taken towards reaching Samaria. It reiterates that the mission of the church and the saving plan of God could be accomplished not by specially commissioned apostles alone, but by those who are 'full of the Spirit and wisdom' (6:3) and are prepared to carry out his commission, even in a hostile environment. For Luke, the Samaritan mission is an integral part of the *Heilsgeschichte* which is anticipated in Lk. 9:51-56 and is legitimized in Acts 8:4-25. It is the Samaritan mission, not the Gentile mission, that primarily marks a decisive turning point in the development of the early Church, as the former paves the way for the latter. Though it is unorganized from a human point of view, it is rooted in the divine plan and authority of Jesus, commissioned by the risen Lord, emerges out of the divine context of persecution, is confirmed by the descent of the Holy Spirit and sanctioned by the apostolic involvement. It is portrayed as equally valid with the Jewish mission and as the fulfilment of the prophetic and eschatological hope of reunion and restoration. Luke's portrayal will also imply the need for the early Church to continue its mission to other Samaritans and also to the Gentiles. The Samaritan mission, which is initiated by Hellenistic Christianity, is the consequence of the persecution at Jerusalem and by linking it to the persecution Luke intends to show that the Hellenistic Christians are acting in the divine plan of God in fulfilling the anticipated mission of Jesus. The double rejection motif – the Samaritan rejection of Jesus in the beginning of the Gospel narrative (Lk. 9:51-56) and the rejection of the Hellenists at Jerusalem in the beginning of the Acts narrative (Acts 8:4) – play a significant part in the portrait of the Samaritan mission. This, in turn, could be linked to the extension of mission after the rejection of Jesus at Nazareth, and to the rejected prophets of the Old Testament. The origin of Samaritan Christianity, which is to be seen in the light of this double rejection motif in Luke-Acts as well as in the light of the longstanding hostility of the Jews towards the Samaritans, appears to point towards the great success of the gospel in a hostile environment. Now, Luke is able to say: 'Meanwhile the church throughout Judea, Galilee, and Samaria had peace and was built up; living in the fear of the Lord and in the comfort of the Holy Spirit, it increased in numbers' (Acts 9:31).

Finally, the implication of this study further opens up the possibility of exploring the legitimation device Luke applies elesewhere in Luke-Acts, especially with sections where he deals with the poor, the children, the role of women, the mission of Paul and the like. It may also invite issues on the purpose of Luke-Acts, as there are strong signals in the Samaritan references of an 'internal' apologetic probably directed against some factions of the early Church.

BIBLIOGRAPHY

Abbott-Smith, G., *A Manual Greek Lexicon of the New Testament* (3rd edn.; Edinburgh: T. & T. Clark, 1973).

Adna, Jostein and Kvalbein, Hans (eds), *The Mission of the Early Church to Jews and Gentiles* (WUNT 127; Tübingen: Mohr Siebeck, 2000).

Agua, A. Del, 'The Lucan Narrative of the "Evangelization of the Kingdom of God": A Contribution to the Unity of Luke-Acts', in J. Verheyden (ed.), *The Unity of Luke-Acts* (BEThL CXLII; Leuven: Leuven University Press, 1999), pp. 639–61.

Albright, W.F., 'Simon Magus as the "Great Power" of God', in J. Munck, *The Acts of the Apostles*, Appendix VII (AB 31; rev. W.F. Albright and C.S. Mann; New York: Doubleday, 1967), pp. 305–8.

Alexander, L.C.A., 'Luke's Preface in the Context of Greek Preface-Writing', *NovT* 28 (1, 1986), pp. 48–74.

—— 'Sisters in Adversity: Retelling Martha's Story', in George J. Brooke (ed.), *Women in the Biblical Tradition* (SWR 31; Lampeter: The Edwin Mellen Press, 1992), pp. 167–86.

—— *The Preface to Luke's Gospel* (SNTSMS 79; Cambridge: Cambridge University Press, 1993).

—— '"In Journeyings Often": Voyaging in the Acts of the Apostles and in Greek Romance', in C.M. Tuckett (ed.), *Luke's Literary Achievement* (JSNTSup.116; Sheffield: Sheffield Academic Press, 1995), pp. 17–39.

—— 'Narrative Maps: Reflection on the Toponomy of Acts', in M. Daniel Carroll R., *et al.* (eds), *The Bible in Human Society*, Essays in Honour of John Rogerson, (JSOTSup.200: Sheffield: Sheffield Academic Press, 1995), pp. 17–57.

—— 'The Preface to Acts and the Historians', in Ben Witherington III (ed.), *History, Literature and Society in the Books of Acts* (Cambridge: Cambridge University Press, 1996), pp. 73–103.

—— 'Fact, Fiction and the Genre of Acts', *NTS* 44 (1998), pp. 380–99.

—— 'The Acts of the Apostles as an Apologetic Text', in M. Edwards, M. Goodman, and S. Price (eds), *Apologetics in the Roman Empire: Pagans, Jews and Christians* (Oxford: Oxford University Press, 1999), pp. 15–43.

—— 'Reading Luke-Acts from Back to Front', in J. Verheyden (ed.), *The Unity of Luke-Acts* (BEThL CXLII; Leuven: Leuven University Press, 1999), pp. 419–46.

Alon, G., 'The Origin of the Samaritans in the Halakhic Tradition', in *idem, Jews, Judaism and the Classical World: Studies in Jewish History in the Times of the Second Temple and Talmud* (trans. Israel Abrahams; Jerusalem: The Magnes Press, 1977), pp. 354–73.

—— *The Jews in their Land in the Talmudic Age, 70-640 CE*, vol. II (Jerusalem: The Magnes Press, 1984).

Anderson, H., 'Broadening Horizons: The Rejection of Nazareth Pericope of Luke 4:16-30 in the light of Recent Critical Trends', *Int* 18 (1964), pp. 259–75.

Anderson, Robert T., 'The Elusive Samaritan Temple', *BA* 54 (2, 1991), pp. 104–7.

—— 'Samaritans', in D.N. Freedman (ed.), *ABD* V (New York: Doubleday, 1992), pp. 940–47.

Anderson, R.T. and Giles, T., *The Keepers: An Introduction to the History and Culture of the Samaritans* (Peabody, MA: Hendrickson Publishers, 2002).

—— *Tradition kept: The Literature of the Samaritans* (Peabody, MA: Hendrickson Publishers, 2005).

Arlandson, J.M., *Women, Class and Society in Early Christianity: Models from Luke-Acts* (Peabody: Hendrickson Publishers, 1997).

Arndt, William F., *Saint Luke* (St. Louis: Concordia Publishing House, 1956).

Arnold, B.T., 'Luke's Characterising Use of the Old Testament in the Book of Acts', in B. Witherington III (ed.), *History, Literature, and Society in the Books of Acts* (Cambridge: Cambridge University Press, 1996), pp. 300–23.

Arrington, F.L., *The Acts of the Apostles* (Peabody, MA: Hendrickson, 1988).

Avi-Yonah, Michael (ed.), *History of the Holy Land* (London: Weidenfeld & Nicolson, 1969).

—— 'Historical Geography of Palestine' in Safrai and Stern (eds), *The Jewish People in the First Century* I (CRINT; Philadelphia: Fortress Press, 1974), pp. 78–116.

Baarda, T., 'The Shechem Episode in the Testament of Levi: A Comparison with other Traditions', in J.N. Bremmer and F.G. Martinez (eds), *Sacred History and Sacred Texts in Early Judaism. A Symposium in Honour of A.S. Van der Woude* (Kampen: Kok Pharos Publishing House, 1992), pp. 11–73.

Bailey, J.A., *The Traditions Common to the Gospels of Luke and John* (NovTSup.7; Leiden: E.J. Brill, 1963).

Barclay, John, 'Apologetics in the Jewish Diaspora', in John R. Bartlett (ed.), *Jews in the Hellenistic and Roman Cities* (London: Routledge, 2002), pp. 129–48.

Barrett, C.K., *Luke the Historian in Recent Study* (Philadelphia: Fortress Press, 1970).

—— *The Gospel According to John: An Introduction with Commentary and Notes on the Greek Text* (2nd edition; London: SPCK, 1978).

—— 'Light on the Holy Spirit from Simon Magus (Acts 8:4-25)', in J. Kremer (ed.), *Les Actes des Apôtres: Traditions, Rédaction, Théologie* (BEThL 48; Paris-Gembloux: Duculot; Louvain: Louvain University Press, 1979), pp. 281–95.

—— *The Acts of the Apostles: A Critical and Exegetical Commentary*, 2 vols., (Edinburgh: T. & T. Clark, 1994, 1998).

—— 'The Historicity of Acts', *JTS* new series 50 (2, 1999), pp. 515–34.

Barthes, R., *Critical Essays* (trans. R. Howard; Evanston: Northwestern University Press, 1972).

—— *S/Z: An Essay* (trans. Richard Miller, Oxford: Basil Blackwell, 1974).

—— *Image, Music and Texts* (New York: Hill and Wang, 1977).

—— 'Structural Analysis of a Narrative from Acts X–XI', in A.M. Johnson, Jr. (ed.), *Structuralism and Biblical Hermeneutics: A Collection of Essays* (Pennsylvania: The Pickwick Press, 1979), pp. 109–43.

Barton, J (ed.)., *The Cambridge Companion to Biblical Interpretation* (Cambridge: Cambridge University Press, 1998).

Bauckham, R., 'The Scrupulous Priest and the Good Samaritan: Jesus' Parabolic Interpretation of the Law of Moses', *NTS* 44 (1998), pp. 475–89.

—— 'The Restoration of Israel in Luke-Acts', in J.M. Scott (ed.), *Restoration: Old Testament, Jewish, and Christian Perspectives* (JSJSup.72; Leiden: E.J. Brill, 2001), pp. 435–87.

—— (ed.), *The Book of Acts in Its First Century Setting.vol.4: The Book of Acts in Its Palestinian Setting* (Grand Rapids: Wm.B. Eerdmans Publishing Co., 1995).

Bauernfeind, O., *Die Apostelgeschichte* (ThHKNT 5; Leipzig: Deichert, 1939).

Beardslee, W.A., *Literary Criticism of the New Testament* (Philadelphia: Fortress Press, 1969).

Beasley-Murray, G.R., *Baptism in the New Testament* (Exeter: Paternoster press, 1962).

Beavis, M.A., '"Expecting Nothing in Return": Luke's Picture of the Marginalised', *Int* 48 (1994), pp. 357–68.

Berger, K., 'Propaganda und Gegenpropaganda im Frühen Christentum: Simon Magus als Gestalt des Samaritanischen Christentums', in Lukas Bormann, *et al.* (eds), *Religious Propaganda and Missionary Competition in the New Testament World*, Essays honouring Dieter Georgi (Leiden: E.J. Brill, 1994), pp. 313–17.

Bergmeier, R., 'Die Gestalt des Simon Magus in Act 8 und in der simonianischen Gnosis-Aporien einer Gesamtdeutung' in *Das Gesetz im Römerbrief und andere Studien zum Neuen Testament* (WUNT 121; Tübingen: Mohr Siebeck, 2000), pp. 238–46.

Best, E., 'Spirit-Baptism', *NovT* 4 (1960), pp. 236–43.

Betz, H.D., 'The Cleansing of the Ten Lepers (Luke 17:11-19)', *JBL* 90 (1971), pp. 314–28.

—— *The Greek Magical Papyri in Translation* (Chicago: The University of Chicago Press, 1986).

Beyschlag, K., 'Zur Simon-Magus-Frage', *ZTK* 68 (1971), pp. 395–415.

—— *Simon Magus und die christliche Gnosis* (WUNT 16; Tübingen: Mohr Siebeck, 1974).

Bickerman, E.J., *From Ezra to the Last of the Maccabees* (New York: Schocken, 1962).

—— *The Jews in the Greek Age* (Cambridge, MA: Harvard University Press, 1988).

Black, M., *An Aramaic Approach to the Gospels and Acts* (3rd edn.; Clarendon Press, Oxford, 1967).

Blass, F. and Debrunner, A., *A Greek Grammar of the New Testament and Other Early Christian Literature* (trans. and ed. Robert W. Funk; Chicago: The University of Chicago Press, 1961).

Blomberg, C.L., *Interpreting the Parables* (Leicester: Apollos, 1990).

—— *Neither Poverty nor Riches: A Biblical Theology of Material Possessions* (NSBT 7; Leicester: Apollos, 1999).

Bock, D.L., *Proclamation from Prophecy and Pattern: Lukan Old Testament Christology* (JSNTSup.12; Sheffield: JSOT Press, 1987).

—— *Luke1:1-9:50 and 9:51-24:53* (BECNT; Grand Rapids: Baker Book House, 1994, 1996).

—— 'Proclamation from Prophecy and Pattern: Luke's Use of the Old Testament for Christology and Mission', in C.A. Evans and W.R. Stenger (eds), *The Gospels and the Scriptures of Israel* (JSNTSup.104; Sheffield: Sheffield Academic Press, 1994), pp. 280–307.

Böhm, M., *Samarien und die Samaritai bei Lukas: Eine Studie zum religionshistorischen und traditionsgeschichtlichen Hintergrund der lukanischen Samarientexte und zu deren topographischer Verhaftung* (WUNT: Reihe 2. 111; Tübingen: Mohr Siebeck, 1999).

Bosch, David J., *Transforming Mission: Paradigm Shifts in Theology and Mission* (ASMS 16; Maryknoll, NY: Orbis Books, 1991).

Bovon, Francis, *Luke the Theologian: Thirty-three Years of Research (1950–1983)* (PTMS 12; Allison Park: The Pickwick Press, 1987).

—— *Luke I: A Commentary on the Gospel of Luke 1:1-9:50* (trans. Christine M. Thomas; ed. Helmut Koester; Minneapolis: Fortress Press, 2002).

Bowman, J., 'Contact Between Samaritan Sects and Qumran', *VT* 7 (1957), pp. 184–9.

—— *The Samaritan Problem: Studies in the Relationships of Samaritanism, Judaism and Early Christianity* (PTMS 4; Pittsburgh: The Pickwick Press, 1975).

—— (trans. and ed.), *Samaritan Documents: Relating to Their History, Religion and Life* (Pittsburgh: The Pickwick Press, 1977).

—— 'The History of the Samaritans', *AbrN* 18 (1978/79), pp. 101–15.

Brawley, R.L., *Luke-Acts and the Jews: Conflict, Apology, and Conciliation* (Atlanta: Scholars Press, 1987).

—— *Centering on God: Method and Message in Luke-Acts* (Louisville: Westminster/John Knox Press, 1990).

Brodie, T.L., 'Towards Unravelling Luke's Use of the Old Testament: Luke 7:11-17 as an *Imitatio* of 1 Kings 17:17-24', *NTS* 32 (1986), pp. 247–67.

—— 'Towards Unravelling the Rhetorical Imitation of Sources in Acts: 2 Kings 5 as One Component of Acts 8, 9-40', *Bib* 67 (1986), pp. 41–67.

—— 'The Departure for Jerusalem (Luke 9,51-56) as a Rhetorical Imitation of Elijah's Departure for the Jordan (2 Kings 1,1-2,6)', *Bib* 70 (1989), pp. 96–109.

—— 'Luke-Acts as an Imitation and Emulation of the Elijah-Elisha Narrative', in E. Richard (ed.), *New Views on Luke and Acts* (Collegeville, MN: The Liturgical Press, 1990), pp. 78–85, 172–4.

Brown, R.E., *The Birth of the Messiah* (Garden City: Doubleday, 1977).

Brown, Schuyler, *Apostasy and Perseverance in the Theology of Luke* (Rome: Pontifical Biblical Institute, 1969).

Bruce, F.F., 'The Acts of the Apostles: Historical Record or Theological Reconstruction?', *ANRW* II.25.3 (1985), pp. 2570–2603.

—— *The Book of Acts* (revised edition; Grand Rapids: Wm.B. Eerdmans Publishing Co., 1988).

—— *The Acts of the Apostles: The Greek Text With Introduction and Commentary* (third revised and enlarged edition; Grand Rapids: Wm.B. Eerdmans Publishing Co., 1990).

Bruners, W., *Die Reinigung der zehn Aussätzigen und die Heilung des Samariters Lk 17,11-19: Ein Beitrag zur lukanischen Interpretation der Reinigung von Aussätzigen* (Stuttgart: Katholisches Bibelwerk, 1977).

Büchsel, F., 'ἀλλογενής', *TDNT* I, ed. G. Kittel, pp. 266–7.

Bull, Robert J., 'A Note on Theodotus' Description of Shechem', *HTR* 60 (1967), pp. 221–8.

—— 'An Archaeological Context for Understanding John 4:20', *BA* 38 (2, 1975), pp. 54–9.

Bultmann, R., *The History of the Synoptic Tradition* (New York: Harper & Row, 1963).

—— *Theology of the New Testament* I (London: SCM Press, 1968).

Byrskog, S., *Story as History – History as Story: The Gospel Tradition in the Context of Ancient Oral History* (WUNT 123; Tübingen: Mohr Siebeck, 2000).

Cadbury, H.J., *The Making of Luke-Acts* (London: Macmillan, 1927).

Caird, G.B., *The Gospel of St Luke* (PNTC; Harmondsworth: Penguin Books, 1963).

Callan, T., 'The Preface of Luke-Acts and Historiography', *NTS* 31 (1985), pp. 576–81.

Calvin, John, *The Acts of the Apostles 1-13* (trans. John W. Fraser and W.J.G. McDonald; ed. D.W. Torrance and T.F. Torrance; London: Oliver and Boyd, 1965).

Capper, Brian, 'The Palestinian Cultural Context of Earliest Christian Community of Goods', in R. Bauckham (ed.), *The Book of Acts in Its First Century Setting*. vol. 4: *The Book of Acts in Its Palestinian Setting* (Michigan: Wm.B. Eerdmans Publishing Co., 1995), pp. 323–56.

Carroll, J.T, and Green, J.B., *The Death of Jesus in Early Christianity* (Peabody, MA: Hendrickson, 1995).

Casey, R.P., 'Simon Magus', in Lake and Cadbury (eds), *Beginnings of Christianity: Part I. The Acts of the Apostles, vol. v. Additional Notes to the Commentary* (London: Macmillan and Co. Ltd., 1933), pp. 151–63.

Cassidy, Richard J., *Society and Politics in the Acts of the Apostles* (Maryknoll, NY: Orbis Books, 1987).

Chang, C.S., *A New Examination of Samaritan Origins and Identity in the Light of Recent Scholarship* (PhD Dissertation; Sydney: University of Sydney, 1990).

Charlesworth, J.H. (ed.), *Old Testament Pseudepigrapha*, 2 vols., (Garden City, NY: Doubleday and Co., 1983–1985).

Clark, Andrew C., 'The Role of the Apostles' in Marshall and Peterson (eds), *Witness to the Gospel: The Theology of Acts* (Grand Rapids: Wm. B. Eerdmans Publishing Co., 1998), pp. 169–90.

Clarke, W.K.L., 'The Use of the Septuagint in Acts', in F.J. Jackson and K. Lake (eds), *The Beginnings of Christianity: Part I. The Acts of the Apostles*, vol. II (London: Macmillan, 1922), pp. 66–105.

Cogan, M., 'For We, Like You, Worship Your God: Three Biblical Portrayals of Samaritan Origins', *VT* 38 (3, 1988), pp. 268–92.

Coggins, R.J., *Samaritans and Jews: The Origins of Samaritanism Reconsidered* (Oxford: Basil Blackwell, 1975).

—— 'The Samaritans and Acts', *NTS* 28 (1982), pp. 423–34.

—— 'The Samaritans in Josephus', in L.H. Feldman and G. Hata (eds), *Josephus, Judaism, and Christianity* (Leiden: E.J. Brill, 1987), pp. 257–73.

—— 'The Samaritans and the Northern Israelite Tradition', in Tal and Florentin (eds), *Proceedings of the First International Congress of the Société d'Études Samaritaines (Tel-Aviv, April 11-13, 1988)* (Tel-Aviv University: Chaim Rosenberg School for Jewish Studies, 1991), pp. 99–108.

—— 'Jewish Local Patriotism: The Samaritan Problem', in Siân Jones and Sarah Pearce (eds), *Jewish Local Patriotism and Self-Identification in the Graeco-Roman Period* (JSPSup.31; Sheffield: Sheffield Academic Press, 1998), pp. 66–78.

—— 'Issues in Samaritanism', in J. Neusner and Alan J. Avery-Peck (eds)., *Judaism in Late Antiquity, Part III: Where We Stand: Issues and Debates in Ancient Judaism* I (Leiden: E.J. Brill, 1999), pp. 63–77.

Cohen, Abraham (ed.), *Hebrew-English Edition of the Babylonian Talmud: Minor Tractates* (London: The Soncino Press, 1984).

Cohen, S.J., *From the Maccabees to the Mishnah* (Philadelphia: The Westminster Press, 1987).

—— 'Ioudaios: "Judean" and "Jew" in Susanna, First Maccabees, and Second Maccabees', in Hubert Cancik, Hermann Lichtenberger and Peter Schaefer (eds), *Geschichte-Tradition-Reflexion: Festschrift fuer Martin Hengel zum 70. Geburtstag*, vol. I (Tübingen: Mohr, 1996), pp. 211–19.

Coleridge, M., *Birth of the Lukan Narrative* (JSNTSup.88; Sheffield: JSOT Press, 1993).

Collins, J.J., 'The Epic of Theodotus and the Hellenism of the Hasmoneans', *HTR* 73 (1980), pp. 91–104.

Collins, M.F., 'The Hidden Vessels in Samaritan Traditions', *JSJ* 3 (1972), pp. 97–116.

Conzelmann, H., *The Acts of the Apostles* (Philadelphia: Fortress Press, 1987).

—— *The Theology of St Luke* (London: Faber & Faber, 1960).

Creed, J.M., *The Gospel According to St. Luke* (London: Macmillan Co. Ltd., 1953).

Cross, F.M., 'The Discovery of Samaria Papyri', *BA* 26 (1963), pp. 118–19.

—— 'Aspects of Samaritan and Jewish History in Late Persian and Hellenistic Times', *HTR* 59 (1966), pp. 201–11.

—— 'Papyri of the Fourth Century BC from Daliyeh', in D.N. Freedman and J.C. Greenfield (eds), *New Directions in Biblical Archaeology* (Garden City, NY: Doubleday, 1969), pp. 45–69.

—— 'The Papyri and their Historical Implications', in P.W. Lapp and N.L. Lapp (eds), *Discoveries in the Wadi Ed-Daliyeh* (AASOR 41; Cambridge, MA., 1974), pp. 17–29.

—— 'A Reconstruction of the Judean Restoration', *JBL* 94 (1975), pp. 4–18.

Crown, A.D (ed.), *The Samaritans* (Tübingen: J.C.B. Mohr, 1989).

—— 'The Samaritan Diaspora' in *idem* (ed.), *The Samaritans* (Tübingen: J.C.B. Mohr, 1989), pp. 195–217.

—— 'Redating the Schism between Judaeans and the Samaritans', *JQR* 82:1-2 (1991), pp. 17–50.

—— 'Another Look at Samaritan Origins', in A.D. Crown and L. Davey (eds), *New Samaritan Studies of the Société d'Etudes Samaritaines* (vol. III & IV), Essays in Honour of G.D. Sixdenier (Studies in Judaica No.5; University of Sydney: Mandelbaum Publishing, 1995), pp. 133–55.

—— 'The Samaritans, their Literature and the Codicology of their Manuscripts', *BAIAS* 15 (1996–97), pp. 87–104.

—— 'Qumran, Samaritan *Halakha* and Theology and Pre-Tannaitic Judaism', in M. Lubetski, *et al.* (eds), *Boundaries of the Ancient Near Eastern World*, A Tribute to Cyrus H. Gordon (JSOTSup.273; Sheffield: Sheffield Academic Press, 1998), pp. 420–41.

Cullmann, O., 'Samaria and the Origins of the Christian Mission' in Cullmann, *The Early Church* (London: SCM Press, 1956), pp. 185–92.

Culpepper, R.A., 'Story and History in the Gospels', *RevE* 81 (1984), pp. 467–77.

Cunningham, Scott, *'Through Many Tribulations': The Theology of Persecution in Luke-Acts* (JSNTSup.142; Sheffield: Sheffield Academic Press, 1997).

Curtius Rufus, Quintus, *The History of Alexander the Great* (trans. John Yardley, Harmondsworth: Penguin, 1984).

Daise, M., 'Samaritans, Seleucids, and the Epic of Theodotus', *JSP* 17 (1998), pp. 25–51.

Danby, Herbert, *The Mishnah, Translated from the Hebrew with Introduction and Brief Explanatory Notes* (Oxford: Oxford University Press, 1933).

Danker, F.W, *Jesus and the New Age: A commentary on St. Luke's Gospel* (Philadelphia: Fortress Press, 1988).

—— (ed.), *A Greek-English Lexicon of the New Testament and other Early Christian Literature* (3rd edition; Chicago: The University of Chicago Press, 2000).

Davies, J.H., 'The Purpose of the Central Section of St. Luke's Gospel', in F.L. Cross (ed.), *SE* 2 (TU 87; Berlin, 1964), pp. 164–73.

Davies, W.D and Allison, Dale C., *A Critical and Exegetical Commentary on the Gospel According to Saint Matthew*, vol. II (Matthew VIII-XVIII) (Edinburgh: T. & T. Clark, 1991).

Denaux, A., 'Old Testament Models for the Lukan Travel Narrative: A Critical Survey', in C.M. Tuckett (ed.), *The Scriptures in the Gospels* (Louvain: Leuven University Press, 1997), pp. 271–305.

Denova, R.I., *The Things Accomplished Among Us: Prophetic Tradition in the Structural Pattern of Luke-Acts* (JSNTSup.141; Sheffield: Sheffield Academic Press, 1997).

Derrett, J.D.M., 'Simon Magus (Acts 8:9-24)', *ZNW* 73 (1982), pp. 52–68.

—— 'Law in the New Testament: Fresh Light on the Parable of the Good Samaritan', *NTS* 10 (1964–65), pp. 22–37.

—— 'The Samaritan Woman's Purity (John 4:4-52)', *EvQ* 60 (4, 1988), pp. 291–8.

De Saussure, F., *Course in General Linguistics* (New York: McGraw Hill, 1966).

Dexinger, F. and Pummer, R. (eds), *Die Samaritaner* (Darmstadt: Wiss. Buches, 1992).

Dexinger, F., 'Limits of Tolerance in Judaism: The Samaritan Example', in E.P. Sanders, *et al.* (eds), *Jewish and Christian Self-Definition*, vol. II (London: SCM Press, 1981), pp. 88–114.

—— 'Samaritan Origins and the Qumran Texts', in Crown and Davey (eds), *New Samaritan Studies of the Société d'Etudes Samaritaines (vols. III and IV), Essays in Honour of G.D. Sixdenier* (Studies in Judaica, No.5; The University of Sydney: Mandelbaum Publishing, 1995), pp. 169–84.

—— 'Samaritan and Jewish Festivals: Comparative Considerations', in Crown and Davey (eds), *New Samaritan Studies of the Société d'Etudes Samaritaines (vols. III and IV), Essays in Honour of G.D. Sixdenier* (Studies in Judaica, No.5; The University of Sydney: Mandelbaum Publishing, 1995), pp. 57–78.

Dibelius, M., *Studies in the Acts of the Apostles* (London: SCM Press, 1956).

Dickerson, P.L., 'The Sources of the Account of the Mission to Samaria in Acts 8:5-25', *NovT* 39 (3, 1997), pp. 210–34.

Dietrich, W., *Das Petrusbild der lukanischen Schriften* (BWANT 14; Stuttgart: Kohlhammer, 1972).

Dion, P.E and Pummer, R., 'A Note on the "Samaritan-Christian Synagogue" in Ramat-Aviv', *JSJ* 11 (2, 1980), pp. 217–22.

Donaldson, T.L., 'Moses Typology and the Sectarian Nature of Early Christian Anti-Judaism: A Study in Acts 7', *JSNT* 12 (1981), pp. 27–52.

Doran, R., '2 Maccabees 6:2 and the Samaritan Question', *HTR* 76 (1983), pp. 481–5.

Drane, J.W., 'Simon the Samaritan and the Lukan Concept of Salvation History', *EQ* 47 (3, 1975), pp. 131–7.

Drury, J., *Tradition and Design in Luke's Gospel* (Atlanta: John Knox Press, 1976).

Dunn, J.D.G., *Baptism in the Holy Spirit: A Re-examination of the New Testament Teaching on the Gift of the Spirit in Relation to Pentecostalism Today* (London: SCM Press, 1970).

—— 'Spirit-and-Fire Baptism', *NovT* 14 (1972), pp. 81–92.

—— 'Judaism in the Land of Israel in the First Century', in J. Neusner (ed.), *Judaism in Late Antiquity, Part II. Historical Syntheses* (HOS; Leiden: E.J. Brill, 1995), pp. 229–61.

—— *The Acts of the Apostles* (Narrative Commentaries; Valley Forge: Trinity Press International, 1996).

Dupont, J., *The Sources of Acts: The Present Position* (London: Darton, Longman & Todd, 1964).

—— 'The Salvation of the Gentiles and the Theological Significance of Acts', in *The Salvation of the Gentiles: Essays on the Acts of the Apostles* (trans. J.R. Keating, New York: Paulist Press, 1979), pp. 11–33.

—— 'Community of Goods in the Early Church', in *The Salvation of the Gentiles: Essays on the Acts of the Apostles* (trans. J.R. Keating, New York: Paulist Press, 1979), pp. 85–102.

Edwards, Mark, 'Simon Magus, the Bad Samaritan', in M. Edwards and S. Swain (eds), *Portraits: Biographical Representation in the Greek and Latin Literature of the Roman Empire* (Oxford: Clarendon Press, 1997), pp. 69–91.

—— et al. (eds), *Apologetics in the Roman Empire: Pagans, Jews, and Christians* (Oxford: Oxford University Press, 1999).

Egger, R., *Josephus Flavius und die Samaritaner: Eine terminologische Untersuchung zur Identitätsklärung der Samaritaner* (Freiburg: Vandenhoeck & Ruprecht, 1986).

—— 'Josephus Flavius and the Samaritans', in A. Tal and M. Florentin (eds)., *Proceedings of the First International Congress of the Société d'Etudes Samaritaines*, Tel-Aviv, April 11-13, 1988 (Tel-Aviv University: Chaim Rosenberg School for Jewish Studies, 1991), pp. 109–14.

Ehrhardt, Arnold, *Acts of the Apostles* (Manchester: Manchester University Press, 1970).

Ellis, E.E., *The Gospel of Luke* (NCB; London: Nelson, 1966).

Enslin, M.S., 'Luke and the Samaritans', *HTR* 36 (1943), pp. 277–97.

—— 'The Samaritan Ministry and Mission', *HUCA* 51 (1980), pp. 29–38.

Ervin, H., *Conversion-Initiation and the Baptism in the Holy Spirit* (Peabody, MA: Hendrickson, 1984).

Esler, P.F., *Community and Gospel in Luke-Acts: The Social and Political Motivations of Lucan Theology* (Cambridge: Cambridge University Press, 1987).

—— 'Jesus and the Reduction of Intergroup Conflict: The Parable of the Good Samaritan in the Light of Social Identity Theory', *BI* 8 (4, 2000), pp. 325–57.

Evans, Craig A., '"He Set His Face": A Note on Luke 9,51', *Bib* 63 (1982), pp. 545–8.

—— '"He Set His Face": Luke 9,51 Once Again', *Bib* 68 (1987), pp. 80–4.

—— 'Luke's Use of the Elijah/Elisha Narratives and the Ethics of Election', *JBL* 106 (1987), pp. 75–83.

—— *Luke* (NIBC; Peabody, MA: Hendrickson Publishers, 1990).

Evans, Craig A. and S. Talmon (eds)., *The Quest for Context and Meaning: Studies in Biblical Intertextuality in Honor of James A. Sanders* (BI Series 28; Leiden: E.J. Brill, 1997).

Evans, C.F., 'The Central Section of St Luke's Gospel', in D.E. Nineham (ed.), *Studies in the Gospels: Essays in Memory of R.H. Lightfoot* (Oxford: Basil Blackwell, 1957), pp. 37–53.

—— *Saint Luke* (London: SCM Press, 1990).

Farris, S., *Hymns of Luke's Infancy Narratives* (JSNTSup.9; Sheffield: JSOT Press, 1985).

Feldman, L.H., 'Josephus' Attitude Toward the Samaritans: A Study in Ambivalence', in M. Mor (ed.), *Jewish Sects, Religious Movements, and Political Parties, Proceedings of the third Annual Symposium of the Philip M. and Ethel Klutznick Chair in Jewish Civilization held on October 14-15, 1990* (SJC 3; Nebraska: Creighton University Press, 1992), pp. 23–45, now reprinted in Feldman, L.H., *Studies in Hellenistic Judaism* (Leiden: E.J. Brill, 1996), pp. 114–36.

Feldman, L.H. and Hata, G. (eds), *Josephus, Judaism, and Christianity* (Leiden: E.J. Brill, 1987).

Ferreiro, Alberto, 'Simon Magus: The Patristic-Medieval Traditions and Historiography', *Apocrypha* 7 (1996), pp. 147–65.

—— 'Simon Magus, Dogs, and Simon Peter', in A. Ferreiro (ed.), *The Devil, Heresy and Witchcraft in the Middle Ages*, Essays in Honor of J.B. Russell (Leiden: Brill, 1998), pp. 45–89.

Fichtner, J., 'πλησίον', *TDNT* VI, ed. G. Friedrich, pp. 312–15.

Fiensy, David A., 'The Composition of the Jerusalem Church', in Bauckham (ed.), *The Book of Acts in Its First Century Setting.Vol.4: The Book of Acts in Its Palestinian Setting* (Grand Rapids: Wm.B. Eerdmans Publishing Co., 1995), pp. 213–36.

Fiorenza, E.S. (ed.), *Aspects of Religious Propaganda in Judaism and Early Christianity* (Notre Dame: University of Notre Dame Press, 1976).

—— 'Miracles, Mission, and Apologetics: An Introduction', in *eadem* (ed.), *Aspects of Religious Propaganda in Judaism and Early Christianity* (Notre Dame: University of Notre Dame Press, 1976), pp. 1–25.

Fitzer, G., 'σύνδεσμος', *TDNT* VII, ed. G. Friedrich, p. 858.

Fitzmyer, J.A., *The Gospel According to Luke*, 2 vols. (Garden City, NY: Doubleday, 1981, 1985).

—— *Luke the Theologian: Aspects of his Teaching* (New York: Paulist Press, 1989).

—— 'The Use of the Old Testament in Luke-Acts', *SBLSP 1992* (ed. E.H. Lovering; Atlanta: Scholars Press, 1992), pp. 524–38.

—— *The Acts of the Apostles: A New Translation with Introduction and Commentary* (AB; Garden City, New York: Doubleday and Co., 1998).

Forbes, Greg W., *The God of Old: The Role of the Lukan Parables in the Purpose of Luke's Gospel* (JSNTSup.198; Sheffield: Sheffield Academic Press, 2000).

Ford, J.M., 'Can We Exclude Samaritan Influence From Qumran?', *RevQ* 6 (1, 1967), pp. 109-29.

—— *My Enemy is My Guest: Jesus and Violence in Luke* (New York: Orbis Books, 1984).

Fossum, J.E., 'Samaritan Demiurgical Traditions and the Alleged Dove Cult of the Samaritans', in R. Van den Broek and M.J. Vermaseren (eds), *Studies in Gnosticism and Hellenistic Religions*, presented to G. Quispel on the Occasion of his 65th Birthday (Leiden: E.J. Brill, 1981), pp. 143–160.

—— *The Name of God and the Angel of the Lord: Samaritan and Jewish Concepts of Intermediation and the Origin of Gnosticism* (WUNT 36; Tübingen: J.C.B. Mohr, 1985).

—— 'Samaritan Sects and Movements', in A.D. Crown (ed.), *Samaritans* (Tübingen: J.C.B. Mohr, 1989), pp. 293–389.

Franklin, E., *Christ the Lord: A Study in the Purpose and Theology of Luke-Acts* (London: SPCK, 1975).

Freed, Edwin D., 'Samaritan Influence in the Gospel of John', *CBQ* 30 (1968), pp. 580–7.

—— 'Did John Write His Gospel Partly to Win Samaritan Converts?', *NovT* 12 (1970), pp. 241–56.

Freyne, Sean, 'Behind the Names: Samaritans, *Ioudaioi*, Galileans', in S.G. Wilson and M. Desjardins (eds), *Text and Artefact in the Religions of Mediterranean Antiquity*, Essays in Honour of Peter Richardson (SCJ 9; Canada: Wilfrid Laurier University Press, 2000), pp. 389–401.

Friedrich, G., 'Lukas 9:51 und die Entrückungschristologie des Lukas', in P. Hoffmann, *et al.* (eds), *Orientierung an Jesu: Festschrift für J.Schmid* (Freiburg: Herder, 1973), pp. 48–77.

Furness, J.M., 'Fresh Light on Luke 10:25-37', *ExpTim* 80 (1968-69), p. 182.

Garrett, S.R., *The Demise of the Devil: Magic and the Demonic in Luke's writings* (Minneapolis: Fortress Press, 1989).

Gasque, W.W., *A History of the Criticism of the Acts of the Apostles* (Grand Rapids: Wm.B. Eerdmans Publishing Co., 1975).

Gaster, M., *The Samaritans: Their History, Doctrines, and Literature* (London: Oxford University Press, 1925).

Gaventa, B.R., 'Toward a Theology of Acts: Reading and Rereading', *Int* 42 (2, 1988), pp. 146–57.

Giblin, C.H., *Destruction of Jerusalem according to Luke's Gospel: A Historical-Typological Model* (AnBib 107; Rome: Pontifical Biblical Institute, 1985).

Gill, David W.J and Conrad Gempf (eds), *The Book of Acts in Its First Century Setting. vol. 2: The Book of Acts in Its Graeco-Roman Setting* (Grand Rapids: Wm.B. Eerdmans Publishing Co., 1994).

Gnilka, J., *Die Verstockung Israels: Isaias 6, 9-10 in der Theologie der Synoptiker* (SANT 3; Munich: Kösel, 1961).

Godet, F., *A Commentary on the Gospel of St. Luke*, 2 vols. (Edinburgh: T. & T. Clark, 1888–89).

Goodman, M., *The Ruling Class of Judea* (Cambridge: Cambridge University Press, 1987).

Goulder, M.D., 'The Samaritan Hypothesis', Appendix (ii), in Goulder (ed.), *Incarnation and Myth: The Debate Continued* (London: SCM Press Ltd., 1979), pp. 247–50.

—— *Luke: A New Paradigm*, 2 vols. (JSNTSup.30; Sheffield: JSOT Press, 1989).

Grabbe, L.L., 'Josephus and the Reconstruction of the Judean Restoration', *JBL* 106 (2, 1987), pp. 231–46.

—— 'Betwixt and Between: The Samaritans in the Hasmonean Period', *SBLSP 1993* (Atlanta: Scholars Press, 1993), pp. 334–47.

Gray, Rebecca, *Prophetic Figures in Late Second Temple Jewish Palestine: The Evidence from Josephus* (Oxford: Oxford University Press, 1993).

Green, Joel B. (ed.), *Hearing the New Testament: Strategies for Interpretation* (Grand Rapids: Wm. B. Eerdmans Publishing Co., 1995).

—— *The Gospel According to Luke* (Grand Rapids: Wm.B. Eerdmans Publishing Co., 1997).

—— 'From "John's Baptism" to "Baptism in the Name of the Lord Jesus": The Significance of Baptism in Luke-Acts', in S.E. Porter and A.R. Cross (eds), *Baptism, the New Testament and the Church*, Historical and Contemporary Studies in Honour of R.E.O. White (JSNTsup.171; Sheffield: Sheffield Academic Press, 1999), pp. 157–72.

Greenwood, D., *Structuralism and the Biblical Text* (New York: Mouton Publishers, 1985).

Greimas, A.J., *Structural Semantics: An Attempt at Method*, trans. D. McDowell, *et al.* (Lincoln: University of Nebraska Press, 1983).

—— 'Structure and History', in A.M. Johnson, Jr. (ed.), *Structuralism and Biblical Hermeneutics: A Collection of Essays* (PTMS 22; Pennsylvania: Pickwick Press, 1979), pp. 57–74.

—— 'The Interpretation of Myth: Theory and Practice', in P. Maranda and E. Koengaes Maranda, *Structural Analysis of Oral Tradition* (Philadelphia: University of Pennsylvania, 1971), pp. 81–121.

Gundry, R.H., *Matthew: A Commentary on His Literary and Theological Art* (Michigan: Wm.B. Eerdmans Publishing Co., 1982).

Haar, Stephen, *Simon Magus: The First Gnostic?* (BZNW 119; Berlin: Walter de Gruyter, 2003).

Haenchen, E., 'Gab es eine vorchristliche Gnosis?', *ZTK* 49 (1952), pp. 316–49.

—— *The Acts of the Apostles: A Commentary* (Oxford: Basil Blackwell, 1971).

—— 'Simon Magus in der Apostelgeschichte', in K.W. Tröger (ed.), *Gnosis und Neues Testament* (Gütersloh: Mohn, 1973), pp. 267–79.

Hagner, Donald A., *Matthew 1-13*, WBC vol. 33a (Dallas: Word Books Publishers, 1993).

Hahn, F., *Mission in the New Testament* (London: SCM Press, 1965).

Hall, Bruce, 'From John Hyrcanus to Baba Rabbah' in A.D. Crown (ed.), *The Samaritans* (Tübingen: J.C.B. Mohr, 1989), pp. 32–54.

Hamilton, R.W., *Guide to Samaria-Sebaste* (Amman: Hashemite Kingdom of Jordan Department of Antiquities, 1953).

Hamm, Dennis, 'What the Samaritan Leper Sees: The Narrative Christology of Luke 17:11-19', *CBQ* 56 (1994), pp. 273–87.

Harnack, A., *The Acts of the Apostles* (trans. J.R. Wilkinson; London: Williams & Norgate, 1909).

Havelaar, Henriette, 'Hellenistic Parallels to Acts 5:1-11 and the Problem of Conflicting Interpretations', *JSNT* 67 (1997), pp. 63–82.

Hemer, C.J., *The Book of Acts in the Setting of Hellenistic History* (ed. C.H. Gempf; WUNT 49; Tübingen: J.C. Mohr, 1989).

Hengel, M., *Between Jesus and Paul: Studies in the Earliest History of Christianity* (London: SCM Press, 1983).

—— *Earliest Christianity* (London: SCM Press, 1986).

—— *The 'Hellenization' of Judaea in the First Century after Christ* (London: SCM Press, 1989).

—— 'The Political and Social History of Palestine from Alexander to Antiochus III (333-187 BCE)', in W.D. Davis & L. Finkelstein (eds), *The Cambridge History of Judaism*, vol. II (Cambridge: Cambridge University Press, 1989), pp. 35–78.

—— 'The Geography of Palestine in Acts', in R. Bauckham (ed.), *The Book of Acts in Its First Century Setting. vol. 4: The Book of Acts in Its Palestinian Setting* (Grand Rapids: Wm.B. Eerdmans Publishing Co., 1995), pp. 27–78.

Hill, Craig C., *Hellenists and Hebrews: Reappraising Division within the Earliest Church* (Minneapolis: Fortress Press, 1992).

Hjelm, Ingrid, *The Samaritans and Early Judaism: A Literary Analysis* (CIS 7, JSOTSup.303; Sheffield: Sheffield Academic Press, 2000).

Hjelmslev, L., *Prolegomena to a Theory of Language* (Madison: University of Wisconsin, 1961).

Holladay, C.R., *Fragments from Hellenistic Jewish Authors* I (Chico, CA: Scholars Press, 1983).

Holum, K.G., 'Caesarea and the Samaritans', in R.L. Hohlfelder (ed.), *City, Town and Countryside in the Early Byzantine Era* (EEM 120, Byzantine Series I; Boulder, 1982), pp. 65–73.

Horsley, R.A., *Galilee: History, Politics, People* (Valley Forge: Trinity Press International, 1995).

Hull, J.H.E., *The Holy Spirit in the Acts of the Apostles* (London: Lutterworth Press, 1967).

Hultgren, A.J., *The Parables of Jesus: A Commentary* (Grand Rapids: Wm.B. Eerdmans Publishing Co., 2000).

Hultgren, A.J and Haggmark, S.J (eds), *The Earliest Christian Heretics: Readings from their Opponents* (Minneapolis: Fortress Press, 1996).

Isser, Stanley J., *The Dositheans: A Samaritan Sect in Late Antiquity* (SJLA 17; Leiden: E.J. Brill, 1976).

—— 'Jesus in the Samaritan Chronicles', *JJS* 32 (2, 1981), pp. 166–94.

Jacobson, R., 'The Structuralists and the Bible', *Int* 28 (2, April 1974), pp. 146–64.

Jameson, F., *The Prison House of Language: A Critical Account of Structuralism and Russian Formalism* (Princeton: Princeton University Press, 1972).

Jeremias, J., *Jesus' Promise to the Nations* (London: SCM Press, 1956).

—— *Jerusalem in the Time of Jesus: An Investigation into Economic and Social Conditions during the New Testament Period* (Philadelphia: Fortress Press, 1969).

Jervell, J., 'The Lost Sheep of the House of Israel: The Understanding of the Samaritans in Luke-Acts', *Luke and the People of God: A New Look at Luke-Acts* (Minneapolis: Augsburg Publishing House, 1972), pp. 113–32.

—— 'The Mighty Minority', *ST* 34 (1980), pp. 13–38.

—— 'The Future of the Past: Luke's Vision of Salvation History and Its Bearing on His Writing of History', in B. Witherington III (ed.), *History, Literature and Society in the Book of Acts* (Cambridge: Cambridge University Press, 1996), pp. 104–26.

—— *Die Apostelgeschichte* (KEKNT; Göttingen: Vandenhoeck & Ruprecht, 1998).

Johnson, Jr., A.M., 'Structuralism, Biblical Hermeneutics, and the Role of Structural Analysis in Historical Research', in *idem* (ed.), *Structuralism and Biblical Hermeneutics: A Collection of Essays* (PTMS 22; Pennsylvania: Pickwick Publications, 1979), pp. 1–28.

—— 'Philip the Evangelist and the Gospel of John', *AbrN* 16 (1976), pp. 49–72.

Johnson, L.T., *The Literary Function of Possessions in Luke-Acts* (SBLDS 39; Missoula, Montana: Scholars Press, 1977).

—— *Sharing Possessions: Mandate and Symbol of Faith* (Philadelphia: Fortress Press, 1981).

—— *The Gospel of Luke* (Sacra Pagina Series 3; Collegeville, MN: The Liturgical Press, 1991).

—— *The Acts of the Apostles* (Sacra Pagina Series 5; Collegeville, MN: The Liturgical Press, 1992).

Jones, A.H.M., *The Cities of the Eastern Roman Provinces* (rev. M. Avi-Yonah, *et al.*; 2nd edition; Oxford: Clarendon Press, 1971).

Käsemann, E., *Essays on New Testament Themes* (Philadelphia: Fortress Press, 1964).

Kasher, A., *Jews and Hellenistic Cities in Eretz-Israel: Relations of the Jews in Eretz-Israel with the Hellenistic Cities during the Second Temple Period (332 BCE-70 CE)* (TSAJ 21; Tübingen: Mohr, 1990).

—— 'Josephus on Jewish-Samaritan Relations under Roman Rule (BCE 63-CE 70)', in A.D. Crown and L. Davey (eds), *New Samaritan Studies of the Société d'Etudes Samaritaines* (vol. III & IV), Essays in Honour of G.D. Sixdenier (Studies in Judaica No.5; University of Sydney: Mandelbaum Publishing, 1995), pp. 217–36.

Keck, L.E., 'Will the Historical-Critical Method Survive? Some Observations', in R.A. Spencer (ed.), *Orientation by Disorientation: Studies in Literary Criticism and Biblical Literary Criticism, Presented in Honor of William A Beardslee* (PTMS 35; Pittsburgh: Pickwick Press, 1980), pp. 115–27.

Kee, H.C., *Understanding the New Testament* (New Jersey: Prentice-Hall, Inc., 1983).

—— *To Every Nation Under Heaven: The Acts of the Apostles* (Harrisburg: Trinity Press International, 1997).

Kilgallen, J.J., 'The Function of Stephen's Speech (Acts 7:2-53)', *Bib* 70 (1989), pp. 173–93.

Kilpatrick, G.D., 'ΛΑΟΙ at Lk. 2:31 and Acts 4:25, 27', *JTS* new Series 16 (1965), p. 127.

Kingsbury, Jack D., *Matthew: Structure, Christology and Kingdom* (Philadelphia: Fortress Press, 1975).

—— *Conflict in Luke: Jesus, Authorities, Disciples* (Minneapolis: Fortress Press, 1991).

Kippenberg, H.G., *Garizim und Synagogue: Traditionsgeschichtliche Untersuchungen zur samaritanischen Religion der aramäischen Periode* (Berlin: W.de Gruyter, 1971).

Klauck, Hans-Josef, *Magic and Paganizm in Early Christianity* (trans. Brian McNeil; Edinburgh: T. & T. Clark, 2000).

Klutz, T.E., *With Authority and Power: A Socio-stylistic Investigation of Exorcisms in Luke-Acts* (PhD Thesis; Sheffield: Sheffield University, 1995).

Koch, D.A., 'Geistbesitz, Geistverleihung und Wundermacht: Erwägungen zur Tradition und zur lukanischen Redaktion in Act 8:5-25', *ZNW* 77 (1986), pp. 64–82.

Koester, C.R., 'The Saviour of the World (John 4:42)', *JBL* 109 (4, 1990), pp. 665–80.

Koester, H., *Introduction to the New Testament,* vol. II: *History and Literature of Early Christianity* (Philadelphia: Fortress Press, 1982).

Kollmann, Bernd, 'Philippus der Evangelist und die Anfänge der Heidenmission' *Bib* 81 (4, 2000), pp. 551–65.

Kraabel, A.T., 'New Evidence of the Samaritan Diaspora has been Found on Delos', *BA* 47 (1, 1984), pp. 44–7.

Kraemer, R.S., 'On the Meaning of the term "Jew" in Greco-Roman Inscriptions', *HTR* 82 (1989), pp. 35–53.

Kremer, J., *Pfingstbericht und Pfingstgeschehen: Eine exegetische Untersuchung zur Apg 2,1-13* (SBS 63-64; Stuttgart: KBW, 1973).

—— (ed.), *Les Actes des Apôtres: Traditions, Rédaction, Théologie* (BEThL 48; Paris-Gembloux: Duculot: Louvain: Louvain University Press, 1979).

Kurz, W.M., *Reading Luke-Acts: Dynamics of Biblical Narrative* (Louisville: Westminster Press, 1993).

Lake, K., and Cadbury, H.J, *The Beginnings of Christianity*. Part I: *The Acts of the Apostles*, vol. IV: *English Translation and Commentary* (London: Macmillan, 1933).

Lampe, G.W.H., *The Seal of the Spirit* (London: Longmans, Green & Co., 1951).

Larkin Jr., William J., 'Mission in Acts', in William J. Larkin Jr. and Joel F. Williams (eds), *Mission in the New Testament: An Evangelical Approach* (ASMS 27; Maryknoll, NY: Orbis Books, 1998), pp. 170–86.

Lerner, Berel Dov, 'Samaritans, Jews and Philosophers', *ExpTim* 113 (5, 2002), pp. 152–6.

Levi-Strauss, C., *The Raw and the Cooked: Introduction to a Science of Mythology* I (trans. J. & D. Weightmann; New York: Harper & Row, 1969).

—— 'Structure and Form: Reflections on a Work by Vladimr Propp', *Structural Anthropology* II (trans. Monique Layton, New York: Basic Books, 1976), pp. 115–45.

Levine, Amy-Jill (ed.), *A Feminist Companion to Luke* (London: Continuum, 2003).

Levine, L.I., *Caesarea under Roman Rule* (Leiden: Brill, 1975).

—— *The Ancient Synagogue: The First Thousand Years* (New Haven: Yale University Press, 2000).

Liddell, H.G and Scott, R., *A Greek-English Lexicon* (With a revised supplement, 9th edn., rev. Henry Stuart Jones; Oxford: Clarendon Press, 1996).

Lieu, Judith, *The Gospel of Luke* (Peterborough: The Epworth Press, 1997).

Lightley, J.W., *Jewish Sects and Parties in the Time of Jesus* (London: The Epworth Press, 1925).

Lindars, B. (ed.), *The Gospel of John* (NCB; London: Morgan and Scott, 1972).

Lindemann, A., 'Samaria und Samaritaner im Neuen Testament', *WuD* 22 (1993), pp. 51–76.

Loewe, R., 'Salvation is not of the Jews', *JTS* new series 32 (2, 1981), pp. 341–68.

Lohse, E., 'Missionarisches Handeln Jesu nach dem Evangelium des Lukas', *TZ* 10 (1954), pp. 1–11.

Lucian, *Lucian*, ed. and trans. A.M. Harmon *et al*, 8 vols., (LCL; London: Heinemann, 1913–1967).

Lüdemann, G., *Untersuchungen zur simonianischen Gnosis* (GTA 1; Göttingen: Vandenhoeck & Ruprecht, 1975).

—— 'The Acts of the Apostles and the Beginnings of Simonian Gnosis', *NTS* 33 (1987), pp. 420–6.

—— 'Acts of the Apostles as a Historical Source', in J. Neusner, *et al.* (eds), *The Social World of Formative Christianity and Judaism*, Essays in Tribute to H.C. Kee (Philadelphia: Fortress Press, 1988), pp. 109–25.

—— *Early Christianity according to the Traditions in Acts* (trans. John Bowden; London: SCM Press, 1989).

Luz, Ulrich, *The Theology of the Gospel of Matthew* (Cambridge: Cambridge University Press, 1995).

—— *Matthew 8-20: A Commentary* (trans. James E. Crouch; Minneapolis: Fortress Press, 2001).

Maccini, R.G., 'A Reassessment of the Woman at the Well in John 4 in Light of the Samaritan Context', *JSNT* 53 (1994), pp. 35–46.

Macdonald, J., *The Theology of the Samaritans* (London: SCM Press, 1964).

Maddox, R., *The Purpose of Luke-Acts* (ed. J. Riches; Edinburgh: T. & T. Clark, 1982).

Magen, Y., 'Mount Gerizim and the Samaritans', in F. Manns and E. Alliata (eds), *Early Christianity in Context: Monuments and Documents* (SBF 38; Jerusalem: Franciscan Printing Press, 1993), pp. 91–148.

Marcus, R., 'Alexander the Great and the Jews', in R. Marcus (trans.), Josephus' *Works: Jewish Antiquities* (Books IX-XI), vol. VI (Cambridge, MA: Harvard University Press, 1937), Appendix C, pp. 512–32.

Mare, W. Harold, 'Acts 7: Jewish or Samaritan in Character?', *WTJ* 34 (1, 1971), pp. 1–21.

Margalith, Othniel, 'The Political Background of Zerubbabel's Mission and the Samaritan Schism', *VT* 41 (3, 1991), pp. 312–23.

Marshall, I.H., *Luke: Historian and Theologian* (Grand Rapids: Zondervan, 1970).

—— 'The Resurrection in the Acts of the Apostles', in W.W. Gasque and R.P. Martin (eds), *Apostolic History and the Gospel*, Biblical and Historical Essays presented to F.F. Bruce on his 60th Birthday (Exeter: The Paternoster Press, 1970), pp. 92–107.

—— *The Gospel of Luke: A Commentary on the Greek Text* (Exeter: Paternoster Press, 1978).

—— *The Acts of the Apostles: An Introduction and commentary* (Leicester: IVP, 1980).

—— *The Acts of the Apostles* (NTG; Sheffield: Sheffield Academic Press, 1992, 1997).

Marshall, I.H., and Peterson (eds), *Witness to the Gospel: The Theology of Acts* (Grand Rapids: Wm. B. Eerdmans Publishing Co., 1998).

Matthews, C.R., 'Philip and Simon, Luke and Peter: A Lukan Sequel and Its Intertextual Success', *SBLSP 1992* (ed. E.H. Lovering; Atlanta: Scholars Press, 1992), pp. 133–46.

—— *Philip: Apostle and Evangelist: Configurations of a Tradition* (NovTSup.105; Leiden: E.J. Brill, 2002).

McCown, C.C., 'The Geography of Luke's Central Section', *JBL* 57 (1938), pp. 56–66.

—— 'Gospel Geography: Fiction, Fact and Truth', *JBL* 60 (1941), pp. 1–25.

McKenzie, S.L., *The Trouble with Kings: The Composition of the Book of Kings in the Deuteronomistic History* (Leiden: E.J. Brill, 1991).

Meeks, W.A., *The Prophet-King: Moses Traditions and the Johannine Christology* (NovTSup.14; Leiden: E.J. Brill, 1967).

—— 'Simon Magus in Recent Research', *RSR* 3 (1977), pp. 137–42.

Meier, J.P., 'The Historical Jesus and the Historical Samaritans: What can be said?', *Bib* 81 (2, 2000), pp. 202–32.

—— 'The Samaritans', in *idem*, *A Marginal Jew: Rethinking the Historical Jesus*, vol. 3 (New York: Doubleday, 2001), pp. 532–49.

Menken, M.J.J., 'The Position of σπλαγχνίζεσθαι and σπλάγχνα in the Gospel of Luke', *NovT* 30 (1988), pp. 107–14.

Menzies, R.P., 'Spirit and Power in Luke-Acts: A Response to Max Turner', *JSNT* 49 (1993), pp. 11–20.

—— *Empowered for Witness: The Spirit in Luke-Acts* (Sheffield: Sheffield Academic Press, 1994).

Metzger, B.M., *A Textual Commentary on the Greek New Testament* (London: United Bible Societies, 1971).

Mikolasek, A., 'The Samaritans: Guardians of the Law against the Prophets', in A.D. Crown & L. Davey (eds), *New Samaritan Studies of the Société D'Etudes Samaritaines (vols. III and IV), Essays in Honour of G.D. Sixdenier* (Studies in Judaica, No.5; The University of Sydney: Mandelbaum Publishing, 1995), pp. 85–94.

Miyoshi, M., *Der Anfang des Reiseberichts Lk. 9:51-10:24: Eine Redaktionsgeschichtliche Untersuchung* (AnBib 60; Rome: Pontifical Biblical Institute, 1974).

Moessner, D.P., 'Luke 9:1-50: Luke's Preview of the Journey of the Prophet like Moses of Deuteronomy', *JBL* 102 (1983), pp. 575–605.

—— 'Paul and the Pattern of the Prophet like Moses in Acts', in *SBLSP 1983* (ed. K.H. Richards; CA: Scholars Press, 1983), pp. 203–12.

—— '"The Christ Must Suffer": New Light on the Jesus-Peter, Stephen, Paul Parallels in Luke-Acts', *NovT* 28 (1986), pp. 220–56.

—— *Lord of the Banquet: The Literary and Theological Significance of the Lukan Travel Narrative* (Minneapolis: Fortress Press, 1989).

Montefiore, C.G., *The Synoptic Gospels*, 2 vols. (New York: Ktav, 1968).

Montgomery, J.A., *The Samaritans: The Earliest Jewish Sect: Their History, Theology and Literature* (Philadelphia: John C. Winston, 1907; reprinted, New York: Ktav, 1968).

Moore, S., *Literary Criticism and the Gospels: The Theoretical Challenge* (New Haven: Yale University Press, 1989).

Mor, M., 'The Persian, Hellenistic and Hasmonaean Period', in A.D. Crown (ed.), *The Samaritans* (Tübingen: J.C.B. Mohr, 1989), pp. 1–18.

—— 'The Samaritans and the Bar-Kokhbah Revolt', in A.D. Crown (ed.), *The Samaritans* (Tübingen: J.C.B. Mohr, 1989), pp. 19–31.

—— (ed.), *Jewish Sects, Religious Movements, and Political Parties, Proceedings of the third Annual Symposium of the Philip M. and Ethel Klutznick Chair in Jewish Civilization held on October 14-15, 1990* (SJC 3; Nebraska: Creighton University Press, 1992).

Morabito, v. , *et al* (eds), *Samaritan Researches, vol. V: Proceedings of the Congress of the SES 1996/1997* (Studies in Judaica, No.10; University of Sydney: Mandelbaum Publishing, 2000).

Moule, C.F.D., 'Once More, Who were the Hellenists?', *ExpTim* 70 (1958–59), pp. 100–2.

—— *An Idiom-Book of New Testament Greek* (2nd edn.; Cambridge: Cambridge University Press, 1960).

Moulton, J.H. and Milligan, G., *The Vocabulary of the Greek Testament* (London: Hodder and Stoughton Ltd., 1930, reprinted 1972).

Munck, J., *Paul and the Salvation of Mankind* (London: SCM, 1959).

—— *The Acts of the Apostles* (AB; New York: Doubleday & Co., 1967).

Munro, W., 'The Pharisee and the Samaritan in John: Polar or Parallel?', *CBQ* 57 (4, 1995), pp. 710–28.

Neagoe, A., *The Trial of the Gospel: An Apologetic Reading of Luke's Trial Narratives* (Cambridge: Cambridge University Press, 2002).

Neil, William, *Acts* (NCBC; Grand Rapids: Wm.B. Eerdmans Publishing Co., 1973).

Neusner, J. (ed.), *Judaism in Late Antiquity, Part II: Historical Syntheses* (HOS; Leiden: E.J. Brill, 1995).

Neusner, J. and Avery-Peck (eds), *Judaism in Late Antiquity, Part III: Where We Stand: Issues and Debates in Ancient Judaism* I (Leiden: E.J. Brill, 1999).

Neyrey, J.H. (ed.), *The Social World of Luke-Acts: Models for Interpretation* (Peabody, MA: Hendrickson, 1991).

Nock, A.D., 'Paul and the Magus', in Lake and Cadbury (eds), *The Beginnings of Christianity. Part I: The Acts of the Apostles, vol. V: Additional Notes to the Commentary* (London: Macmillan and Co., Ltd., 1933), pp. 164–88.

—— *Essays on Religion and the Ancient World I and II* (Harvard: Harvard University Press, 1972).

Nolland, J., *The Gospel of Luke*, 3 vols. (WBC; Dallas: Word Books, 1990–1994).

Oakman, D.E., 'Was Jesus A Peasant? Implications for Reading the Samaritan Story (Lk. 10:30-35)', *BTB* 22 (3, 1992), pp. 117–25.

Oepke, 'ἀπώλεια', *TDNT* I, ed. G. Kittel, p. 397.

Ogg, G., 'The Central Section of the Gospel according to St. Luke', *NTS* 18 (1971–72), pp. 39–53.

O'Neill, J.C., 'The Connection between Baptism and the Gift of the Spirit in Acts', *JSNT* 63 (1996), pp. 87–103.

Oppenheimer, Aharon, 'The 'Ammei Ha-Aretz, the Christians, and the Samaritans', in *The 'Am Ha-Aretz: A Study in the Social History of the Jewish People in the Hellenistic-Roman Period* (trans. I.H. Levine; Leiden: E.J. Brill, 1977), pp. 218–38.

O' Toole, R.F., *The Unity of Luke's Theology: An Analysis of Luke-Acts* (GNS 9; Wilmington: Michael Glazier, 1984).

Oulton, J.E.L., 'The Holy Spirit, Baptism, and Laying on of Hands in Acts', *ExpTim* 66 (1954–55), pp. 236–40.

Palmer, P.M. and R.P. More, *The Sources of The Faust Tradition: From Simon Magus to Lessing* (New York: Octagon Books Inc., 1966).

Pamment, Margaret, 'Is there Convincing Evidence of Samaritan Influence on the Fourth Gospel?', *ZNW* 73 (1982), pp. 221–30.

Parrot, Andre', *Samaria: The Capital of the Kingdom of Israel* (London: SCM Press, 1958).

Parsons, M.C., *The Departure of Jesus in Luke-Acts: The Ascension Narratives in Context* (JSNTSup.21; Sheffield: Sheffield Academic Press, 1987).

Parsons, M.C and Pervo, R.I, *Rethinking the Unity of Luke and Acts* (Minneapolis: Fortress Press, 1993).

Parsons, M.C. and Tyson, J.B. (eds), *Cadbury, Knox and Talbert: American Contributions to the Study of Acts* (Atlanta: Scholars Press, 1992).

Patte, D., *What is Structural Exegesis?* (Philadelphia: Fortress Press, 1976).

—— *The Gospel According to Matthew: A Structural Commentary on Matthew's Faith* (Philadelphia: Fortress Press, 1987).

—— *Structural Exegesis for New Testament Critics* (Minneapolis: Fortress Press, 1989).

Pervo, R.I., *Profit with Delight: The Literary Genre of the Acts of the Apostles* (Philadelphia: Fortress Press, 1987).

—— 'Must Luke and Acts Belong to the Same Genre?', *SBLSP 1989* (ed. David J. Lull; Atlanta: Scholars Press, 1989), pp. 309–16.

Pesch, R., Pesch, *Jesu ureigene Taten?* (Freiburg: Herder, 1970).

—— *Apostelgeschichte*, 2 vols. (EKKNT 5; Zürich: Benziger, 1986).

Peterson, David, 'The Motif of Fulfilment and the Purpose of Luke-Acts', in B.W. Winter and A.D. Clarke (eds), *The Book of Acts in Its First Century Setting. Vol. I: The Book of Acts in Its Ancient Literary Setting*, pp. 83–104.

Phillips, Thomas E., 'Reading Recent Readings of Issues of Wealth and Poverty in Luke and Acts', *CBR* 1 (2, 2003), pp. 231–69.

Philo, *Works*, ed. F.H. Colson, G.H. Whitaker, J.W. Earp and R. Marcus, 12 vols. (LCL; Cambridge, MA: Harvard University Press, 1929–1953).

Pilgrim, Walter E., *Good News to the Poor: Wealth and Poverty in Luke-Acts* (Minneapolis: Augsburg Publishing House, 1981).

Plummer, A., *A Critical and Exegetical Commentary on the Gospel According to St. Luke* (ICC; 4th edn.; Edinburgh: T. & T. Clark, 1913).

Plumptre, E.H., 'The Samaritan Elements in the Gospels and Acts', *The Expositor*, first series, VII, (1878), pp. 22–40.

Porter, Stanley E., 'The "We" Passages', in David W.J. Gill and Conrad Gempf (eds), *The Book of Acts in Its First Century Setting. vol. 2: The Book of Acts in Its Graeco-Roman Setting* (Grand Rapids: Wm.B. Eerdmans Publishing Co., 1994), pp. 545–74.

Powell, M.A., *What is Narrative Criticism?* (Minneapolis: Fortress Press, 1990).

—— *What are they Saying about Acts?* (Mahwah: Paulist Press, 1991).

Praeder, S.M., 'The Problem of First Person Narration in Acts', *NovT* 29 (1987), pp. 193–218.

Prior, M., *Jesus the Liberator: Nazareth Liberation Theology (Luke 4:16-30)* (Sheffield: Sheffield Academic Press, 1995).

Pummer, Reinhard, 'The Samaritan Pentateuch and the New Testament', *NTS* 22 (1976), pp. 441–3.

—— 'The Present State of Samaritan Studies: I', *JSS* 21 (1976), pp. 39–61.

—— 'The Present State of Samaritan Studies: II', *JSS* 22 (1977), pp. 27–47.

—— 'New Evidence for Samaritan Christianity?', *CBQ* 41 (1979), pp. 98–117.

—— 'Genesis 34 in Jewish Writings of the Hellenistic and Roman Periods', *HTR* 75 (2, 1982), pp. 177–88.

—— *The Samaritans* (Leiden: E.J. Brill, 1987).

—— 'Argarizin: A Criterion for Samaritan Provenance?', *JSJ* 18 (1, 1987), pp. 18–25.

—— 'Samaritan Material Remains and Archaeology' in A.D. Crown (ed.), *The Samaritans* (Tübingen: J.C.B. Mohr, 1989), pp. 135–77.

—— 'How to Tell a Samaritan Synagogue from a Jewish Synagogue', *BAR* 24 (3, 1998), pp. 24–35.

—— *Early Christian Authors on Samaritans and Samaritanism: Texts, Translations and Commentary* (TSAJ 92; Tübingen: Paul Siebeck, 2002).

Pummer, R. and Roussel, M., 'A Note on Theodotus and Homer', *JSJ* 13 (1–2, 1982), pp. 177–82.

Purvis, J.D., *The Samaritan Pentateuch and the Origin of the Samaritan Sect* (Cambridge: Harvard University Press, 1968).

—— 'The Fourth Gospel and the Samaritans', *NovT* 17 (3, 1975), pp. 161–98.

—— 'The Samaritans and Judaism', in Robert A. Kraft and G.W.E. Nickelsburg (eds), *Early Judaism and its Modern Interpreters* (Philadelphia: Fortress Press, 1986), pp. 81–98.

—— 'The Samaritan Problem: A Case Study in Jewish Sectarianism in the Roman Era', in B. Halpern and J.D. Levenson (eds)., *Tradition in Transformation*, F.M. Cross Festschrift (Indiana, 1986), pp. 350–83.

—— 'The Samaritans', in W.D. Davies and Louis Finkelstein (eds), *The Cambridge History of Judaism*, vol. II: *The Hellenistic Age* (Cambridge: Cambridge University Press, 1989), pp. 591–613.

—— 'Samaria (City)', *ABD* V (1992), pp. 914–21.

Rabbinowitz, J. (trans.), *Midrash Rabbah: Deuteronomy* (London: The Soncino Press, 1983).

Rappaport, Uriel, 'The Samaritans in the Hellenistic Period', in A.D. Crown and L. Davey (eds), *New Samaritan Studies of the Société d'Etudes Samaritaines* (vol. III & IV), Essays in Honour of G.D. Sixdenier (Studies in Judaica No.5; University of Sydney: Mandelbaum Publishing, 1995), pp. 271–88.

Ravens, D., 'The Role of the Samaritans and the Unity of Israel', in *idem, Luke and the Restoration of Israel* (JSNTSup.119; Sheffield: Sheffield Academic Press, 1995), pp. 72–106.

Read-Heimerdinger, J., *The Bezan Text of Acts: A Contribution of Discourse Analysis to Textual Criticism* (JSNTSup.236; Sheffield: Sheffield Academic Press, 2002).

Rengstorf, K.H., 'σημεῖον', *TDNT* VII, ed. G. Friedrich, pp. 200–69.

—— 'The Election of Matthias', in W. Klassen and G.F. Snyder (eds), *Current Issues in New Testament Interpretation*, Essays in honour of O. Piper (London: SCM Press, 1962), pp. 178–87.

Resseguie, J.L., 'Interpretation of Luke's Central Section (Luke 9:51-19:44) since 1856', *SBT* 5 (1975), pp. 3–36.

Richard, E., *Acts 6:1-8:4: The Author's Method of Composition* (SBLDS 41; Missoula, 1978).

Ringgren, H., 'Luke's Use of the Old Testament', *HTR* 79 (1986), pp. 227–35.

Robbins, V.K., 'By Land and By Sea: The We-Passages and Ancient Sea Voyages', in C.H. Talbert (ed.), *Perspectives on Luke-Acts* (Edinburgh: T. & T. Clark, 1978), pp. 215–42.

Roberts, A. and J. Donaldson (eds), *The Ante-Nicene Fathers* I (rev. A Cleveland Coxe; Grand Rapids: Wm. B. Eerdmans Publishing Co., 1975), original version 1870.

—— *The Clementine Homilies: Ante-Nicene Christian Library*, XVII (Edinburgh: T. & T. Clark, 1870).

Rohrbaugh, Richard L., 'The Pre-industrial City in Luke-Acts: Urban Social Relations', in J.H. Neyrey (ed.), *The Social World of Luke-Acts: Models for Interpretation* (Peabody, MA: Hendrickson Publishers, 1991), pp. 125–49.

Rowley, H.H., 'Sanballat and the Samaritan Temple', *BJRL* 38 (1955–56), pp. 166–98.

—— 'The Samaritan Schism in Legend and History', in B.W. Anderson and W. Harrelson (eds), *Israel's Prophetic Heritage* (New York: Harper and Row, 1962), pp. 208–22.

Ruddick, C.T., 'Behold, I Send My Messenger', *JBL* 88 (1969), pp. 381–417.

Rudolph, K., 'Simon– Magus oder Gnosticus? Zur Stand der Debatte', *ThR* 42 (1977), pp. 278–359.

Sacchi, Paolo, 'The Samaritans', in *idem, The History of the Second Temple Period* (JSOTSup.285; Sheffield: Sheffield Academic Press, 2000), pp. 152–9.

Sanders, E.P., *Jesus and Judaism* (London: SCM Press, 1985).

Sanders, Jack T., *The Jews in Luke-Acts* (London: SCM Press, 1987).

—— 'Who is a Jew and Who is a Gentile in the Book of Acts?', *NTS* 37 (1991), pp. 434–55.

Sandmel, S., *Anti-Semitism in the New Testament* (Philadelphia: Fortress Press, 1978).

Scharlemann, M.H., *Stephen: A Singular Saint* (AnBib 34; Rome: Pontifical Biblical Institute, 1968).

Schmidt, Francis, *How the Temple Thinks: Identity and Social Cohesion in Ancient Judaism* (The Biblical Seminar 78; Sheffield: Sheffield Academic Press, 2001).

Schmidt, Thomas E., *Hostility to Wealth in the Synoptic Gospels* (JSNTSup.15; Sheffield: Sheffield Academic Press, 1987).

Schneemelcher, W. and R.McL. Wilson (eds), *New Testament Apocrypha*, 2 vols. (Cambridge: James Clarke & Co., 1992).

Schürer, E., *The History of the Jewish People in the Age of Jesus Christ (175 BC-AD 135)*, 3 vols. (rev. and ed. G. Vermes, *et al.*; Edinburgh: T. & T. Clark, 1973–1987).

Schur, N., *History of the Samaritans* (Frankfurt am Main: Verlag Peter Lang, 1989).

Schwartz, Seth, 'The "Judaism" of Samaria and Galilee in Josephus' Version of the Letter of Demetrius I to Jonathan (*Antiquities* 13.48-57)', *HTR* 82 (4, 1989), pp. 377–91.

Scobie, C.H.H., 'The Origins and Development of Samaritan Christianity', *NTS* 19 (1972–73), pp. 390–414.

—— 'The Use of Source Material in the Speeches of Acts III and VII', *NTS* 25 (1978–79), pp. 399–421.

Scott, James M., 'Luke's Geographical Horizon', in David W.J. Gill and Conrad Gempf (eds), *The Book of Acts in Its First Century Setting. vol. 2: The Book of Acts in Its Graeco-Roman Setting* (Grand Rapids: Wm.B. Eerdmans Publishing Co., 1994), pp. 483–544.

—— (ed.), *Restoration: Old Testament, Jewish, and Christian Perspectives* (JSJSup.72; Leiden: E.J. Brill, 2001).

Scroggs, R., 'The Earliest Hellenistic Christianity', in J. Neusner (ed.), *Religions in Antiquity* (Leiden: E.J. Brill, 1968), pp. 176–206.

Seccombe, David, 'The New People of God', in Marshall and Peterson (eds), *Witness to the Gospel* (Grand Rapids: Wm. B. Eerdmans Publishing Co., 1998), pp. 349–72.

Sellin, G., 'Lukas als Gleichniserzähler: Die Erzählung vom barmherzigen Samariter (Lk. 10:25-37)', *ZNW* 65 (1974), pp. 166–89; *ZNW* 66 (1975), pp. 19–60.

Shafer, Grant R., 'Further Samaritan Motifs in Stephen's Speech (Acts 7:2-53)', in Vittorio Morabito, *et al* (eds), *Samaritan Researches, vol. V: Proceedings of the Congress of the SES 1996/1997* (Studies in Judaica, No.10; University of Sydney: Mandelbaum Publishing, 2000), pp. 2.03-2.12.

Sheeley, S.M., *Narrative Asides in Luke-Acts* (JSNTSup.72; Sheffield: Sheffield Academic Press, 1992).

Shelton, James B., *Mighty in Word and Deed: The Role of the Holy Spirit in Luke-Acts* (Peabody, MA: Hendrickson Publishers, 1991).

Shepherd, W.H., *The Narrative Function of the Holy Spirit as a Character in Luke-Acts* (SBLDS 147; Atlanta: Scholars Press, 1994).

Simon, Marcel, *St Stephen and the Hellenists in the Primitive Church* (London: Longmans, Green and Co., 1958).

Smith, G.A., *Historical Geography of the Holy Land* (25th edn.; London: Collins, 1931).

Smith, M., 'The Account of Simon Magus in Acts 8', in *Harry Austryn Wolfson Jubilee Volume* (English section, vol. 2; Jerusalem: American Academy for Jewish Research, 1965), pp. 735–49.

—— *Palestinian Parties and Politics that Shaped the Old Testament* (New York: Columbia University Press, 1971).

Spencer, F.S., *The Portrait of Philip in Acts: A Study of Roles and Relations* (JSNTSup.67; Sheffield: Sheffield Academic Press, 1992).

Spiro, A., 'Stephen's Samaritan Background', Appendix V, in J. Munck, *The Acts of the Apostles* (AB 31; rev. W.F. Albright and C.S. Mann; New York: Doubleday, 1967), pp. 285–300.

Spivey, R.A., 'Structuralism and Biblical Studies: The Uninvited Guest', *Int* 28 (2, April 1974), pp. 133–45.

Squires, John T., 'The Function of Acts 8:4-12:25', *NTS* 44 (1998), pp. 608–17.

Stanton, G., 'Samaritan Incarnational Christology?' in M. Goulder, *Incarnation and Myth: The Debate Continued* (London: SCM Press Ltd., 1979), pp. 243–6.

Stenhouse, Paul (trans.), *The Kitab Al-Tarikh of Abu'l Fath* (Sydney: Mandelbaum Trust, 1985).

Sterling, G.E., *Historiography and Self-Definition: Josephos, Luke-Acts and Apologetic Historiography* (Leiden: E.J. Brill, 1992).

—— '"Opening the Scriptures": The Legitimation of the Jewish Diaspora and the Early Christian Mission', in David P. Moessner (ed.), *Jesus and the Heritage of Israel: Luke's Narrative Claim upon Israel's Legacy* (Harrisburg, PA: Trinity Press International, 1999), pp. 199–227.

Stern, E. and Magen, Y., 'Archaeological Evidence for the First Stage of the Samaritan Temple on Mount Gerizim', *IEJ* 52 (1, 2002), pp. 49–57.

Stern, M., *Greek and Latin Authors on Jews and Judaism*, 3 vols. (Jerusalem: Israel Academy of Sciences and Humanities, 1974, 1980, 1984).

Stoops, Robert F., Jr., *Miracle Stories and Vision Reports in the Acts of Peter* (PhD Thesis; Cambridge, MA: Harvard University, 1982).

—— 'Patronage in the *Acts of Peter*', *Semeia* 38 (1986), pp. 91–100.

Strabo, *The Geography of Strabo*, 8 vols., with an English translation by Horace Leonard Jones (London: Heinemann, 1917–1932).

Strelan, Rick, 'Recognizing the Gods (Acts 14:8-10)', *NTS* 46 (2000), pp. 488–503.

—— 'The Running Prophet (Acts 8:30)', *NovT* 43 (1, 2001), pp. 31–8.

Stuhlmacher, P., 'Matt 28:16-20 and the Course of Mission in the Apostolic and Post-apostolic Age', in Adna and Kvalbein (eds), *Mission of the Early Church to Jews and Gentiles* (WUNT 127; Tübingen: Mohr Siebeck, 2000), pp. 17–43.

Talbert, C.H., *Luke and the Gnostics: An Examination of the Lucan Purpose* (Nashville: Abingdon Press, 1966).

—— *Literary Patterns, Theological Themes and Genre of Luke-Acts* (SBLMS 20; Missoula: Scholars Press, 1974).

—— *Reading Luke: A Literary and Theological Commentary on the Third Gospel* (New York: Crossroad, 1982).

Tannehill, R.C., *The Narrative Unity of Luke-Acts: A Literary Interpretation*, 2 vols. (Philadelphia: Fortress Press, 1986, 1990).

—— *Luke* (Nashville: Abingdon Press, 1996).

Taylor, N.H., 'Stephen, the Temple, and Early Christian Eschatology', *RB* 110 (1, 2003), pp. 62–85.

Tcherikover, V.A., *Hellenistic Civilization and the Jews* (Philadelphia: Fortress Press, 1966).

Thornton, T.C.G., 'The Samaritan Calendar: A Source of Friction in New Testament Times', *JTS* new Series vol. 42 (October 1991), pp. 577–80.

—— 'Anti-Samaritan Exegesis Reflected in Josephus' Retelling of Deuteronomy, Joshua, and Judges', *JTS* new series vol. 47 (1, April 1996), pp. 125–30.

Tiede, David L., 'Religious Propaganda and the Gospel Literature of the Early Christian Mission', *ANRW* II.25.2 (1984), pp. 1705–29.

—— 'Glory to Thy People Israel', *SBLSP 1986* (ed. Kent H. Richards; Atlanta: Scholars Press, 1986), pp. 142–51.

Tipei, John P., *The Laying on of Hands in the New Testament* (PhD Thesis; Sheffield: University of Sheffield, 2000).

Tomson, P.J., 'Gamaliel's Counsel and the Apologetic Strategy of Luke-Acts', in J. Verheyden (ed.), *The Unity of Luke-Acts* (BEThL CXLII; Leuven: Leuven University Press, 1999), pp. 585–604.

Torrey, C.C., 'Medina and Polis, and Luke 1:39', *HTR* 17 (1924), pp. 83–90.

Tsedaka, B., 'Samaritanism – Judaism or Another Religion?', in M. Mor (ed.), *Jewish Sects, Religious Movements, and Political Parties, Proceedings of the third Annual Symposium of the Philip M. and Ethel Klutznick Chair in Jewish Civilization held on October 14-15, 1990*, (SJC 3; Nebraska: Creighton University Press, 1992), pp. 47–51.

Tuckett, C.M (ed.), *Luke's Literary Achievement* (JSNTSup.116; Sheffield: Sheffield Academic Press, 1995).

—— *Luke* (NTG; Sheffield: Sheffield Academic Press, 1996).

—— (ed.), *The Scriptures in the Gospels* (Louvain: Leuven University Press, 1997).

Turner, Max, *Power from on High: The Spirit in Israel's Restoration and Witness in Luke-Acts* (JPTS 9; Sheffield: Sheffield Academic Press, 1996).

Tushingham, A.D., 'A Hellenistic Inscription from Samaria-Sebaste', *PEQ* 104 (1972), pp. 59–63.

Tyson, J.B., 'The Gentile Mission and the Authority of Scripture in Acts', *NTS* 33 (1987), pp. 619–31.

—— (ed.), *Luke-Acts and the Jewish People: Eight Critical Perspectives* (Minneapolis: Augsburg, 1988).

—— *Images of Judaism in Luke-Acts*, South Carolina: University of South Carolina Press, 1992).

Van der Horst, P.W., 'Samaritans and Hellenism', in *Hellenism – Judaism – Christianity: Essays on their Interaction* (Kampen: Kok Pharos Publishing House, 1994), pp. 48–58.

—— 'Samaritans and Hellenism', in D.T. Runia (ed.), *SPA VI* (1994), pp. 28–36.

Verheyden, J., 'The Unity of Luke-Acts: What are we up to', in Verheyden (ed.), *The Unity of Luke-Acts* (BEThL CXLII; Leuven: Leuven University Press, 1999), pp. 3–56.

—— (ed.), *The Unity of Luke-Acts* (BEThL CXLII; Leuven: Leuven University Press, 1999).

Vermes, Geza, *The Complete Dead Sea Scrolls in English* (New York: Allen Lane The Penguin Press, 1997).

Via, Dan O., 'Parable and Example Story: A Literary-Structuralist Approach', *Biblica* 1 (1974), pp. 105–133.

—— *Kerygma and Comedy in the New Testament: A Structuralist Approach to Hermeneutic* (Philadelphia: Fortress Press, 1975).

Vink, J.G., 'The Date and Origin of the Priestly Code in the Old Testament', in *The Priestly Code and Seven Other Studies* (Leiden: E.J. Brill, 1969), pp. 52–3.

Waitz, H., 'Die Quelle der Philippusgeschichten in der Apostelgeschichte 8,5-40', *ZNW* 7 (1906), pp. 340–55.

Walsh, J.T., '2 Kings 17: The Deuteronomist and the Samaritans', in J.C. De Moor & H.F. Van Rooy (eds), *Past, Present, Future: The Deuteronomistic History and the Prophets* (Leiden: E.J. Brill, 2000), pp. 315–23.

Walton, Steve, *Leadership and Lifestyle: The Portrait of Paul in the Miletus Speech and 1 Thessalonians* (Cambridge: Cambridge University Press, 2000).

Weatherly, J.A., *Jewish Responsibility for the Death of Jesus in Luke-Acts* (JSNTSup.106; Sheffield: JSOT Press, 1994).

Wehnert, J., *Die Wir-Passagen der Apostelgeschichte: Ein lukanisches Stilmittel aus jüdischer Tradition* (GTA 40; Göttingen: Vandenhoeck & Ruprecht, 1989).

Weiss, Herold, 'The Sabbath among the Samaritans', *JSJ* 25 (2, 1994), pp. 252–73.

Wellhausen, J., *Kritische Analyse der Apostelgeschichte* (Berlin: Weidmann, 1914).

Wenham, David., *The Parables of Jesus: Pictures of Revolution* (London: Hodder & Stoughton, 1989).

Wenham, J.W., 'Synoptic Independence and the Origin of Luke's Travel Narrative', *NTS* 27 (1980–81), pp. 507–15.

Whaley, E.B., 'Josephus' *Antiquities* 11.297-347: Unravelling the Evidence Regarding the Founding of the Gerizim Temple and the Background of the Samaritan Religious Community', in M. Mor (ed.), *Jewish Sects, Religious Movements, and Political*

Parties: Proceedings of the third Annual Symposium of the Philip M. and Ethel Klutznick Chair in Jewish Civilization held on October 14-15, 1990 (SJC 3; Nebraska: Creighton University, 1992), pp. 1–21.

Wilcox, M., *The Semitisms of Acts* (Oxford: Clarendon Press, 1965).

Williams, C.S.C., *A Commentary on the Acts of the Apostles* (BNTC; London: A. & C. Black, 1957).

Williamson, H.G.M., 'The Historical Value of Josephus' *Jewish Antiquities* XI, 297-301', *JTS* 28 (1977), pp. 49–66.

Wilson, R. McL., 'Simon, Dositheus and the Dead Sea Scrolls', *ZRGG* 9 (1957), pp. 21–30.

—— 'Simon and Gnostic Origins', in J. Kremer (ed.), *Les Actes des Apôtres: Traditions, Redaction, Theologie* (BEThL 48; Gembloux-Leuven: Leuven University Press, 1979), pp. 485–91.

Wilson, S.G., *The Gentiles and the Gentile Mission in Luke-Acts* (SNTSMS 23; Cambridge: Cambridge University Press, 1973).

—— *Luke and the Law* (SNTSMS 50; Cambridge: Cambridge University Press, 1983).

Wilson, S.G. and M. Desjardins (eds), *Text and Artefact in the Religions of Mediterranean Antiquity*, Essays in Honour of Peter Richardson (SCJ 9; Canada: Wilfrid Laurier University Press, 2000).

Witherington III, Ben, *The Acts of the Apostles: A Socio-Rhetorical Commentary* (Michigan: Wm.B. Eerdmans Publishing Co., 1998).

—— (ed.), *History, Literature, and Society in the Books of Acts* (Cambridge: Cambridge University Press, 1996).

Woods, Edward J., *The 'Finger of God' and Pneumatology in Luke-Acts* (JSNTSup.205; Sheffield: Sheffield Academic Press, 2001).

Wright, G.E., 'The Samaritans at Shechem', *HTR* 55 (1962), pp. 357–66.

—— *Shechem: The Biography of a Biblical City* (New York: McGraw-Hill, 1965).

Yamauchi, E.M., *Pre-Christian Gnosticism: A Survey of the Proposed Evidences* (London: Tyndale Press, 1973).

—— 'Gnosticism and Early Christianity', in Wendy E. Helleman (ed.), *Hellenization Revisited* (Lanham: University Press of America, 1994), pp. 29–61.

York, J.O., *The Last Shall be First: The Rhetoric of Reversal in Luke* (JSNTSup.46; Sheffield: JSOT Press, 1991).

Young, Brad H., *The Parables: Jewish Tradition and Christian Interpretation* (Peabody, MA: Hendrickson Publishers, 1998).

Zangenberg, Jürgen, '"Open Your Eyes and Look at the Fields": Contacts between Christians and Samaria According to the Gospel of John', in Vittorio Morabito, *et.al* (eds), *Samaritan Researches, vol. V: Proceedings of the Congress of the SES 1996/1997* (Studies in Judaica, No.10; University of Sydney: Mandelbaum Publishing, 2000), pp. 3.84–3.94.

Zeitlin, S., 'The Names Hebrew, Jew and Israel', *JQR* 43 (1952/53), pp. 365–79.

Zevit, Z., 'The Gerizim-Samarian Community in and between Texts and Times: An Experimental Study', in C.A. Evans and S. Talmon (eds), *The Quest for Context and Meaning: Studies in Biblical Intertextuality in Honor of James A. Sanders* (BI Series 28; Leiden: E.J. Brill, 1997), pp. 547–72.

Index of Authors